American Democracy in Peril

American Democracy in Peril

Eight Challenges to America's Future

SEVENTH EDITION

William E. Hudson

Providence College

Los Angeles | London | New Delhi
Singapore | Washington DC

Los Angeles | London | New Delhi
Singapore | Washington DC

FOR INFORMATION:

CQ Press
An Imprint of SAGE Publications, Inc.
2455 Teller Road
Thousand Oaks, California 91320
E-mail: order@sagepub.com

SAGE Publications Ltd.
1 Oliver's Yard
55 City Road
London EC1Y 1SP
United Kingdom

SAGE Publications India Pvt. Ltd.
B 1/I 1 Mohan Cooperative Industrial Area
Mathura Road, New Delhi 110 044
India

SAGE Publications Asia-Pacific Pte. Ltd.
3 Church Street
#10-04 Samsung Hub
Singapore 049483

Copyright © 2013 by William E. Hudson

CQ Press, an Imprint of SAGE Publications, Inc.

CQ Press is a registered trademark of Congressional Quarterly, Inc.

Cover Design: Anne C. Kerns, Anne Likes Red, Inc.

Photo © Pete McArthur/Corbis

Printed in the United States of America

Library of Congress Cataloging-in-Publication Data

Hudson, William E., 1948–

American democracy in peril : eight challenges to America's future/William E. Hudson.—7th ed.

p. cm.
Includes bibliographical references and index.

ISBN 978-1-4522-2675-0 (pbk.)

1. United States—Politics and government—Textbooks.
2. Democracy—United States—Textbooks. I. Title.

JK31.H86 2013
320.473—dc23   2012004939

This book is printed on acid-free paper.

Acquisitions Editor: Charisse Kiino
Editorial Assistant: Nancy Loh
Production Editor: Astrid Virding
Copy Editor: Taryn Bigelow
Typesetter: C&M Digitals (P) Ltd.
Proofreader: Scott Oney
Indexer: Molly Hall
Cover Designer: Anne C. Kerns, Anne Likes Red, Inc.
Marketing Manager: Jonathan Mason
Permissions Editor: Adele Hutchinson

SUSTAINABLE FORESTRY INITIATIVE

Certified Chain of Custody
Promoting Sustainable Forestry
www.sfiprogram.org
SFI-01268

SFI label applies to text stock

12 13 14 15 16 10 9 8 7 6 5 4 3 2 1

To the memory of my parents,
Maxine Smith Hudson
and
E. Kenneth Hudson,
both democrats

Contents

Tables and Figures

Preface

The preface to the sixth edition of this book began on a hopeful note—that Barack Obama's election might bring about major progress toward addressing the challenges to democracy delineated in this book. Yet it also included a caution: "The fundamental forces that have brought about trivialized elections, radical individualism, citizen disengagement, and inequality remain and will not be changed by a single election outcome. . . . the institutions of the national security state remain in place and constitute an ongoing challenge to democracy. . . . Business's privileged position in our politics remains strong . . . the many veto points within our constitutional arrangements will certainly bedevil his initiatives." Unfortunately, the caution rather than the hopeful note has characterized the Obama presidency.

A reader of this edition will be able to trace systematically how each of these challenges has impeded the hope for change embodied in Obama's election. Foremost has been the way the dysfunctional institutional structure of the national government stands in the way of crafting effective reforms. When institutional gridlock nearly led to a government default in the 2011 debt ceiling crisis, most Americans were horrified with their ineffectual government. Opinion polls showed historic lows in confidence in government and Congress. Even one of the bond rating agencies, Standard and Poor's, downgraded the country's credit rating not because of the state of the economy but over skepticism about the political system's ability to address future fiscal challenges. The majority of citizen voters who chose change in 2008 had little reason to believe in "government by the people."

Recent events have reinforced the other challenges to democracy. The economic crisis has only exacerbated economic inequality as the top 1 percent of Americans seem to have bounced back from the Great Recession while the rest have seen their incomes continue to stagnate and decline. The 1 percent versus the 99 percent has entered into our language, thanks to the Occupy Wall Street movement, indicating a new awareness of inequality in our society. Although many Americans expected that financial crisis would lead to profound reform, the banking industry has used its privileged position to soften efforts to hold it in line.

An activist conservative majority on the Supreme Court has moved in new directions, as in the *Citizens United* decision, to undermine democratic rule. It stands as a potential block to progressive economic and social reform. And the national security state, even as conflict in Iraq and Afghanistan has wound down, remains a potent force directing societal resources, in an era of fiscal austerity, toward the military-industrial complex. In the ways described here, American democracy's peril has only increased since the sixth edition of this book was published.

This new edition has been revised extensively to reflect democracy's peril in the current era:

- The historic and far-ranging impact of the Obama presidency, including the intense partisan conflict that has accompanied it, is incorporated throughout the book.
- A detailed analysis of the tortured politics surrounding health care reform, the repeated threats of government shutdown due to gridlock over deficit reform, and the use of institutional vetoes to prevent effective economic stimulus measures.
- A reorganized elections chapter (5) that looks at the undemocratic structure of elections, the electoral college, and legal obstacles to voting; the role of the media in elections, including new social media; and how hyper-partisanship has undercut the role of political parties as institutions providing citizens effective control over government policy.
- A complete revision of both chapter 6 on the privileged position of business and chapter 7 on economic inequality reflecting the impact of the Great Recession of 2008.
- A revised final chapter (8) that details how the institutions of the national security state derailed the ability of the Obama administration to substantially alter the goals and methods of the military industrial complex.

While examples and references to events of recent years have been added to keep the text current, instructors will find that the basic arguments of most chapters remain unchanged from earlier editions. Even when addressing a generation of students who were small children during the Clinton presidency, I have not shied away from retaining historical references and facts. I find that my own students are very curious about the defining events of earlier decades, such as Watergate, the Vietnam War, and the civil rights movement, that were not often covered in depth in their high school history classes. That these events have much to do with the challenges to democracy discussed in this book make their inclusion a useful stimulus to teaching about them.

This book was written primarily for college students in their first course in American government. Its purpose is to stimulate them to think about how the facts they learn about American politics relate to democratic ideals. Like many Americans, students are frighteningly complacent about democracy—they assume that as long as periodic elections are held, democracy has been achieved. They remain complacent about democracy even while they are skeptical about government effectiveness. I seek to shake up this complacency by showing how current political practices not only fail to achieve democratic ideals but may themselves constitute threats to democracy's very existence. Contemporary American democracy is in peril because too few Americans understand the challenges it faces.

I have received many helpful comments and reactions to the book from students and faculty colleagues across the country. Most gratifying have been those comments that refer to the utility of the book for stimulating class discussion. As I wrote in the preface to the first edition, my primary aim in writing the text was to encourage student reaction to its arguments. I knew that I probably would not persuade all students by what I had to say, but I hoped to say it in a way that would engage their attention and involve them in democratic conversation. From what readers tell me, this book continues to accomplish this goal.

As in previous editions, my introduction offers a review of the history of democratic theory in terms of four "models" of democracy, giving the reader a set of criteria against which to evaluate the challenges discussed later. Then, throughout the book, I argue my own point of view regarding each challenge in as persuasive a manner as I can. I aim to stimulate and engage the reader in thinking critically about these challenges, rather than presenting the "neutral" and "objective" discussion common to most textbooks. The arguments represent my personal conclusions about these challenges, based on many years of study and teaching. Students may well find my positions controversial, and they may discover that some other political scientists—perhaps including their own instructor—are inclined to disagree.

Each chapter concludes with a "Meeting the Challenge" section aimed at stimulating a positive discussion of what policies or reforms may be needed to address the challenge described in the chapter. This edition also retains an updated set of open-ended thought questions at the end of each chapter that were formulated to provoke debate about key arguments and to further encourage critical thinking about the subject matter. Many new works have appeared in the past few years that relate to this book's themes, and I have added those that I consider most illuminating to the lists of suggested readings—including titles marked with an asterisk, which argue views contrary to my own—at the end of the chapters. Following those brief bibliographic recommendations are short lists of websites relating directly to chapter themes, and these lists too have been updated to reflect the fast-paced changes in the cyber world.

The events of the past few years have reinforced my conviction, expressed in prefaces to previous editions, that the future of democratic politics in the United States depends on meeting the challenges presented in this book. If America is to succeed in promoting democracy around the world, we need to acknowledge and address the shortcomings of our own democracy. Creating a more peaceful and democratic world, where Americans can once again feel secure from terror and hostility, will require that we resolve to correct and improve democracy within our own borders. I believe strongly that, at this time in history, Americans need to pay attention to the quality of our democracy. That this book may contribute to promoting a conversation about the issue in political science classrooms is my greatest satisfaction as its author. Any reader of the present edition who would like to converse with me regarding any issue in these pages may contact me at bhudson@providence.edu.

Acknowledgments

Political science colleagues at institutions across the country have proved to be helpful partners in improving how this book "works" in the classroom. I continue to be grateful to my Providence College colleagues for their generous encouragement and thoughtful suggestions. This edition benefited as well from the capable work of two student research assistants: Danielle Turcotte and Danielle Ladd.

The late Ed Artinian, founder of Chatham House, made this book possible, and his skill in promoting it was the major factor in its success. I will be always grateful for Ed's support and encouragement over the years and happy to have had the opportunity to know and work with him. I am grateful that CQ Press is keeping much of Ed's legacy alive through support of the texts he published, including this one. It has been a pleasure to work with Brenda Carter, Charisse Kiino, and the other expert staff at the press. I appreciate their professionalism and strong support for *American Democracy in Peril.*

I also would like to thank the reviewers who provided valuable insights and recommendations for the seventh edition:

Clay Arnold, University of Central Arkansas

J. Robert Baker, Wittenberg University

Paul Brink, Gordon College

Jeremy Busacca, California State Polytechnic University, Pomona

Dave Colnic, California State University, Stanislaus

Taylor Dark, California State University, Los Angeles

Finally, thanks to my wife, Loreto Gandara, who continues to inspire me to keep writing about American democracy. She had the insight, when this book was conceived, to suggest that *peril* was the best word to describe what ails our democracy.

Models of Democracy

As I would not be a slave, *so I would not be a* master. *This expresses my idea of democracy. Whatever differs from this, to the extent there is a difference, is no democracy.*

—ABRAHAM LINCOLN

DEMOCRACY IS A complicated concept. The dictionary definition, "government (or rule) by the people," seems simple, but once we begin to think about the components of the definition, complexities arise. What does "government" or "rule" mean? Does "government by the people" mean that all the people are directly responsible for the day-to-day operation of government? Or is a scheme of representation acceptable? If so, what sort of scheme? How should it be organized? Elections? How often and for which offices? Does "government" have special meaning in a democracy? What is its proper scope? Who decides what is proper? The people, again? How is this decision made and expressed? And who are "the people," anyway? Everyone who lives in the governed territory, or citizens only? What is a citizen? Can newly arriving people (immigrants) become citizens? Under what rules? Should "the people" include everyone or just those with a stake in the community, say, property holders? Should certain groups of people, such as criminals and traitors, be excluded from citizenship? This is just the beginning of a list of questions we could make about the meaning of "government by the people." Notice that in this short list of questions, such additional complex concepts as representation, citizen, and elections are mentioned and suggest additional questions. The search for answers to all these questions is the concern of democratic theory, the branch of scholarship that specializes in elucidating, developing, and defining the meaning of democracy.

Opposite: *Abraham Lincoln, 1863.*

Photo courtesy of Matthew Brady.

If we move beyond dictionary definitions and ask Americans what they think about democracy, we find additional layers of complexity. Americans associate diverse and often contradictory characteristics of their political system with democracy. Most Americans believe that democracy requires majority rule, but at the same time they consider the protection of minority rights from the will of the majority to be a key component of democracy. In fact, most Americans place considerable emphasis on the importance of freedom from governmental interference in their lives as the crucial ingredient of democracy. The individualistic American values democracy because it helps her or him to lead a personal life freely, without government getting in the way. At the same time, patriotic Americans believe that democracy imposes obligations—the duty to vote, for example, or to support the government in times of crisis such as war. Many Americans associate democracy with particular constitutional features, such as the separation of powers and the Bill of Rights. These same Americans would be surprised to see democracy performing quite well in political systems possessing neither of those features; Great Britain is one example. For some, American economic arrangements, usually described as the free enterprise system (capitalism), are a part of democracy. Others, as we later see, believe that capitalism is a threat to political equality and, hence, to democracy. Given these differing views, one can understand why the essay contest on the topic "What Democracy Means to Me" remains a continuing tradition in American schools.

If we are to analyze various challenges to democracy intelligently, we need to clarify some of this confusion about what "democracy" means. We need some sophisticated standards to use in evaluating the degree and kind of threat each of the challenges we examine poses for democratic politics. For example, what democratic characteristics and values does increasing economic inequality or a growing military-industrial complex threaten? This introduction presents an overview of some of the basic concepts of democracy as found in democratic theory. It offers a base to be used in evaluating the challenges to contemporary democracy. Democratic theory is presented here in terms of four distinct "models" of democracy.[1] Each model provides a different understanding of democracy as it has been interpreted by different groups of political theorists. Four different models are needed because democratic theorists have not agreed on what procedures, practices, and values must be emphasized for "government by the people" to be realized. The discussion of the models also provides a brief summary of the major issues and questions raised in modern democratic theory over the past two hundred years. Although some of the ideas in the models were first presented long ago, I believe each of them offers a viable alternative conception of democracy that is relevant to the United States today. The reader, however, should be warned that the discussion of democratic theory presented here is not meant to be a comprehensive review of this voluminous topic. Many important issues are not raised, and some important theorists are not discussed. Readers interested in a more thorough review of democratic theory should consult the works listed in the Suggestions for Further Reading at the end of this introduction.

The models discussed in this chapter are derived from writings on democracy since the eighteenth century. Only in the past two hundred years have humans had experience with democratic government in large nations. The theorists of what I call *modern* democracy agree that democratic politics is possible on such a scale, and they premise their discussions on that assumption. But before the emergence of modern democratic theory, certain historical experiences and political ideas prepared the way for these theorists. Those precursors to modern democratic theory are discussed in the next section.

Precursors to Modern Democratic Theory

Democracy is an ancient concept. The idea of people participating equally in self-rule antedates recorded human history and may be as old as human society itself.[2] From recorded history we know that the ancient Greeks had well-developed and successful democratic societies among their various forms of government. Several Greek city-states, most notably Athens, organized governments that involved the direct participation of their citizens in governing.[3] The Athenian Assembly (Eccle-sia), composed of all male citizens, met more than forty times each year to debate and decide all public issues.[4] Officials responsible for implementing Assembly decisions were either elected or chosen by lot; their terms of office usually lasted one year or less. From historical accounts and the analyses of classic Greek philosophers such as Plato and Aristotle, we know that Greek democracy involved many of the key concepts and practices associated with modern democracy. Political equality, citizen participation—and in Athens, usually *lively* participation—the rule of law, and free and open discussion and debate were all part of Greek democratic practice.[5] Nevertheless, the Greek form of democracy had characteristics that limited it as a model for modern democracy.

The first and most obvious limitation was scale. The Greeks assumed the city-state to be the appropriate size for the polity. Their democracy was carried out within this small territory among several thousand citizens, a condition permitting face-to-face interaction in a single public assembly. Political interaction beyond the scale of the city-state involved either diplomacy or conquest—hardly a democratic procedure. During the fourth and fifth centuries B.C., when Athenian democracy was at its height, Athens ruled its conquered territories in a decidedly undemocratic manner. The idea that democracy could encompass more than a few thousand citizens in a single city-state would have been absurd to Greek democrats.

A second limitation of Greek democracy was its exclusivity.[6] Although all male citizens participated in governing themselves in Athens, this group constituted a minority of the people who actually lived in Athens and were governed by the laws of the Ecclesia. The most obvious exclusion was the female half of the population (an exclusion that would prevail, until quite recently, in modern democracies). Likewise, the enormous slave population, larger than the number of free citizens (about three slaves for each two citizens), had no right to political participation.[7] According to some scholars, one of the ironies of Greek democracy was that its existence depended to a great extent on the slave economy, which permitted citizens the leisure to perform public duties.[8] In addition to slaves and women, a large population of free individuals, immigrants from other Greek cities and other parts of the world, were denied citizenship rights even though they had lived in Athens for generations and its laws governed their lives. The Greek conception of democracy did not include the modern notion that democracy should provide opportunities for political participation to all (with only a few exceptions) who live within a polity and are subject to its laws.

Despite its limitations, Greek democracy remained the Western world's most complete expression of the ideal of "rule by the many" for two thousand years after its demise. Among the numerous empires, monarchies, oligarchies, and tyrannies that followed, the Greek experience remained an inspiration to those who sought to provide power to ordinary citizens to govern themselves. Until the eighteenth century, the few experiments with democratic government, like the Greek experience, involved political regimes encompassing limited geographic areas and small populations. During the Middle Ages and later in various locales, from Italian city-states to Swiss cantons, democratic experiments achieved some success, but scale and exclusivity continued to limit democracy. As in Greece, democracy meant all citizens gathering together in one assembly to make laws; size remained a practical limitation on the relevance of democracy to the governance of large nation-states.

Not surprisingly, given this experience, political theorists assumed that democracy was feasible only in small states where face-to-face interaction of the entire citizenry could occur. For example, the great eighteenth-century French political theorist Montesquieu argued that the ability of citizens to perceive the public good easily, which he considered a requisite of democratic government, was possible only in a small republic.[9] Even the influential democratic theorist Jean-Jacques Rousseau, of the same period, assumed a polity the size of his native Geneva to be the appropriate context for the application of his theories.[10] Only in a small state, where people could meet together in the relative intimacy of a single assembly and where similarity of culture and interests united them, could individuals discuss and find the public good.

By the end of the eighteenth century, events began to overtake the small-state view of democracy and to stimulate a more expansive and modern conception. Inspired by the Enlightenment values of liberty and equality, political activists agitated for more popular forms of government. These democratic aspirations provoked two key events in the history of democracy—the American and French

Revolutions. Because these popular revolutions occurred in large nation-states, satisfying democratic aspirations required moving beyond the small-state limitation. Conceptions of democracy had to be developed to provide for popular government among millions living in large territories.

The idea of democratic *representation* offered the mechanism to solve the dilemma of organizing democratic government over a large territory.[11] The American and French revolutionaries intended to make democracy work through popularly elected assemblies—state legislatures and Congress in the United States and the National Assembly in France. Representative assemblies made democracy feasible in large nation-states, even if the direct participation of the entire people in a single democratic assembly was impossible; representatives would speak on behalf of their constituents. In his famous essay No. 10 in *The Federalist*, James Madison went so far as to turn the conventional wisdom of the political theorists on its head. He argued that representative democracy in a large territory would lead to a more stable popular government than was possible in a small democracy. The introduction of the concept of democratic representation in practice and theory opened the way for the modern conception of democracy.[12]

Along with the idea of representation, a set of political ideas found in the political philosophy called *liberalism* was influential in the emergence of modern conceptions of democracy. Liberal political philosophy was articulated first in the work of the sixteenth-century English philosopher Thomas Hobbes and later in the work of the seventeenth-century English theorist John Locke.[13] Although neither Hobbes nor Locke, as we soon see, would be considered a democrat, their ideas about the nature of political life were influential in modern conceptions of democracy.

Liberal theorists begin with two basic assumptions about human nature: (1) Humans are reasonable creatures who can use their reason to improve their social existence; and (2) humans are self-interested, that is, concerned with their individual well-being. Based on these two assumptions, theorists such as Locke and Hobbes argued that political society comes into being through a "social contract" among reasonable, self-interested individuals. These individuals understand the need for political order because they desire prosperity and security. For Hobbes, the social contract replaced a chaotic "state of nature" in which selfish individuals spend their lives engaged in a "war of all against all," making human life "solitary, poor, nasty, brutish and short." Locke had a more benign view of the state of nature, arguing that most reasonable humans could understand the laws of nature and the need to restrain their selfishness for the good of the community. But because some individuals might sometimes be unreasonable and likely to violate the natural rights of others, prudent people should see the advantage of forming a political society with their fellow citizens to protect themselves. Furthermore, this social contract would place "natural" rights on a more secure and stable basis than they had in the state of nature. According to Locke, government, not the

why only trade matter?

goodwill of humans, would become the guardian of natural law. Despite their differing conceptions of the actual "state" of the state of nature, Hobbes and Locke agreed that reasonable individuals would prefer the security of a social contract.

The purpose of the social contract, and of the government that follows from it, was to maximize the opportunity for individual self-fulfillment. Liberalism was distinguished from medieval and ancient political theories because it identified the individual, his or her rights, and the need for self-fulfillment as the goals of the political order. Individual goals, rather than the glory of God or some universal notion of "the Good"—the sorts of goals assumed in earlier political theory— were the proper end of government.[14] For liberals, government existed to allow individuals to pursue whatever individual "goods" they desired. Individualism meant that each person, informed by reason, was the best judge of what was to be valued in life. The function of government was limited to protecting each individual's natural rights to "life, liberty, and property."

Among these individual rights, liberals counted the right to property especially important. For Locke, the natural—that is, God-given—right to property was central to human existence. The main reason individuals would leave the state of nature and form a political commonwealth was the protection of that right: "The great and chief end of Men's uniting into Commonwealth's, and putting themselves under government, is the preservation of their Property."[15] Since protection of property and other rights is the reason people placed themselves under the authority of a government, it follows logically that government itself should not be allowed to interfere in the exercise of those rights. This liberal commitment to limited government means that individuals have broad leeway in acquiring and disposing of property, free of governmental control.

Obviously, such a view of government and individual rights of property was very compatible with the emergence of capitalist economic relations. Capitalist entrepreneurs in the late eighteenth and early nineteenth centuries sought to be free of the dictates of government. They found liberal political theory especially supportive of their efforts to accumulate wealth and make investments based on their individual estimates of profitability, rather than on the dictates of government. Adam Smith, for example, argued in his *Wealth of Nations,* published in 1776, that economic prosperity, not chaos, would be the result if markets were allowed to function free of governmental interference—a view quite consistent with Locke's notions of property rights and limited government.

Liberal political ideas clearly imply a capitalist or free-enterprise economic order. To what extent does liberalism also imply democratic politics? Liberalism emphasizes that individuals in a society are equally entitled to the protection of their rights and that all humans are equal in forming a social contract. Most Americans associate these liberal political values with democracy. The association is understandable because our American *liberal* democracy has been greatly influenced by our liberal political culture. Nevertheless, liberal thought, although not incompatible with democratic politics, does not lead necessarily to popular control of government.

Neither Hobbes nor Locke favored democratic government. Hobbes, in fact, felt that a liberal society could be best protected if, as part of the original social contract, people turned over all power to a single absolute sovereign (the *Leviathan*), who would provide law and order, protecting citizens in return for their absolute obedience. He so distrusted selfish human nature that he could see no way to control it except with an authoritarian government. But keep in mind that Hobbes advocated authoritarian government for *liberal* ends—to protect individuals' freedom to benefit from their labors.[16] In this respect, Hobbes's position is similar to the public statements of some modern military dictators—such as Chile's former president Augusto Pinochet—who claim they must hold absolute power to protect law-abiding citizens and "free enterprise" from "communists and subversives."[17]

Locke favored some citizen participation in government, but he assumed that participation would be restricted to citizens who had a full stake in the commonwealth—namely, property holders. Although all citizens were obligated to obey government, having consented to the social contract that created it, Locke believed that only citizens with "estate" possessed the capacity for rationality that governing required.[18] Liberals required of government only that it protect individual liberty and not meddle beyond that limited sphere. For this purpose, a nondemocratic government, as long as its powers were limited, might be more trustworthy than a democratic one.

So liberalism does not lead inevitably to democracy. Nevertheless, there are elements in the liberal vision that do suggest democratic politics. For example, both Hobbes and Locke believed that free individuals participated *equally* in the formation of the initial compact that establishes the state. Therefore, they saw no distinctions among people that could justify different political rights for different individuals. So even though differences between citizens may arise in the actual control of government, the foundation of the state rests on the initial consent of all citizens, irrespective of differences in wealth or social status. Furthermore, the initial social contract means that government itself has a democratic obligation to understand that its powers derive from the initial consent of citizens and to enforce laws and protect political rights equally. Failure to do so constitutes justification for revolution. These potentially democratic sentiments find sublime expression in the American Declaration of Independence, which both embodies liberal doctrine and calls for democratic revolution:

> We hold these truths to be self-evident, that all men are created equal, that they are endowed by their Creator with certain unalienable Rights, that among these are Life, Liberty, and the pursuit of Happiness. That to secure

these rights, Governments are instituted among Men, deriving their just powers from the consent of the governed. That whenever any Form of Government becomes destructive of these ends it is the Right of the People to alter or to abolish it, and to institute new Government, laying its foundation on such principles and organizing its powers in such form, as to them shall seem most likely to effect their Safety and Happiness. . . .

Certainly these liberal ideas provided fruitful stimulus to inspire Americans to democratic revolution.

The significance of liberal ideas for modern conceptions of democracy is clearly evident in the first of the four models I describe in this chapter, the Protective Democracy model. Like all the models to follow, this set of ideas shows three things: (1) how one group of "democrats" value citizen participation; (2) what they think the purposes of government are, or should be; and (3) what political arrangements they find most consistent with their thoughts on the first two items. In the pages that follow, I describe each of the four models: Protective Democracy, Developmental Democracy, Pluralist Democracy, and Participatory Democracy.[19] Toward the end of the chapter, a table summarizes and compares the four.

Protective Democracy

Protective Democracy is a model of democracy that advocates popular control of government as a means of protecting individual liberty. Its most explicit formulation is found in the work of two nineteenth-century British political philosophers, Jeremy Bentham and James Mill, who favored democratic government as the best means for securing a liberal society. Bentham, founder of the philosophy of *Utilitarianism,* believed that a capitalist, market society, as described by Smith and implicit in liberal theory, was most likely to achieve the Utilitarian ideal of "the greatest good for the greatest number." He and his disciple Mill believed that for a capitalist society to flourish, it needed government officials who would pass laws nurturing market relations and who would be restrained from using their powers to enrich themselves at the expense of the rest of society.[20]

Bentham and Mill believed that the democratic institutions of universal male suffrage, the secret ballot, a free press, and most of all, frequent elections offered the best chance of keeping government under control. For them, democracy was a method for protecting *both* citizens and capitalism's market relationships: "A democracy, then, has for its characteristic object and effect, the securing of its members against oppression and depredation at the hands of those functionaries which it employs for its defense."[21]

If members of society were self-interested and competitive, as assumed, then voters would be vigilant against government officials bent on violating their liberties. Voters would be ready to punish (at the polls) government officials who raised taxes too severely or whose policies reduced voters' incomes. Bentham and Mill were willing to embrace universal suffrage, even though that meant including in the electorate the poor, people with no property, and the working class. They were confident that middle-class political leaders like themselves could lead the lower class to support liberal, pro-market governments. After all, in their Utilitarian philosophy, the long-run best interest of even the poor lay in the successful operation of the market society. (This belief is still widely held in the United States, as in the "trickle down" economics of many conservative Republicans.)

Bentham's and Mill's confidence in the support of the poor and propertyless for liberal values contrasted sharply with earlier liberal anxiety about the participation of the poor. Just a few years earlier, in 1787, the American founders also had expressed an essentially liberal view of the role of the government. In the *Federalist* No. 10, James Madison asserts that "the protection of [the diversity of the faculties of men from which the rights of property originate] is the first object of government."[22] To Madison, the chief danger to limited government (a liberal goal) was the emergence of factions that might gain control of governmental power and use it in their own interest and against that of the rest of society. Of particular concern was a potential faction comprising the majority of citizens without property, who might use government to inflate the currency, abolish debts, or appropriate property directly.

This concern with the dangers of popular participation, or the "excesses of democracy," as the founders put it, was a major factor precipitating the Constitutional Convention of 1787. Many of the institutional arrangements established in the Constitution were intended to reduce the potential for a democratic majority to threaten individual liberty. Among the most important was the system of separation of powers, which divides lawmaking power among different institutions: the presidency, Congress, and the judiciary. In addition, Congress is divided into two branches, whose members are elected under different electoral schemes. This division of power ensured that even if a passionate majority were to succeed in capturing control of one institution of government, the other, separate institutions would manage to check the potentially tyrannical institution. Several articles of the Constitution—and especially the Bill of Rights—also contain specific limitations on governmental power as a means to protect individual liberty. All these provisions were intended to create a government that anyone bent on tyranny, whether a faction of the majority or a minority, could not easily use to that end.

Combining the institutional vision of the American founders with the democratic theory of Bentham and Mill suggests our first distinctive model of democracy. Protective Democracy values democratic institutions and procedures to the extent that they protect and nurture a liberal, capitalist, market society.

According to this model, democracy exists so that free, competitive individuals can enjoy maximum freedom to pursue material gain (see Table I.1 on page 19). Some individuals may choose other objectives for their lives, but the basic assumption is that most people are motivated primarily to seek wealth. These dedicated capitalists are likely to be interested in, and participate in, politics only to the extent necessary to protect their freedom in the marketplace.

Liberalism heavily influences the Protective Democracy model, in which the prime purpose of government is the protection of individual liberty and property. In fact, the limits that government imposes are needed precisely because threats to property are inherent in an acquisitive and competitive human nature. For its part, government should never threaten property rights and should always protect individual liberty. And since the natural human tendencies toward material greed and political tyranny live in government leaders as well, individual liberty can best be protected if there are also clear and strong limits on government. Political institutions such as the separation of powers, federalism, and bicameralism are intended to limit the power of the government so that it will not behave in a tyrannical manner.

Political participation within these institutions provides further protection because citizens will be vigilant in protecting their freedoms. Although Protective Democracy is very concerned with equality in political rights, such as voting, and with equal protection under the law, Protective democrats are less concerned about the existence or threat of material inequality in society; in fact they assume that such inequality will exist.

Developmental Democracy

As we have seen, the Protective model of democracy rests upon a negative view of human nature—democracy's first aim is to prevent the inherent selfishness, acquisitiveness, and even evil of humankind from controlling the state to the detriment of individual liberty. In sharp contrast to this negative view, the Developmental model of democracy takes a much more positive view of people, especially people in a democratic society. Writing in the nineteenth century, John Stuart Mill (James Mill's son) declared that man is not simply a "consumer and appropriator" (as assumed in the Protective model), but also an "exerter, developer, and enjoyer of his capacities."[23] As a result, people in democratic societies can come to possess "civic virtue," which permits them to look beyond their self-interest to the well-being of all of society. Through participation in governmental institutions and the affairs of their communities, people develop a broad appreciation of the public good and what it requires. They become public-spirited *citizens*.

The concept of the good citizen is central to the model we call Developmental Democracy. This conception of democratic citizenship is widely embraced in

American society, not only in civics textbooks but also by such "good government" groups as the League of Women Voters. "Good citizens" are knowledgeable about, interested in, and active in government and civic affairs. They vote regularly, inform themselves on public issues, write to their elected representatives, and sometimes serve in public office. Democracy is desirable because it provides these opportunities.

Through their active involvement, good citizens contribute to the well-being of their communities, but they also receive something in return. Because democracy requires that citizens involve themselves in the community, it is a means for educating people, enhancing their capacity to improve themselves as well as their government. Democratic citizenship is an intellectual exercise, requiring ordinary people to make constant decisions about political issues and candidates. In making these judgments, citizens talk to one another, learn from one another, and develop their own intelligence.[24] Their active involvement in democratic institutions develops their character in a more fully human direction.[25] In being responsible for public affairs, people learn to be more responsible human beings. The virtue of democracy is that it develops these positive aspects of human character. In sum, the Developmental model sees democracy as having a moral value and purpose—it requires good citizens and thus develops good people. Like the Protective model, the Developmental model accepts the need for representative democracy, but only because of the impracticality of a more direct form of democracy. According to John Stuart Mill,

> The only government which can fully satisfy all the exigencies of the social state is one in which the whole people participate; . . . any participation, even in the smallest public function is useful. . . . But since all cannot, in a community exceeding a single small town, participate personally in any but some very minor portion of the public business, it follows that the ideal type of a perfect government must be representative.[26]

Even though the Developmental model accepts the need for representation, as indicated in the last lines of the quotation above, the emphasis rests on the people's active control of their "deputies." In such a relationship, citizens must be full and active participants in both electing their representatives and monitoring their activities. This view of representation is quite different from that of the proponents of the Protective Democracy model. The Protective democrats, like Madison, thought representation improved on direct democracy because an elite, potentially more civic-minded than ordinary citizens, would control day-to-day policy making. The Developmental democrats, expecting and encouraging *all* citizens to be civic minded, accept representation only as a practical necessity.

For most of American history, this Developmental model of democracy dominated Americans' interpretation of their political life. This view became ascendant during the Jacksonian era, when suffrage was extended to nearly all white males, and the spirit of the common man dominated the frontier. This democratic spirit led the French observer Alexis de Tocqueville to conclude in the 1830s that "the people reign over the American political world as God rules over the universe."[27] From Abraham Lincoln to Woodrow Wilson, American political leaders articulated this vision of Developmental Democracy, and their views were reiterated in schoolroom texts and in the writings of political philosophers.

Toward the middle of the twentieth century, however, some intellectuals began to question the Developmental model's accuracy as a description of actual political practice in the United States. This questioning led them to develop our next interpretation of democracy, Pluralist Democracy.

Pluralist Democracy

To a considerable extent, the Developmental model represents a democratic ideal—if political society were organized according to this model, popular control of government would be assured. But is it possible for such a political regime to exist? This key question troubled social scientists observing the emergent democratic regimes in such nations as the United States, Britain, and France at the turn of the twentieth century. The question was especially troubling because social scientists saw a political reality that differed greatly from the ideals represented in the Developmental model.

For example, instead of seeing average citizens actively engaged in political affairs, they observed that most ordinary people seemed to be apathetic and uninformed about politics. That left day-to-day governance in the hands of a political elite: party leaders, officeholders, "notables," and journalists. Moreover, average citizens were far from equal in their ability to influence public officials; some seemed to have more interest in politics and greater resources for contact with political leaders. Democratic constitutions alone, they concluded, did not seem to create the sort of democratic politics described in the Developmental model.

Among political theorists, these observations about the gap between the democratic ideal and political reality led to two different responses. The first social scientists to describe the gap, in the early years of the twentieth century, saw it as evidence that democracy was impossible. These "elitist" theorists—Roberto Michels, Gaetano Mosca, and Vilfredo Pareto—argued that the experience with democratic institutions proved that democracy could never be achieved.[28] As they saw it, the ideas of democracy and democratic constitutions only hid the reality of elite control of politics and government. For these theorists, the actual practice of democracy differed little from politics in authoritarian or oligarchical regimes because a small "political class" inevitably ruled all societies. A democratic constitution did not change this fundamental "iron law of oligarchy."

By the middle of the twentieth century, another group of social and political scientists formulated an alternative response to the elitists' conclusion about the impossibility of democracy. If the actual practice of politics in "democratic" regimes did not measure up to the democratic ideal, then instead of giving up on democracy altogether, they suggested redefining democracy to fit actual political practice. Rather than let the standards of the Developmental model define democracy, the "revisionists" sought to redefine democracy by careful observation of politics as it was actually practiced in societies such as the United States.

In 1954, Bernard Berelson, Paul Lazarsfeld, and William McPhee made this argument in their book *Voting*, which was based on a sophisticated survey of a sample of citizens in Elmira, New York, at the time of the 1948 presidential election.[29] They found that the behavior of Elmira's citizens differed significantly from the democratic ideal as presented in the Developmental model. Most citizens' levels of knowledge about the election were quite low. More important, there was great variation in the level of political interest and participation—some people were highly interested and involved, others passive and apathetic, and still others showed moderate interest. Overall, there were not many "good citizens" among the population they studied.

But Berelson, Lazarsfeld, and McPhee did not conclude that these "facts" were a threat to democracy. Instead, they wrote that this mixture of involvement and apathy contributed positively to the stability of democratic politics:

> How could mass democracy work if all the people were deeply involved in politics? Lack of interest by some people is not without its benefits, too. . . . Extreme interest goes with extreme partisanship and might culminate in rigid fanaticism that could destroy democratic processes if generalized throughout the community. Low affect toward the election . . . underlies the resolution of many political problems; votes can be resolved into a two party split instead of fragmented into many parties. . . . Low interest provides maneuvering room for political shifts necessary for a complex society. . . . Some people are and should be highly interested in politics, but not everyone is or needs to be.[30]

Thus, for these authors apathy among some citizens, even among a large portion of a society, could be considered a positive dimension of democracy. In fact, too many "good citizens," as described in the Developmental model, would constitute a danger to orderly democratic politics.

If democracy is not to be defined by the activism of its citizens, how do democratic regimes differ from authoritarian ones? For the Pluralists, the answer to this question is *competitive elections.* This answer might seem paradoxical, given the quotation above concerning the dangers of electoral participation, but to the Pluralists, elections provide an opportunity for even apathetic and passive citizens to choose their political leaders. This choice distinguishes democratic regimes from authoritarian ones. Since Pluralists assume that the political elite will make actual policy decisions, the role of democratic citizens lies primarily and almost exclusively in their capacity to choose among alternative political leaders. As Joseph Schumpeter put it in a famous definition of democracy, "The democratic method is that institutional arrangement for arriving at political decisions in which individuals acquire the power to decide by means of a competitive struggle for the people's vote."[31] Elections are important not because they provide *direct* citizen involvement in governance but because they allow citizens to choose whom their rulers will be. For the Pluralists, this mechanism ensures that political leaders will remain responsive to the general preferences of the people and at the same time have the flexibility to make intelligent policy decisions without intrusive public meddling.

For the periods between elections, Pluralists assign to interest groups the important role of providing democratic responsiveness.[32] Most citizens, Pluralists observe, are not very aware of day-to-day governmental policy making, but leaders of interest groups represent average citizens in those policy debates. Because some interest group represents almost everyone's interests, the activities of interest group leaders are an effective democratic channel for the expression of the public's wants and needs. Moreover, interest group leaders possess the knowledge and institutional skills to influence policy making that ordinary people lack. They actively compete with leaders of other interest groups on a daily basis to convince elected officials to enact policies that they favor.

For their part, elected officials seek to please as many groups as possible as a means of maximizing electoral support. To achieve that goal, they must fashion compromises satisfactory to a wide variety of groups. Government policies represent democratic compromises reflecting the preferences of numerous interest groups and their members. Some Pluralists argue that even the concerns of those *not* represented by an interest group are taken into account in these compromises because politicians need to worry about the preferences of "potential" interest groups that might form if unaffiliated citizens become too dissatisfied with a policy compromise. For Pluralists, therefore, interest group activity and regular, competitive elections produce a democratic system that is responsive to the popular will, even though an elite is responsible for day-to-day governing and most citizens are relatively uninvolved in politics.

Finally, Pluralists emphasize that successful democratic politics rests on a base of social diversity. Society consists of many different and competing groups, interests, and associations, and government must be responsive to the legitimate aspirations of all these interests while it protects the right of various groups to exist. Pluralists believe that democracy can thrive only if the many and various associations that make up society express themselves politically.[33] Consequently, the concentration of power in the state, in a social class, or in any single part of society is the complete opposite of democracy. As long as power is widely dispersed among many groups, all provide a check against the accumulation of hegemonic power by any one of them. The competition among aspiring government leaders, the fairness of elections, the free interplay of interest groups, and the formulation of democratic compromises can work only if no single group is able to monopolize power and limit competition, undermine free elections, restrict interest groups, and bias policy compromises.

The Pluralist model emerged as social scientists observed apathetic, uninterested, and uninformed citizens in democratic societies. Based on their observations, they concluded that earlier democratic theorists, including those who created the Developmental model, had overestimated the capacity of most people to participate as active, democratic citizens. If most people were not interested in political affairs, it seemed logical to look to the active political elite as guardians of democratic values and participants in policy formation. Most ordinary citizens could be assigned the less-demanding (although still important) role of voting in periodic elections to choose among alternative leaders. The basis of the Pluralist conception was the intermittent and indirect, even remote, participation of most people in political affairs.

Participatory Democracy

But why are citizens apathetic? The Pluralists assume political apathy to be a natural inclination—unless political affairs directly affect their immediate interests, most people prefer to focus on their private concerns. In the 1960s, however, political activists and political theorists began to question this Pluralist assumption. They formulated a conception of Participatory Democracy, which sees apathy as a result of lack of opportunities for significant participation, rather than as a fundamental disposition of humanity. If most people preferred to concern themselves with their private affairs rather than with public ones, it was because of the structure of social institutions, not human nature. For Participatory democrats, the solution to citizen apathy lay in restructuring political and social institutions so that citizens could learn, through participation, the value and joys of democratic citizenship.

The Participatory model, although it has antecedents in the earlier Developmental model, arose from the political turbulence of the 1960s. Its earliest formulations came from the manifestos of student political activists in such organizations as Students for a Democratic Society (SDS) and the Student Nonviolent Coordinating Committee (SNCC). In 1962, a small group of SDS members gathered in Port Huron, Michigan, to formulate a declaration of principles, the Port Huron Statement, which included a call for "a democracy of individual participation."[34] Political, social, and economic institutions were to be reformed to make them more conducive to participation. In the South, the black and white student activists of SNCC attempted to put participatory ideals into practice in their efforts to register black voters. The battles for civil rights and later against the Vietnam War provided arenas to test the capacity of mass participation to influence public policy.

While students practiced Participatory Democracy in the streets, a number of political scientists challenged the then dominant Pluralist interpretation of American politics in scholarly journals.[35] They questioned whether the elite-dominated politics celebrated by the Pluralists merited the label "democratic." They charged that the Pluralists were complacently praising the virtues of American politics while ignoring the structures that prevented the development of a more authentic democratic politics. Pluralists were criticized for claiming that interest groups offered wide representation to societal interests when many Americans did not belong to any voluntary associations and not all groups had equal access to policymakers. Most important, for discounting the ideals of democratic citizenship in the name of "realism," Pluralists were accused of ignoring and undermining analysis of how more effective structures of democratic participation might be constructed.

The Participatory model, as presented by theorists such as Carol Pateman, differs from previous models in its emphasis on the importance of democratic participation in nongovernmental as well as governmental institutions. The Developmental model (like the Protective and Pluralist models) views the democratic problem as subjecting governmental institutions and decisions to popular control. Participatory democrats agree with the need to control the government democratically, but they also point out that in modern industrialized societies it is not only government that makes authoritative decisions that individuals must obey or that has the capacity to apply sanctions to those who do not obey. Individuals are subject to the rules and dictates of their employers, unions, schools, churches, and other institutions. In fact, the authoritative decisions of these institutions usually have a more direct impact on people's lives than do government policies. The decisions an employer makes regarding salary, working conditions, or layoffs can have an immediate and, if adverse, devastating effect on an employee's life. In comparison to these decisions, the national government's choice to pursue a manned rather than an unmanned space program, or a local government's determination about which streets to pave, is remote or unimportant to most people.

In most cases, nongovernmental decisions are made in hierarchical, bureaucratic organizations, in an authoritarian manner, without any of the procedures and protections we associate with democracy. Participatory democrats think that the absence of democracy in these nongovernmental settings undermines both the capacity of citizens to function democratically and the overall quality of a society's democracy. The model presents three related arguments to support this idea. First, the lack of participatory opportunities in the workplace, the school, and the union deprives citizens of the chance to influence those decisions that are most important to them. An opportunity to nurture those qualities of citizenship valued by the Developmental theorists is lost when people are unable to influence decisions that directly affect their lives. Democratic participation would be much more meaningful if people could see such participation affecting decisions with direct impact on their day-to-day lives.

Second, people are apt to acquire nonparticipatory habits when subjected to an authoritarian environment on a regular basis. After spending the day following orders without question at the factory, a worker cannot be expected to return home in the evening to act like the civics textbook's inquiring, skeptical, self-actualizing citizen. Students who are taught primarily to obey authority in school are not likely to grow into effective democratic citizens. Third, Participatory democrats argue that a society can hardly be called democratic when so many socially and politically relevant choices are in the hands of people who are not democratically accountable. For example, corporate officials sometimes make decisions—such as deciding to close a factory—that affect the well-being of a whole community. The inability of the community's citizens to influence that decision is as indicative of a lack of democracy as their inability to influence the local property tax rate.

For Participatory democrats, the way to hold those who make decisions accountable is to expand participatory opportunities in society. Democracy is a

On a snowy day in March, the citizens of Elmore, Vermont, practice Participatory Democracy at their town meeting.
AP Photo/Toby Talbot.

concept that is not only relevant to government; it should be implemented in all instances where authoritative decisions affecting people's lives are made. Workers should be able to participate democratically in the running of their factories, students and faculty their schools and universities, and welfare recipients the welfare department. Through meaningful participation in these environments, people will acquire the capacity to be more effective participants in influencing government. For Participatory democrats, creating effective democracy in our industrialized and bureaucratized society requires a radical restructuring of institutions to increase people's control over the decisions that affect their lives.

The Models Compared

Table I.1 compares and summarizes the characteristics of the four models of democracy described in this chapter. In the table, the purpose (goal, end) that the model assigns to democracy uniquely defines that model. The Protective model values democracy because democratic institutions are thought to provide the best protection for individual liberties, particularly economic ones such as the right to individual control of property. Developmental Democracy considers democratic politics the best method of developing the personal qualities associated with its idea of the "good citizen." Pluralists value the social diversity and system stability that democratic institutions encourage. And for the Participatory democrats, democracy is worthwhile because it permits people to participate in decisions that affect their lives. Each model's unique character seems to derive from the central purpose or goal it expects democracy to accomplish.

Other dimensions of the table direct our attention to values and characteristics the models share. For example, the Developmental and Participatory models obviously have a lot in common. Each assumes a positive view of human nature—people are thought to be capable of rising above their narrow self-interest. Through participation in democratic procedures and institutions, citizens acquire the quality of civic virtue, which enables them to evaluate public issues in terms of the public interest. Consequently, we should expect and encourage people to be active participants in political affairs to enrich both society and the individual. Both of these models also agree on the need for political and social equality in democratic societies. When citizens come together to discuss the needs of the community, no artificial distinctions of political or social status should override the commonality of citizenship.

The differences between the Developmental and Participatory models center on their different evaluations of the impact of economic relationships on democratic politics. Developmental democrats do not view economic inequalities or class differences as significant barriers to equal citizenship. They emphasize the potential that all citizens enjoy, no matter what their economic resources, to participate fully in governmental institutions. In contrast to this governmental focus,

TABLE I.1   Models of Democracy Compared

	Protective Democracy	Developmental Democracy	Pluralist Democracy	Participatory Democracy
Goal or purpose	Protect liberty (market relations and private property)	Nurture citizenship	Protect and promote diversity	Foster participation
Role of citizens	Passive	Active	Passive	Active
Institutional mechanisms	Separation of powers and representation	Representation	Interest groups and elections	Neighborhood assemblies and workers' councils
Equality	Political	Political and social	Political	Economic, political, and social
Human nature	Selfish and acquisitive	Capable of civic virtue	Selfish and acquisitive	Capable of civic virtue

Participatory democrats focus on the importance of social relationships, particularly economic ones that lie outside government. For them, full and active participation in government alone cannot fulfill the requirements of democracy, which also entails popular control of authoritative decisions in corporations, factories, unions, and schools. Moreover, social and economic inequality may impede the functioning of even political democracy. This broader view makes greater economic equality both a prerequisite for more meaningful participation and a likely consequence of popular power over economic decision making.

Like the Developmental and Participatory models, the Protective and Pluralist models share a common view of human nature. Both adopt the pessimistic position that humans are primarily selfish and acquisitive creatures, concerned primarily with increasing and maintaining their private wealth. From this assumption follows these models' shared expectation that most people will have only limited interest in public affairs. Moreover, especially for the Pluralists, the average person's limited interest and participation in politics are quite acceptable, for they contribute to the stability of the system and the liberty of all. If people are naturally rapacious and interested in their own welfare, their active involvement in government will only produce factional conflict and, if one faction wins, potential violations of liberty. Because both models assume that political leaders (elites) make most of the decisions, even in a democracy, many political scientists would label these *elitist* models of democracy.

The Pluralist and Protective democrats also agree that equality in a democracy need only apply to political rights and opportunities. They expect social and economic inequalities to affect the degree of actual participation, but these conditions reflect a natural reality that does not disturb them. Political leaders, whether elected representatives or interest group leaders, will probably possess higher social standing and greater affluence, but that elite status will not interfere with their ability to speak and act for their constituents and followers, according to these two models. Universal suffrage and competitive elections are enough in themselves to ensure equal representation for all economic interests. Furthermore, the "one person, one vote" idea ensures that the voting power of the many will counterbalance the potential political advantages of the affluent few.

THE DISCUSSION SO FAR may have left some readers a bit confused. The preface promised that this chapter would offer a definition of democracy as a standard against which to judge alternative challenges to the well-being of democracy. However, instead of a single definition, I have presented four very different models, each claiming to provide a description of democratic politics. It appears that one of the challenges democracy faces is that no one can agree on what it means! What conclusions about the concept of democracy can be drawn from these various models? Can we identify some essential characteristics of democracy that will facilitate our identifying its challenges?

First, the models suggest that a part of the meaning of democracy is a continuing discussion of the meaning of democracy. The reader should note that these models have evolved historically in response to practical efforts to establish and maintain democratic regimes during the past two hundred years. Democratic politics has been a new experience for humankind; it is understandable that conceptions of it remain in formation. There is obviously no single, authoritative blueprint for how democracy can be achieved. Instead, democratic politics involves a constant discussion among citizens about how best to organize their political life.

Despite the differences among the models, we can identify certain common elements that seem to have emerged during humankind's two-century discussion about democracy. First, all models assume that democracy means popular rule—that is, government based on popular sovereignty (as opposed, say, to the divine right of kings) and subject to popular control. The models differ on how popular control is to be expressed, but all merit the label "democratic" because they assume the need for control by the people. Second, all models assume political equality. None questions the fact that democracy requires all citizens to possess equal political rights, even though the models differ on the capacity of individuals to take equal advantage of those rights. What differentiates these models from authoritarian theories of government is the absence of any argument in favor of an aristocracy or of assigning a privileged political role to any preordained class or group in society. Third, all assume the need for political liberty. Democratic discussion and popular control of governmental actions can occur only if all people feel free to express themselves and to try to influence government. In sum, these three values—popular rule, equality, and liberty—constitute the core of democracy's definition. All those who honestly call themselves democrats embrace these concepts.

The differences among these models do not mean that the models are mutually exclusive. Embracing one does not necessarily require a total rejection of the others. Instead of containing a wholly distinctive definition of democracy, each emphasizes different values consistent with the other models and an implicit global definition of democracy. The Protective model, for example, stresses the importance of individual liberty and the need to protect liberty from governmental infringement. Participatory democrats would object to the Protective democrats' preoccupation with property rights but would agree with the need to preserve the generic liberties required for free and open political participation. Pluralists emphasize the necessity of social diversity for effective democracy; the other models do not question this need. The Developmental model calls attention to the value of good democratic citizenship, while the Participatory model emphasizes the value of searching for new ways for democratic citizens to make social decisions that control their lives. I do not mean to suggest that the disagreements among adherents of the various models are merely cosmetic—only that certain common values underlie them all.

Finally, these four models do not exhaust all the theoretical possibilities for conceptualizing democracy. Those who think and write about democracy have developed a wide variety of ways of thinking about the concept, and the practice of democracy has varied in a multitude of ways across time and throughout the world. A careful examination of these variants can lead one to many different democracy models. British political scientist David Held, for example, identifies *nine* distinct models of democracy in his comprehensive review of the concept.[36] Nor do these four models, as presented here, focus on all the key issues of concern to democratic theorists. For example, in recent years many theorists have written about the importance of deliberation as a key aspect of the democratic ideal (an issue that will be touched on in subsequent chapters). These theorists argue that one advantage democracy offers over other forms of government is the opportunity for reasoned deliberation, in public, over the best policies that ought to be pursued. In a democracy, when a public problem or issue arises, people can think through together what should be done to address it and are thereby more likely to find successful solutions. One can find advocates of deliberative democracy among theorists who otherwise see democracy through the lens of different ones of the four models presented in this chapter. For example, some who support the Protective model consider the separation of powers and checks and balances, which that model emphasizes, conducive to public deliberation.[37] Other proponents of deliberative democracy emphasize the merits of widespread popular participation in public deliberation, and they can be classed as Participatory democrats.[38]

What the four democratic models presented here suggest, and what this chapter shows, is that democracy remains, even after much practical experience with democratic institutions throughout the world, an ideal to be continually sought after, rather than a settled system to be complacently admired. People in many countries, including the United States, strive to achieve democratic ideals. They aim to subject public decisions to popular control, to protect individual civil rights and liberties, to expand political equality, to encourage participation in decisions that affect people's lives, to foster social diversity, and to promote good citizenship. Nevertheless, nowhere—not even in the United States—have these ideals been achieved. Partly the reason is that our definitions of these ideals, like our definition of democracy, continually change. For example, in 1840 universal white male suffrage seemed to satisfy the aspirations of most American democrats; in the United States of the twenty-first century, the exclusion of women and nonwhites from voting is rightly considered a gross violation of democratic principles.

We can see, therefore, that the achievement of the democratic ideal is so difficult because the ideal itself is so demanding. The limitations of human nature and social organization are always barriers in the way of successful democracy. Sometimes doing things undemocratically is just simpler than wrestling with democratic procedures. Impatience with the demands of democracy often tempts some people in democracies to bypass democratic procedures.[39] Another way in which democracy is demanding is in the time and energy that democratic citizenship requires—time many people would prefer to devote to their private affairs. Also, despite the almost universal lip service given to democratic ideals in the modern world, not everyone believes in democracy. Active opposition from individuals and groups opposed to democratic aspirations is surely a significant barrier to the achievement of democratic ideals. Whether it is a government such as Saudi Arabia's or Cuba's, a segment of society such as the southern whites who opposed the civil rights movement of the 1960s, or the economic interests of corporate officials who resist public efforts at regulation, the opponents of democracy remain powerful in every country and in every segment of society. With such opposition, the world will never be absolutely "safe for democracy."

This recognition of the fragility of democratic political institutions brings us to the main point of this book. Observers of democratic politics are continually identifying threats to the future and well-being of democracy. When studying these challenges, several questions need to be asked: First, what is the implicit or explicit model of democracy that each particular challenge seems to confront? Does the seriousness of the particular challenge diminish or increase depending on the model? Does the challenge threaten underlying values differently in the various models? Second, to what extent does the threat discussed undermine the democratic values of all the models, of democracy itself? Is the challenge to democratic values so serious that Protective, Pluralist, Developmental, and Participatory democrats should be equally concerned? Finally, what does analysis of the various threats to democracy tell us about the models themselves? Which model of democracy seems to offer the best chance of overcoming the challenges American democracy faces in the modern world? In other words, how should our politics be structured if we are to thrive as a democratic society?

Suggestions for Further Reading

Dahl, Robert. *On Democracy.* New Haven, CT: Yale University Press, 1998. The most prominent American democratic theorist sums up his ideas on why democracy is the preferred system.

Dunn, John. *Democracy: A History.* New York: Atlantic Monthly Press, 2005. A readable meditation on the concept of democracy.

Hayek, Friedrich A. *The Political Order of a Free People.* Chicago: University of Chicago Press, 1979. A brilliant and thorough exposition of the case for the Protective Democracy model.

Held, David. *Models of Democracy.* 3rd ed. Cambridge, UK: Polity Press, 2006. Presents nine models to describe the history of democratic theory.

Macpherson, C. B. *The Life and Times of Liberal Democracy.* Oxford: Oxford University Press, 1977. A comprehensive review of the theoretical ideas underpinning the models of democracy presented in this chapter.

Miller, James E. *Democracy Is in the Streets.* New York: Simon & Schuster, 1987. A history of Students for a Democratic Society (SDS) that focuses on the political ideas of student activists in the 1960s.

Nino, Carlos Santiago. *The Constitution of Deliberative Democracy.* New Haven, CT: Yale University Press, 1996. The late, renowned Argentinian scholar and human rights activist offers an intricate reflection on the relation between constitutionalism and democracy, and he proposes a theory of Deliberative Democracy to overcome the limitations of existing conceptions.

Pateman, Carole. *Participation and Democratic Theory.* Cambridge: Cambridge University Press, 1970. A prominent democratic theorist dissects the Participatory model.

Sandel, Michael J. *Democracy's Discontent: America in Search of a Public Philosophy.* Cambridge, MA: Harvard University Press, 1996. An elegantly written and clear argument calling for a public philosophy that moves beyond the "procedural republic" of liberal rights and entitlements to a democracy grounded in the civic republican tradition and citizen self-government.

Tilly, Charles. *Democracy.* New York: Cambridge University Press, 2007. A comparative empirical study of the social forces that lead toward and away from democratic regimes.

CHAPTER 1

The First Challenge: Separation of Powers

Nothing human can be perfect. Surrounded by difficulties, we did the best we could; leaving it with those who should come after us to take counsel from experience, and exercise prudently the power of amendment.

—GOUVERNEUR MORRIS

The evils we experience flow from the excess of democracy.

—ELBRIDGE GERRY

WE AMERICANS tend to equate democracy with our particular constitutional structure. When I ask students to define democracy, several always respond, "Democracy means a separation of powers—checks and balances between the branches of government." Like many Americans, these students identify democracy with government as it is practiced in the United States, and it is only a short leap then to define democracy in terms of the central feature of our constitutional structure: the separation of powers. This tendency is reinforced in the news media, in schools, and in statements by government officials, all of whom treat the Constitution reverentially, including the ideas of separation of powers and checks and balances.[1] In fact, whenever there is a crisis in American government, the standard solution proposed is to seek a restoration of "proper governmental checks and balances."

Idea of checks & Balances in Democracy

Opposite: *During the State of the Union address on January 25, 2011, President Barack Obama is applauded by Vice President Joe Biden and House Speaker John Boehner, each representing one of the separate institutions that must agree to make laws.*

© Pablo Martinez Monsivais/Pool/Corbis.

[handwritten: seperat seperation of govt assosiated w/ democracies]

The thesis of this chapter is that Americans are mistaken to equate the separation of governmental powers with democracy. In practice, especially in recent years, the constitutional separation between branches of government, particularly that between Congress and the presidency, has undermined the capacity of Americans to control their government. In their zeal to protect individual liberty—the central value of the Protective Democracy model—the authors of the Constitution erected barriers to majority rule that have always impeded democracy and now, after more than two hundred years, have produced perpetually stalemated government. For most of our history, we managed to overcome the antimajoritarian bias of the Constitution through a combination of presidential leadership and political party organization. This system offered a temporary and partial solution to governmental deadlock, but over the past few decades even this partial system has no longer worked. Divided government, in which different political parties control Congress and the presidency, has compounded the defects of the separation of powers in making the government inefficient, unresponsive, and unaccountable. Even during periods of unified government in recent years, separation of powers tends to lead to gridlock. Our eighteenth-century Constitution has become a major obstacle to achieving democratic government in the twenty-first century.

[handwritten: DIVISION = Defects]

The Founders' Work

Both the signers of the Declaration of Independence and the drafters of the Constitution can be classified, in the terminology of the democracy models, as "Protective democrats." They believed that the purpose of a democracy—or a *republic,* their term for representative democracy—was the protection of individual liberty. Their great fear was a tyrannical government that ignored individual rights and ruled without the consent of the governed. For the revolutionaries, however, the danger of tyranny emanated from a very different source than the tyranny the Constitution's authors feared. In 1776, a tyrannical executive, specifically King George III and his royal governors in the colonies, motivated the movement for independence. Only eleven years later, in 1787, the men who gathered to draft a new constitution worried mainly about the tyranny of popularly elected legislatures. What in the experience of the new American republic had caused this shift in concern?

During and after the Revolutionary War, most states enacted constitutions reflecting the popular spirit and republican enthusiasm that the Revolution had produced. Because the revolutionaries distrusted political executives, the new state constitutions lodged most power in the legislatures. These institutions were structured to permit maximum responsiveness to popular majorities. State legislators were typically chosen in annual elections so that their constituents would have plenty of opportunity to hold them accountable. Accountability through annual elections was carried farthest in the radical Pennsylvania constitution, which required that before it could become law, legislation had to be passed twice, with an election between the two votes, permitting voters an opportunity to ratify directly the actions of their representatives. Although all states required voters to own some property, property qualifications were modest enough in most states so that suffrage was widespread (at least among white males). Voters also tended to elect representatives very much like themselves, producing state legislatures dominated by farmers and tradesmen, most with minimal education but with personal interests and concerns reflective of those who elected them.[2] Given the weakness of the national government under the Articles of Confederation, the democratic majorities in the state legislatures were the centers of power in the new American nation.

Fear of and dissatisfaction with these state legislatures, particularly their democratic character, are what brought the founders to Philadelphia for the purpose of revising the Articles during that hot summer in 1787.[3] As Governor Edmund Randolph of Virginia put it, "Our chief danger arises from the democratic parts of our [state] constitutions. . . . None of the constitutions have provided sufficient checks against democracy."[4] The founders had two major complaints against the state legislatures. First, they considered state government too chaotic, with annual elections producing frequent turnover and legislators too prone to enacting the transitory passions of their constituents into law. Second, and more serious, the founders were dismayed at the sorts of laws being enacted in the states, particularly laws to inflate currency and abolish debts. Most of the convention delegates regarded those laws as a despotic attack on fundamental rights of property—the consequence of debtor majorities in the states taking over state governments and promoting their interests at the expense of the propertied minority. Even where a propertyless majority did not control state government, such a majority might resort to violent acts to support their interests—acts that the inept and overresponsive legislatures were ill equipped to control. When, just a year before the convention, a revolt by debtors in western Massachusetts (called "Shays' Rebellion") was put down with great difficulty by the state militia, the worst fears of the critics of state constitutions seemed to have been confirmed.

Historians debate vigorously the motives and purposes of the men who wrote the Constitution. Was the Constitutional Convention an antidemocratic counterrevolution of wealthy and propertied Americans seeking to preserve their wealth and power from a democratic citizenry? Or was it simply an attempt by prudent statesmen, concerned that the new nation would dissolve into violence and chaos, to establish the structure of a stable representative democracy?[5] Whichever characterization of the founders' motives is true, the record of the convention provides much evidence that controlling tyrannical majorities was the major agenda item. The result of the convention's work, the US Constitution, reflects that concern, for it is a masterly creation whose central purpose is preventing the "tyranny" of a majority.

The new Constitution restricted majority tyranny in two principal ways. First, it established a strong national government that would be capable of countering any tyrannical majority in a state. The central government gained new powers, such as the power to coin money and regulate commerce, and new instruments, such as a standing army, to enable it to overcome any state government that fell under the control of a factional interest. Even though the convention did not go as far as James Madison wanted it to in giving the national government a veto over state legislation, it did replace the weak government under the Articles with a national government with muscle. But what prevented the national government from being subjected to a tyrannical majority? The answer was the second principal feature of the Constitution: the structure of governmental institutions that we now call the "separation of powers."

The central impetus of the separation of powers was to give the individuals controlling each of the government branches only partial control over the enactment of law, but control they could exercise independently of those controlling the other branches. The separate political base of each branch was the guarantee that the occupants of the different branches would be politically independent of one another and capable of acting autonomously. For example, the president was to be chosen by a special Electoral College that was completely independent of Congress. Likewise, the president had no role in the election of members of Congress. This logic was carried further in the separate election processes for the two houses of Congress: members of the House of Representatives elected directly every two years in congressional districts, and senators chosen by state legislatures, with only one-third of the Senate picked at any one time. And these politically independent actors, a president and the two houses of the bicameral Congress, all had to agree before any laws were enacted.

Although the Electoral College never operated in the way intended in choosing the president, and although we now elect senators directly, the separation of powers structure remains an excellent means of preventing a political majority from easily controlling government. A president elected to office with a massive popular majority in a national constituency cannot count on enacting into law the political platform he campaigned on because a majority of members of Congress, selected in a separate election process in their individual constituencies, may oppose the president's programs. Because of the separation of powers, voters are free—a freedom that they exercise, as we later see, with increasing regularity—to vote simultaneously for a president who favors one set of policies and for a congressional representative who opposes those same policies. Even if, in a given election, a majority of voters choose both a president and a majority of members of Congress who agree on a set of policies, the two-thirds of senators who are not chosen in that election can block those policies. If in the "midterm" congressional elections that come in the middle of a president's term, voters choose to send to

Washington a decisive majority of representatives to enact a particular policy, that policy can be blocked by a presidential veto that needs the votes of only thirty-four senators to avoid being overridden. Add to this series of cross-checks a judiciary made up of members with life tenure and the power to strike down what they consider unconstitutional legislation, and one has an excellent mechanism for frustrating majority rule.

The author of this system, James Madison, understood its political logic quite well. In *Federalist* No. 51, he argues that succeeding occupants of the various government branches will jealously protect the constitutional prerogatives of their particular branch and seek to prevent the other branches from accumulating too much power. For the separation of powers to work, "the interest of the man must be connected with the constitutional rights of the place."[6] In this way, "ambition" would "counteract ambition" as wary presidents would check the powers of Congress and members of congress would keep a watchful eye on power-hungry presidents. With their political independence from one another lodged in their independent electoral bases, the practical ability of the occupants of the different branches to check the power of the other branches was secured. In such a system, Madison and the other founders believed, no tyrannical majority could simultaneously control all the relevant policymakers, and thus the rights of minorities were secure.

The Jeffersonian Model

The separation of powers structure erected formidable barriers in the way of forming a coherent governing majority in the United States, but it did not take long after the ratification of the Constitution for the ingenious politicians of the period to develop a means of uniting the branches of government behind a popular government. The key to uniting the branches was the political party, and the first practitioner of the method was the third US president, Thomas Jefferson.

The founders abhorred the idea of political parties; their prevention had been one of the goals of the Constitution. For James Madison in 1787, parties were "factions," groups united by a common "passion" or "interest" adverse to the interests of other citizens. But in the first decade of the new Republic, its leaders, including Madison, came to find the political party an indispensable institution for organizing voters and their representatives. By the end of the century, two vigorous political parties contested for power throughout the nation: the Federalists and the Democratic-Republicans. In a hard-fought election in 1800, the Democratic-Republican Party led by Thomas Jefferson decisively defeated the Federalists and captured the presidency and large majorities in both the Senate and the House of Representatives. As president, Jefferson, to a much greater extent than his Federalist predecessor, John Adams, used his position as national party leader to organize Congress on behalf of his political program and policies.[7] He devised a new model of government that could mobilize the country on behalf of an electoral majority in spite of the separation of powers. This model of govern-ment, which political scientist James MacGregor Burns labeled the "Jeffersonian model," has been the strategy for organizing coherent and responsible democratic government since Jefferson's presidency.

In the past two hundred years of American history, there have been frequent punctuations of creative democratic leadership producing policy innovation. During each of these creative periods, a dynamic president has used the Jeffersonian model to build an electoral majority and then, with the support of party majorities in Congress, to bridge the separation of powers to enact new policies. These periods, with which we associate the names of our greatest presi-dents—Jackson, Lincoln, Theodore Roosevelt, Wilson, Franklin Roosevelt, and Lyndon Baines Johnson—all had in common the Jeffersonian model. In contrast, periods of divided government, when different parties control Congress and the presidency, have allowed the separation of powers structure to impede the devel-opment of coherent policies. These have been periods of stalemate and deadlock, when no one seems to be in charge of government. Our history seems to show that, given the constitutional structure, the Jeffersonian model of leadership is a requisite for democratic change to occur.

Although the Jeffersonian model has been the historical strategy for successful democratic politics in the United States, it does not overcome completely the antimajoritarian bias of the separation of powers. First, it permits only episodic periods of majority rule. Divided government remains a continuing possibility as long as the presidency and the two houses of Congress are elected independently. This is why we have come to associate democratic change in the United States with short periods of policy innovation followed by long periods of stasis. In addi-tion, presidents are usually under tremendous pressure to enact their programs swiftly, in the first two years of office, for fear that the midterm congressional elections will bring a hostile majority into Congress. The result is incompletely enacted programs and a muddled record of presidential performance.

Second, because of the separation of powers structure, the president has only limited control over the members of his own party in Congress. Members of Congress are dependent on electoral majorities in their individual constituencies, not on the national party organization or on the president's national majority. Sometimes the support of an individual constituency requires defying the presi-dent and the national majority, as both recent Republican and Democratic presi-dents have learned when their own party followers in Congress failed to support their policies. Consequently, even with a partisan majority in Congress, a presi-dent sometimes cannot employ the Jeffersonian model because of the recalci-trance of a minority within his own party.

And third, bicameralism continues to impede unified governmental action even when the same political party controls both houses of Congress. The differ-ent electoral constituencies of the Senate and House thwart their ability to craft common policies.[8] The unrepresentative character of the Senate—in which each state, regardless of population, has the same voice—presents additional obstacles to majority rule. The 450,000 residents of Wyoming, for example, have the same representation in the Senate as the 32 million residents in California, giving the vote of a lucky Wyoming citizen 66 times the weight of a fellow citizen who happens to live in California.[9] And the Senate's tradition of the filibuster, which allows a minority of forty senators to block legislation, presents an additional barrier to majority rule.

Although the Jeffersonian model has been a partial solution to the bias toward governmental stalemate inherent in the separation of powers, a critical requisite of its operation—one-party control of both the presidency and Congress—has been a rarity in recent years. Since 1956, one-half of presidential elections—seven of fourteen—have returned to office a president of one party and a Congress controlled by the other.[10] Because this situation is now so common, most Americans do not realize that divided government produced as a result of a presidential election was once extremely rare. Between 1832 and 1952 it occurred only three times. As Table 1.1 shows, prior to 1952 divided government was almost exclusively a product of midterm congressional elections, when voters sometimes voted in a congressional majority opposed to the sitting president. The midterm elections of 1994, 2006, and 2010 seemed to follow that older pattern, with Republicans gaining control of Congress in 1994 and 2010 and Democrats in 2006. In the 1996 and 2000 presidential elections, voters once again opted for divided government as Presidents Clinton and George W. Bush assumed office facing at least one congressional house controlled by the opposing party. Both Bush's reelection in 2004 and President Barack Obama's victory in 2008 were more in line with the traditional pattern, as a one-party triumph produced a partisan sweep and unified government. Following both these partisan sweeps, the hand-wringing of some political commentators about the dangers to "checks and balances" that partisan control of both ends of Pennsylvania Avenue represented underscored the novelty of unified government in the modern era. Many Americans do not recognize that the historical tradition had been unified partisan control after a presidential election.

TABLE 1.1   Divided Government by Type of Election, 1832–2010

	Presidential	*Midterm*
1832–1898	3	11
1900–1952	0	4
1954–2010	7	11

Source: Adapted from Morris P. Fiorina, "An Era of Divided Government," *Political Science Quarterly* 107 (Fall 1992): 390. Data updated to reflect elections after 1992.

A variety of explanations have been offered for the increasing frequency of divided government after 1952, including the decline of partisanship among voters, the greater reelection resources of congressional incumbents, gerrymandered congressional districts, and conscious choice by the electorate.[11] Some political scientists pointed to voters' weaker attachment to political parties as a crucial factor in more divided government. More voters, particularly among the highly educated and more affluent—a crucial "swing" voter group in close elections—became ticket-splitters in the 1960s through the 1980s, voting for candidates of different political parties for different offices in a single election.[12] A few observers of this phenomenon even claimed that voters were consciously choosing divided government as a way of achieving competing policy outcomes.[13] A voter would choose a Republican president to hold the line on taxes and a Democratic member of Congress to protect valued social programs. Recently some political scientists, citing renewed partisan attachments among voters and less ticket-splitting, have begun to argue that the era of divided government may be coming to an end, as the 2004 and 2008 elections suggest.

Even if unified governments become more common, the prevalence of divided government over the last few decades brought concern for the consequences of the separation of powers system onto the political agenda. Partisan division between the branches prevented the country's coping with our constitutional system in the traditional manner—the Jeffersonian model. Instead, Americans had to observe the full effects of negotiating policy between politically independent institutions with separate policy agendas, political interests, and claims to democratic legitimacy. Even the periods of unified partisan control under Clinton in his first two years, Bush from 2002–2006, and Obama from 2008–2010 seemed not to overcome governmental gridlock as the Jeffersonian model had done in the past. The result has been a continuing spectacle of contentious and stalemated government, leaving unaddressed many important policy problems: inadequate health care, dependence on foreign oil supplies, failure to control rising deficits and debt, continuing economic inequality, deteriorating infrastructure, and global warming. No wonder citizens have little confidence in American political institutions.

The Separation of Powers and Democratic Values

The founders' preoccupation with the democratic value *liberty* (the central concern of the Protective model) caused them to construct an institutional structure that interfered with achieving two other key democratic values. First, in their zeal to prevent majority tyranny, they created a structure insufficiently *responsive* to political majorities. Responsiveness to citizens is an underlying concern of all the models discussed in the introduction, but it is of special concern to proponents of the Participatory and Developmental models. Second, the separation of powers design has so fragmented and divided responsibility for government policy that it has become impossible to hold elected officials *accountable* for their actions. Accountability is also an assumed attribute of all the models, including the Pluralist model, which defines the democratic citizen's key role as passing judgment on the performance of officials at election time. Such a judgment cannot be made effectively when the separation of powers obscures who is responsible for governmental conduct.

Responsiveness

Although democrats can sympathize with the founders' concern for protecting minority rights and preventing majority tyranny—objectives all democrats share—the separation of powers creates a problem for responsive democratic politics. The system is incapable of distinguishing between majorities that are tyrannical and those that are not tyrannical; it frustrates all majorities, regardless of their objectives. The system creates a series of roadblocks at which a minority interest can prevent change that a democratic majority supports. An electoral majority may send to Washington a House of Representatives prepared to enact policies they favor only to have those policies voted down in the Senate, in which less-populated states are overrepresented and two-thirds of the senators have not faced the electorate in the most recent election. Alternatively, the president may be a minority instrument, employing the veto to prevent enactment of legislation—a veto that can be made override-proof with the cooperation of only thirty-four senators. Or a president elected to office with a majority mandate for change may face opposition from elected majorities in either house of Congress that are committed to a very different mandate. Separation of powers provides a constitutional structure that is inherently biased against change, even when change has the support of an overwhelming majority of citizens.

The separation of powers system was *intended* to reduce the responsiveness of government. Because of their fear of majority tyranny, the founders wanted to "cool" democratic passions by passing them through several independent institutions.[14] In addition, they believed in the classical liberal ideal of limited government. Separation of powers served this ideal by providing a permanent conservative bias to government; a minority could easily block the passage of new policies. Or competing institutions claiming responsiveness to different electoral majorities would check each other's ability to pass any measure. Even large popular majorities in favor of a policy had to fight through numerous barriers before innovative laws could be passed. As a result, government could act in response to democratic majorities only slowly and in a limited way. Defenders of the separation of powers, including the founders themselves, usually have justified this blanket frustration of all majorities by arguing that enduring majorities backing wise and useful policies will eventually succeed. They believe that the system will stop wrongheaded proposals passionately backed by a transitory majority but that, if a proposal has genuine merit, it will succeed through several election cycles in bringing to power supporters in all branches and then be enacted into law. As one defender puts it, the separation of powers was intended "to protect liberty from an immoderate majority while permitting a moderate majority to prevail."[15]

Separation of powers in a democratic political system, then, is based on a proposition about its consequences for democratic majorities: Tyrannical, immoderate, and unwise majorities will be blocked; non-tyrannical, moderate, and wise majorities will eventually succeed. Does our two-hundred-year experience with the separation of powers confirm this proposition? An easy "objective" test would be quite difficult to construct, for observers of the historical record are likely to differ over whether majority-backed policies that have not succeeded or were long delayed were or were not "immoderate," "unwise," or "tyrannical." An evaluation of the issue would require detailed argumentation about individual policies and historical episodes. I believe that such a detailed review of our history would show that the separation of powers has impeded the enactment of numerous moderate, just, and wise policies. Over the past two hundred years, this system has worked repeatedly to frustrate and divide popular majorities. Even with the partial amelioration of the Jeffersonian model, our constitutional system has made the enactment of every policy innovation a protracted struggle. As a result, many popular programs and policies have failed to be enacted or have been put into place only after years of debate, discussion, and compromise, which dilute their effects. Because of this bias against policy innovation, government *is* smaller in the United States than in other industrialized nations, but our government also provides fewer and less generous social programs even though public opinion supports more expansive ones.

For example, until the passage of the Affordable Care Act in 2010 (not to be fully implemented until 2014), the United States was the only industrialized, democratic nation in the world that did not guarantee all its citizens access to health care. By the middle of the last century, in other democratic countries, citizen demand for access to health care produced a variety of government policies to provide either universal health insurance or government-subsidized health care services. According to public opinion polls, the same majority preference for universal health care coverage that produced such programs elsewhere has existed in the United States for over half a century.[16] But since the administration of President Franklin Roosevelt in the 1930s, minority special interests have been able to manipulate the separation of powers system to block numerous attempts to enact universal health insurance.[17] Although separation of powers is supposed to impede only unwise policies, in the case of health insurance it has helped to produce the most complex and expensive system in the world, one that leaves about 50 million Americans without health care coverage and many others inadequately covered.[18] Even if the Affordable Care Act takes effect in 2014 and ameliorates this problem, the decades of delay in its enactment demonstrates the lack of responsiveness to broad majority preferences of American governmental institutions for decades.

I could cite numerous other examples of the separation of powers impeding governmental responsiveness to majority preferences. The blockage of civil rights legislation by a minority of southern congressmen in the 1940s, 1950s, and 1960s; the National Rifle Association's continuing obstruction of reasonable gun control legislation; the failure to enact meaningful campaign finance reform; the decade-long delay in enacting a minimal family leave policy; the continuing failure to control greenhouse gas emissions that produce global warming; and the inability to resolve the problem of a growing national debt are just a few. Even in a time of national emergency, after the terrorist attacks of September 2001, the two houses of Congress and the president were deadlocked for more than two months over a plan to nationalize airport security. The inherent bias of the separation of powers structure against majorities supporting change inhibits governmental responsiveness to serious problems, citizen concerns, and substantive policy innovation.[19] In a recent comparative study, political scientists Alfred Stepan and Juan J. Linz find that the high number of veto points in the American separation of powers structure impedes enactment of programs to mitigate economic inequality, giving the United States the highest level of inequality of any established democracy.[20] Given this system, it is not surprising that most Americans have less and less confidence in governmental institutions. The perception that "those politicians in Washington can't seem to get anything done" reflects an awareness of the inherent unresponsiveness of government. What Americans need to understand is that the unresponsiveness is built into the separation of powers structure.

Governmental unresponsiveness is most often associated with periods of divided government, but the separation of powers system places roadblocks in the way of policy innovation even when a single party controls both Congress and the presidency. In the past, the Jeffersonian model was a means of sometimes overcoming institutional division to enact progressive policies, but the political autonomy of members of Congress, their ability to gain election in their districts independently of the president, means that even a congressional majority of his own party does not guarantee support for the president's program. And the Senate's filibuster rule usually gives the opposition party a potential veto over presidential initiatives if the Senate majority numbers less than sixty. In the late 1970s, President Jimmy Carter discovered that substantial Democratic Party majorities in both houses of Congress were not enough to enact his legislative agenda, including his major proposal for a comprehensive energy policy. When Bill Clinton assumed the presidency in 1993, after twelve years of divided government, many observers expected that a more politically savvy president would be able to mobilize congressional Democrats to carry out his electoral mandate. Clinton found that most of his fellow Democrats cared little about the promises he had made to the country as a whole, or about the success of his presidency, but focused mainly on how the legislation would affect their constituencies and the special interests that funded their campaigns.[21] Like Carter before him, Clinton found uniting his own party around his initiatives a challenge and a Republican opposition united against most all that he wanted to do. Early on he had to abandon an effort to stimulate the economy with a job creation package in the face of a Republican Senate filibuster. His deficit reduction package, including tax increases (that eventually would be credited with fueling the economic boom of the 1990s and producing a budget surplus), barely passed the House and squeaked through the Senate only when Vice President Al Gore broke a tie vote. After the embarrassing defeat of his health reform plan, the Republicans captured majorities in both Houses in 1994, forcing Clinton to cope with divided government for the balance of his tenure.

Although separation of powers seems most likely to frustrate liberals who advocate progressive, majoritarian reforms such as national health insurance, conservative Republicans, like Clinton's successor George W. Bush, have found "checks and balances" to be equally effective in blocking their favored reforms. In his first six months in office, President George W. Bush was able to take advantage of slim Republican majorities in both houses of Congress to enact his central campaign promises—a large and controversial tax cut and a major education reform—the No Child Left Behind Act.[22] In both cases, he was forced to modify his original proposals to accommodate moderate Republicans and certain key Democrats whose support was needed to pass the legislation.[23] Despite a relatively clear-cut presidential victory in 2004 and expanded Republican majorities in the House and Senate, the president and his conservative supporters found themselves frustrated when the Social Security and tax reform initiatives that Bush had campaigned on foundered within months of his reelection. These domestic initiatives could not overcome resistance from key moderate Republicans or pick up enough Democratic votes in the Senate to neutralize the threat of filibusters. Bush conservatives thus learned the same lesson that Clinton liberals had learned from the failure of health care reform: A decisive electoral victory is not sufficient to overcome the obstacles to change that are inherent in the separation of powers structure. Those obstacles block responsiveness to conservative and liberal majorities alike.

President Barack Obama's first two years in office seemed to mark a revival of the Jeffersonian model and its capacity to bring about substantial change despite the separation of powers. Obama gained office through a decisive electoral victory with about 53 percent of the popular vote and an overwhelming electoral vote margin.[24] Democrats also expanded their control of Congress to a seventy-eight-seat majority in the House and, eventually, the magic sixty-vote filibuster-proof majority in the Senate. Coming to power at the height of the most severe economic downturn since the Great Depression, the challenge facing the new president and Congress was to revive the moribund economy and relieve the distress of the Great Recession. Democrats were able to use their control of both branches to enact major new legislative initiatives. Among these, the passage of the Affordable Care Act of 2010, which finally achieved the progressive goal of universal health insurance, was the signature achievement. In addition, Obama signed into law a major economic stimulus package; financial regulatory reform; student loan reform; new regulation of credit cards, tobacco, and food safety; gay rights to serve in the armed services; and extensions of unemployment, food stamp, and Medicaid assistance to ease the effects of the recession. Several key reforms passed the House, including climate change mitigation through cap and trade, immigration reform, and new campaign finance reforms, but failed to pass the Senate.[25] Despite the overall legislative success, after two years both Obama and Congress had grown immensely unpopular, leading to the Republicans recapturing control of the House after 2010 and reducing the Democrats' Senate majority.

Obama's 2008 campaign promise to bring change to Washington meant not only accomplishing new legislative achievements, like reform of health care, but also altering the atmosphere of partisan conflict. Upon taking office, Obama appealed to bipartisanship as a means of accomplishing his goals. Not content to follow solely the partisan logic of the Jeffersonian model, Obama hoped he could gain Republican backing for parts of his agenda. Understanding better the logic of the separation of powers and the opportunity "checks and balances" offered to a minority, the Republicans consistently rebuffed the administration's bipartisan appeals and adopted a policy of consistent opposition. In the face of such partisan gridlock, Obama soon discovered that the complications of the legislative process in the separation of powers system undermined his policy initiatives, forcing him to water down their effectiveness and enact them through a prolonged and drawn-out process that undermined their popularity. We can see these factors at work in the enactment of the two most prominent legislative achievements of the first two years: the economic stimulus and the Affordable Care Act.

In his first few weeks in office, Obama's first priority was enacting a substantial economic stimulus package. Even as it designed its initial proposal, the administration had to take into account the potential roadblocks of the separation of powers that might derail any stimulus. Because it would need two or perhaps three Republican votes to overcome a filibuster in the Senate (the election of Democratic Senator Al Franken in Minnesota was at that time not settled and Pennsylvania Republican Senator Arlen Specter had not yet shifted his allegiance to the Democrats, which eventually would give them sixty Senate votes), tax cuts constituted about 40 percent of the administration's initial stimulus proposal even though most economists considered direct government spending more effective than tax cuts in stimulating the economy.[26] Obama and his advisers also hoped the tax cuts would help gain the votes of "Blue Dog Democrats," Democratic House members elected in conservative districts many of which Republican candidate John McCain had won in 2008. The logic of separation of powers meant that these members perceived their reelection prospects in terms of individual voting records that attract support in their conservative districts rather than the overall success of the Obama presidency. To court these Blue Dogs, the overall size of the stimulus, $787 billion, also was kept lower than economists recommended to cover what was a $2 trillion drop in GDP.[27] In the end, this smaller, less robust stimulus did bring an end to the recession and the decline in jobs, but it did not prove strong enough to bring about forceful economic growth. Unemployment remained mired at about 9 percent for Obama's entire first term and left the perception of ineffectual economic leadership. In 2010, as the economy seemed to stagnate, several of Obama's advisers advocated a second stimulus package, yet enacting one was impossible given congressional roadblocks.[28] The continuing weak economy fueled the Republican surge in the 2010 midterms, bringing a Republican majority in the House and a smaller Democratic majority in the Senate. Now with divided government, response to public demand for government action on the economy proved impossible. In the fall of 2011, a new jobs proposal from the Obama administration met solid rejection from House and Senate Republicans. The public's central demand for action on job creation could not be met because of legislative gridlock.

Obama's signature legislative achievement, the Affordable Care Act, also emerged from the legislative process in a distorted form because of roadblocks inherent in the separation of powers. As with the stimulus bill, the initial design of the health care proposal reflected the administration's calculation of what was needed to overcome legislative barriers rather than what would most effectively and efficiently provide universal health care. Rejecting at the outset any consideration of a single payer universal insurance plan favored by liberal Democrats, the administration opted for an approach it hoped might attract some Republican support.[29] The administration plan involved maintaining the current employer-based private health insurance system for most workers. For workers without employer-based coverage, the plan involved creation of state-level health insurance exchanges through which competing insurance companies would offer coverage to individuals and small businesses. This approach, including a mandate that all individuals purchase insurance coverage through either their employer or the exchange, was similar to the Massachusetts health care program enacted by former Republican Governor Mitt Romney and to one Republican Senators had advocated as an alternative to the Clinton health care reform plan in 1993. In proposing a plan with a conservative Republican pedigree, the administration hoped for some bipartisan support for health reform, but in the end this was not to be. Also, to prevent the sort of full-scale health industry assault on their proposal that had brought down the Clinton plan, the administration negotiated agreements with the health insurance industry, health care providers, and pharmaceutical makers to gain their support. In deference to concerns of liberal Democrats, initial legislative drafts provided for a "public option" in the health exchanges—a government-run plan that would compete with private insurers in providing coverage. Liberals expected the public option to set standards for cost and quality that competing private coverage would have to meet.

Despite a plan with bipartisan roots and support from the health care industry, passing the Affordable Care Act proved an arduous and drawn-out process, stymied repeatedly by the veto points in the separation of powers system. This complex and, to most of the public, baffling process alienated the public and undermined public support for the eventual legislation. Three separate House committees were involved in drafting the House bill in the spring of 2009 and, in the face of united Republican opposition, would have to report out a bill with Democratic votes alone. One, the House Commerce Committee, insisted on a watered down version of the public option to gain support from the Blue Dog Democrats on the committee.[30] Despite prolonged negotiations in the House, that chamber was poised to pass a bill prior to the August congressional recess as Obama preferred, but meeting this deadline would be impossible in the Senate. There, the legislation was bogged down in the Senate Finance Committee, chaired by Senator Max Baucus of Montana, who was attempting to forge a compromise with the Republican members of the committee. Although most observers saw little chance any Republicans would accept any compromise (and in the end no Republicans supported the bill), Baucus allowed Republican members to drag out the discussions beyond the August recess. In the meantime, opponents of the legislation, particularly on right wing talk radio and Fox cable TV, were filling the airwaves with hysterical and distorted denunciations of the legislation, claiming imminent "government takeover" of health care and "death panels" that would force euthanizing of senior citizens. When members of Congress returned to their districts in August 2009, they were met at town meetings with crowds of "Tea Party" supporters screaming their opposition to health care reform based largely on these false claims. Intense media coverage of these events, including the false claims, significantly undermined public support. While a strong majority of the public had favored health care reform in the spring, by August support had fallen below 50 percent where it would remain for the balance of legislative consideration.[31]

When Congress reconvened in the fall, attention focused on the Senate, where the Finance Committee finally approved draft legislation without any Republican votes. If health care reform was to pass the Senate, supporters would need the votes of all sixty Democrats to break an inevitable Republican filibuster. This reality gave every individual Democratic senator enormous leverage to extract concessions in return for a vote and several took full advantage of this leverage.[32] For his vote, Connecticut Senator Joe Lieberman demanded elimination of the public option. Senator Mary Landrieu of Louisiana demanded a special provision providing additional Medicaid funds for her state. Most blatant of all was the notorious "Cornhusker Kickback," a concession to Nebraska's Senator Ben Nelson for special Medicaid funding for his state. Widespread coverage of these special deals tainted the public perception of health care reform, fed public cynicism, and undermined further public support. Little of this coverage, however, explained how these special interest "kickbacks" resulted from the logic of separation of powers and the leverage, in particular, the filibuster gave individual senators to trade their votes for special interest deals.

Even as public dismay over the prolonged conflict over health care reform eroded public support, both houses of Congress managed to pass versions of reform before the end of 2009. Only negotiations between the two houses to reconcile the more conservative Senate version with the more liberal House version seemed necessary to enact this historic legislation. Then, a Massachusetts bombshell blasted new institutional roadblocks to passage. In a special election to replace the late Edward Kennedy, voters in the predominantly Democratic state of Massachusetts elected upstart Republican Scott Brown, who had campaigned against health care reform. Now, without the sixty Democratic votes needed to end a Senate filibuster, any hope for final passage of health reform seemed impossible. Salvation came only when the Democrats devised a scheme to enact the legislation without a second Senate vote subject to the filibuster rule. Rather than convene a conference committee to reconcile the House and Senate versions of the legislation, the House simply enacted the Senate version. As a result of this legislative maneuver, however, the House had to accept the more conservative Senate version without the public option. In addition, small modifications of the enacted legislation were made in a separate bill enacted as a budget reconciliation measure that could not be filibustered in the Senate. So, by this convoluted process, the Affordable Care Act became law.

As noted before, in terms of purely passing legislation, the first two years of the Obama presidency ought to be heralded a success. Not only were significant initiatives enacted, but most, such as credit card reform, banking regulatory reform, and student loan reform, were quite popular with the public. Even health care reform initially earned public praise, only losing majority support as the reform debate dragged on and still remaining favorable to a large segment of the public when signed into law. Yet, despite legislative success, positive perception of Obama's performance declined steadily throughout his first two years. Much of the decline was tied to the stagnant economy.[33] Here the roadblocks of the separation of powers that impeded a more effective policy response directly contributed to public perception of Obama's presidency.

These same roadblocks required accepting modifications that reduced policy effectiveness in response to special interest pressures. Some of the decline in popular support for the Affordable Care Act, for example, came from health care reform supporters who perceived the elimination of the public option as fatally undermining reform. In the end, Obama's muddled legislative record, necessitated by the need to overcome institutional barriers, failed to achieve a clear response to the demands for political change that had propelled him to office.

The separation of powers not only blocks responsiveness to electoral majorities but also creates opportunities for well-placed minority interests to prevail over majority interests. In creating obstacles to majority tyranny through the separation of powers system, the framers made possible minority tyranny. Sometimes this tyranny can come from a single politician occupying a key veto point in the legislative process—as with the concessions Senators Lieberman, Landrieu, and Nelson exacted for their votes on health reform. In a particularly famous incident of a single legislator enacting a price for his support, the Republican legislative leadership in 1995 found it impossible to reduce milk price subsidies as a part of a comprehensive package of federal budget cuts.[34] Although reduced spending was a key objective of the Republican conservative agenda, Republican representative Gerald Solomon, whose New York district includes many dairy farmers, was not about to sacrifice their interests for the larger goal of budget restraint. As chairman of the Rules Committee, he demanded (and gained) restoration of the full subsidy before allowing the budget bill to reach the floor of the House. The capacity of many members of Congress thus to extract special interest favors for constituents is largely responsible for the phenomenon of "pork barrel spending" that pundits so loudly condemn. What many fail to understand, however, is that responsiveness, even to narrowly based constituent interests, follows directly from the Madisonian constitutional structure.

Special interests are adept at exploiting conflicts between the branches and between the two houses of Congress to insert their minority preferences when major legislation is being enacted. Typically, enactment of an important government program—such as the Medicare prescription drug program passed in 2003—requires reconciling differing versions favored by the House, the Senate, and also the executive branch. Responding to a clear need among senior citizens for relief from the rising costs of prescription drugs, majorities in both houses (including both Democrats and Republicans) and the Bush administration supported creation of a new prescription drug program.[35] Conflict over the legislation focused on how the program should be structured. The simplest, cheapest, and most straightforward way would have been merely to add coverage of prescription drugs to the existing Medicare program; many members of Congress, particularly Democrats but also some Republicans, favored such an approach. However, the pharmaceutical industry feared that if drug costs were to be paid directly by Medicare, the federal government might use its bargaining power as a major drug consumer to negotiate lower drug prices (and lower profits for drug companies)—a practice followed in all industrialized countries except the United States. The health insurance industry, meanwhile, also wanted an opportunity to profit from the new benefit, which it would not be able to do if the assistance was provided directly through Medicare. These industries played the pressure and veto points within the separation of powers system perfectly to see that their preferences were achieved—at the cost of adequate drug coverage for seniors.

When the House and the Senate pass different versions of legislation, which they often do, a conference committee consisting of members from both houses meets to hammer out a single version, which is then returned to each house for final approval. Conference committees, usually meeting in secret, offer many opportunities to lobbyists to insert their preferences into the final legislation. When a conference committee on the differing Senate and House versions of the prescription drug bill convened, lobbyists for the pharmaceutical and health care industries leapt into action. With the assistance of conferees from both houses (who had received generous campaign contributions from both industries in the past), these lobbyists made sure that the conference agreement returned to both houses for final enactment leaned toward the more industry-friendly House version—and they even added new provisions not included in either of the versions enacted earlier. The result was a complex and confusing program that requires Medicare enrollees to choose among varying drug benefit plans offered by dozens of different health insurers, that cover only some of their costs, require very high out-of-pocket payments from those seniors who need the most drugs, provide expensive subsidies to health insurance companies to ensure their participation, forbid the government from negotiating lower drug costs from the drug companies, and, because of these latter two provisions, will be enormously expensive to taxpayers.[36] Although many senators and congressmen, especially Democrats, objected to the special interest provisions inserted into the final version, they had no choice but to support it or be labeled opponents of a prescription drug benefit.

As the legislation began to be implemented in 2005, dissatisfaction with the program rose, and many seniors objected to the bewildering complexity of choosing an appropriate drug plan.[37] Taxpayers began to realize that the generous subsidies to health insurers and the prohibition on negotiating lower drug prices made the program much more expensive than the Bush administration had projected. But who were disgruntled citizens to hold accountable for this unsatisfactory and expensive program? Even though the Republican administration and Republican congressional leadership had pushed the special interest perks in the bill, many Democrats had been forced, in the end, to vote for the flawed program as well. Given the complexity of the legislative process under a separation of powers system, voters find it almost impossible to single out which politicians or political party to blame for bad policy decisions. Which brings us to the other major flaw in the separation of powers structure: the obstacles it raises to holding government accountable.

Accountability

The accountability of elected officials to those they represent is crucial to *representative* democracy. The famous democratic theorist Jean-Jacques Rousseau did not believe that people could rule themselves through representatives because he did not trust representatives to make laws in their constituents' best interests rather than in their own. Proponents of representative democracy, however, held that the problem Rousseau raised could be overcome if the representatives were required to face the electorate at regular intervals. At election time, the represented would be able to review the governmental record of their representatives and decide whether they had been well served. Between elections, elected officials would exercise their duties responsibly because they knew their constituents would hold them accountable for their actions at the next election. This system of accountability of representatives to the represented means that citizens must be able to evaluate the performance of elected officials: Those who have performed well should be reelected; those who have done poorly should be rejected.

The American separation of powers system hopelessly muddles the ability of citizens to hold their representatives accountable. Under this system, the president and Congress share responsibility for public policy and governmental performance, but they are held accountable separately. At election time, not only must citizens form a judgment about governmental performance (already a challenging task for most of us), but they must also sort out responsibility for that performance between the president and Congress (and between the House of Representatives and the Senate!). Determining this responsibility would be in itself a monumental task—requiring hours of research on separate issues—but it is made impossible by the way incumbents of both branches distort their records. The president and members of Congress routinely take credit for governmental successes while blaming the other branch for any failures.

The politics surrounding Obama's first term illustrate well the challenge voters face in holding government accountable in a separation of powers system. As was explained above, the failure of the president to successfully address the country's sluggish economy and continuing high unemployment, with the perception of unresponsiveness thus created, led to an electoral swing toward the Republicans in the 2010 midterm election. This swing demonstrated the electorate's discontent with Washington policymakers and a desire that action be taken to revive the economy and address other issues like rising government debt. Republicans also benefitted from the very different electorate that voted in 2010 from that of 2008. In 2008, voting turnout was much larger as is usually the case in presidential years, especially among young, poorer, and minority voters who had flocked to the polls in record numbers to support Obama. In 2010, these core Obama supporters largely stayed home while a populist surge of anti-Obama "Tea Party" supporters gave their votes to Republican candidates. Given separation of powers, the consequence of voters shifting allegiance served not to create conditions to more successfully address Washington's failure to revive the economy. Instead, with a new Republican House majority, divided government was now in place with gridlock, not action to address national problems, the likely outcome.

In the months following the Republican House takeover, the public witnessed a depressing spectacle of vituperative partisanship, political brinkmanship, and failure to pass constructive policy measures. Despite continued high joblessness, during most of 2011, the parties deadlocked over the issues of deficits and debt while pushing any effort to promote job growth to the background. Upon taking office, House Republicans decided to use their new leverage of control of one congressional chamber to force their agenda of smaller government and lower taxes.[38] This strategy culminated in a showdown over lifting the federal debt ceiling during the summer of 2011. Normally raising the debt ceiling is a routine vote that authorizes the US Treasury to issue additional treasury bonds to cover

The separation of powers structure gave House Speaker John Boehner and the Republican leadership the ability to force a crisis over raising the debt ceiling in July 2011 to extract concessions from President Obama on the federal budget.

© Pete Marovich/ZUMA Press/Corbis.

debt that already has been incurred. Raising the debt ceiling itself does not increase the debt nor does it authorize any additional indebtedness. If the debt ceiling is not raised, the consequences are momentous—the country would be in default, unable to pay its debts, something that has never happened in US history. Nevertheless, House Republicans seized on the symbolism of the debt ceiling to demand that either Obama and congressional Democrats agree to their position on taxes and spending or they would not vote to raise the debt ceiling. The Democrats, for their part, viewed the Republican spending cut proposals as too draconian and refused to consider cuts without also increasing taxes on wealthy Americans, something the Republicans refused to entertain. The result was deadlock.

As the deadline approached for either the ceiling to be raised or America to be in default, Republicans, in control of the House, and Democrats, in control of the Senate and presidency, faced off like gunfighters at the OK Corral. Each party claimed to represent majority will—having come to control their institutions through electoral victories in separate elections; neither was about to accede to the others' demands.[39] In the end, at the eleventh hour, a compromise was reached to raise the debt ceiling while deferring decisions on deficit reduction to a twelve-member "super committee" of Congress members, evenly divided between the two parties, that would produce a proposal by the following November. Although a large faction of House Republicans, to the end, advocated default rather than raising the debt ceiling, the fears of the financial turmoil that would result led the Republican leadership to support raising the ceiling, with the help of Democratic votes in the House. The political maneuvering over the debt ceiling and the near default dismayed both the financial markets and the American public. In the weeks following, Standard and Poor's, a major bond rating agency, downgraded the United States' AAA bond rating, citing deficiencies in America's governance structure as the reason.[40] At the same time, job approval ratings for both the president and Congress plummeted. By the fall of 2011, only 9 percent of the public, a historic low, approved of the job Congress was doing and 89 percent of the public expressed distrust of government to do the right thing.[41]

As could have been easily predicted as the debt ceiling was negotiated in August, the November deadline for the "subcommittee" to negotiate the deal that could not be done in August came and went without a deal. The subcommittee approach ignored the political reality of divided government under the separation of powers. The two parties differed fundamentally over how to reduce government spending and each controlled competing institutions. The Republicans insisted on reducing deficits through spending cuts alone while the Democrats insisted on some increased taxes targeted at the wealthiest Americans as part of the mix. In the end, the deadlock focused on the 2001 Bush tax cuts scheduled to expire at the end of 2012. The Republicans refused to agree to any deal that did not make these cuts permanent while the Democrats would never agree to extend any of the Bush tax cuts without excluding those for high earners. Since each party had the institutional clout to back up their positions—the Republicans controlled the House, the Democrats the Senate and the presidency—neither needed to accede to the other. For both, awaiting the outcome of the 2012 elections in the hope that institutional control would shift in their favor trumped abandoning their policy positions. But would a new election, given the logic of separation of powers, provide a clear answer?

As the 2012 elections approached, the electorate seemed in the mood to hold governmental leaders accountable for poor performance. Not only was the public dissatisfied with inaction on the deficit; it continued to want decisive action to spur job growth as the economy continued to sputter. Throughout 2011 and early 2012, Obama and congressional Republicans were unable to agree on effective job creation measures. As had occurred when the "super committee" failed to reach a budget deal, each party pointed the finger at the other for the deadlock over both deficits and economic performance—a muddying of accountability made easy in the separation of powers system.[42] In light of this dissatisfaction with government, who and how could voters hold their elected representatives accountable? Vote against all incumbents? This strategy, given divided government, would produce a Republican in the White House and a Democratic House—hardly a formula to end partisan gridlock. Return unified control to the Democrats? This strategy works only if one concludes policy deadlock is primarily the fault of Republicans. Give unified control to Republicans? Again, a good strategy only if Democrats alone could be blamed. Placing blame squarely on one or the other, however, cannot be done, based solely on overall government performance, since separation of powers and divided government give the parties joint control of outcomes. In its evaluation of elected representatives, the public senses this conundrum as it disapproves by a similar margin the performance of both congressional Republicans and Democrats. Given the division of responsibility and accountability under separation of powers, assigning clear credit and blame to either party for what government does is an impossible task.

The dilemma voters faced in 2012 is inherent in the separation of powers structure. If both branches of government share responsibility for policy, why shouldn't a citizen avoid the nearly impossible task of sorting out responsibility for policy failures and hold officials accountable by simply voting against incumbents in both branches at once? Such a solution might be reasonable if members of the same political party controlled both Congress and the presidency, but when control is divided between the parties, it places a dissatisfied citizen in an absurd position: A majority of citizens' voting against incumbents in both branches would "punish" the party in control of one branch by awarding it control of the other. The logic of separation of powers—shared responsibility for policy making, combined with accountability through separate elections—makes holding officials accountable for policy failure extremely difficult.

Meanwhile, congressional incumbents of both parties can avoid responsibility when running for reelection by blaming deficits or other failed policies on the administration or by claiming that, whatever the collective congressional responsibility for the problems, they *individually* have not contributed to them.[43] Given the way the separation of powers system muddles responsibility for policy, assessing the truth of such claims is nearly impossible for even the most conscientious citizen. Not surprisingly, despite widespread dissatisfaction in the country with Congress as a whole and growing uneasiness about many domestic issues, incumbent members of Congress are usually reelected.[44]

The separation of powers renders a muddled message as well when voters seek to acknowledge policymakers' responsibility for success. On the strength of a robust economy, in 1996 President Clinton handily won reelection. One might see a Democratic presidential victory as a strong voter endorsement of the policies Clinton had pursued during the previous four years, but in the same election, voters returned to power those who had opposed those policies, giving the Republicans majorities in both House and Senate. In 1998, despite Clinton's continued popularity, Republicans argued for impeaching him over revelations of his sexual liaison with a White House intern, Monica Lewinsky. Although they hoped this action might bring them gains in the midterm elections, in a marked reversal of the normal historical pattern in "off-year" elections, in which the party not occupying the White House normally gains, the Republicans lost a substantial number of House seats and failed to gain seats in the Senate. Despite this reversal, the lame-duck Republican Congress proceeded to impeach Clinton, and the Senate went ahead to try (and eventually acquit) him in early 1999, clearly ignoring popular will. As constitutional scholar Kathleen Sullivan has pointed out, the behavior of Congress in Clinton's impeachment turned Madison's constitutional theory on its head: Instead of level-headed representatives cooling the passions of a wild democratic majority, the American people in 1998 were the level-headed ones who signaled to their passionate and partisan representatives not to pursue an unnecessary impeachment effort.[45] Unfortunately, however, the constitutional system, which left Republicans in control of Congress despite reduced majorities in both houses, allowed congressional leaders to pursue their wrongheaded attempt at impeachment despite public wishes.

Along with providing citizens an opportunity to punish their representatives for policy failures or reward them for policy successes, accountability is supposed to ensure more responsible behavior from representatives between elections. But rather than ensuring such responsible behavior, the separation of powers instead opens up opportunities for special interests to gain legislation favorable to themselves. This process has been at work over the past three decades as Congress and several presidential administrations have promoted deregulation in banking and corporate oversight. New Deal regulatory agencies and procedures established in the 1930s to prevent corporate abuse were dismantled. When such deregulation led to disastrous results, first in the savings and loan collapse of the 1980s, then in corporate scandals such as that surrounding the Enron collapse in 2001, and more recently in the 2008 financial crisis and its aftermath, the separation of powers impeded the process of holding lawmakers accountable for the consequences of their actions. Since voters could not easily understand whether the president or Congress, or who in Congress, might be to blame for the bad policies leading to these disasters, they could not hold the responsible persons accountable, opening the door to further bad policy making. A detailed look at the history of, and connections among, these scandals shows what happens when lawmakers escape accountability.

The savings and loan (S&L) scandal of the 1980s was an ominous precursor to the larger financial crisis of 2008. Since the 1930s, most savings and loan institutions, which traditionally specialized in providing home mortgages, were insured through a governmental agency called the Federal Savings and Loan Insurance Corporation (FSLIC). Like its counterpart in banking, the Federal Deposit Insurance Corporation (FDIC), the FSLIC was intended to assure depositors of the safety of their deposits by guaranteeing them with the full faith and credit of the US government. If a savings and loan institution became insolvent, the FSLIC insurance fund would pay to every depositor the full value of his or her deposit up to a set amount ($100,000 in the 1980s). The purpose of this system was to create consumer confidence in S&Ls and prevent the kind of disastrous "runs" on failing institutions that had occurred with the banks in the 1930s. Backing up this system was careful FSLIC regulation of the industry to make sure that S&Ls made prudent loans and concentrated primarily on providing mortgages to home buyers.

For fifty years, this system worked very well, buttressing a successful industry. In the 1980s, however, both Republican President Reagan and the Democratic Congress supported legislation easing the regulation of savings and loans while maintaining the commitment to depositors.[46] Then both parties turned a blind eye as unscrupulous investors took advantage of the new, looser regulations to burden S&Ls with risky loans, usually in areas outside their traditional business of home mortgage financing. When those loans went bad in the late 1980s, Congress was forced to pass legislation bailing out the industry, saddling taxpayers with a bill of approximately $500 billion to be paid over the next decade. Voters were unable to hold either political party accountable for this massive governmental failure because, through the shared power in the separation of powers system, both were equally responsible for it, and both parties conspired to keep the issue out of the 1988 and 1992 presidential elections.[47] The muddling of accountability permitted by the separation of powers allowed officials in both branches to act irresponsibly in their oversight of the savings and loan industry. All knew that citizens would never be able to hold any one branch or party responsible for the mess because both were culpable.

Because they had not been held accountable for the S&L debacle, lawmakers remained unrepentant about their role in allowing it to happen and were therefore open to the pressure for additional special interest legislation that it inspired. Because they all had played a role in failing to warn investors of the S&Ls' shaky condition, the Big Six (now Big Five) accounting firms faced substantial losses in the early 1990s from investor lawsuits.[48] To limit such losses— eventually the firms would pay $1 billion in damages—and protect itself from liability in any comparable future business failure, the accounting industry mobilized its lobbyists and made generous campaign contributions to both Republicans and Democrats, ensuring that both parties would be responsive to its concerns. Winning a first victory by blocking attempts to enact legislation to regulate its activities more closely, the industry next became a strong advocate of legislation to restrict investor lawsuits. It got its wish when Congress enacted the Private Securities Litigation Reform Act of 1995. The initiative for that law had formed a part of Newt Gingrich's "Contract with America," but unlike other key parts of that campaign platform, it also drew strong support from powerful Democrats, such as Connecticut Senator Christopher J. Dodd. Later in the decade, the accounting industry achieved another major victory when, under pressure from both Democrats and Republicans, the Securities and Exchange Commission (SEC) chairman, Arthur Levitt, was forced to withdraw proposed regulations to bar accounting firms from consulting for the same firms they audited. The accounting industry's political success in deflecting government regulation in the 1990s would prove to be a key factor in the first American business scandal of the twenty-first century, the collapse of Enron.

The Enron Corporation, led by its CEO, Kenneth Lay, had been a major political player and advocate of government deregulation throughout the 1980s and 1990s.[49] Although Enron generally favored Republican politicians who shared Lay's libertarian ideology, it was careful to contribute to the campaigns of key Democrats as well. The giant energy corporation lobbied actively at both state and federal levels to reduce government regulation, not only of the energy industry—its major interest—but also of business generally.[50] These efforts paid off in energy deregulation in the 1990s and in specific rulings by the SEC exempting the company from Depression-era laws limiting executives' ability to create and invest in overseas partnerships.[51] These partnerships led eventually to Enron's downfall, when it was revealed that executives had used them to hide financial losses from Enron investors. Falling energy and stock prices brought exposure of these losses in late 2001, and the corporation was forced into bankruptcy. Enron's auditing firm, Arthur Andersen, then faced its own crisis for having failed to discover and report what was happening at Enron, and the situation worsened when it was discovered that its employees had started shredding Enron files after the SEC investigation into Enron began.[52] Many observers suspected that Andersen's failure to audit Enron more closely had been influenced by its interest in retaining its substantial consulting business with the firm—a relationship made possible by the accounting industry's earlier success in blocking government regulation of such conflicts of interest. The fact that the Private Securities Litigation Reform Act of 1995 now limited Andersen's liability in investor lawsuits may also have reduced its incentive to look too closely at Enron's books.

As with the S&L and Enron scandals, the separation of powers system diffused responsibility for the banking crisis that led to the Great Recession of 2008, leaving voters a difficult task in holding anyone responsible.[53] The financial crisis developed in 2007 over defaults in "subprime" mortgages—a class of home mortgages given to people whose low income or poor credit history normally would not qualify them to receive a mortgage. Around 2000, as housing prices rose dramatically and mortgage interest rates fell, many lenders began to write these subprime mortgages, promising borrowers that their monthly payments would remain low and that rising home prices would permit them to sell their property at a profit if they got into financial difficulty. Financial deregulation allowed mortgage companies to develop a variety of loans, such as variable rate mortgages (a mortgage payment would rise as interest rates rose), no-down-payment loans, and loans at low "teaser rates" that ballooned after the first few years. At the same time, Wall Street modified the way it packaged mortgage securities to sell to investors so that the risk associated with the subprime loans was hidden. When rising mortgage rates and falling house prices in 2007 began causing people to default on their subprime mortgages, many large banks and other investors found themselves holding mortgage securities that included these risky loans. The resulting millions of dollars in losses forced the Federal Reserve and Congress—much as had occurred in the S&L crisis of the 1980s—to attempt a $700 billion bailout of the entire banking system. Taxpayers were made to assume the consequences of the actions of irresponsible mortgage lenders and of the financial institutions that bought the risky mortgages they sold. Again, Washington policymakers have largely escaped accountability for the banking crisis, as both parties point fingers at each other and no one is held responsible.

The Parliamentary Alternative

If the separation of powers now inhibits governmental responsiveness to majorities and muddles accountability, achieving these democratic values would require concentration of policy-making power in a single institution—what political scientists call "unified government." In 1789, the founders associated unified government with tyranny because the existing examples of such governments, usually ones that concentrated power in the monarchy, were clearly authoritarian regimes. After the eighteenth century, however, a democratic variant of unified government was devised as European democrats came to power in their countries. This form of unified government, called a *parliamentary system,* is the most widespread form of democratic government in the world. Among the world's most industrially advanced democracies, the United States is the only one with a separation of powers system rather than a parliamentary system.[54]

The founders' attempt to craft the world's first large-scale representative democracy could not draw on the experience with mass-based political parties and party-organized legislatures that would bring about the evolution of parliamentary systems in nineteenth-century Europe. Had they the opportunity to consider this alternative in 1787, they, too, might have opted for a parliamentary structure.[55] Unlike the authors of our Constitution, modern Americans are able to consider such a democratic alternative to our separation of powers system and whether it might provide better opportunities to achieve responsive and accountable government. In doing so we would be following the recommendation of Gouverneur Morris "to take counsel from experience"—in this case the experience of parliamentary democracies—to identify ways to improve our constitutional structure.

In a parliamentary system, both executive and legislative powers are concentrated in a "government" composed of members of whichever party or coalition of parties has a majority in a democratically elected legislature (or parliament). This government consists of a prime minister, who is usually the leader of the legislative majority party, and a cabinet that the prime minister selects from among her or his legislative majority. Cabinet ministers head the various executive departments (or ministries, as they are usually called) and, under the direction of the prime minister, supervise the day-to-day operation of the government bureaucracy. In exercising their executive roles, the prime minister and cabinet function much as the president and the cabinet in the American system do, except that they serve simultaneously as elected representatives in the legislature—a dual status that is constitutionally prohibited in our separation of powers system.

As legislative leader, the parliamentary government is responsible for initiating and passing all legislation. Its policy proposals are discussed, debated, and always strongly criticized by the legislative opposition, but with rare exception its proposals are also enacted into law. The government can pass its legislative program because it can count on the support of the members of its party or coalition, who possess the majority of votes in the legislature. Thus when a prime minister is elected to power in a parliamentary system, he or she can expect to be able to enact the governmental agenda promised to the voters during the election campaign. Political parties play a much more powerful and important role in a parliamentary system than we are accustomed to in the United States. In the legislature, whether they are among the majority or in opposition, individual legislators in a parliamentary system follow the directions of their party leaders when voting on legislation. They must do so because the party leaders control their ability to run under the party label at election time—a major difference from the American system of primary elections, which has largely eliminated the ability of party leaders to control who runs under a party label. In a parliamentary system, any legislator who votes against the leadership can expect to find someone nominated in his or her place for the next election. In addition, advancement to positions of governmental power, such as a cabinet post, is under the control of party leaders, providing an additional incentive for ambitious legislators to submit to party discipline.

Question Time in the British House of Commons requires Conservative Prime Minister David Cameron to publicly respond to pointed questions about government policy from opposition Labour Party members.

© PRESS ASSOCIATION/epa/Corbis.

Political parties in most parliamentary systems are also more closely associated with consistent sets of public policy positions than are those in the United States. Within the American Republican and Democratic Parties, one finds officeholders advocating a wide variety of specific policy positions. They can do so because each is elected on the basis of his or her individual legislative record, not on the collective record of the political party. In a parliamentary system, it is that collective record that a party member must defend when running for election; therefore, policy differences usually exist between parties, not within them.

Because of the sharper definition of what a party stands for and because parties have the power to enact their promises when elected, voters in a parliamentary system focus much more on party than on any other factor at election time. National legislative elections are contests between political parties, each presenting its party program and seeking control of government to carry it out. This is very different from American elections, which involve contests between hundreds of individual legislative candidates who run on individual policy platforms, for which they can promise no more than to be advocates within the complex separation of powers system.

When a political party wins an election in a parliamentary system, the party and its leader, the prime minister, control all the governmental levers of power needed to enact their legislative mandate. Responsiveness in carrying out the will of its electoral majority is obviously not a problem. But what about accountability? Accustomed as we are to the checks inherent in the separation of powers, Americans are apt to regard the awesome power of a parliamentary prime minister with alarm. What is to prevent such a powerful individual from using this power to pursue an undemocratic agenda? How can one be sure that a prime minister, once in office, will not act tyrannically?

The appearance of unrestrained power does not coincide with the reality of the political position of prime ministers in most parliamentary systems. Prime ministers are constrained and held democratically accountable in their exercise of power in three ways. First, their political parties hold them accountable. Although leaders can normally count on discipline from the members of their party in the legislature, those same members can collectively remove the prime minister if they become dissatisfied with his or her leadership. British Prime Minister Margaret Thatcher was forced to resign in 1990 because members of her Conservative Party feared that her leadership would result in defeat for the party at the next election. In 2007, Labour Prime Minister Tony Blair suffered the same fate, when party leaders eased him from power in response to dissatisfaction among party rank and file with his support for the Iraq War. Second, a prime minister can lose the parliamentary majority if enough members of that majority defect to the opposition. This result can come about either because some members of the prime minister's own party defect or, in the case of a multiparty governing coalition (given party discipline, this is the more likely scenario), because one of the coalition parties withdraws its support. Finally, and most important, citizens hold prime ministers and their governments accountable in parliamentary systems. Although they possess unified control of government while in power, prime ministers know that eventually, at the next election, they will need to defend their exercise of power to the voters. Unlike the separation of powers system, the parliamentary system offers no possibility of deflecting responsibility for governmental performance onto another branch of government or the opposition party. Consequently, in making every governmental decision, prime ministers and their governments must be sensitive to how these decisions will affect the people who will decide at the next election whether the government should continue in power.

The contrast between the ability of a parliamentary system and that of the American separation of powers system to hold a head of government accountable for his or her behavior was revealed in the controversy over President Bill Clinton's impeachment. Removing an individual prime minister from office, as the cases of Margaret Thatcher and Tony Blair show, is easier and carries with it less constitutional significance than removal of an American president. Prime ministers are merely heads of government; they do not carry with them the quasi-monarchical character of a president, who also is head of state. Moreover, although prime ministers are important political leaders, who tend to dominate their governments and—in the current era of highly personalized campaigning and media coverage—to become the primary symbols of governmental power, they remain simply heads of a collective leadership that is composed of their cabinet and party majority in parliament. Although in most parliamentary systems modern prime ministers are more than "first among equals," their power derives from the collective leadership that backs them up. Therefore, if an individual prime minister is removed, for whatever reason, between elections, the collective party leadership remains in power, promoting the programs and policies the electorate endorsed in the last election. How different from the act of removing an American president! Since a president is elected separately from Congress and embodies alone (albeit in combination with the vice president) the will of the voters who elected him, removing a president between elections constitutes a reversal of the previous presidential election. In a democracy, this is an awesome decision that cannot be made easily.

The founders understood how serious it would be to remove a president in the system they had devised, and that caused them to ponder at length how it would be accomplished. The solution they came up with was impeachment, based on a procedure developed in eighteenth-century Britain to remove the king's ministers.[56] In an era before the development of the modern parliamentary system, the king appointed government ministers whom Parliament could remove only through impeachment and proof of "high crimes and misdemeanors." The process was a quasi-judicial one, although Parliaments of the era often abused it to remove officials on political grounds. As the practice of having the parliamentary majority appoint ministers evolved in the nineteenth century, impeachment was no longer needed. Everyone understood that all ministers, including the prime minister, served only so long as they had the confidence of a parliamentary majority; no legal process proving "guilt" was required to be rid of them.

Impeachment and conviction in a Senate trial of treason, bribery, or "high crimes and misdemeanors" remain, however, the only means of removing American presidents between elections. This quasi-legal standard, to be administered in the quasi-judicial proceeding of a Senate trial, created the dilemma that

Congress wrestled with and that distracted the country through most of 1998. Whereas even his strongest defenders agreed that President Clinton's conduct was reprehensible, demeaning of his office, and immoral, the constitutional standard required proof that his actions constituted high crimes and misdemeanors. In the end, a majority of senators voted that they did not.

The Advantages of a Parliamentary System

In a parliamentary system, dealing with a prime minister who had committed a sexual transgression like Clinton's would have occurred on a basis more suitable to the nature of the transgression. Political judgments, rather than quasi-legal judgments, would govern the decision. The decision would not involve a determination of someone's individual guilt or innocence but more appropriate considerations of accountability as a democratic leader and ability to be responsive to the electorate.[57] In Clinton's case, his own party would have had to make a judgment regarding his political viability in light of the revelation of his tawdry sexual liaison and his attempt to cover it up. The months-long preoccupation and distraction from other issues that Clinton's impeachment engendered would not have occurred. In the end, he would have been held accountable, through his political party, to those most important in this situation—the American people.

In more than just the removal of a head of government, the operation of parliamentary systems seems superior to that of our separation of powers system in providing both responsiveness and accountability.[58] Elections produce mandates that those elected have the power to carry out. Voters can select, through their ballots, which party's policy proposals they prefer and can actually expect them to be implemented. They can also hold governments accountable. Citizens in a parliamentary system are able to evaluate clearly and unambiguously whether the government has served them well or poorly. In making that evaluation, they are assisted by the political opposition party or parties, which naturally seek to expose the governing party's failures and offer themselves as an alternative. In such a system, citizens can use their strongest tool—elections—much more effectively than is possible under a separation of powers system. The ambiguity, confusion, and obfuscation of who is or is not responsible for governmental action are not possible in a unified government system.

Parliamentary government—which, as mentioned earlier, is universal in the developed world except the United States—seems to be related also to the long-term stability of democracies. Although the United States has maintained a stable democracy under the separation of powers—or what in the study of comparative politics is called the "presidential" system—it seems the exception among such regimes.[59] Experience elsewhere in the world suggests that the institutional conflict between presidents and legislatures inherent in presidential regimes frequently leads to the demise of democracy. That has been the case in parts of the developing world, especially Latin America, where presidential democracy has often been tried. In most cases, when a crisis cannot be resolved between president and congress, either an elected president with military backing assumes dictatorial powers in defiance of the congress, or a military coup replaces both. Although many economic and cultural factors play a role in such antidemocratic coups, evidence is strong that a separation of powers regime seems to facilitate undemocratic crisis resolution. Political scientist Fred W. Riggs, in a comprehensive 1992 study of democracies in developing countries, found that every one of thirty-three presidential regimes had experienced at least one antidemocratic coup, whereas only about one-third of the forty-three parliamentary regimes had suffered such a disruption.[60] Although many Americans consider separation of powers a key factor in the stability of our democracy, such studies suggest that our democratic culture and economic prosperity allow our democracy to succeed in spite of—not because of—the separation of powers!

Objections to a Parliamentary System in the United States

Despite the argument of the previous section, Americans are likely to be nervous about any movement toward a parliamentary regime. The idea of institutional checks and balances is such a settled and familiar part of our constitutional history that many are likely to be worried about what we might lose in modifying the system. Even those who have been convinced that parliamentary democracy could produce more responsive and accountable government still might argue that these benefits would be purchased at too high a cost. Separation of powers, even though it presents barriers to democracy, remains a useful deterrent to tyranny. Defenders of the separation of powers usually offer three arguments on its behalf: Separation of powers decreases the chance of majority tyranny; it provides a useful bias toward limited government; and it constitutes a check on the abuse of power.

The specter of majority tyranny was, of course, the primary rationale for the American separation of powers from the beginning. But it is a rationale based on an unproven assumption: that majority tyranny is somehow a greater danger than minority tyranny.[61] The founders, who were preoccupied with the former, set up a system that, as we have seen, actually facilitates the latter. If tyranny is the danger, instead of solving the problem, the separation of powers creates a system in which well-placed minorities can pursue their interests at the expense of other minorities or even the majority. A more productive way to avoid tyranny would be to rely on the democratic ethos of citizens. As the noted political theorist Robert Dahl argues, "The protection of minority rights can be no stronger than the commitment of the majority of citizens to preserving the primary democratic rights of all citizens, to maintaining respect for their fellow citizens, and to avoiding the adverse consequences of harming a minority."[62]

Also, American political history offers little evidence to support the founders' fear of majority tyranny. Rather than a group united by a single-minded "passion or interest," majorities in American politics tend to be large coalitions representing widely varying interests.[63] In a large and diverse country such as the United States, even without institutional checks and balances, a governing majority would include many different groups with overlapping memberships. In such a situation, building a consensus behind any policy measure would involve a process of accommodating multiple preferences and interests. James Madison realized this himself when he argued in *Federalist* No. 10 that the size and social diversity of the United States were the principal check against majority tyranny. Institutional checks and balances were only an "auxiliary precaution," but one that, I have argued, does not discriminate between tyrannical and benign majority preferences. By reforming the separation of powers as suggested above, we can facilitate majority rule in America without significant risk of majority tyranny.

Along with their concerns about majority tyranny, the founders, being good classical liberals, were interested in limiting government. As shown earlier, their handiwork has succeeded in establishing an institutional bias in favor of limited government. Attempts to introduce policies that will expand the role of government into a new area or activity—even when such policies are popular with a majority of citizens—are easily blocked. Realizing this, defenders of the separation of powers often accuse its critics of advocating more unified government merely as a way of promoting an activist ideological agenda.[64] This fear is probably justified: Contemporary liberals (not the classical kind) do believe that a majority of citizens would support a more activist government if the restraints on political change inherent in the separation of powers were removed.

But why should one of the central issues of our time—activist versus limited government—be decided by the bias of our constitutional structure, rather than democratically, through political debate, discussion, and competitive elections? Political conservatives who favor a smaller, less-activist government should pursue their goal through open processes of political competition; they should persuade a democratic majority that such a government is in the majority's interest. Those conservatives who defend separation of powers because they support its bias toward limited government are supporting a particular constitutional structure because they believe it promotes their ideological agenda.

In recent years, however, some conservatives have found the separation of powers an obstacle to their policy preferences. They have discovered that our institutional structure is biased not so much in favor of limited government as against innovation and change. Anyone wishing to expand the existing size and scope of government is at a disadvantage, but so is anyone who wishes to reduce government below the size it has reached. In the twentieth century, liberals did succeed, despite the separation of powers and employing the Jeffersonian model, in expanding the responsibilities of the federal government (although, as argued earlier, not as much as occurred in parliamentary democracies). Conservatives who came to power in the executive branch with the presidential elections of the 1980s and in the legislative branch in 1994 found the separation of powers and divided government to be obstacles to their political agenda. Part of the preoccupation of many House Republicans, particularly the group first elected in 1994, with the attempt to impeach President Clinton in 1998 may have been tied to their frustration over how he had blocked their political agenda. Liberals, paradoxically, found Democratic control of the opposing branches useful for protecting established programs. President George W. Bush, after his reelection victory in 2004, found his effort to enact his "ownership society"—a series of broad reforms of existing domestic programs, including Social Security—entirely blocked.[65] If, as conservatives believed, there was a substantial majority in the country in favor of reducing the size of government, separation of powers proved not a force in favor of more limited government but a structure that impeded a democratic movement on its behalf.

A third argument usually given in defense of the separation of powers is that it provides an institutional check on the abuse of power. Usually proponents of this argument point to the important role that Congress has taken in investigating abuses of executive power in the past few decades. The Senate Watergate hearings, 1970s hearings on abuses by the FBI and the CIA, the Iran-*contra* hearings in the 1980s, and the 1990s hearings on Clinton administration campaign finance dealings are examples of a politically independent Congress looking into abuses of executive power. However, despite the institutional capacity to check the president, there is no guarantee that Congress will use its institutional power. During most of his presidency, George W. Bush had little to fear from congressional oversight as he asserted wide-ranging presidential authority and engaged in what critics consider abuses comparable to those committed prior to the 1970s. With Republican control of both houses of Congress between 2002 and 2006, Bush had a relatively free hand in reinstituting an imperial presidency (see chapter 8 for a more extensive discussion of expanded presidential power), and congressional acceptance of Bush's actions served to legitimize his expansion of presidential power among an electorate that is accustomed to relying on institutional checks, rather than partisan and electoral ones, against the abuse of power. Even when the Democrats regained congressional control in 2006, the logic of the separation of powers impeded their ability to limit unilateral presidential power in areas such as foreign and military affairs and bureaucratic management. The Bush administration stonewalled congressional oversight attempts through assertions of "executive privilege" that impeded access to key documents and testimony from presidential staffers. Separation of powers allowed the president, asserting the privileges of a constitutionally independent branch of government, to insulate many of his administration's actions from legislative, and consequently public, scrutiny.[66]

The main point that needs to be made in response to this question is that although a parliamentary regime does reduce *institutional* checks on abuse of power by one branch or another, it increases other kinds of checks on such abuses. In a parliamentary system, responsibility for monitoring governmental abuses would shift to the political opposition and the electorate as a whole. The party in opposition would have great incentive to be vigilant in looking for abuses because, once exposed, such issues could be the basis for electoral defeat of the government and a return of the opposition to power. Since a governing party would have to take responsibility for abuses that occurred while it controlled the government, its members would have to take responsibility for any abuses of power during their tenure in office. That concern for accountability to the electorate led British Parliament members, even those in the governing Labour Party, to be much more critical of Prime Minister Tony Blair's use of misleading intelligence prior to the Iraq War than the Republican majorities in the US Congress were of similar actions by the US president. Blair was forced to respond directly to detailed critiques of his policy in parliamentary Question Time, while President Bush avoided any direct confrontation with his critics. In parliamentary systems, when incidents such as Watergate, the Iraq War debacle, or the Katrina disaster occur, they produce governmental resignations and often new elections in which the electorate can pass judgment directly on the abuses that have occurred. In the United States, we rely instead on long, drawn-out hearings or judicial investigations in which the electorate is simply an observer. At the end of the investigations, responsibility for the abuses usually remains unclear—which is not surprising, given the way the separation of powers muddles responsibility for governmental actions—and the resolution is obscured by complicated legal proceedings. A parliamentary form of government would shift responsibility for monitoring governmental abuse to the more democratic process of competition between government and opposition, followed by the voters' judgment.

Meeting the Challenge: Bridging the Separation of Powers

Although most critics of the separation of powers system would be delighted if the United States were to adopt a parliamentary form of government, few expect Americans to embrace such a drastic reform. Nevertheless, reformers believe that changes could be made within the separation of powers system that, while falling short of creating a true parliamentary system, would introduce quasi-parliamentary features. These reforms would permit more unified government, reviving at the least the possibility that the Jeffersonian model of government could again become viable. In fact, most reform advocates would go beyond the Jeffersonian model to ensure permanent and continuing unified government.

Strengthening political parties is central to most calls for reform. In both the parliamentary system and the Jeffersonian model, political parties are the keystone supporting the effective operation of the government structure. Unfortunately, in 1789 the American founders did not understand the critical role of political parties in organizing democratic government and ensuring its responsiveness and effectiveness. They equated *party* (a word they used interchangeably with *faction*) with the small personal cliques surrounding individual leaders in the British Parliament, and they could not have foreseen how, as parliamentary systems were organized in Europe in the late nineteenth century, their leaders would make parties the linchpin of responsible and effective democratic government. Had the founders been able to observe the effective marriage of party politics with a unified parliamentary system, they might have decided not to separate the executive and the legislature.[67] Even so, as we saw in tracing the evolution of the Jeffersonian model, before the ink was dry on the Constitution they were using parties to bridge the separation between president and Congress.

Understanding this need for strong parties, many of America's most distinguished political scientists have been leading advocates of strong political parties.[68] In 1950, the American Political Science Association (APSA) went so far as to publish an official report advocating various measures to strengthen parties.[69] If parties could be revived as strong, disciplined, and coherent political organizations, according to reformers, the separate branches would act in a unified manner, and at election time voters would be able to both hold the governing party accountable and make clear choices between the parties. The hope of the reformers, and I include myself among them, was that more ideologically coherent and unified parties alone might inject more responsiveness and accountability into the system. In fact, in recent years the parties have evolved in the direction reformers hoped, becoming more unified, differentiated from one another, and ideologically distinct. Yet to a degree perhaps unappreciated by political scientists who saw coherent parties alone as a formula for a more responsive and accountable politics, today's more unified parties compete in a context of the separation of powers system that itself continues to frustrate responsiveness and accountability. As the Republican Party has demonstrated during the Obama years, separation of powers and associated institutional rules like the filibuster simply offer a unified party the tools to frustrate responsiveness and obscure accountability. If strong party competition is to bring the sort of responsiveness and accountability one associates with parliamentary government, fundamental institutional reforms are needed.

A key first step would be to abolish the filibuster rule in the Senate. Up to the 1980s, the filibuster was invoked only rarely on only crucial legislation.[70] Since the late 1980s, however, filibusters have been used more and more frequently until, in the past two years, they have become routine.[71] This gives a unified partisan minority in the Senate the capacity to routinely block the majority's legislation—a form of minority tyranny. Since 2009, nearly every measure considered in the Senate, including routine administrative appointments, has required a super majority of sixty votes to break a filibuster. The Senate must revise its rules to end this antimajoritarian practice by abolishing the filibuster and returning to the democratic norm of majority rule.

Even with more ideologically coherent and unified parties, as long as the president and individual Congress members are elected independently of one another, they will seek to establish independent political bases organized around their individual political performance. Although strong and organized parties make them more effective collectively, they also need to be made individually accountable for collective outcomes. Rather than having to answer for those collective outcomes, however, individual politicians prefer to go it alone. Because divided government results from ticket splitting—voters choosing a president of one party and congressional representatives of another—several reform proposals seek to limit or prevent this practice. One would be simply to restore the option of straight-party-ticket voting, which no longer exists in thirty-one of the fifty states. In all states, providing separate party slates for all federal offices as a voting option might reduce ticket splitting. Another more radical proposal, team ticket ballots, would require voters to choose both a president and their congressional representatives with a single vote, virtually assuring the winning president of a majority in the House and probably one in the Senate. More important, it would link the political fates of all members of Congress to their party's presidential candidate. Individual congressional candidates would have to convince voters to select not only themselves but also their party's presidential candidate. A third reform would be to hold elections for Congress in presidential election years two weeks after the presidential election. The delay would give the newly elected president a chance to appeal to the voters who had just elected him to support his party's candidates for Congress. A system along these lines in France helped President François Mitterrand obtain legislative control for his party after both the 1981 and 1988 presidential elections and President Jacques Chirac to do so in 2001.[72] A more dramatic reform would ensure presidential control of Congress by giving the president-elect's party automatic bonus seats to provide majorities in both houses.

These reforms would increase the likelihood of unified government in presidential election years, but divided government could still return and muddle accountability in midterm elections. To prevent this, midterm elections simply should be abolished by making both House and Senate terms four years. This would place the entire House and the one-third of the Senate up for election in a given year on the same election cycle and responsive to the same electorate. A more radical variant would require all members of the Senate to stand for election every four years. In addition, abolition of midterm elections would give a president with the support of partisan majorities in both houses more time to put in place a policy program before being subject to voter judgment. With more time, voters would be better able to evaluate whether a party's policies were effective or not.

In addition to these electoral changes, reformers suggest a number of changes in the relations between the separate branches to create quasi-parliamentary government.[73] One would be to amend the Constitution so that members of Congress could serve in the president's cabinet and head executive branch agencies. Another would require presidents periodically to submit to questions either before congressional committees or before the entire Congress, as happens in most parliamentary regimes. Some reformers also suggest that the president should have the power to dissolve Congress and call new congressional elections, which would allow him to appeal directly to the people to elect new representatives if he thought Congress was an obstacle to enacting a coherent government program. Congress, also, ought to have the power to force new elections, including for the president, through votes of no confidence in both chambers. This latter seems an especially important democratic measure if the proposal above to eliminate midterm elections were adopted. Legislators in a democracy need to have the ability to turn to the voters in the face of discontent with the executive. The basic premise of all these proposals is that elements of parliamentary-style government can be introduced into the American constitutional structure that would retain the form of the separation of powers while instituting the reality of more unified government.

The separation of powers challenges democracy by impeding responsiveness to legitimate majority interests and by muddling the accountability of representatives to citizens. The institutional checks in our constitutional structure offer many opportunities for minority interests to block needed change and reform. The fact that politicians must share policy making with those in other institutions permits them to blame others for policy failures and thereby escape accountability to the people. Unfortunately, democrats must realize that the sorts of constitutional reforms discussed in this chapter are not likely to be adopted easily. Among the barriers to progressive change built into our constitutional structure is a complex amendment process that was designed to impede change. In addition, two centuries of indoctrination concerning the "sanctity" of our constitutional arrangements have made most Americans reluctant even to consider changes, despite massive institutional failure. Although Americans seem less and less confident in the performance of their governmental institutions, they tend to blame the current occupants of those institutions, rather than the institutional structure. Much public education will be needed to convince the American public that reconsideration, as the founders intended, of a portion of our constitutional arrangements—the separation of powers—might be the way to better and more democratic government.

Thought Questions

1. This chapter argues that the separation of powers system reflects the outlook of the Protective Democracy model. Why? What about the other models? Analyze separation of powers from the perspective of each of the other models. From which perspectives can you develop arguments supportive of separation of powers, and which suggest more support for a parliamentary system?

2. Suppose the founders had adopted a parliamentary system: How would American history have been different? Pick a crucial moment from history and analyze how it might have been different if America had had a parliamentary system. For example, how might Prime Minister Abraham Lincoln have handled the threatened secession of the Southern states?

3. Suppose that, having been persuaded by this chapter's argument, the American people amended the Constitution to create a parliamentary system: How might such a change affect the party system? Would we continue to have two dominant (Republican and Democratic) parties? Or would a multiparty system evolve? How would such a development affect responsiveness and accountability in an American parliamentary system?

4. A parliamentary system, according to this chapter, would be superior to separation of powers in achieving democratic accountability and responsiveness. But what other political values would you want to consider before adopting as momentous a constitutional change as proposed here? How would those values be affected under each alternative system?

5. Political leaders in parliamentary systems, such as prime ministers, must have long experience in national government before rising to the leadership of their party and, hence, governmental power. In contrast, American presidents, because of the separation of powers system, can come to power with little or no experience in national government and politics. Dwight Eisenhower, Ronald Reagan, Bill Clinton, and George W. Bush are examples of men whose first national elective office was president of the United States. What are the advantages and disadvantages of these alternative patterns of recruitment to national office?

Suggestions for Further Reading

Burns, James MacGregor. *The Deadlock of Democracy.* Englewood Cliffs, NJ: Prentice Hall, 1963. A classic statement of the political consequences of separation of powers and how Americans have coped with them for the past two hundred years.

Dahl, Robert A. *How Democratic Is the American Constitution?* 2nd ed. New Haven, CT: Yale University Press, 2003. In this book, Dahl evaluates the Constitution as an instrument of democratic government and finds it not as democratic as it should be.

Fiorina, Morris. *Divided Government.* New York: Macmillan, 1991. A thorough analysis of why partisan division between the president and Congress has increased over the past four decades.

*Goldwin, Robert A., and Art Kaufman, eds. *Separation of Powers—Does It Still Work?* Washington, DC: American Enterprise Institute, 1986.

*————, and William Schambra, eds. *How Democratic Is the Constitution?* Washington, DC: American Enterprise Institute, 1980. This collection and *Separation of Powers* contain articles arguing various points of view on the extent to which the separation of powers and other aspects of the Constitution are democratic.

Johnson, Haynes, and David Broder. *The System: The American Way of Politics at the Breaking Point.* Boston: Little, Brown, 1996. Two of America's best journalists offer a blow-by-blow account of the defeat of Clinton's health care proposal. The tale provides a close-up view of how the separation of powers works in practice to frustrate innovative and progressive policy.

*Jones, Charles O. *Separate but Equal Branches: Congress and the Presidency.* 2nd ed. New York: Chatham House, 1999; and *The Presidency in a Separated System.* 2nd ed. Washington, DC: Brookings Institution, 2005. In these two works, a renowned American government scholar defends the wisdom of the separation of powers.

Linz, Juan, and Arturo Valenzuela, eds. *The Failure of Presidential Democracy.* Vol. 1. Baltimore: Johns Hopkins University Press, 1994. Distinguished political scientists compare the performance of presidential (separation of powers) and parliamentary systems around the world and find parliamentary ones both more democratic and more stable. Linz's essay argues strongly that presidential democracies are prone to collapse and replacement by authoritarian governments.

*Mayhew, David. *Divided We Govern: Party Control, Lawmaking, and Investigations, 1946–2002.* 2nd ed. New Haven, CT: Yale University Press, 2005. Mayhew argues that divided government has not made any difference for the enactment of "a standard kind of important legislation" and documents his claim with a thorough analysis of legislative enactments over the past fifty years. But he does not consider whether these enactments were responsive to democratic majorities; he ignores the accountability issue.

*Palazzolo, Daniel J. *Done Deal? The Politics of the 1997 Budget Agreement.* New York: Chatham House, 1999. A case study of legislative success under divided government.

Sundquist, James L. *Constitutional Reform and Effective Government.* Washington, DC: Brookings Institution, 1986. Also two follow-up volumes published by Brookings, *Beyond Gridlock? Prospects for Governance in the Clinton Years and After* (1993), and *Back to Gridlock? Governance in the Clinton Years* (1995). A well-argued case for fundamental changes in the separation of powers, including an interesting history of the origins of the constitutional structure and the two-century debate it has engendered. The two follow-up volumes are based on conferences that examined Sundquist's arguments in the light of Clinton's first term.

*Presents points of view that disagree with the arguments presented in this chapter.

Selected Websites

http://thomas.loc.gov. The Library of Congress site for gaining access to legislative information and all government agencies.

www.ipl.org/div/potus/jmadison.html. A site on the Internet Public Library with information about James Madison and links to related sites.

www.whitehouse.gov. The official White House website.

CHAPTER 2

The Second Challenge:
The Imperial Judiciary

*If the policy of the government upon vital questions affecting the whole
people is to be irrevocably fixed by decisions of the Supreme Court . . . the
people will have ceased to be their own rulers.*
— ABRAHAM LINCOLN, FIRST INAUGURAL ADDRESS

*Scarcely any political question arises in the United States that is not
resolved, sooner or later, into a judicial question.*
— ALEXIS DE TOCQUEVILLE

THE 2000 PRESIDENTIAL ELECTION resulted in one of the most controversial decisions ever from the United States Supreme Court. *Bush v. Gore* ended several
weeks of intense legal maneuvering by lawyers representing the presidential contenders. At issue were the twenty-five electoral votes of the state of Florida, which
would give one of the candidates the Electoral College majority needed to win the
election. The lawyers were arguing over how and whether disputed votes cast in
the very close Florida election should be recounted. Since the close of the polls on
election night, the Bush camp had sought to halt any recounting of disputed ballots because their candidate held a razor-thin lead of a few hundred votes in the
unofficial results. Gore's lawyers were pressing for hand recounts of ballots in
several counties where a variety of imperfections in the ballots suggested that the
initial vote tallies were flawed. On the evening of December 12, 2000, after a
month of wrangling in both state and federal courts, the Supreme Court

---

Opposite: *A familiar Washington D.C. sight: protestors outside the Supreme Court seeking to
influence the decisions of the justices inside. In this case, the constitutionality of the individual mandate of the Affordable Care Act.*

AP Photo/Charles Dharapak.

announced its final decision. In a 5–4 ruling, the Court's majority, all conservative Republicans, overturned a decision of the Florida Supreme Court and mandated an end to vote counting in Florida, effectively handing that state's electoral votes to Republican candidate George W. Bush. As a result, Bush became the first president in over a century to assume the presidency with a bare majority in the Electoral College but without having earned more popular votes than his opponent. He was also the first president ever to gain office by means of a decision by the Supreme Court.

In the months that followed this unique event in American history, political scientists and legal scholars commented on it in numerous books and articles. Political scientists tended to be critical of the Court's intervention, and legal scholars, in the main, found the majority's reasoning justifying the intervention weak.[1] In contrast to the reaction among scholars, however, the public at large and most of the popular media seemed to accept the Court's resolution of the election dispute with equanimity. Why, after all, be surprised about the Supreme Court deciding a presidential election? Doesn't the Supreme Court make authoritative decisions in nearly all areas of American life? On many of the most important issues of interest to the public? The political scientists and legal scholars critical of the election outcome should not be surprised that most Americans would respond to these questions in the affirmative. In recent decades, Americans have seen the Court intervene decisively on a host of controversial issues, including abortion, school prayer, affirmative action, school vouchers, flag burning as symbolic speech, campaign finance reform, the death penalty, federalism, Internet pornography, and so on. The Court's intervention to settle a disputed presidential election thus seemed not so unusual, given the many other issues that the Court decides.

This easy acceptance of the Supreme Court's role in the 2000 election reflects the propensity of modern Americans to look to the judiciary, particularly the Supreme Court, to decide controversial political issues. As the observation by Tocqueville quoted at the beginning of this chapter reminds us, looking to the courts to resolve public conflicts is an old American habit. Nevertheless, we now seem to be even more addicted to it than when Tocqueville visited America in the 1830s. In the nineteenth century, for example, Americans did not expect the courts to decide presidential elections. In the election of 1876, a somewhat similar dispute over the allocation of electoral votes was resolved not by recourse to a lawsuit in federal court but by a special, congressionally appointed commission.[2] Accordingly, many of the scholarly critics of the *Bush v. Gore* decision argued that Congress, not the Court, should have been the ultimate arbiter of this electoral dispute as well. But in our time, the judicial branch of government has become a more active policymaker, using the power of judicial review—the power to judge whether laws or actions of government officials are consistent with the Constitution—to rule authoritatively on political conflicts. Even when the constitutionality of governmental actions is not at stake, the courts are frequently the arena in which parties to political conflict seek to advance their policy goals. It seems that much of American politics has become *judicialized.* The courts, not the legislatures, are the arena in which important policy questions are resolved. This chapter examines whether this judicialization of American politics is consistent with democratic values. Is the judicial resolution of important political matters democratic? Does the expansion of judicial power in American politics constitute a challenge to our democracy?

For people who (as I did) grew up in the 1950s and 1960s and consider themselves political progressives or liberals, the notion that the judiciary, particularly the Supreme Court, might be considered an undemocratic force seems like heresy. The Court, led during most of those years by Chief Justice Earl Warren, seemed to be our government system's best defender of democratic values. In 1954, when the power of southern Democrats in Congress effectively blocked national legislation to protect the civil rights of American blacks, the Court, in the historic *Brown v. Board of Education of Topeka, Kansas,* decision, declared the segregation of public schools to be unconstitutional. Many regard that decision as a key inspiration to the civil rights movement of the next decade, which tore down the edifice of Jim Crow segregation and secured greater political rights for blacks and, eventually, other minorities. The Warren Court also promoted enhanced recognition of key democratic rights in decisions that expanded free speech, mandated regular reapportionment of state legislatures according to the principle of "one person, one vote," protected freedom of the press, and provided new protections to those accused of crimes. For many political liberals, Court decisions promoting individual reproductive rights—first in *Griswold v. Connecticut* in 1965 (striking down a state law that prohibited the sale of contraceptives) and then, in perhaps the most controversial decision of the era, *Roe v. Wade* in 1973 (guaranteeing women the individual right to decide whether to have an abortion)—seemed to be significant expansions of democratic rights. Liberals praised the decisions of that era and came to see an activist judiciary as the prime defender and promoter of democratic values.[3]

Not all Americans agreed. Political conservatives denounced the Court's activism, arguing that it was usurping the legitimate power of elected representatives to determine public policy.[4] Disagreement over the substance of Supreme Court decisions drove much of the conservative rhetoric; opposition to desegregation motivated the "Impeach Earl Warren" signs scattered along southern roadsides in the 1960s. But many thoughtful conservatives raised principled objections, arguing that the judiciary was mandating policies that would be more suitably settled through deliberation in representative legislatures. During that era "judicial activism"—the theory that judges should not be afraid to overturn legislative enactments in the pursuit of just outcomes—became the conventional liberal position, and "judicial restraint"—the belief that judges should defer to elected representatives in their decisions—became associated with political conservatism.

Liberals also came to see the courts as an arena for defending the politically weak from powerful interests and for promoting the public interest in opposition to predatory private interests. In the 1960s and 1970s, activists in environmental protection, consumer protection, civil rights and liberties, and other liberal causes routinely sought to promote their policy objectives by suing powerful interests in court rather than fighting them in Congress or state legislatures. Many activists saw legislatures as under the thumb of influential special interests, while the insulation of judges from political pressure made them more receptive to liberal claims regarding individual rights and their definition of the public interest. By the 1980s, conservative opponents of such liberal activism began to advocate tort reform, or limiting the ability to seek the redress of a wrong (a tort) in the courts. The judiciary seemed to be the liberal-friendly arena of American politics, while electoral institutions were under the sway of reactionary forces. Most liberals at the time did not reflect on the fundamental distrust of democratic politics that such a view implied, nor did they imagine that the judiciary might not remain supportive of their goals.

The ideological tenor of the American judiciary has altered significantly since the early 1970s. In response to the perceived liberal activism of the Warren Court, Republican conservatives made appointment of politically conservative judges a major political objective. They demanded judges who would show "judicial restraint," who would be "strict constructionists" (merely applying the law, not making it), and who would interpret the Constitution according to the "original intent" of the framers. Republican presidents have appointed most of the federal judiciary over the past thirty years, including five of the nine current members of the Supreme Court. Yet this Republican domination of the appointment power, while it has produced a more ideologically conservative judiciary, has not led to a necessarily more restrained one.[5] In fact, as is more fully documented later in this chapter, current Supreme Court justices, as well as many of the judges on lower federal courts, have been as activist in promoting their conservative ideological preferences as an earlier generation was in promoting liberal ones. In fact, the conservative political activism of the current Supreme Court, as reflected in *Bush v. Gore,* is more typical of the Court's history than was the short period of its mid-twentieth-century liberal activism.[6]

This chapter evaluates the judiciary's role according to democratic values, not the ideological bias of its decisions at a particular time. Viewed in this light, the power of the courts over public policy in contemporary America is a significant challenge to our democracy. The federal judiciary's insulation from political control and democratic accountability, although justified when it performs its adjudicatory responsibilities, becomes a danger when it moves into the policy-making arena. I examine this challenge to democracy in a review of how the Supreme Court has used its power of *judicial review,* the legal doctrine that is the source of its influence over public policy, to usurp the democratic policy-making function. The next section begins with an examination of why the judiciary is inherently the "least democratic branch," in its structure and its decision-making processes and in the antimajoritarian—hence democratically problematic—character of judicial review.

The Least Democratic Branch

The people rule in modern democracies, as pointed out in the introduction, through representatives elected in free and open elections. Representative democracy assumes that over time, through the process of democratic elections, the will of the majority of the people will be expressed in the policies that those representatives enact. In the United States, both the presidency and Congress reflect this democratic logic. The president obtains his position by means of a democratic electoral process, even though the majority's will is then translated through a democratically flawed Electoral College system (as we explore in chapter 5). And members of both the House of Representatives and the Senate, at least since the passage of the Seventeenth Amendment (providing for the direct election of senators), also gain their positions by public election. Although one may question whether these democratic electoral processes ultimately result in decisions that express the people's will—indeed, the previous chapter did so in claiming that the separation of powers frustrates popular rule—the process of election is at least intended to create such a linkage. There is, however, nothing democratic about the process of selecting Supreme Court justices and other federal judges. Nor is that process intended to subject judges to democratic control; on the contrary, the mode of their selection is intended to insulate them from majority will.

The president has the power to appoint federal judges, including members of the Supreme Court, with the advice and consent of the Senate. Article III of the Constitution provides that once appointed, judges have life tenure and cannot be removed from the bench except by impeachment, nor can their salaries be reduced. Life tenure and security of compensation are intended to insulate judges from political pressures, allowing them to make unpopular decisions without fear of retribution either from those who appointed them or from the public at large.[7] In the previous chapter, separation of powers is faulted for impeding the people's ability to make elected representatives responsive and hold them accountable. The federal judiciary, by design, is expected to be neither responsive nor accountable to the people. Why in a democracy would one want such a nondemocratic institution?

The standard answer to this question is the need for judicial impartiality, given the fundamental functions of a court system. The primary job of the courts is to adjudicate disputes—whether between the government and a defendant in a criminal case about someone's guilt or innocence or between two parties to a civil lawsuit. In our adversarial system, judges referee the legal conflicts brought to their courts by hearing the facts of a dispute, applying relevant laws, and rendering a decision. Insulating judges from political pressure is intended to ensure their impartiality in adjudicating such conflicts. Parties to a civil suit can feel more confident that their dispute will be resolved fairly if neither can use access to the political system to pressure the judge. The defendant in a criminal case would have cause to worry if the judge had to fear that his or her decision in a case might draw retribution from the very government officials conducting the prosecution. Insulation of judges from political, even democratic, pressures makes sense when it comes to their adjudicatory role.

The democratic problem arises because the process of adjudication, applying laws to particular cases, inevitably involves a legislative aspect. When applying the law, a judge must resolve any ambiguities that exist in the relevant legal statute and decide what it means in the context of a particular case. For example, Congress has passed legislation forbidding colleges and universities from revealing student grades to third parties without the student's permission. Does this statutory protection of student privacy mean that a professor cannot require students to grade each other's quizzes as part of a peer-learning exercise? If a student objecting to such peer learning sued a professor under the statute, a court would have to determine whether peer grading constituted a violation of student privacy.[8] In the process the judge would make law, in effect, determining whether the public policy protecting student privacy encompassed peer grading.

When public policy is shaped in such a manner, a judge's accountability to the democratic process becomes an issue. Is the judge's policy choice consistent with the people's will? How, without the controlling power of an election, can the people hold a judge accountable? When a judge interprets a statute in the ordinary course of determining whether it applies to the situation raised in a particular case, as in the student privacy example, the solution is simple: If the judge's interpretation of the statute is contrary to the will of elected legislators, the judge's policy choice can be corrected by amending that particular statute to clarify the legislative intent. The problem becomes more complex, however, when federal judges exercise the power of judicial review.

The United States is one of only a few countries in the world in which the federal judiciary has the power to invalidate a law or official action by declaring it inconsistent with a basic law—in the United States, our Constitution.[9] Such judicial review applies to both federal and state-level laws and officials. In many democracies, the policy decisions of elected legislatures and the executive officials responsible either to them or to the electorate are inviolate. Legislatures, because of their more democratic character, are usually seen as the most appropriate arbiters of constitutional intent. In the United States, however, judicial review gives to unelected judges—the federal judiciary in general, and ultimately the Supreme Court—the ability to overrule the people's elected representatives by declaring legislation or executive acts to be unconstitutional. The courts are thus empowered to do more than just determine how a law applies to a particular case; they are authorized even to declare that the statute itself should not be allowed—in effect repealing it. Elected representatives who disagree with such a ruling by the judiciary cannot respond by simply amending the statute in question, as they can when a simple difference of interpretation of the meaning or legislative intent of a statute is at issue. Once the court system has determined that a statute (or portion of a statute) is unconstitutional, the only recourse available to the people and their representatives to overrule the judiciary is to undertake some extraordinary action, such as amending the Constitution itself. As one constitutional scholar defines the situation, "The central function, and it is at the same time the central problem, of judicial review [is that] a body that is not elected or otherwise politically responsible in any significant way is telling the people's elected representatives that they cannot govern as they'd like."[10]

The question for democrats is this: Can judicial review, the substitution of the will of unelected judges for that of elected representatives, be justified, and if so, on what basis? Before we examine the arguments relevant to this question, the next section offers a brief historical review of the origins of judicial review and the Supreme Court's record of judicial activism in using this power.

A Brief History of Judicial Review

Many textbook treatments of the Supreme Court's power of judicial review describe two alternative philosophies for its exercise: *judicial restraint* versus *judicial activism*.[11] Justices are said to exercise judicial restraint when their decisions do not reflect their personal values and policy preferences but adhere closely to the law and to precedent. When using restraint, they also are careful to defer to the choices of elected representative bodies on policy questions. Judicial activists, by contrast, are said "to promote their preferred social and political goals."[12] Activist judges are not afraid to overturn laws enacted by elected representatives in order to advance their preferred policies. When the history of the judiciary is viewed according to these definitions, it is clear that the Supreme Court has always been more activist than restrained. It has not hesitated to intervene in some of the country's most crucial political conflicts, such as slavery and the structure of industrial society, often overturning the will of the people's elected representatives. Nor, in most cases, has the Court acted to promote democratic values through its decisions; instead, its activism has more often been intended as a means of reining in democracy. We can see evidence of this propensity in the very origins of the practice of judicial review.

The text of the Constitution makes no mention of judicial review and assigns no such power to the judiciary. Unlike Article I's lengthy enumeration of specific legislative powers assigned to Congress, Article III vests the "judicial power" in the "supreme Court, and in such inferior Courts as the Congress may from time to time ordain and establish," but it does not explain what is contained in that judicial power. In the first legislation passed under the new Constitution, the Judiciary Act of 1789, Congress provided for the required "inferior Courts" but again offered no directive assigning to the courts the power to review the constitutionality of laws. There is, however, evidence that many of the delegates to the Constitutional Convention assumed that the Supreme Court would have this power. In state ratification debates, several Constitution proponents argued that it would, and Alexander Hamilton affirmed this notion in *Federalist* No. 78.[13] Yet many at that time, including Thomas Jefferson, feared that with such a power the Court would usurp the legitimate authority of the other branches.[14] Without any explicit grant of power in the Constitution itself, judicial review therefore had to be, in the words of constitutional scholar Alexander Bickel, "summoned up out of the constitutional vapors" by Chief Justice John Marshall in the 1803 decision *Marbury v. Madison.*[15]

Marshall's decision was the first and perhaps the most brilliant example of the Supreme Court's judicial activism. As a partisan Federalist and political opponent of President Jefferson, Marshall was anxious to use the Court as a restraint on the president and Congress. The Federalists had lost control of both those branches in the 1800 election, and they feared that Jefferson might use his political power to enact radical legislation. The judiciary, however, was firmly in Federalist hands as a consequence both of judicial appointments made prior to 1800 and of many lame-duck appointments, including Marshall's, by President John Adams prior to Jefferson's inauguration in 1801. Fortunately, as it turned out for Marshall, not all those whom Adams had appointed received their official, written commissions before the inauguration. Once in power, Jefferson instructed his secretary of state, James Madison, not to deliver the commissions to these unfortunates. One, Mr. Marbury, brought suit before the Supreme Court, demanding that Madison send him his letter of commission. Marshall seized upon this case as the perfect vehicle for asserting the power of judicial review, thereby establishing the Federalist judiciary as a safeguard against Jefferson's government, with the certainty that the Court would be obeyed.

In his decision, Marshall agreed that Madison was wrong to deny Marbury his commission but decided against Marbury on a technicality: Marbury's mistake was going directly to the Supreme Court to seek redress of his grievance. The Judiciary Act of 1789 had given the Supreme Court original jurisdiction, the right to hear a case directly, when citizens sued to force a federal official to do his duty. But in thus attempting to add to the Court's original jurisdiction beyond what had been explicitly assigned in the Constitution, Marshall declared, Congress had violated the Constitution, and therefore that portion of the Judiciary Act was overturned. The Court, Marshall said, had no power to order Madison to send Marbury his commission, but at the same time, he was asserting the Court's more significant power to overturn an act of Congress. This assertion of judicial review infuriated Jefferson and Madison, but because the substantive decision had affirmed their action, they did not—as Marshall knew they would not—defy the

Court.[16] Marshall had achieved his aim of establishing the judiciary as a check on the potential "evils" of democracy.

Marshall's motives in asserting the power of judicial review were not purely partisan. Judicial review, he argued, derived from the logic of constitutional government and the nature of judicial power.[17] In enacting a constitution, the American people had opted that government be limited by the principles in that document. If any ordinary law conflicted with the Constitution, judges were obliged to rule in favor of constitutional principle, necessitating overturning the law. As Marshall wrote in *Marbury v. Madison:*

> [T]hose who have framed written constitutions contemplate them as forming the fundamental and paramount law of the nation. . . . [A]n act of the legislature, repugnant of the constitution is void. . . . It is emphatically the province and duty of the judicial department to say what the law is. Those who apply the rule to particular cases, must of necessity expound and interpret the rule. If two laws conflict with each other, the courts must decide on the operation of each.
>
> So if a law be in opposition to the constitution . . . the court must determine which of these conflicting rules governs the case. This is of the very essence of judicial duty.[18]

Although Marshall's decision never explicitly makes the assertion, it implies that the Supreme Court is the final arbiter in interpreting the Constitution. In the words of a later chief justice, Charles Evans Hughes, "The Constitution is what the judges say it is."[19] This claim of judicial supremacy, as Lincoln's warning quoted at the beginning of this chapter suggests, would not go uncontested in American political life, but the power of judicial review and the power of the Supreme Court to determine the constitutionality of the decisions of other political decision makers would be a fundamental reality of American politics over the next two hundred years.

Once the principle of judicial review was established, the Supreme Court was slow to exercise it again in a federal matter. Although Marshall had acted decisively to assert the power of judicial review, never again under his leadership did the Court overturn an act of Congress (see Table 2.1). Marshall did exercise judicial review in overturning state laws; many of those decisions affirmed the supremacy of the federal government over the states and offered expansive interpretations of congressional powers.[20]

The next time the Supreme Court overturned congressional legislation was in the infamous 1857 *Dred Scott v. Sandford* decision, perhaps the worst and clearly the most politically disastrous Supreme Court decision ever.[21] In the majority opinion, Chief Justice Roger B. Taney—Marshall's successor—rejected the attempt of a black slave, Dred Scott, to obtain his freedom. Scott's owner had taken him to live in part of what is now Minnesota, then a federal territory in which slavery had been prohibited by the Missouri Compromise of 1820. Now back in Missouri, a slave state, Scott claimed that his prolonged sojourn in a free territory should make him permanently free. With the support of his fellow southerners on the Court, Taney saw the case as an opportunity to place a constitutional barrier against any congressional attempt to limit slavery. His opinion declared that the Missouri Compromise legislation's attempt to divide western territories equally into slave and free zones was unconstitutional because Congress had no power to forbid slavery anywhere. Slaves, in the Taney Court's eyes, were property, not persons; any law forbidding slavery violated the right of property. In the process, the Taney Court also declared that black people, whether slave or free, could never be American citizens. This unequivocal prohibition of congressional action on the central issue of the time and the preemptive exclusion of blacks from any future citizenship rights inflamed opponents of slavery in the North and, historians agree, contributed to the coming of the Civil War.

Sobered by this example of the disastrous potential of judicial activism, the post–Civil War courts might justifiably have been reluctant to use judicial review to overturn congressional legislation thereafter, but instead they became more assertive in exercising their power in the second half of the nineteenth century. In the 1883 *Civil Rights Cases,* the Supreme Court overturned the Civil Rights Act of 1875, which had forbidden racial discrimination in public accommodations, such as hotels, theaters, and restaurants. The 1875 act was one of several civil rights laws that Congress had passed to implement the Thirteenth, Fourteenth, and Fifteenth Amendments, which were meant to protect the rights of the newly freed slaves and integrate them into American society as full-fledged citizens.[22] In the *Civil Rights Cases* the Court imposed a very narrow interpretation on the Fourteenth Amendment, saying that it only applied to discrimination by state governments and not discrimination by private individuals or corporations. In this and other decisions restricting the application of the post–Civil War constitutional amendments, the Court gave a green light to the South's Jim Crow laws consigning blacks to political and social inferiority. In 1896, the Court endorsed the then-widespread practice of legally mandated segregation with its "separate but equal" doctrine in *Plessy v. Ferguson.* With these decisions, the Supreme Court destroyed the promise of full citizenship for black Americans expressed in the Thirteenth through Fifteenth Amendments—and the promise would remain unfulfilled until the 1960s. In sharp contrast to the mid-twentieth-century Court, revered by liberals for protecting civil rights, the nineteenth-century Court, from *Dred Scott* through *Plessy,* was a major force for actively denying African Americans their civil liberties.

At the same time that the Supreme Court was interpreting the Fourteenth Amendment narrowly as it applied to black civil rights, it gave the amendment an expansive interpretation as a tool to protect the economic rights of corporations. From the 1890s until the 1930s, the Court would use the Fourteenth Amendment's guarantee that no state could "deprive any person of life, liberty, or property, without due process of law" as grounds to strike down numerous state

TABLE 2.1   Supreme Court's Exercise of the Power of Judicial Review, 1789–2009

Years	Supreme Court Decisions Overruled	Acts of Congress Overturned	State Laws Overturned	Ordinances Overturned
1789–1800, Pre-Marshall	0	0	0	0
1801–1835, Marshall Court	3	1	18	0
1836–1864, Taney Court	4	1	21	0
1865–1873, Chase Court	4	10	33	0
1874–1888, Waite Court	13	9	7	0
1889–1910, Fuller Court	4	14	73	15
1910–1921, White Court	5	12	107	18
1921–1930, Taft Court	6	12	131	12
1930–1940, Hughes Court	21	14	78	5
1941–1946, Stone Court	15	2	25	7
1947–1952, Vinson Court	13	1	38	7
1953–1969, Warren Court	45	25	150	16
1969–1986, Burger Court	52	34	192	15
1986–2005, Rehnquist Court	39	38	97	21
2005–, Roberts Court	7	4	10	2

Source: David O'Brien, *Storm Center: The Supreme Court in American Politics,* 9th ed. (New York: Norton, 2011), 31.

and federal laws that regulated business power and provided protection to workers. The first step came in *Santa Clara County v. Southern Pacific Railroad* (1886), when Chief Justice Morrison Waite, with the support of other former corporate lawyers on the Court, declared corporations to be "legal persons" entitled to protection under the Fourteenth Amendment.[23] Thirty years earlier, to protect slavery, the Taney Court had argued that human beings in slavery were property, not persons; now, the Waite Court, to protect business power, found corporations to be not merely a type of property, but persons.[24] In the 1905 *Lochner v. New York* decision, the Court would explicitly enunciate the doctrine that a substantive "right of contract" implicit in the Fourteenth Amendment's due process clause limited states' ability to regulate business. In this case, the Court struck down a New York state law intended to limit the number of hours that bakers could be required to work. In a famous dissenting opinion, Justice Oliver Wendell Holmes Jr. castigated his majority colleagues for imposing their laissez-faire and Social Darwinist economic philosophy through their decision.

In the "*Lochner* era" that followed this decision and lasted into the 1930s, the Court would strike down many state and federal economic regulations, including protections of the right to form labor unions, child labor laws, minimum wage laws, and other measures to protect workers and the public from the consequences of industrialization. While its inventive interpretation of the Fourteenth Amendment allowed the Court to constrain state governmental efforts to mitigate those consequences, the laissez-faire justices used a narrow interpretation of the Constitution's commerce clause (which gives Congress the power to regulate interstate commerce) to undermine congressional attempts to regulate business. For example, in *U.S. v. E. C. Knight Co.* (1895) the Court ruled that the Sherman Antitrust Act could not be used to break up the American Sugar Refining Company, even though the company controlled the refining of 98 percent of the sugar sold in the United States.[25] The Court's majority claimed that "commerce succeeds to manufacture, and is not a part of it," thereby preventing Congress from regulating any aspect of the production of goods, even if they later were to be sold across state lines. In making this artificial distinction between commerce and production, the Court had "at a stroke . . . immunized from congressional regulations major elements of the national economy, including manufacturing, oil production, agriculture, and mining."[26] Ironically, in view of its restrictions on state governments in *Lochner,* this narrow construction of Congress's commerce power was portrayed as a defense of state governments from congressional interference in economic regulation. The laissez-faire Supreme Court justices of the 1880s to the 1930s were determined that neither the state nor federal legislatures would be allowed to interfere with business.

Franklin Roosevelt's New Deal legislation, enacted to bring the country out of the Great Depression of the 1930s, came in direct conflict with the laissez-faire philosophy of the Supreme Court. Between 1934 and 1936, the Hughes Court in twelve decisions struck down a total of eleven New Deal policies, rendering the government nearly helpless to alleviate the economic distress of the country.[27] In desperation, Roosevelt proposed to Congress a controversial "court packing" plan to expand the size of the Court, allowing him to appoint new justices. That measure became unnecessary when Justice Owen Roberts changed his position on the commerce power in the 1937 case *National Labor Relations Board v. Jones & Laughlin Steel Corporation,* creating a new liberal majority by voting to endorse the federal government's power to protect workers' right to join labor unions. This pivotal switch marked a turning point in the Court's interpretation of the commerce power, giving Congress expansive powers to legislate on economic matters for the next fifty years. Over the next five decades the focus of judicial activism would shift from economic concerns to civil rights and civil liberties. (Only recently has the Court returned to a more narrow construction of the commerce power, as I discuss later.)

Political conservatives of the 1960s portrayed judicial activism as an invention of the Warren Court (1953–1969), under Chief Justice Earl Warren, even though, as we have seen, activism has been a recurrent tendency throughout Supreme Court history. The Warren Court, however, drew new attention to its role as a significant policy-making institution by its willingness to use its power to expand civil rights for black Americans, as in the landmark *Brown v. Board of Education* (1954) decision; to provide new protections for the rights of criminal defendants (*Gideon v. Wainwright,* 1963, and *Miranda v. Arizona,* 1966); to ensure equal

electoral representation (*Baker v. Carr*, 1962); to restrict prayer in s
v. Vitale, 1962); and to protect controversial political speech (*B*
Ohio, 1969). The Warren Court was in fact activist, as Table 2.1 sh
of the number of state and federal laws it overturned—although hardly more so
than the Courts that have ruled in the years since Earl Warren left the bench in
1969. Because the Warren Court's decisions were perceived as favoring a liberal
ideology, however, liberals as well as conservatives of that era came to regard both
the Supreme Court as an institution and the practice of judicial activism itself as
inherently liberal. This perception continued into the 1980s, as justices appointed
during the Warren era continued to serve on the Court. Many of the decisions
most associated with liberal activism were actually made by the Court led in those
later years by the conservative Chief Justice Warren Burger. Among those cases,
the controversial 1973 *Roe v. Wade* decision striking down state laws restricting
abortion seemed to be the most influential in mobilizing political conservatives
against liberal judicial activism.

Although political conservatives had begun demanding the appointment of
politically conservative judges in the 1960s—such appointments had been a
campaign promise of Republican President Richard Nixon in 1968—
conservatives began to focus more intently on influencing Court appointments
after *Roe v. Wade*. Much of the rhetoric that conservatives adopted to advocate
change on the Court was couched in terms of judicial philosophy, rather than
political ideology: They demanded the selection of judges who would be
committed to judicial restraint and to "strict constructionism"—that is, to
interpreting the Constitution according to its literal meaning, or the "original
intention" of the framers, rather than "legislating" from the bench. In reality,
however, conservative Republican presidents Nixon, Ford, Reagan, and George
H. W. Bush sought to appoint justices who were ideologically acceptable to the
party's right wing.

By the 1980s, as the complexion of the Court had begun to change in a more
conservative direction, its decisions began to modify many of the liberal Court
decisions of the Warren era and its immediate aftermath. Already, beginning in
the 1970s, the Burger Court had relaxed the restrictions on police interrogation
and searching of criminal suspects that had been established in *Miranda* and other
decisions of the Warren Court. By the 1990s, *Roe v. Wade* had been modified
extensively, permitting state legislatures and Congress to restrict, although not to
prevent altogether, a woman's access to abortion. The ideological complexion of
the Supreme Court had changed, but there was little sign that it was becoming
any more "restrained." As indicated in Table 2.1, the rate at which the Court
overturns federal, state, and local legislation has not abated since the days of the
Warren Court.

After the appointment of Associate Justice Steven Breyer in 1994, membership
on the Supreme Court remained unchanged until 2005. During this period, the
Court often split 5–4 on key issues, with the five conservative justices who formed

the majority in *Bush v. Gore* willing to use the undemocratic power of judicial review actively to advance conservative political goals. The core members of this majority—Chief Justice William Rehnquist, Justice Antonin Scalia, and Justice Clarence Thomas—were committed to substantially diminishing the latitude the Court has extended to Congress since 1937 to legislate on any matter it deems of national concern.[28] These three justices were in general sympathy with the tenets of the Federalist Society, an organization of conservative lawyers and judges who argue that the post–New Deal expansion of federal power violates states' rights and ought to be rolled back. Scalia and Thomas, especially, seem sympathetic to the "Constitution in Exile" movement of certain legal activists who believe that the "true" Constitution was banished from American politics when the Court abandoned strict limitations on state and federal power after 1937.[29] During this period, two less ideological but still conservative justices, Sandra Day O'Connor and Anthony Kennedy (the other two members of the *Bush v. Gore* majority), joined the federalist core to rule that the commerce clause does not allow Congress to ban guns near schools (*United States v. Lopez*), to apply the Americans with Disabilities Act to state government employees (*Board of Trustees of the University of Alabama v. Garrett*), or to authorize rape victims to sue their assailants in federal court (*United States v. Morrison*). Despite the familiar conservative mantra of judicial restraint and respect for precedent, these decisions were an opening wedge of systematic judicial attack on Congress's ability to legislate in the areas of environmental protection, civil rights, health care, and education.

New appointments to the Supreme Court since 2005 have maintained the 5–4 ideological division. George W. Bush appointed John Roberts to replace Chief Justice Rehnquist upon the latter's death in 2005 and Samuel Alito to replace Justice O'Connor when she retired in 2006. The Roberts and Alito appointments did not alter the overall ideological split on the Court but their appointments moved the Court somewhat to the right because both were more closely associated with conservative legal activists, such as those in the Federalist Society, than the justices they replaced. President Obama's appointments of Sonia Sotomayor and Elena Kagan replaced two of the justices on the Court's liberal wing—Justice David Souter and Justice John Paul Stevens, respectively. As a result of these appointments, the Roberts Court retains a conservative majority but one with a stronger ideological flavor and more prone to conservative judicial activism.[30]

Two decisions underscore this greater propensity to conservative judicial activism on the Roberts Court. The first, *District of Columbia v. Heller,* overturned a local ordinance prohibiting the ownership of guns in Washington, DC, asserting for the first time, in Justice Scalia's majority opinion, an individual right to own firearms based on the Second Amendment. Prior Court decisions always had interpreted the "right of the people to keep and bear arms" to be a collective right to form state militias and not an individual right. Scalia claimed to base his opinion on an originalist reading of the constitutional text, a view effectively refuted in Justice Stevens's scathing dissent that documented Scalia's selective use of historical evidence. Even conservative constitutional experts have pointed to Scalia's flawed reading of history and propensity in *Heller* to a loose interpretation of the constitutional text in the interest of an ideologically determined outcome— precisely the charge conservatives have leveled at "liberal activists" for decades.[31] The second, even more egregious example of conservative activism came in *Citizens United v. the Federal Election Commission.* Since the passage of the 1907 Tilman Act, federal law had prohibited corporations from contributing to political campaigns and restricted their political involvement. Several federal laws and previous Supreme Court decisions always had held that corporations did not possess the same free speech rights as individuals. In a novel interpretation, *Citizen's United* overturned a prohibition of corporate campaign advertisements in the 2002 Bipartisan Campaign Reform Act (BCRA), citing a violation of corporate first amendment rights. (The implications of this decision for democratic elections will be examined in detail in chapter 5.) The case underscored the conservative majority's propensity to judicial activism because the case plaintiff, Citizen's United, initially did not raise a constitutional issue but only questioned the FEC's interpretation of the law. The conservative justices themselves decided to declare the act unconstitutional.[32]

This brief historical review indicates that the Supreme Court has been, in the main, an activist presence in American political life. Over time, as Table 2.1 shows, its activist presence—as represented by the number of legislative actions overturned—has grown. The mere volume of such interventions by an unelected judiciary should be worrisome to democrats. Even more alarming is the willing- ness of justices from both ends of the political spectrum to substitute their own value and policy judgments for those of elected legislatures. In any political sys- tem, policy making involves trade-offs between alternative policy goals and often profound moral choices. Democracy is meant to lodge the difficult responsibility for weighing these trade-offs with the people, usually through their elected repre- sentatives. It rejects the notion that any group of "philosopher-kings" can do a better job of making those choices. Yet, as this brief historical review shows, the Court often sets itself up as a panel of philosopher-kings who are willing to sub- stitute their policy judgments for those of elected representatives. In the next section, I examine in more detail two specific cases in which I believe the justices acted as philosopher-kings, when the more democratic decision would have been to defer to the policy judgments of elected legislators.

Two Cases of Judicial Usurpation

My two examples, *Roe v. Wade* and *United States v. Morrison,* demonstrate judicial usurpation from opposite ends of the ideological spectrum. Conservatives view the Supreme Court's 1973 decision in *Roe v. Wade* as the worst example of liberal judicial activism, as it struck down state laws prohibiting abortion in the first trimester of pregnancy. In this case, the justices articulated a policy that substituted their judgment regarding a morally complex issue for that of legislatures in the various states. The other example, *U.S. v. Morrison,* shows how justices with a conservative political agenda that favors limiting the power of the federal government substituted their judgment for that of Congress itself by limiting congressional authority under the commerce clause. In this 2000 decision, as in other so-called federalism cases, the current conservative majority has signaled the beginning of a new era of conservative judicial activism that has all the signs of the judicial "usurpation" that conservatives have long denounced in decisions such as *Roe.*

The 1973 abortion decision arose from a case brought by a Texas woman, identified as "Jane Roe" in the court documents, who had been prevented from obtaining an abortion under Texas law. That law, dating from 1854, resembled statutes passed by many states in that era to prohibit abortion except when performed to save the life of the mother.[33] Earlier, most states had either placed no restrictions on abortion or had proscribed the procedure only after "quickening"—the time of the fetus's first movement in the womb—but by the early twentieth century, many had adopted restrictive abortion statutes similar to the Texas one. By the 1960s, however, about half the states—not including Texas—had again liberalized their abortion laws to allow abortion when pregnancy risked the physical or mental health of the mother, when the child was likely to be born with grave mental or physical defects, and in cases of rape or incest. And by 1972, four states—Hawaii, New York, Washington, and Alaska— had enacted laws that allowed largely unrestricted abortion in the first trimester of pregnancy. In sum, the legal status of abortion at the time of *Roe* was very much in flux, as states considered various ways to resolve the complex moral issues involved.

The *Roe* decision effectively halted this state legislative activity by imposing a common federal policy. Under the Court's mandate, state law could not interfere with a woman's decision to have an abortion in the first trimester of pregnancy, although the states could impose restrictions designed to preserve maternal health in the second trimester and could prohibit abortions in the third.[34] The Court majority argued that state laws regulating first trimester abortions violated a women's right to privacy. As in *Griswold v. Connecticut* (which in 1965 had overturned laws restricting the sale of contraceptives), the Court found that a right to privacy regarding matters of reproduction and sexual intimacy was implicit in the Constitution and that this was a substantive right guaranteed to persons through the Fourteenth Amendment's due process clause. One difference between *Roe* and *Griswold,* however, was that in the case of abortion, exercising this right to privacy involved destruction of a fetus, which raised further questions. Should the fetus also be regarded as a "person" under the Fourteenth Amendment and thus invested with guaranteed rights? And, if so, how should these fetal rights be weighed against the privacy rights of the mother?

In defending the Texas statute, the state's lawyers argued that life begins at conception and that the fetus is a person whose life the state is compelled to protect. In its decision, the Court acknowledged the state's interest in the potential life of the fetus but did not agree that that interest could be based on a definition of the fetus as a person. Opting to be agnostic on the question of when life begins, the Court held that since there was no consensus on the matter among doctors, philosophers, and theologians, it "need not resolve the difficult question." In effect, the Court acknowledged that the legality of abortion hinged on balancing a woman's privacy right against the state's legitimate interest in fetal life, but it ruled that the Texas legislature could not assert that right from conception. According to the Court majority, "By adopting one theory of life, Texas may [not] override the rights of the pregnant woman." The Court's answer to these questions in *Roe v. Wade* so provoked the ire of abortion opponents that abortion has continued to be one of the most contentious national policy issues into the new century.

As *Roe*'s critics charge, the problem with the decision was that, while acknowledging uncertainty about when life begins, the justices gave no constitutional rationale why Texas should not be allowed to assume that it begins at conception and to regulate abortion in accordance with that assumption. Given the theological, scientific, and philosophical uncertainties, the Texas legislature's understanding was as reasonable as an assumption that life does not begin at conception. As one constitutional scholar put it, "Why wasn't Texas free—free as a constitutional matter, free under the Fourteenth Amendment—to proceed on the basis of the assumption that a pre-viable unborn child is no less a subject of justice than a post-viable unborn child or a born child?"[35] One does not have to agree with the Texas legislature's theory about the beginning of life to acknowledge that it should have the power to strike a balance, based on that theory, between fetal rights and those of women. For democrats, striking the proper balance between competing rights and moral values under conditions of uncertainty is the job of democratically elected representatives deliberating in legislatures—not that of unelected judges. Viewed in this light, the Court in *Roe* simply substituted its judgment about how the potential life of a fetus should be weighed for that of the Texas legislators. From a democratic perspective, this seems a clear case of judicial usurpation of legislative power.

From the perspective of the larger political system, moreover, the impact of *Roe* has been destructive to the ongoing democratic deliberation about abortion. With its decision, the Court effectively arrested the deliberation and legislative activity in the states regarding abortion; instead, it nationalized and constitutionalized the issue. Rather than arguing with one another about how the complex moral issues surrounding abortion should be resolved in law, abortion opponents and proponents have since focused all their energies on either denouncing or defending *Roe*. What had been in the late sixties a constructive period of accommodation and compromise among contending ideological and moral interests

Formal group portrait at the Supreme Court in Washington, DC, taken in 2010. Seated, from left, are Associate Justices Clarence Thomas, Antonin Scalia, Chief Justice John Roberts, Associate Justices Anthony M. Kennedy, and Ruth Bader Ginsburg. Standing, from left, are Associate Justices Sonia Sotomayor, Stephen Breyer, Samuel Alito Jr., and Elena Kagan.

AP Photo/Pablo Martinez Monsivais, File.

became, by the late 1970s, a rancorous fight over absolutist positions pitting the constitutional "rights" of the unborn against those of women. Even defenders of *Roe* acknowledge this point—as Justice Ruth Bader Ginsburg wrote in a 1985 article, "[M]ajoritarian institutions were listening and acting. Heavy-handed judicial intervention was difficult to justify and appears to have provoked, not resolved, conflict."[36] Eventually *Roe* had the effect of greatly politicizing the Court itself, as pro-choice and pro-life forces mobilized to evaluate nominees to the bench based on their perceived positions on *Roe*. Looking back over the past thirty years, it seems clear that *Roe*'s impact on the democratic political process has not been a positive one.

In fact, the political reaction to *Roe* contributed substantially to the current ideological complexion of the Supreme Court. By the 1980s, abortion concerns and their connection to judicial appointments had become a standard element of electoral politics. For both parties, but especially for Republicans, positions on abortion became a litmus test in nominations for Congress and the presidency. At the same time, using *Roe* as a rallying cry, conservative groups began a concerted effort to place right-wing judges on federal district and appeals courts, as well as the Supreme Court, and to prevent the nomination of liberals. During the past twenty years, contention over the abortion issue has exacerbated several hard-fought political conflicts over Supreme Court nominations, including the defeat of Reagan nominee Robert Bork and the eventual confirmation of the first President Bush's appointee Clarence Thomas. In the past, judicial nominations never produced such highly visible conflicts. During both the Reagan and George H. W. Bush presidencies, however, conservatives had considerable success in shaping the judiciary: By the 1990s, not only could they count on a narrow 5–4 conservative majority on the Supreme Court, but their appointees were also well placed on lower federal courts to actively mold the law according to conservative ideology.

Although the abortion issue has driven much of the politics around judicial appointments, it has not been a central concern of the conservatives actually serving on the bench. More important to them have been questions about the proper role of the federal government. For many conservative justices, especially the late Chief Justice Rehnquist, a major objective has been to restore the concept of dual federalism to the government system. Dual federalism, a doctrine that guided the pre-1937 Court, claims that the Constitution carves out separate "sovereign" spheres for the federal and state governments, and these conservatives argue that post–New Deal Congresses have repeatedly gone beyond their constitutionally enumerated powers to interfere with the prerogatives of state government. In particular, they believe that the broad interpretation of the power to regulate interstate commerce, which has justified congressional legislation over virtually every aspect of American life, needs to be limited so as to return more power to state governments. In a series of decisions in the 1990s, the Court took major steps toward cutting into congressional power by interpreting the commerce clause more narrowly.

My second example of judicial usurpation involves a 2000 decision reining in Congress's power under the commerce clause: *United States v. Morrison.* The stage had been set for *Morrison* five years earlier in *United States v. Lopez,* in which the Rehnquist Court struck down the Gun-Free Schools Act of 1990, ruling that Congress had not proved in the legislation how the commerce clause allowed it to prohibit the presence of firearms within 1,000 feet of schools. Thus, for the first time since 1936, the Court cited a too-broad claim of the power to regulate commerce as grounds for overturning an act of Congress.[37] In the wake of *Lopez,* some Court observers thought that the decision was merely a warning to Congress to legislate more carefully and to make more explicit in legislation the links to its power to regulate commerce.[38] In *Morrison,* however, the Court's conservative majority demonstrated that its goals were more ambitious, as it directly called into question the extent of Congress's power under the commerce clause, not simply— as seemed to be the case in *Lopez*—seeking to monitor how Congress implemented its power.

Morrison involved a case arising under the Violence Against Women Act of 1994, which authorized victims of rape and other gender-motivated crimes to sue their attackers in federal court. In crafting this legislation, unlike the Gun-Free Schools Act, the lawmakers had gone to great lengths to document the impact of violence against women on the economy, making explicit Congress's judgment that its legislation was justified under the commerce clause.[39] In the same year that the legislation passed, two members of the Virginia Polytechnic Institute football team, Antonio J. Morrison and James Crawford, raped Christy Brzonkala, a freshman at the college. After the university permitted Morrison to return to school, even though its disciplinary system had found him guilty, Brzonkala sued Morrison and Virginia Tech in federal court. On May 16, 2000, in a 5–4 decision, the Court rejected Brzonkala's suit on the grounds that neither the commerce clause nor section 5 of the Fourteenth Amendment gave Congress the power to authorize rape victims to sue their attackers in federal court.

In his discussion of the commerce clause in the majority opinion, Chief Justice Rehnquist resurrected the distinctions between economic and noneconomic power that the Court had deployed so effectively to restrain federal power in the first part of the twentieth century. Congress had no power to allow victims to seek compensation in federal court because, in his words, "gender-motivated crimes of violence are not, in any sense of the phrase, economic activity."[40] What about the congressional findings showing the impact of gender-related violence on the economy? Although Congress believed that the evidence indicated a substantial link between such violence and interstate commerce, Rehnquist simply dismissed this evidence as "not sufficient, by itself, to sustain the constitutionality of commerce clause legislation."[41] Later in the opinion, the chief justice indicated that Congress cannot be allowed to justify its legislation under the commerce clause with such evidence. To do so, he writes, "would allow Congress to regulate any crime as long as the nation-wide, aggregated impact of that crime has substantial effects on employment, production, transit, or consumption."[42] Rehnquist's opinion makes clear that the Supreme Court, not Congress, will henceforth determine and possibly limit Congress's authority under the commerce clause—a clear reversal of the Court's practice since 1937.

As in *Roe*—but this time on behalf of a conservative objective—the Court majority in *Morrison* was asserting its power to substitute its own judgment for that of elected representatives. In his dissent, Justice David Souter took the majority to task for that substitution, arguing for a more restrained interpretation of judicial power:

> The fact of such a substantial effect is not an issue for the courts in the first instance, but for the Congress, whose institutional capacity for gathering evidence and taking testimony far exceeds ours. By passing legislation, Congress indicates its conclusion, whether explicitly or not, that facts support its exercise of the commerce power. The business of the courts is to review the congressional assessment not for soundness but simply for the rationality of concluding that a jurisdictional basis exists in fact.[43]

In sum, Souter points out, elected representatives in Congress are better judges of what the commerce power requires than are the appointed members of the judiciary. Even if Rehnquist were correct in warning that nearly any action might be regulated under the commerce clause as long as Congress could show some economic impact, from a democratic point of view, the need for such action must be a political judgment made by representatives accountable to the people and not by unelected judges.[44] This recognition of legislative authority has been the tacit interpretation by both the Court and Congress since the New Deal. The current Court's attempts to block congressional action can only undermine the capacity of democratic majorities to address genuine national needs.

So as not to leave any doubt about the Court's intention to limit congressional power, Rehnquist included in the *Morrison* opinion one of the strongest assertions ever of the Court's supremacy in interpreting the Constitution. Referencing a similar assertion in a 1958 Warren Court decision (*Cooper v. Aaron*), Rehnquist describes the Court as "the ultimate expositor of the Constitution," which will not defer to Congress's judgment as to the extent of congressional power. The Rehnquist Court's willingness to assert its superiority over the other branches of the federal government marked an extension of judicial authority beyond that claimed by the Warren and Burger Courts, which generally employed such rhetoric in asserting the Court's power over the states.[45] *Morrison* was but one example of the Rehnquist Court's determination not to defer to Congress. As one legal scholar put it, "The current [Rehnquist] Court increasingly displaces Congress's view with its own without much more than a passing nod to Congress's factual findings or policy judgments."[46] As a former clerk and admirer of Rehnquist, Chief Justice Roberts shows every sign of continuing the trend of reining in Congress. The Supreme Court's willingness to override the judgments of an elected legislature seems rooted in a fundamental distrust of democracy and democratic institutions.[47] This distrust of democracy was evidenced further in 2000 when the Court took it upon itself to resolve the dispute over the Florida presidential vote, rather than leave the issue to be resolved in Congress.

Despite their many differences, decisions such as *Roe* and *Morrison* pose a similar challenge to democracy. In both cases, the Supreme Court assumes a policy-making role in defiance of the preferences of elected legislatures even though the constitutional justification for doing so is extremely weak. Justices sensitive to democratic governance should have been willing to defer to the judgment of elected legislators in these instances rather than take on the policy-making responsibility themselves. Even if one believes that the Court made the "correct" decision in either of these cases—that the Court's policy was preferable to that of the legislatures—a democrat has to be concerned when unelected judges usurp the power of elected representatives. These two cases, as well as the historical review in the previous section, point out the inherently countermajoritarian character of judicial review. As the Court has become increasingly activist over the past few decades, the overall impact of its exercise of power on American governance has become more threatening to representative democracy. From John Marshall to the Roberts Court, those who fear democracy have promoted judicial review as a bulwark against popular majorities.

This brings us back to the question raised earlier in the chapter: Can the exercise of judicial review—the substitution of the will of unelected judges for that of elected representatives—be justified, and if so, on what basis? In the next section, we enter into the realm of constitutional theory to see if there is a satisfactory answer to that question.

Can Judicial Review Be Made Consistent With Democracy?

Constitutional scholars offer two alternative theoretical approaches to how the judiciary should go about exercising its power of judicial review so that the exercise might be consistent with democratic governance. The first holds that judges should decide the cases before them solely through application of principles derived from the written text of the Constitution. Adherents of this view refer to themselves as "strict constructionists," and as we shall see, they often make the additional claim that when any interpretation of constitutional language is needed beyond the "plain meaning" of the text, such interpretation should be based on the "original intent" of the framers. The second approach argues the necessity of going beyond the text to identify constitutional principles that have evolved over time, as Americans come to understand how those original principles apply to new situations and changing historical circumstances. This latter approach portrays the Constitution as a living document, whose basic principles must be understood with reference to changes in social mores and values.

Although political conservatives are often identified with the strict constructionist approach and political liberals with the living Constitution one, neither approach is necessarily linked with a particular ideology. As described earlier in this chapter, the "*Lochner* era" Court's artful use of the Fourteenth Amendment places the conservative justices of that time firmly in the living Constitution camp.[48] Nor is either approach related, in practice, to judicial activism or judicial restraint, as the active reversal of laws and previous court decisions based on judges' own social goals has been characteristic of judges advocating both approaches.

Strict constructionists believe that adherence to the constitutional text provides the best protection against judicial policy making and offers the best assurance that Court decisions will be democratic. If decisions are based solely on the constitutional text, they argue, judges cannot be applying their own preferences in their decisions but only requiring what the Constitution itself requires. Moreover, because the Constitution and its amendments were ratified by the people in democratic processes, their application in overturning subsequent statutes involves merely implementing the people's more profound democratic will as expressed in the fundamental law. According to one defender of this approach, "When a court strikes down a popular statute or practice as unconstitutional, it may also reply to the resulting public outcry: 'We didn't do it—you did.'"[49] So when the Supreme Court strikes down a local ordinance prohibiting a march by neo-Nazis, or a state law preventing flag burning, or a federal law limiting how much money candidates can spend on their campaigns, it is only applying the clear text of the First Amendment: "Congress shall make no law . . . abridging the freedom of speech."

The last sentence points, as many readers may have realized, to a basic flaw in the strict constructionist approach. If, as this approach suggests, constitutional interpretation requires merely an application of the literal text of the Constitution, there is a problem: Applying constitutional language always requires a judgment regarding what the language means as related to a particular situation. In the three examples of free speech provided in the sentence above (all taken from actual Court decisions), the crucial step in applying the First Amendment is determining whether an action constitutes "free speech"—a decision the words alone cannot define. In each, one can see that making such a determination is neither obvious nor uncontroversial. In the flag-burning case, for example, the Court's finding that burning the flag is a form of symbolic political speech has been quite controversial, although it is a reasonable understanding of how political views are sometimes conveyed. To say that interpreting the Constitution requires only applying its text thus ignores the ambiguity inherent in even seemingly simple concepts, such as free speech, when they are applied to the real world. The nature of most constitutional language compounds this problem, as it consists largely of very general terms and concepts that are susceptible to multiple interpretations. Phrases such as "due process of law," "equal protection of the laws," "unreasonable search and seizure," and "cruel and unusual punishment" do not lend themselves to precise or totally noncontroversial interpretation.

What constitutes free speech, such as burning a flag as a form of symbolic speech, will always be open to interpretation and controversy.

Photo courtesy of David Furst/Getty Images.

To get around this difficulty of ambiguous language, strict constructionists usually seek to derive meanings with reference to the "original intent" of the framers. By determining what the words meant to those who chose them and then applying those meanings to the particular issues at hand, judges can avoid any accusation that their decisions impose their own values or policy preferences. Such interpreters of original intent claim to be merely applying the will of the framers, presumably codified democratically through the process that ratified the Constitution, rather than their own will. According to Edwin Meese III, attorney general under President Ronald Reagan, combining the constitutional text with attention to original intent provides a judicial standard that prevents the Court from imposing what it thinks is "sound public policy" rather than "deference to what the Constitution—its text and intention—demands."[50] If Meese's view is correct, judicial review in the strict constructionist/original intent mode cannot be undemocratic because it involves no subjective interpretation by judges but merely the objective application of constitutional principle.

There are two serious problems with the idea of original intent as a democratic standard of interpretation. First, determining original intent itself is a highly subjective process fraught with opportunities for judges to slip in their own policy preferences. Nowhere did the framers provide a clear commentary on what their intentions were in coming up with the language of the Constitution. The authors of the initial constitutional document conducted their work in Philadelphia in secret and without an official transcript. Several participants—most notably James Madison—published their own notes and recollections of the proceedings, often long after the events, but all of those offer incomplete and fragmentary records of the debates. Often the *Federalist Papers* are cited as evidence of the framers' intent, but the collected articles record only the opinions of their three authors (Madison, Alexander Hamilton, and John Jay) and, rather than dispassionate expositions of textual meaning, are polemical essays intended to influence votes in the New York Constitutional Convention.

In interpreting the documentary evidence that does exist, one needs to determine precisely who counts as a framer. Should one count only the delegates to the Philadelphia Convention? But what of the participants in the states' ratifying conventions who gave the Constitution its democratic sanction? Or the members of the various Congresses and state legislatures that wrote and ratified amendments? Compounding this problem is evidence of disagreement among the framers themselves—whether in Philadelphia, at the ratifying conventions, or in Congress or state legislatures—about the meaning of constitutional language. Former Justice William J. Brennan argues that much of the ambiguity that befuddles constitutional interpreters today is a logical product of these disagreements among the framers, who, Brennan writes, "hid their differences in cloaks of generality."[51] In sum, applying the original intent standard requires the same subjective judgment that its proponents decry in much judicial interpretation and that its application is supposed to eliminate.

Second, even if we could unambiguously identify original intent, one might question whether intentions held in the eighteenth and nineteenth centuries can be or should be applicable to contemporary policy issues. A sincere democrat would wonder, first of all, about the legitimacy of insisting that the democratic intentions of a previous generation prevail over those of the present generation. Judicial review adhering to a standard of original intent gives such precedence to ancestral preferences, yet many democratic theorists have questioned whether prior generations can legitimately bind subsequent ones. Thomas Jefferson, for one, wrote to his friend James Madison that "the earth belongs . . . to the living. . . . the dead have neither powers nor rights over it."[52] Indeed, by contemporary standards the majority intent expressed in the Constitution and many of its amendments would hardly seem democratic, given the exclusion of women, blacks, Native Americans, and even propertyless men from participation in the process of ratification.

Even if one accepted such intergenerational binding as a legitimate component of a constitutional democracy—the amendment process, after all, allows younger generations to alter the work of previous ones—serious questions remain about whether meanings once applied to constitutional concepts continue to be relevant and acceptable in the contemporary culture. For example, at the time the Eighth Amendment first prohibited "cruel and unusual punishments," public flogging and branding were common practice; it is doubtful that the amendment's authors intended it to prohibit such commonly accepted punishments. Nevertheless, were a community to reinstitute such practices in modern America, surely even the most committed partisan of original intent would consider such punishments to be "cruel and unusual."[53] Clearly, changes in society and cultural mores must influence how constitutional provisions are understood over time. In fact, many who praise the framers' work cite their foresight in writing a document composed of general principles that can be adapted to changing times. This adaptability has been key to making the US Constitution the longest-lived such document in the world. An absolute commitment to a standard of original intent in judicial review would be a perfect formula for undermining our Constitution's legitimacy and perhaps for bringing about its demise.

In practice the strict constructionists, or "originalists," have been as activist in formulating novel constitutional doctrines out of the text as the most ardent advocates of a loosely construed, living Constitution. The Court's conservative majority, most of whom claimed to adhere to the strict constructionist/originalist camp, proved quite adept at promoting conservative policy objectives through artful reinterpretation of constitutional principles. Their advocacy of "dual federalism," in *Morrison* and other decisions mentioned earlier, rested not on explication of specific constitutional language, but on creative interpretation of what the federal structure established in the Constitution means.[54] For example, in a series of cases seeking to limit Congress's ability to extend to employees of state governments the same labor law and antidiscrimination protections that are provided to private sector workers, the Court articulated a doctrine of state governments' "sovereign immunity" from lawsuits brought by their own citizens in either state or federal courts unless the state government gives its consent. This doctrine is derived by combining claims about the nature of sovereignty as articulated in English common law, including the notion of the "sovereign immunity of the King," with the conservative majority's understanding of the "structure and history" of federalism, rather than by citing any explicit constitutional language.[55] At the same time, in a manner reminiscent of the post-*Lochner* Courts of the first half of the twentieth century, then Chief Justice Rehnquist cited the commerce clause in striking down state government environmental protections and business regulations that were more stringent than those passed at the federal level. In the eyes of that Court, Congress's power to regulate commerce did not permit it to authorize women to sue their assailants or to prohibit guns near schools, but it was the perfect excuse to prevent the states from rigorously regulating business activities within their boundaries.[56] For these strict constructionists, apparently, the Constitution's language could easily be construed to limit the ability of both the federal and state governments to protect workers or to regulate business.

The claim that judicial review can be democratized through strict adherence to the Constitution's text, informed by the original intent of the framers, thus fails through a combination of the infeasibility of the theory itself and the actual practice of its proponents. What, then, of the opposing theory of drawing fundamental constitutional principles from the Constitution understood as a living document?

This less-restrictive approach has the advantage of recognizing the practical necessity of assigning contemporary meanings to constitutional language and concepts. Its starting point is rejecting the fiction that the text, combined with a search for original intent, can provide some objective, unambiguous guidance for Court decisions. Judicial review inevitably requires providing content to vague, open-ended constitutional provisions such as "due process," "freedom of speech," or "equal protection of the laws" in the context of the particular cases brought before the Court. According to this view, the Supreme Court should be guided by what it regards as "fundamental values," which may supersede any aims that Congress, the president, or state governments wish to pursue.[57] For example, a state legislature's desire to honor the American flag and prevent its desecration by banning flag burning must give way to the more fundamental value of protecting symbolic means of open political dissent. The First Amendment text alone—"no law . . . abridging the freedom of speech"—offers no clear guidance in this case. Is flag burning "speech"? No framer ever spoke to the issue because there was no official flag when the Bill of Rights was adopted. Free speech, in this case, is given meaning in terms of the judicially identified value to democracy of not preventing citizens from expressing their political views, particularly dissenting ones, even through incendiary means.

What is to be the source of the fundamental values that should guide judicial review? Different theorists in the living Constitution camp propose varied means of identifying such values.[58] Some look to historical analysis or social science to inform the search, while others rely on notions of natural law or the findings of moral philosophy. Many advocates of this approach even suggest that the judge's sense of what values are widely shared among the public should guide his or her decisions. Whatever the source, however, a reliance on fundamental values ultimately involves having judges apply their own value choices in making decisions.[59] This approach makes judges the guardians of American values and judicial review the means to monitor whether the rest of the political system adheres to those values.

The living Constitution approach thus rests on the appealing notion that wise judges are watching over the actions of government officials and reviewing laws to make sure they do not result in harm to society. This is an especially attractive idea when the harm happens to be something I want to prevent. To return to the flag-burning example, although I prefer to wave flags myself, I value open political dissent even when obnoxious means are used, and I think it is important to democracy. Therefore, I am happy that the Supreme Court strikes down flag-burning statutes. Nevertheless, we have to recognize that this approach to constitutional interpretation explicitly places in the hands of elite guardians the responsibility for determining which values will be implemented—that is, our governance in regard to these values. Many antidemocratic political philosophers, beginning with Plato, have advocated such an arrangement as the best form of governance, but democrats realize that to rely on elite guardians requires assuming that they will always be wise. Because history and experience have shown that assumption not to be true, democrats choose to rely on the wisdom of the people in the long run, rather than on any group of elite guardians, including unelected judges.[60] The premise of judicial review is that elite judges are better at determining what values are fundamental and at balancing conflicting values than are the elected officials they overrule. Even democrats may be tempted by such a notion when they agree with the judges, but the notion must be understood nevertheless as a profoundly undemocratic one.

Neither strict constructionist nor living Constitution approaches succeed in making judicial review democratic, and both permit striking down laws enacted by democratically elected legislatures. The first champions an infeasible standard of keeping true to the framers' intent—a standard that even its adherents cannot meet in practice. The second admits the inevitability of a judge's values being reflected in court decisions, but whatever the claimed source of the fundamental values informing those decisions, the outcome of judicial action remains elitist and undemocratic. Of the two approaches, the strict constructionist may be the more dangerous to democracy. The strict constructionist/originalist justices claim not to be imposing their own values in making decisions; they say they are only interpreting what the Constitution's words require. But as shown in the examples cited earlier, in practice their decisions mold those interpretations to be consistent with their ideological preferences. Adherence to the text and the search for the framers' intent become merely a smoke screen to obscure the undemocratic nature of judicial review. In comparison, the advocates of a living Constitution are more honest about the inevitability of judges' injecting their own values into their decisions, and the acknowledgment at least opens the way to an open discussion about the sources of those values.

The leading constitutional theories regarding the interpretive role of judges, then, fail to democratize the concept of judicial review. Does this mean that judicial review must remain at odds with democracy? Before reaching that conclusion, we need to consider another possibility that seeks to limit the scope of judicial review to make it consistent with democracy.

In his now-classic work *Democracy and Distrust,* constitutional theorist John Hart Ely seeks to tame judicial review by placing it at the service of democratic processes. While not contesting the undemocratic nature of judicial review, Ely identifies a role that unelected guardians might play in protecting democratic politics. Elaborating on a suggestion made by Justice Harlan Stone in a famous footnote to a 1938 court decision, *United States v. Carolene Products Co.,* Ely argues that judicial review should be limited to two functions: ensuring that the political process remains democratic and preventing a majority from discriminating against the democratic representation of a "discrete and insular minority."[61]

The first function would focus the Supreme Court on processes of elections, representation, and the arenas through which citizens debate and deliberate on public policy. The goal would be to ensure that the widest range of opinions and issues are represented in the political process. Ely's "representation-reinforcing" approach recognizes that a particular majority at a given point in time might try to freeze representative institutions to prevent new majorities from forming. In such cases, judicial review could be a tool to unblock the process to permit continual forming and re-forming of democratic majorities. A historical example might be the apportionment of state legislatures prior to the 1960s. At that time, many state legislatures failed to reapportion seats on a regular basis to reflect population changes. As a result, rural districts were vastly overrepresented in state legislatures in comparison to cities, but the rural majorities refused to authorize reapportionment, so as to remain in power. In the 1962 *Baker v. Carr* decision, the Supreme Court mandated regular legislative reapportionment on the basis of "one person, one vote." Judicial review in cases such as this, according to Ely, does not involve the judiciary's imposing its substantive values on a legislative majority, but instead mandates a process to allow truly democratic majorities to form.[62]

The second function that Ely, following Stone, assigns to judicial review is to facilitate the representation of minorities in the political process.[63] This role would include much of the Warren Court's efforts, beginning with *Brown v. Board*, to champion the civil rights and inclusion of blacks, other ethnic minorities, and women, who had been systematically discriminated against. An electoral majority may deny to minority groups the fundamental rights of participation, such as the right to vote, to express political opinions, to assemble, or to form political organizations. In such cases, officials elected by the discriminatory majority cannot be relied upon to open the political system to minorities. As happened in the United States in the 1960s, however, the Supreme Court can use judicial review to intervene to require the inclusion of minorities in the political process.

Ely's process-oriented theory narrows the scope of judicial review and, if properly implemented, serves to enhance the democratic system. It makes the Supreme Court a guardian of democratic processes without investing in it the power to overturn the substantive value choices made by elected officials. Under this theory, a Court would not impose its views on abortion, as it did in *Roe,* or its interpretation of Congress's power to regulate commerce, as it did in *Morrison.* It could, however, overturn attempts to limit fundamental rights of political participation for all or legislation targeted at discrete minorities. To the extent that this theory would allow judges to impose their values, they would necessarily be the "fundamental values" required of a democratic process.

Of course, the success of such a judicial review regime would rest on the restraint of judges, who must not sneak in substantive value choices in the name of protecting democratic processes. The history of judicial activism related earlier should alert us to the creative ways in which judges can apply constitutional theories to advance their own preferences. Even Ely's restricted role seems to leave to the Court the power to decide what particular actions threaten democratic processes and when judicial interventions are needed to protect them. What if a Supreme Court chose to overturn environmental regulations that protect the public's health on the grounds that they somehow undermined democratic processes? As long as the power to define what democracy requires rests with unelected judges, who could deny them? Constitutional theories of whatever stripe, including Ely's process-oriented one, cannot get around the fundamentally undemocratic character of judicial review.

The Judicialization of American Politics as a Challenge to Democracy

If, then, judicial review is inherently undemocratic and cannot be made democratic, the increasing judicial activism of the Supreme Court poses a serious challenge to American democracy. Over the past few decades, as Table 2.1 (on page 77) shows, the Court has been ever more active in using its power of judicial review to overturn acts of Congress and state and local legislation. Moreover, the Court now exercises its power in nearly every aspect of American life—no policy issue is beyond its purview. In just one year—the 2001–2002 term—the Supreme Court decided seventy-five cases setting policy on a wide variety of significant issues.[64] Among the many authoritative policy choices it made were allowing publicly funded vouchers to be used in private religious schools; permitting drug testing of students who wish to participate in extracurricular activities; requiring juries, not judges, to impose the death penalty; preventing state governments from being subject to complaints before federal regulatory agencies; limiting protections for the disabled guaranteed under the Americans with Disabilities Act; and allowing police to conduct random searches of bus passengers to look for drugs. The fact that unelected judges are making so many policy decisions based on the undemocratic doctrine of judicial review has to be problematic for democracy.

In addition to this undemocratic rule of judges, authoritative Supreme Court decisions tend to stifle ongoing democratic deliberation on important public issues. We saw such a distortion of democratic debate on the abortion issue with *Roe v. Wade.* By turning to the Court for the resolution of contentious issues, the conflicting parties in major policy disputes avoid deliberating with each other to find constructive compromises that might earn majority support. Because Court decisions tend to award total victory to one side or the other, they may impede the work of legislatures in seeking accommodation of contending values and interests for the long run. Democratic citizens need to deliberate with one another in their elective legislative arenas rather than take each other to court to resolve public problems. But as long as activist Courts are available to award decisive policy victories, citizens can avoid doing so.

Judicial power, like the separation of powers discussed in the previous chapter, can impede the responsiveness and accountability of democratically elected representatives to their constituents. On the one hand, as long as there is an expectation that contentious issues will be resolved in court, elected officials may avoid addressing them. Casting votes on such highly charged issues as abortion, school vouchers, or campaign finance reform is often difficult for representatives because any vote can cost them important electoral support. When Americans come to expect such issues to be resolved in the Supreme Court, however, legislators can escape the need to address them. On the other hand, once the Court removes from legislative control the resolution of significant public issues, as it did with abortion in 1973, candidates for office are free to take strong and decisive positions on issues as a way to attract votes, without any concern about actually doing anything about those issues once in office. Voters will find it difficult to assert democratic accountability over their elected representatives as long as those representatives are not fully responsible for acting on the issues of concern to them.

In the long run, judicial activism can undermine the democratic capacity of citizens themselves. Looking to wise judicial guardians to solve public problems relieves citizens, just as it does their representatives, from taking responsibility for confronting the issues. Over the past forty years, there has been a marked decline in citizen participation in politics—a challenge to democracy that is examined in detail in chapter 4. While many factors, as we shall see, are associated with this dwindling participation, increasing reliance on activist courts may be a contributing factor. The need to pay attention to electoral politics and vote becomes less urgent if the significant policy decisions are being made by unelected judges rather than by representatives who are accountable to voters. More than one hundred years ago, the legal scholar James Bradley Thayer feared that citizen apathy would be the most dangerous consequence of judicial activism. According to Thayer, even if judicial review is employed to overturn bad laws, it takes away from citizens the capacity to correct legislative errors themselves.

> Judicial review is always attended with a serious evil, namely, that the correction of legislative mistakes comes from the outside, and the people thus lose the political experience, and the moral education and stimulus that comes from fighting the question out in the ordinary way, and correcting their own errors. . . . The tendency of a common and easy resort to [judicial review], now lamentably too common, is to dwarf the political capacity of the people, and to deaden its sense of moral responsibility.[65]

Thayer's comments, expressed in an era when courts were much less active in American political life than they are today, raise a warning that is even more relevant to contemporary judicial activism than it was in his own time.

Political scientist Robert Kagan observes that the increasing judicial activism of recent decades has contributed to a profound change in how political activists seek to influence public policy. Rather than attempting to pursue their policy objectives through electoral politics or legislative lobbying, many individuals and groups have begun to employ a process Kagan calls "adversarial legalism" to achieve their objectives in court.[66] This process involves bringing suit in court to achieve a policy goal instead of seeking enactment of legislation. Whereas the more conventional legislative approach involves promoting the election of representatives who support a particular policy and building a majority coalition behind a policy in a legislature, adversarial legalism sidesteps the need for electoral and legislative coalition building. Instead, advocates find a basis for bringing a court action in a manner that will produce policy change. In this chapter, we have seen how judicial review of the constitutionality of a governmental action or statute, as in *Roe* or *Brown v. Board,* can formulate public policy. But, Kagan argues, this is but one form of policy making through adversarial legalism. Policy can also be changed through a lawsuit seeking a particular interpretation of a statute or forcing adherence to existing regulations. For example, Kagan details how for nearly two decades environmental activists delayed implementation of an economic development project to modernize the Port of Oakland, California, by means of lawsuits requiring satisfaction of federal environmental regulations.[67] These lawsuits had far-reaching impacts on both the economy and the environment of the entire San Francisco Bay area.

The resort to a resolution through the court system after the failure to enact legislation points to a possible explanation for the increasing judicialization of American politics. Contemporary American democracy is imperiled by the combination of challenges discussed in this book that stifle our ability to resolve public conflicts and address serious policy issues. The previous chapter demonstrates how the separation of powers works to discourage responsiveness and accountability. In subsequent chapters, we will see how other challenges similarly interfere with the smooth and effective functioning of our representative institutions. As these institutions have failed to resolve public issues in a democratic manner, distrust of American democracy has grown. Not surprisingly, policy advocates seeking progress on serious problems have sought to get around these blocked democratic processes through resort to our least democratic institution—the judiciary. Using the power of the judiciary becomes an attractive option when distrust of democratic processes grows and when those processes do not work well. The judicialization of our politics, however, does little to solve the defects in the processes; it serves instead to place democracy in further peril.

Meeting the Challenge: Revitalize American Democracy

One obvious measure to correct the judicialization of American democracy would be to abolish judicial review. Since it is doubtful that some future Court would overturn *Marbury v. Madison*, abolition would require amending the Constitution. Recently constitutional scholar Mark Tushnet has proposed an End Judicial Review Amendment (EJRA; see the full text below).[68] The EJRA would prevent the judiciary from overruling the will of democratically elected legislatures, but it would save that portion of constitutional enforcement appropriate to the courts. Courts would retain the power to find acts of individual officials in violation of constitutional principle. For example, if a police chief were to order his department to enforce speeding regulations only against black citizens, under Tushnet's amendment a court could still find such an act in violation of the Fourteenth Amendment's equal protection clause. Nor would the EJRA prevent courts from interpreting statutes in light of their understanding of constitutional principle, but such interpretations, unlike current judicial review of legislation, could be reversed by a legislature. The EJRA would leave intact the court's judiciary functions—adjudicating criminal and civil cases and interpreting statutes—and leave weighing the practical and moral considerations involved in policy making to elected officials. Moreover, with the EJRA, the elective institutions, including Congress, the presidency, and state legislatures, and the people themselves would have to take responsibility for enforcing the Constitution.[69] An amendment to end judicial review of legislation would be a way of returning ownership of the Constitution to the people.

Although Tushnet's call for an amendment banning it has appeal for democrats, many might worry that the amendment overlooks the power of judicial review, appropriately tamed, to be an important defender of democracy.[70] If restricted to protecting key democratic rights and processes—"representation-reinforcing," as John Hart Ely recommends—judicial review could be a bulwark to democracy rather than a challenge. Indeed, the democratic aspect of the history of judicial review—only touched on in our focus on its undemocratic practice—demonstrates that the Supreme Court can enhance our democracy. In decisions such as *Brown v. Board* (supporting full citizenship rights for black Americans), the Pentagon Papers case (protecting freedom of the press), and *Baker v. Carr* (advocating the principle of one person, one vote), as well as numerous decisions protecting free speech, the right to assemble, and so forth, the power of judicial review has been used as a democratic tool. An alternative, "representation-reinforcing" amendment (which also appears below) might preserve this democratic aspect of judicial review while restricting it from going too far in usurping the legislative function. And, like Tushnet's proposed amendment, such an alternative would make explicit in the constitutional text itself, rather than in Court precedent, the meaning and limits of judicial review.

Amending the Constitution to Define Judicial Review

Tushnet's End Judicial Review Amendment (EJRA)

"Except as authorized by Congress, no court of the United States or of any individual state shall have the power to review the constitutionality of statutes enacted by Congress or by state legislatures."

A Possible Representation-Reinforcing Amendment

"Judicial review of the constitutionality of statutes by any federal or state court may occur only when a statute prevents or impedes either the political representation of a discrete and insular minority or the democratic operation of governmental and political processes."

Nevertheless, the prospect of either abolishing or limiting judicial review by constitutional amendment at this stage in American history seems remote. Although it is a fundamentally undemocratic doctrine that has been established and sustained through judicial activism, after two centuries judicial review is a deeply ingrained tradition, enjoying widespread popular support. Even if restricting it might give the people more direct ownership of their Constitution—especially given the cumbersome process required for amending the Constitution—there is little chance that they would make the democratic choice to take possession. We must consider other ways of limiting the Court's use of judicial review to usurp legislative power.

How might judicial review be constrained to focus solely on democratic rights and processes without a constitutional amendment? Perhaps the best approach would be a renewed movement toward judicial restraint within our political and legal culture. More legal scholars need to speak out, as Ely did, in law schools and within the legal profession, for representation-reinforcing judicial review, and constitutional experts need to work out in detail how such an approach might work. A movement among lawyers, judges, and political scientists could influence Supreme Court appointments by persuading presidents to nominate and senators to confirm candidates sympathetic to the need for judicial restraint. Conservatives' recent success in placing many ideologically similar judges on the bench provides a model of how a self-conscious movement to mold the judiciary can work. Supreme Court justices themselves can play a role, as Associate Justice Stephen Breyer recently did in calling for more deference to democratically elected representatives.[71] A democratic campaign to urge the selection of judges committed to the use of judicial review only as a tool for protecting the democratic process not only might change judicial decisions, but also might create political support for a constitutional amendment to limit judicial review.

Process-oriented, representation-reinforcing judicial review might be the best form of judicial review for a democracy, but it still would not render the practice itself democratic. Leaving judges alone to defend democratic processes means relying on an undemocratic means to achieve a democratic end. By far the best cure for the undemocratic judicialization of American politics would be, as suggested earlier, an overall renewal of our democratic institutions. Because judicialization is itself a reflection of American democracy's current peril, successfully reversing the trend would require meeting the challenges described throughout this book. Americans will cease to turn to the undemocratic institution of the judiciary to resolve public issues when they are confident that our more representative and responsive institutions are addressing them effectively. A rejuvenated democracy would act to restrain judges from intervening in important disputes on which the people's elected representatives should be allowed to deliberate. No matter how personally distrustful they were of democracy, the Rehnquist majority would not so easily have ventured to decide the presidential election of 2000 if they had not sensed a similar unease in the news media and among the

American people. In sum, the best way of meeting the challenge presented in this chapter would be to respond decisively to those described elsewhere in this book.

Thought Questions

1. With its *Roe v. Wade* decision, the Supreme Court effectively short-circuited an ongoing democratic policy-making process in the states. Had that process been allowed to continue, state by state, what do you think would have happened? How would national policy on abortion have been similar or different?

2. Had the Supreme Court not intervened in the 2000 election in *Bush v. Gore,* the dispute over who won Florida's electoral votes might have continued for many weeks, eventually leaving Congress to sort out the issue. Do you think such a resolution would have been preferable to what occurred? Would it have been more democratic or less so?

3. How would the proponents of the various models of democracy described in the introduction regard judicial review? Which ones would agree that it is a fundamental challenge to democracy? Which ones might be more sympathetic to judicial review in a democracy? Why?

4. Some proponents of judicial review of the substantive merits of public policy argue that it is necessary to protect the country from elected representatives who might choose to enact very bad policies. If, as Ely suggests, the judiciary was confined to monitoring democratic processes and barred from reviewing the content of legislative enactments, there would be no means to prevent a majority constituted by democratic processes from passing even the most outrageously unjust and absurd laws—such as prohibiting houses from being painted in gaudy colors, or, as in one famous hypothetical, prohibiting doctors from removing gall bladders, except to save a patient's life. What do you think of this argument? Are there some things you fear a democratically constituted majority might do that would justify judicial review by elite judges? What would those things be? How might they be addressed without recourse to judicial review?

5. In the wake of the passage of the Affordable Care Act of 2010, several Republican state attorneys general sued in federal court arguing the legislation violated the commerce clause in its federal mandate that all Americans buy health insurance. How might this action be construed as another example of the judicialization of American politics?

Suggestions for Further Reading

*Barnett, Randy E. *Restoring the Lost Constitution: The Presumption of Liberty.* Princeton, NJ: Princeton University Press, 2004. An articulate and well-argued statement of the views of the "Constitution in Exile" movement.

*Breyer, Stephen. *Making Our Democracy Work: A Judge's View.* New York: Knopf, 2010. A Supreme Court justice offers a method for reconciling the living Constitution approach to judicial review with democracy.

Burns, James Macgregor. *Packing the Court: The Rise of Judicial Power and the Coming Crisis of the Supreme Court.* New York: Penguin, 2009. A detailed history of Supreme Court activism most of which, Burns argues, tilts in a conservative direction.

Ely, John Hart. *Democracy and Distrust: A Theory of Judicial Review.* Cambridge, MA: Harvard University Press, 1980. A classic critique of both interpretivism and noninterpretivism, offering Ely's now-famous representation-reinforcing theory of judicial review.

Gillman, Howard. *The Votes That Counted: How the Court Decided the 2000 Presidential Election.* Chicago: University of Chicago Press, 2001. A fair, balanced analysis of *Bush v. Gore* that concludes, in the end, that the justices were wrong to intervene in the election.

Noonan, John T. *Narrowing the Nation's Power: The Supreme Court Sides With the States.* Berkeley: University of California Press, 2002. A Reagan appointee to the federal appeals court mounts a witty and erudite attack on Rehnquist's doctrine of state sovereign immunity.

O'Brien, David M. *Constitutional Law and Politics.* 2 vols. New York: Norton, 2008. A thorough, basic constitutional law collection, including texts of the most important cases along with careful analysis. Keep it as a basic reference.

Rosen, Jeffrey. *The Most Democratic Branch: How the Courts Serve America.* New York: Oxford University Press, 2006. Although the title suggests otherwise, much of this book's argument supports the one in this chapter.

*Tribe, Laurence H., and Michael C. Dorf. *On Reading the Constitution.* Cambridge MA: Harvard University Press, 1991. A defense of judges' identifying "fundamental values" to justify activist decisions.

Tushnet, Mark. *Taking the Constitution Away From the Courts.* Princeton, NJ: Princeton University Press, 1999. An argument that "We the People" should seize the Constitution and make it a populist document.

*Wellington, Harry H. *Interpreting the Constitution: The Supreme Court and the Process of Adjudication.* New Haven, CT: Yale University Press, 1990. Argues that the Supreme Court has a justifiable role in actively determining the meaning of the Constitution on issues such as abortion.

*Wolfe, Christopher. *Judicial Activism: Bulwark of Freedom or Precarious Security?* Lanham, MD: Rowman & Littlefield, 1997. A critic of judicial activism from an originalist perspective offers, nevertheless, an even-handed, readable summary of the pros and cons.

*Presents a point of view that disagrees with the arguments presented in this chapter.

Selected Websites

www.fjc.gov. The Federal Judicial Center provides educational information and research on the federal courts.

www.law.cornell.edu/supct/index.html. Cornell University Legal Information Institute provides a wealth of searchable basic documents related to the Supreme Court, including a comprehensive archive of cases and biographies of the justices.

www.supremecourtus.gov/index.html. Official website of the US Supreme Court.

www.uscourts.gov. Official website of the Administrative Office of the United States Courts, offering information about the entire federal judiciary, including appeals, district, and specialized federal courts.

CHAPTER 3

The Third Challenge: Radical Individualism

I came here to say that I do not recognize anyone's right to one minute of my life. Nor to any part of my energy. Nor to any achievement of mine. . . . I came here to say that I am a man who does not exist for others.
—Ayn Rand, *THE FOUNTAINHEAD*

Each man is forever thrown back on himself alone, and there is danger that he may be shut up in the solitude of his own heart.
—Alexis de Tocqueville

Americans celebrate individual autonomy. This celebration can be found throughout American popular culture, as in the quotation from novelist-philosopher Ayn Rand's *The Fountainhead*. Rand gives these words to the novel's hero, Howard Roark, an architect who succeeds because of his individual brilliance, talents, and efforts despite social pressures to conform to the mediocrity of the broader society. In the novel, the autonomous individual is portrayed as the source (fountainhead) of all that is creative, good, and worthwhile in life; the community, in all its manifestations—government, public opinion, family, social mores—is only an impediment to be overcome. Ironically, for all her celebration of individual uniqueness and creativity, Rand repeats the commonest theme in American mass culture: the virtuous, autonomous individual triumphing in the face of social pressures.

This celebration of the individual hero is a standard formula in such popular genres as the western film and the detective story. Lone cowboy heroes, such as Shane or Rooster Cogburn or the Lone Ranger, come to the rescue of communities

---

Opposite: *Individual autonomy with our electronic devices may be harmless, but carried too far in all realms of life may lead to the radical individualism Tocqueville warned against.*

Photo courtesy of Darrin Klimek/Getty Images.

Individualism is the basis of american politics but has darkside of isolation

of hapless citizens unable to save themselves from evil criminals. Superheroes, whether Spiderman or Superman or Wonder Woman, are on their own in saving the world from dastardly villains. Even when the hero has the help of a cadre of loyal friends, as in the sci-fi western *Star Wars,* the climax depends on the ability of Luke Skywalker, alone, to place his bomb precisely to blow up the imperial Death Star. Success and the triumph of good over evil are products of individual effort. The role of social factors in contributing to individual success—who, for instance, built Luke's star fighter?—remains in the background.

America's celebration of the individual in novels, movies, and television often carries over into our perception of the real world. Economics and politics are usually portrayed in highly individualistic terms. The individual business entrepreneur is celebrated as the source of our prosperity, and the individual political hero—a Franklin Delano Roosevelt or a Martin Luther King Jr.—is the author of political progress. From such portrayals, it would be impossible to know that most businesspeople work in large, hierarchical organizations, or that such historic political achievements as the New Deal and the civil rights movement were products of the efforts of millions of people.

The focus on the individual carries over into how Americans see themselves. Countless studies of American attitudes find that ordinary people are likely to see their personal successes and failures in highly individual terms. Getting into a good college or landing a good job is perceived as the reward for hard work and individual talent. Americans tend not to think about how social institutions and forces, such as a good school system or a growing economy that creates good jobs, make their achievements possible. Failure is also usually attributed to individual factors. During the 1930s, for example, in the throes of the social disaster of the Great Depression, unemployed American workers were likely to blame themselves for their unemployment.[1] Like Howard Roark, most Americans see themselves as sole authors of both their achievements and their failures.

Individualism is certainly an attractive and even democratic aspect of American society. The chance for individual freedom and autonomy has been a major factor in attracting immigrants to American shores. The United States is perceived throughout the world as a place where, to quote a former US Army recruiting slogan, you can "Be all that you can be," free from the constraints of traditional social institutions that elsewhere trap people in particular social roles.[2] Compared to many other countries, the United States is very egalitarian in the opportunities it offers ambitious individuals to use their own initiative, talent, and energies to get ahead. Just as they were one hundred years ago, American cities today are full of individual immigrant entrepreneurs running grocery stores, small restaurants, corner bars, and laundries. The United States continues to attract people from all over the world who are eager to be free to make something of themselves.

Yet for all its positive aspects, American individualism, as the Tocqueville quotation at the beginning of this chapter suggests, has a dark side. Along with freeing people from social constraints, individualism tends to isolate people from one another. To return to western films, the cowboy hero is also a loner. Clint Eastwood's character, "the man with no name," provides the definitive portrayal of this aspect of the cowboy hero as someone so detached from society that no one knows his name. What happens to society when individualism becomes so extreme that people do not need names for each other? Can nameless people "shut up in the solitude of their own hearts" form a democratic society?

Recognition of the dark side of individualism raises the question of whether American celebration of the autonomous individual has been carried to such an extreme that the United States has become a society of isolated individuals. Before analyzing the implications of individualism for American democracy, however, it is useful to identify the sources of this attitude in the American creed and American history.

Individualism in the American Tradition

American national identity, unlike that of most other nations, is based on a set of political ideas: the American creed.[3] People in most other nations understand their national attachment in terms of a common historical experience, usually common ethnicity, and often common religious belief. As a nation of immigrants, the United States contains a diversity of people with different histories, ethnic backgrounds, and religions. What has held the nation together is a widely held commitment to the ideals symbolized in the founding events of the nation—the American Revolution and constitutional ratification—and the principles found in the documents connected to those events. Unlike France, for example, where citizens have more often been divided than united by the political ideals of the French Revolution, in the United States acceptance of the ideals of the American founding is usually thought of as a prerequisite for considering oneself an American, as in the requirement that new citizens learn about the creed and swear allegiance to it before they can be naturalized. Because of the ideological character of our national identity, political crusades, such as McCarthyism in the 1950s, often apply the label "un-American" in accusing citizens of disloyalty to American ideals. Accusing a German or French person of being "un-French" or "un-German" because of their political beliefs would be absurd.

What are these ideals—the American creed—that define American identity? For the most part, they are the ideals of classical liberalism as described in the introduction to this book: limited government, the rule of law, liberty, political equality, and individualism. The political ideas of seventeenth- and eighteenth-century liberal political theorists were given, of course, a particular American cast by the founding events of the American Republic. The Revolution, in particular, employed the ideals of liberalism to achieve democratic ends.[4] Whereas John Locke may have understood liberal ideals to be relevant to the political goals of

English gentleman property holders, the American revolutionaries applied them—especially political liberty, equality, and individualism—to all citizens, as is evident in their Declaration of Independence. The American Revolution produced a democratized version of classical liberalism that became the American creed.

Among the creed's various components, individualism has been a powerful and distinctive influence on how Americans understand themselves and how they understand politics. Alexis de Tocqueville perceived this on his visit to the United States in the 1830s. In fact, he coined the term *individualism* to describe the attitude he found among Americans. This is how he defined it:

> Individualism is a calm and considered feeling that disposes each citizen to isolate himself from the mass of his fellows and withdraw into the circle of family and friends; with this little society formed to his taste, he gladly leaves the greater society to look after itself. . . . Such folk owe no man anything and hardly expect anything from anybody. They form the habit of thinking of themselves in isolation and imagine that their whole destiny is in their hands.[5]

Although Tocqueville had grave concerns about the long-term effect of individualism, Americans embraced individualism with enthusiasm. A society in which individuals are in charge of their own lives, free from social constraint, became our central ideal.

American individualism derives from the classical liberal idea that the individual is at the center of political society. As we saw in the introduction, liberals believe that political society exists to facilitate the individual's ability to pursue individual goals as he or she defines them. The preoccupation of the founders, as revealed in the Constitution and *The Federalist Papers,* with government's role in protecting individual liberty and their concern that government be structured so as not to interfere with it nurtured individualism. From the founding of the Republic, Americans had political institutions that both protected and promoted their ability to pursue individual goals and aspirations. Individualism received further reinforcement as a capitalist market economy, also based on liberal premises, developed in the nineteenth century. Success in the marketplace required thinking primarily of how to achieve individual material goals. Both political and economic institutions in the United States provided a context to support the attitude of Americans that "their whole destiny is in their hands."

Americans have found much to value in individualism, especially the social mobility that is seen to follow from it. In coming to the United States, immigrants have sought to escape rigid social, class, and caste barriers that restrict choice of vocation and social status based on birth. In contrast to "the old country," the United States has been seen as a place where one makes it on one's own based on individual qualities. Such an attitude is found in the comment of a nineteenth-century celebrant of the concept of the American "self-made man," who described the United States as a place where people

> can attain to the most elevated position or acquire a large amount of wealth, according to the pursuits they elect for themselves. No exclusive privileges of earth, no entailment of estates, no civil or political disqualifications, stand in their path; but one has as good a chance as another according to his talents, prudence, and personal exertions.[6]

Americans have always associated individualism with the chance to get ahead based on one's own efforts, free of cultural, social, and political constraints.[7]

Americans also associate individualism with freedom to express their individuality. They value the chance to define for themselves their own ideas of what is good for them. This freedom is claimed for nearly all aspects of life: Americans expect to say, believe, live, eat, and wear whatever they like based on individual choice. Attempts to regulate individual behavior on behalf of the broader good—such as requiring the wearing of seat belts or motorcycle helmets—always meet opposition. As long as they regard such behavior as harmless to others, Americans are quick to demand the right to do whatever they want. Many Americans would easily agree with one of the respondents to a recent survey of American young people who, when asked what was special about the United States, replied, "Individualism, and the fact that it is a democracy and you can do whatever you please."[8]

Although that respondent's claim of autonomy is extreme, it does reflect, as do all American claims of individual freedom and autonomy, a very democratic sentiment: the dignity of each individual and his or her choices about how to conduct his or her life. Such an outlook demands respect for individuals as worthy human beings no matter whether they conform to dominant social mores. Americans from Ralph Waldo Emerson to the hippies of the 1960s to the computer hackers of the 1990s have claimed a right to "do their own thing" as part of their individualistic heritage. Recognizing the right of individuals to choose how they conduct their lives means tolerance for a variety of lifestyles and cultural differences. In this sense, individualism stimulates openness, initiative, and creativity—all positive values that are supportive of a democratic society. Because so many Americans value their individual freedom from social and political constraints, those suffering from overt oppression can appeal to these individualistic values when demanding relief, as blacks and other minorities, homosexuals, and women have done. Americans readily recognize the role individualism can play in reinforcing and expanding democracy.

Unlike most modern Americans, who are likely to perceive individualism as supportive of democracy, Tocqueville, while appreciating its value, was concerned that taken too far, individualism could undermine democracy. He believed that it could easily degenerate into a radical form of individualism that he called "egoism"—a condition that leads a person "to think of all things in terms of himself and to prefer himself to all."[9] A society of egoists (or what I call "radical individualists"), Tocqueville feared, would be vulnerable to despotism. Although individualism helped to free people from external social and political constraints, it also tended to isolate them from one another and thus prevent them from perceiving their common interests. Isolated individuals with no concern for public affairs lose sight of common interests and fail to participate in public life. According to Tocqueville, radical individualism would erode the public-spirited mentality—what some might call "civic virtue"—necessary for the support of a free society. Radical individualists would lose the capacity to notice when a despotic power took control of the state. Without concern for one another's freedom, individuals would be unable to act together to protect anyone's freedom. Tocqueville paints a dark picture of "men, alike and equal, constantly circling around in pursuit of the petty and banal pleasures with which they glut their souls. Each one of them, withdrawn into himself, is almost unaware of the fate of the rest."[10] In this condition, individual citizens succumb one by one to the power of a despotic state. Unable to act together to resist such power, isolated individuals would inevitably lose their freedom to it.

In spite of his fear of the effects of individualism, Tocqueville was somewhat optimistic about the future of democratic government in the United States. The American individualists he met in the 1830s had not yet succumbed to *radical* individualism. The reason for his optimism was another phenomenon he discovered on his travels: the lively civic participation of Americans in both their local governments and nongovernmental associations. He was impressed by the seriousness with which Americans involved themselves in local government, as in the town meetings in New England. Through involvement in public decision making on mundane matters such as repair of local roads, citizens came to understand the relation between their individual well-being and that of the larger community.[11] This understanding was nurtured, as well, in the multitude of civic, religious, and business groups that Tocqueville observed running schools, building churches, organizing festivals, and providing charity. Both local government and nongovernmental associations reminded individualistic Americans of their connection to their fellow citizens. The civic involvement of Americans developed in them the proper "habits of the heart" required for the success of a democracy. By this phrase, Tocqueville meant the unconscious feelings and attitudes or, as he put it, "the whole moral and intellectual state of a people" that guides their behavior.[12] For an individualistic society such as the United States, it was important that these feelings and attitudes include a sense of civic obligation and interconnectedness, or the society would easily slip into egoism. Tocqueville believed that the American society he observed in the 1830s sustained the proper balance by involving individual citizens actively in public affairs. Even though excessive individualism might become a danger to American democracy, Tocqueville concluded that Americans possessed the proper antidote: civic-minded "habits of the heart."

Is what Tocqueville observed in the 1830s still true of the United States today? Do Americans still possess "habits of the heart" conducive to a civic-minded outlook? I believe that we have reason to worry about the balance between individualism and civic virtue in the United States today. American "habits of the heart" have evolved in the direction of less understanding of the social ties that bind us together in a common democratic society and a more selfish preoccupation with our individual selves. Individualism seems to have become excessive—to the point that Tocqueville, visiting the United States today, would probably have grave concern that our healthy democratic individualism was degenerating into the radical form that he called "egoism."

American "Habits of the Heart"

A number of recent sociological studies have documented the growing radical individualism of contemporary Americans. One of the most influential, published in 1985, was *Habits of the Heart,* by a distinguished sociologist, Robert Bellah, and several of his colleagues.[13] Taking their cue from Tocqueville, these investigators interviewed several hundred middle-class Americans about their beliefs and aspirations regarding family, community life, politics, morality, and religion. What they found were people who defined every aspect of their existence in highly individualistic terms. At the same time, they seemed to have lost those habits of the heart conducive to understanding the meaning of community and the interconnectedness of social existence. Bellah and his colleagues found people who defined "personality, achievement, and the purpose of human life in ways that leave the individual suspended in glorious, but terrifying, isolation."[14]

Habits of the Heart begins with a profile of one of the study's interview subjects, under the pseudonym "Brian Palmer," who exemplifies the isolation that they found characteristic of many middle-class Americans. Brian is a successful businessman in his forties who has recently altered his lifestyle dramatically from one dominated by career and moneymaking to a more family-centered existence. A divorce and second marriage precipitated this change, and it came about as a result of much soul-searching on Brian's part about what gave him the most joy and satisfaction: business success or family relationships. What the authors find disturbing about the change in Brian's life is the totally individualistic terms in which he justifies it. His lifestyle change was prompted by "idiosyncratic preference rather than representing a larger sense of the purpose of life."[15] Having devoted his earlier life to career success, he shifted his priorities based simply on what he now sees as giving him more personal satisfaction—wife and family—without any reference to "any wider framework of purpose or belief." For Brian, one's life goals are simply a matter of individual choice at a given moment and are ·

not related to any value system outside oneself or connected with any community norms.

Brian believes that how he lives his life is not connected in any way to the broader community, and this is how he thinks it should be. This outlook is revealed in one comment he makes about the virtues of living in California:

> One of the things that makes California such a pleasant place to live, is people by and large aren't bothered by other people's value systems as long as they don't infringe on your own. By and large, the rule of thumb out here is that if you've got the money, honey, you can do your thing as long as your thing doesn't destroy someone else's property, or interrupt their sleep, or bother their privacy, then that's fine. . . . just do your thing. That works out kind of neat.[16]

Brian's only understanding of his connection to others in his community, their only mutual interest, is that they leave one another alone to pursue their individually determined lifestyles. That he and his neighbors might have a common interest in one another's well-being—that their individual lives may, in some sense, depend on one another—seems to be a concept alien to his understanding of society. Brian appears to be "shut up in the isolation of his own heart"—a situation that is typical, according to Bellah and his associates, of many Americans.

According to these sociologists, this sense of individual isolation carries over into how Americans see their role as democratic citizens. First, they define their own success in terms of their individual efforts through competition in the marketplace—independent of politics and government or cooperation with their fellow citizens.[17] Their personal well-being is not connected to their role as citizens. Second, they tend to think of their civic involvements in altruistic terms—a matter of voluntary service to others and the community. Such involvements are most likely to be with local community organizations, such as a Rotary Club or a local YMCA, rather than a political office, an election campaign, or a political party. Civic involvement is a matter of "getting involved" with like-minded people to do good for the community, independent of one's own interests or personal well-being.

The people interviewed for *Habits of the Heart* tended to divide their conception of the larger political world between the ideal and the real.[18] They would like politics to be similar to what they experience in their civic involvements, a matter of face-to-face interaction based on a spontaneous consensus about what is good for the community. This ideal conception, which Bellah's respondents do not even label "politics," is not, however, their understanding of day-to-day politics as it is associated with national or local government. They believe that a politics of consensus is impossible in a diverse society containing different interests. They therefore conceive of the real world of politics as the "pursuit of differing interests according to agreed on, neutral rules."[19] This real world of politics is seen as a "necessary evil" and an arena dominated by political professionals. It is a world they regard with distaste, a world that individuals enter into only to pursue selfish individual or group interests. Unlike the free economic market—also a world dedicated to pursuit of selfish individual interests—the pursuit of interests through politics is seen as somewhat illegitimate because outcomes are based on "unfair" mobilization of political power. This dynamic is viewed as different from that of free markets, whose outcomes are perceived as a reflection of individual talent and initiative. Because politics, in contrast, is an arena "rewarding all kinds of inside connections, and favoring the strong at the expense of the weak, the routine activities of interest politics thus appear as an affront to true individualism [which rewards individuals for their own effort] and fairness alike."[20]

Because of their radical-individualistic orientations, Americans, according to Bellah, are trapped between two unpalatable conceptions of politics: an ideal one, in which consensus occurs spontaneously between like-minded individuals, such as for the annual community fund drive; and a "realistic" one, where conflicting parties battle to achieve their selfish interests in public policy. Neither conception allows for the formulation of a common *public* good arrived at through democratic discussion among public-spirited citizens with varying interests. Neither calls attention to how the differing interests and problems of individuals may result from common interdependencies and institutional structures. In Tocqueville's terms, Americans have lost the "habits of the heart" that allow them to see how their differing interests are interrelated or how achieving a good for someone else may be connected to one's own good.

Another sociologist, Herbert Gans, has identified similar problems with American individualism through careful analysis of public opinion data. Like Bellah, Gans finds that "popular individualism" characterizes the way middle-class Americans think about themselves and the world they live in.[21] Although less critical of individualism than Bellah, Gans sees similar orientations to politics and citizenship. Most middle-class Americans, he says, are wrapped up in their *micro-social* relations, their relationships with family and like-minded friends. They avoid and ignore *macrosocial* relations—that is, their ties to such formal organizations as Big Government and Big Business, even though these institutions have a great influence over their microsocial relations. People feel in control of their microsocial lives even as they fail to perceive how they are buffeted by events in the macrosocial world. Because they see the macrosociety as not especially relevant to their microsocieties, they tend not to participate in the larger society beyond observing it from afar through the news media (and even this practice is declining) and voting.[22] Gans's description of middle-class Americans preoccupied with microsocial relations calls to mind Tocqueville's description of the individual disposed "to isolate himself from the mass of his fellows and withdraw into the circle of family and friends."

Although Tocqueville's observation suggests that the predominance of microsocial life is deeply rooted in American history and culture, Gans describes several social changes since World War II that have exacerbated popular individualism and severed people's relation to macrosociety, including loosening religious ties, decline of political parties and labor unions, and most important, suburbanization. The postwar explosion of the suburbs followed from the rapid rise in economic prosperity and security that occurred during the period. With increasing economic security, middle-class Americans literally moved away from the communities, urban and rural, in which they had grown up, to settle in brand-new suburbs without the common history that characterized the old communities. As Gans puts it, "In the communities or subdivisions into which they moved, they learned to make friends with strangers on the basis of shared interests rather than shared upbringing or history."[23] Suburban residents shared not only interests but also similar income levels and social status. These new communities were very different from those they came from, where, sharing a common history and perhaps an ethnic identity, they had interacted on a regular basis with people of varying social status.

Isolated in their lifestyle enclaves, like this exclusive New Jersey housing development, Americans lose touch with the concerns of their fellow citizens.

Photo courtesy of David Zimmerman/Getty Images.

As communities of choice, not common history, the suburbs were perfect settings for radical individualistic society. They allowed individuals to live among those people they wanted to associate with—usually people like themselves. They also allowed individuals to choose among different kinds of communities based on individual preference for different styles of living. The result is the "lifestyle enclave"—communities made up of individuals who come together because of a choice of a particular lifestyle.[24] Some of the earliest were retirement communities, which sprang up in Florida and the southwestern states to attract elderly retirees. These communities often exclude residents below a certain age and provide special recreational facilities, such as golf courses and shuffleboard courts, and social activities of interest to older people. By the 1970s, lifestyle enclaves for different kinds of people—condo developments for singles, housing developments of fundamentalist Christians, the Castro district for homosexuals in San Francisco—were springing up throughout the country.

By far the most common lifestyle enclave is the exclusive, upper-middle-class, planned community, usually built around a golf course and protected from outsiders by private security guards. Often, to live in these communities residents must join a homeowners' association that tightly regulates the kinds of homes and the kinds of people (not poor) who can live there. For example, in the 1980s, one such association in an exclusive community in Southern California opposed construction of forty-eight housing units *for senior citizens* on the grounds that they would "attract gangs and dope."[25] Besides such controls over who can live in these communities, the brick walls, security gates, and maze-like street patterns keep outsiders out. In Simi Valley, north of Los Angeles, the entire valley system of exclusive developments can be sealed off from the rest of the world by blocking four freeway exits. As one proud resident bragged, "You'd be stupid to commit a big crime here, because you can't get out. The police can seal this place off in 15 minutes."[26] Choosing to live in a lifestyle enclave allows residents to escape from undesirable people and "solve" the problems of the larger society, such as crime and poverty, by walling themselves off from them.

There is no doubt that residents of places such as Simi Valley are proud of their communities and find their lives there comfortable. Their satisfaction is reflected in such comments as, "We like living in a place with educated people, people who live as we do," and "The people who live here share my values. . . . It's a good socioeconomic climate—conservative, but not stuffy. It's one of the few communities left where you can go shopping and not get hit up by people wanting money."[27] In fact, such residents display more willingness to support their communities—by raising taxes to improve local public schools or special homeowners' assessments to pay for security guards—than we normally associate with individualistic Americans. The reason may be found in the attitudes toward politics that Bellah and his associates discovered: In homogeneous lifestyle enclaves, individualistic residents can practice their ideal brand of consensus politics among like-minded individuals. Because interests, incomes, and values are so similar, there is minimal conflict and no need to work to accommodate differences. But Tocqueville would be alarmed to note that this environment is not conducive to developing democratic "habits of the heart." Learning such habits requires communicating with different sorts of people, seeing different points of view, having the capacity to empathize with someone else's problems. Walling themselves off in lifestyle enclaves may allow people to satisfy their individual aspirations, but it also promotes a radical-individualistic outlook that undermines their capacity to understand, participate in, or even care about the larger macrosociety. Can such people be good democratic citizens?

The Flaws of Libertarianism

At this point, many readers (especially if they are individualistic Americans) may not be concerned about the upsurge of radical individualism among Americans. Many will question whether radical individualism (with Tocqueville's and my fretting notwithstanding) is a problem for a democracy. After all, isn't democracy about people being able to live their lives as they see fit? You may, as Ayn Rand's Howard Roark would, consider the liberty that Brian Palmer and the residents of Simi Valley have to be the "authors" of their own lives as evidence of the success of American democracy, not a threat to it. Why should democratic citizens have to be concerned about an abstraction such as the "public good" if they choose not to be? If some people freely choose to do good works for the less fortunate or concern themselves with macrosocial issues, fine; but why must everyone be so concerned? As long as people obey the law and do not interfere with the rights of others, what difference does it make whether or not they possess public-spirited "habits of the heart"? Shouldn't a real democracy be mainly about preventing community institutions, especially government, from interfering with what individuals choose to think, say, and do?

These rhetorical questions reflect a political ideology known as *libertarianism.* A political ideology is a somewhat systematic set of prescriptions about how government and political life should be organized. While radical individualism reflects a diffuse set of cultural values that orient people toward the whole range of their experience, libertarianism provides a more specific road map for organizing a society to reflect and promote radical individualism. Libertarians believe that people are, and should be, radical individualists—that is, individuals existing independent of and free from obligations to the rest of society. A good government is one that facilitates the ability of individuals to make their individual choices about how they live their lives. Libertarians favor a minimal government whose principal role is protecting individual rights and which itself must not interfere with those rights. In the economic sphere, this model implies a free-market economy with little or no government regulation. In the social sphere, it means that individuals are free to do whatever they want, from taking drugs to playing the violin, without governmental interference, as long as their behavior does not harm or violate the rights of others. According to the libertarians, the obligation of citizens to participate in or support the broader community or public good is minimal. In fact, many libertarians would question the concept of the public good beyond the aggregation of each individual good. As long as individual liberty and autonomy are preserved, the public good is achieved.[28]

Libertarianism, obviously, should strike a chord among individualistic Americans. Some readers may find in the previous paragraph a precise summary of their own personal ideology. In fact, one can find libertarians across the political spectrum in the United States, among people who call themselves liberals and those who say they are conservative, among Democrats and Republicans. Libertarians who call themselves liberals usually are mainly concerned with protecting social and political rights, such as free speech and privacy, and they probably belong to the American Civil Liberties Union (ACLU). Conservative libertarians are more likely to focus on economic rights and to promote free-market economics, and they probably endorsed Ronald Reagan's supply-side economics in the 1980s, George W. Bush's deep tax cuts in 2001, and the budget plan of Congressman Paul Ryan in 2011.[29] The conservative strain of libertarianism has made significant inroads among Republicans represented in the prominence of libertarian-leaning congresspersons like Ryan but also Republican presidential candidate Ron Paul and his son, Kentucky Senator Rand Paul. What libertarians on both the right and left have in common is concern for limiting governmental interference with individual behavior.

The Libertarian Party offers a pristine form of libertarianism that encompasses both economic and social liberties.[30] The Libertarian Party advocates dismantling nearly all government programs; the decriminalization of all drugs, prostitution, and pornography; the elimination of nearly all business regulation; and reducing the size of the military.[31] Although few libertarians belong to, or subscribe to all the tenets of, the Libertarian Party, they take seriously the central premise of libertarianism: A truly democratic society is precisely one in which individuals have maximum freedom to pursue their own goals independent of others in society.

In this section, I argue that this libertarian view of society is flawed. It fails to take into account the many ways in which individuals are inevitably connected to and dependent on one another and on society as a whole. A society in which people concern themselves only with pursuing their individual goals and do not take responsibility for the whole community could not survive. Because we live in society, we cannot avoid being concerned with others and with the good of the collectivity.

To demonstrate the limits of the libertarian vision of society, we can evaluate it in terms of its own goal: the achievement of individual interests and aspirations. Social scientists have devised a number of logical "thought experiments" to show that, in certain situations, totally self-interested individuals cannot achieve even their individual interests without the cooperation of others. One of the simplest and most famous of these is the *prisoner's dilemma.*

Imagine two self-interested partners in crime picked up by the police on suspicion of a rash of burglaries. The police will have the strongest evidence to convict the prisoners if they can convince one of them to inform on his accomplice. Just as in good cop shows on television, the prisoners are separated from one another at the police station and are not allowed to communicate. Each is separately offered the same deal: "Snitch on your friend and admit your crimes, and you'll go free. If you don't talk and your friend does, you'll draw the maximum sentence." Figure 3.1 shows the dilemma each burglar is in.

As radical individualists, each of the two prisoners naturally calculates what is best for "No. 1." Each realizes that his fate is tied to the other's action, but he must decide what is best for himself without communicating with the other. Each worries that the other will snitch and that the price for not doing so is "hard time" (cells B and C). Prisoner A, attempting to maximize his own self-interest, snitches while hoping that B keeps quiet. The same logic, however, leads Prisoner B to do the same, so they both receive long sentences (cell D). Had they been able to cooperate and so avoid confessing, there would have been only evidence enough to put them away for a short time (cell A). The prisoner's dilemma illustrates how individuals' acts of self-interest can be defeating for all involved.

The value of the prisoner's dilemma is that it illustrates the flaw in the intuitive sense of individualistic Americans that the best strategy for success is to "look out for No. 1." Often in the real world we find ourselves in situations like that of the imaginary prisoners: If we look out only for ourselves and ignore the well-being of those around us, we will end up falling short of what we could achieve through cooperation. For example, the political scientist Paul Brace argues that the prisoner's dilemma applies to the strategies that individual American states need to adopt to promote economic development.[32]

In recent years, many state governments have behaved like our burglars. They have competed vigorously to attract businesses to their states by offering big tax breaks and subsidies. Businesses, as one might expect, have taken advantage of this situation by inducing neighboring state governments to engage in "bidding wars" in the offering of such incentives. In some instances, the result has been a state's winning the bidding war to the detriment of its economic development; that is, the incentives it had to offer to attract the businesses exceed the economic benefits the businesses actually bring to the state. At the same time, by lowering tax rates to attract business, the states lose out on revenues to invest in public services, especially education, which support economic development. In the long run,

Burglar A's Options

	Keep Quiet	Snitch
Keep Quiet	Cell A Both A and B get one year	Cell B A goes free while B gets 20 years
Snitch	Cell C B goes free while A gets 20 years	Cell D Both get 10 years

Burglar B's Options

FIGURE 3.1 The Prisoner's Dilemma

public investment in economic growth declines everywhere, eventually hurting even those that competition between states is supposed to benefit: business firms and those they employ. Most economic development specialists today argue that cooperation among states to promote economic development is a better long-run strategy for all states. Through cooperation they can devise policies that place them in cell A in the prisoner's dilemma.

The prisoner's dilemma shows that failure to cooperate with others in pursuit of one's individual self-interest may result in "suboptimization"—failure to achieve as much as could have been achieved through cooperation. Another common thought experiment—the tragedy of the commons—suggests that failure to cooperate may result in more than suboptimization; it can lead to disaster.

Imagine a common grazing land that is home to several families of ranchers. Each family maintains a separate herd of cattle but relies on turning them out into the common pasture to fatten them for market. (Incidentally, reliance on common grazing land remains a major form of ranching in much of the American West today.)[33] Being rugged individualists, each family of ranchers relies on itself to make its living and is not in the habit of communicating with its neighbors, who are also its competitors, about individual business decisions. Being good libertarians, all the ranchers regard any attempt to regulate any aspect of how they run their ranches as a violation of their individual property rights.

One day, while rounding up calves for branding, Rancher Jill notices quite a few bare patches in the pasture and sees that the family's cattle are thinner than last year. She realizes that the common pasture is being overgrazed; there are too many cattle on the land. When she gets back to the ranch house, she calls a family council to decide what to do. What will the family decide? If it acts rationally and in its own self-interest, the family will decide to buy more cattle to compensate for the thinner herd—but this will add even more cattle to the grazing land. When the other families discover the problem, they will do the same. Very quickly, the grazing land will be destroyed, and all the families will be out of the ranching business. This scenario—in which individual rational choices lead to collective failure—is known as the *tragedy of the commons.*

The tragedy of the commons follows inevitably from the logic of the situation. Even though the best solution, obviously, would be to limit the number of cattle allowed on the land to its grazing capacity, such a solution would require some sort of cooperation among the ranchers. They would have to agree collectively to limit the size of their herds and develop some institutional mechanism to enforce the agreement. Because our libertarian ranchers oppose all collective regulation, however, each family can respond to the situation only by changing its individual behavior. In the case of reliance on the common grazing land—an example of what economists call a "common pool resource"—this logic will always lead to abuse and to the eventual depletion of the resource. If any of the ranch families decided individually to limit its herd, it would see its competitors take advantage of that decision by adding to their herds. The only solution is to grab for oneself as much use of the common pool resource as possible before it is all gone.[34]

The tragedy of the commons shows that with common pool resources, the ability of individuals to pursue their individual self-interest independent of and oblivious to one another has to be regulated. If it is not, the individual well-being of all will suffer. This insight is applicable to a whole range of human experience and practical policy problems. Environmentalists are especially sensitive to the tragedy of the commons because the environment is our largest and most obvious common pool resource. Consider clean air. Factories that emit pollutants into the air cannot be expected to limit this discharge voluntarily on their own initiative because cleaning emissions increases production costs and places a factory that does so at a competitive disadvantage with those that do not. The ability to manufacture products while polluting the air, instead of cleaning up emissions, is a common pool resource that smart factory managers will use to their advantage if left free to do so; factories that lower production costs by polluting will win out in competition with those that do not. In this case, free-market competition leads inevitably to the tragedy of the commons. The only way such pollution can be limited is if government, or some other collective institution, regulates the individual's liberty to pollute.

Libertarians underestimate the degree that collective arrangements are needed to achieve a cherished goal—the maximization of individual self-interest. This is the lesson of both the prisoner's dilemma and the tragedy of the commons. Even a society of radical individualists must be sensitive to the necessity of collective action if it is to be successful. In a democracy, an understanding of how individual success is related to cooperation with other individuals is a valuable habit of the heart for all citizens. Such an understanding leads democratic citizens to think about how their own interest relates to the interest of others. Only with this understanding can tragedies of the commons be avoided and prisoners' dilemmas be resolved. Unfortunately, because of our radically individualistic culture, both often ensnare us.

Two Kinds of Liberty

Libertarians also have a flawed understanding of the nature of their key value: liberty. They, like many Americans, tend to think of liberty only as freedom from external constraints on individual behavior. According to this concept, I am free whenever government or other social institutions do not prevent me from pursuing my individual goals. Freedom means being able to use my property as I wish, to speak my mind, to practice my chosen profession, to live where I want, and to worship as I please. Liberty is only in danger when social institutions, especially government, interfere with my ability to do these things. The libertarian perspective assumes that the absence of constraints on individuals satisfies the requirements of liberty.

Many political philosophers consider the concept of liberty to be more complex than simply freedom from constraints on my behavior.[35] Even in a political system that imposed no constraints on my freedom, such freedom would mean nothing unless I also possessed the means to exercise it. *Freedom from* external constraints is only one side of liberty; *freedom to* exercise it is the other. This second component of liberty implies that individuals possess the capacity and power to act; their "freedom to" do so is a product of community resources and social institutions that provide the capacity to exercise one's freedom. A government that does not prevent me from writing what is on my mind, worshipping as I please, or choosing my own profession is essential for liberty. But the absence of such prohibitions means little to me if I have no writing instruments, if there are no churches, or if I cannot find a job. The provision of these resources depends on living in a community that makes them available.

Tyrants understand well these two sides of liberty. In the former Soviet Union, for example, although political dissidents were often imprisoned for criticizing the regime, the main limitation on freedom of expression was through state control of all media. The freedom to publish or disseminate ideas was denied to all but regime supporters. Contemporary tyrannical governments in China and Iran do the same through regulation of Internet access. Without the ability to take advantage of liberty, the absence of constraints on liberty has little value.

Libertarians reply that if you allow free speech *and* free ownership of media, then true liberty of individual expression will automatically exist. Such a view ignores, however, the extent to which free speech, even in a free-market society, depends on social institutions. The widespread dissemination of one's ideas requires access to media outlets such as newspapers, television, radio, publishing firms, and the Internet. Even in the absence of a government monopoly of media outlets, individuals who want to communicate ideas to more than a small circle of friends must employ social institutions. The ability of the owner of a television station, for example, to exercise free speech depends on social networks: the past efforts of those who invented television technology, the widespread ownership of television sets, plus the cooperation and expertise of employees.

The emergence of the Internet and the ability of individuals to disseminate their ideas through their own individual webpages, personal blogs, and interactive sites like Facebook seems to offer new opportunities for speech free from dependence on the social networks required by previous technologies. The evolution of this new medium, however, shows the inevitability of social influence on Internet access. Social institutions define who can access the computer hardware and software needed to use the Internet; what rules access providers use in governing access; what browser software is easily available and how it may channel access; and what government regulations govern use of the medium. No matter what the technology, "freedom to" express one's ideas will always exist within a fabric of social institutions.

The more complex understanding of individual liberty as both *freedom from* and *freedom to* underscores the degree to which an individual's freedom depends on the support of others and society. All one's freedoms depend on a structure of social institutions that provide the means to exercise them. College students, exercising their individual freedom to learn, provide a good example of the need for social support in the practice of freedom. The freedom to pursue higher education would mean nothing if such social entities as colleges and universities did not exist. Their existence is the result of contributions of resources, some going back many years, by many individuals. Admission to a college is a product, in part, of individual talent and effort, but access to elementary and secondary schools is crucial for developing talent. And for most of us, an important prerequisite of freedom to learn is the support of a nurturing family that provides us the wherewithal to learn throughout our schooling. Declaring that no government should prohibit some individuals from acquiring an education does not mean that even strongly motivated and ambitious individuals will be able to learn. Freedom to be educated requires a supportive social environment.

Individuals need more than simply freedom from others and society to attain their goals; they require social support and the cooperation of others if they are to live successful and productive lives. Recently, social scientists have employed the concept of *social capital* to describe the social networks, norms, and trust that benefit individuals.[36] They argue that the development of social capital improves the ability of individuals to cooperate for mutual benefit. In a study of regional governments in Italy, political scientist Robert Putnam discovered that regions with "strong traditions of civic engagement," such as high voter turnout, lots of active community groups, and high levels of awareness of public affairs, had effective governments and were economically prosperous.[37] These regional governments administered successful programs for economic development, child care, and environmental regulation, as well as health clinics, and citizens were largely satisfied with their performance. In contrast, in regions lacking these characteristics, social capital was low. Citizens had a "stunted" conception of citizenship, regarding "public affairs [as] somebody else's business—*i notabili,* 'the bosses,' 'the politicians'—but not theirs."[38] In these regions, mainly in Italy's impoverished south, regional governments were failures: "inefficient, lethargic, and corrupt." Putnam argues that the presence or absence of social capital was deeply rooted in the differing histories of the regions going back to the Middle Ages. Successful regions had long heritages of civic solidarity built on "guilds, religious fraternities, and tower societies for self-defense," whereas unsuccessful regions had heritages of remote despotic government. Social capital, Putnam concludes, "seems to be a precondition for economic development, as well as for effective government."

Putnam identifies three key characteristics of social capital that support good government and economic success: generalized reciprocity, trust, and past success at collaboration. *Generalized reciprocity* is the willingness of an individual to come to the assistance of someone in need, with the understanding that the needy individual will return the favor at some future time. This is the ethic of the frontier barn raising, common in nineteenth-century rural America. When a new family arrived in a community, neighboring farmers would organize a daylong welcoming celebration that featured building a barn for the new family. The recipient of the barn would then be expected to participate in such barn raisings for future community members. The tradition of barn raising was a form of social capital that helped each individual farmer to prosper but also increased the chance that all community members would succeed and none would become a burden on the community. Acts of generalized reciprocity contribute to the development of *trust* between individual community members. Such trust develops "networks of civic engagement" that can be drawn on when cooperative effort is needed, whether for day-to-day public projects or in emergencies. Both trust and generalized reciprocity become historically rooted over time as individuals in a community *collaborate* successfully. This provides the community with a stock of self-perpetuating and self-reinforcing social capital that can be drawn on to solve a wide variety of problems. In his study of Italian regions, Putnam found that regions possessing large amounts of social capital seemed successful in all areas of social existence: culture, economics, and politics; communities without social capital seemed to fail in everything.

It is important to understand that the concept of communities' possessing social capital is quite different from the idealized vision of a consensual community desired by the Americans whom Bellah interviewed. Communities do not need to be made up of totally like-minded individuals, as in Simi Valley, to build social capital. Trust, reciprocity, and a history of successful collaboration can be developed among individuals with differing values, income levels, race or ethnicity, and aspirations.[39] The idea of social capital is that it facilitates and strengthens relations among individuals despite personal differences that might otherwise have interfered with cooperation. Like Tocqueville's "habits of the heart," social capital connects disparate individuals.

The concept of social capital, like the other concepts discussed in this section, implies a more complex understanding of individuality than is to be found either in the radical individualism of many Americans or in libertarian ideology. Libertarians see individuals as atomized, existing independent of one another; in fact, the autonomous individual existing independent of social constraint is their ideal. Social institutions, especially government, and the community of other individuals are external forces apart from the individual. Yet the concepts of social capital, the prisoner's dilemma, the tragedy of the commons, and liberty as "freedom to" suggest that this conception of the individual is unrealistic. Robert Bellah makes the point eloquently:

> We find ourselves not independently of other people and institutions but through them. We never get to the bottom of ourselves on our own. We discover who we are face to face and side by side with others in work, love, and learning. . . . And the positive side of our individualism, our sense of the dignity, worth, and moral autonomy of the individual, is dependent in a thousand ways on a social, cultural, and institutional context that keeps us afloat.[40]

As social beings we are the beneficiaries of those social institutions that nurture us and we also have a moral obligation to help and support those institutions, including political ones.[41] Libertarianism's myopic focus on the individual free of external constraint ignores this individual moral obligation to other individuals and society.

This more complex understanding of individuality should cause concern about the radical individualism of Americans described earlier in this chapter. If Bellah and his colleagues, Gans, and other social commentators are correct about the recent evolution of American culture, individual Americans are less and less aware of their dependence on others and on social institutions. Radically individualistic Americans may be becoming like the burglars caught in the prisoner's dilemma or the ranchers living on the common grazing land—unable, because of their individualistic blinders, to perceive the advantages of cooperation. The dominance of the conception of liberty as freedom from constraint may prevent them from supporting social institutions, such as public schools, that give meaning to those freedoms. Ignorance about their dependence on society may lead Americans to deplete the social capital required for successful economies and governments. If these things come to pass, Americans will have lost the "habits of the heart" that Tocqueville thought were required for successful democratic government.

Our Pathological Politics of Rights and Interests

Americans are not shy about asserting their rights. Much of our politics involves individuals or groups entering the public arena to demand recognition or protection of a right. Pro-choice advocates demand the right to legal abortion; pro-life forces the right to life of the fetus. Smokers claim a right to smoke; nonsmokers the right to smoke-free air. Labor union members assert their right to strike; businesses their right to hire replacements for striking workers. "I demand my rights" is perhaps the most commonly heard phrase in our politics. In the United States, "rights talk" is our predominant form of political discourse.[42]

The American rights tradition is closely linked to our understanding of constitutionalism and democracy. Surveys show that when asked about the content of the Constitution, most Americans refer to the Bill of Rights. When asked to identify the meaning of American democracy, young Americans refer to rights and freedoms.[43] Naturalization ceremonies for new citizens emphasize the rights that citizenship confers on them.[44] This preoccupation with rights reflects, is consistent with, and reinforces American individualism.

A concern for rights is both consistent with and essential to democracy. Individual rights to participate, express one's views, assemble for political purposes, and receive due process from government are necessary conditions for the existence of democracy.[45] The assertion of one's individual rights can be a claim for recognition as a member of a democratic community. In the United States, the assertion of rights has been the principal means that groups—black Americans, women, and others—have used to gain inclusion, equality, and democratic power as citizens. Progress toward making the United States more democratic over time has been largely a process of universalizing rights—bringing more individuals and groups into the democratic community.

Although rights and *rights talk* have been instruments for expanding democracy, the political theorist Benjamin Barber points out that in recent years their democratic and social character has tended to be ignored as rights have become "privatized."[46] Although a democratic understanding of rights recognizes their social origin—the fact that rights are rooted in membership and participation in a democratic community—contemporary Americans seem to consider their rights a private possession unrelated to their political involvement. Increasingly, they claim rights but feel under no obligation to participate in their enforcement. As Barber points out, small-town citizens today demand fire protection as a right but refuse to join the volunteer fire department.[47] Many Americans regard good schools, safe roads, and security from crime in their communities as basic rights but expect to have them without supporting the realistic tax rates that such services require. The radical individualism of Americans seems to blind us to the link between rights and democratic processes.

The radical individualism of American rights talk tends to undermine effective democratic politics.[48] Although concern for and protection of rights are important in a democracy, American rights talk has effectively trivialized the concept of citizens' rights. Traditionally, the assertion of rights was confined to claims for recognition of freedoms that are fundamental to democratic citizenship, such as free speech or the right to a fair trial. Today, however, people tend to turn every want or political preference into a demand for recognition of a right. Assertions of a right to smoke, to carry an assault rifle, to view cable television, or not to wear a motorcycle helmet are a few examples. All these concerns may need to be addressed as matters of public policy, but equating them with such rights as free speech, which are fundamental to democratic liberty, cheapens the fundamental rights. Moreover, discussing all public policy in terms of the existence or absence of a *right* is not the most useful approach to resolving public issues. The assertion of a right is more likely to result in arguments about whether or not such a right should be recognized than in consideration of what course of action is in the public interest.

Because individualistic Americans tend to think about public policy issues in terms of individual rights, no public policy issue is immune to a rights claim. In recent years, these claims have included demands for animal rights and even the rights of inanimate objects. To cite an extreme example, a legal scholar in California has argued for the rights of sand as a way of protecting beaches from development.[49] Such an issue needs to be addressed in terms of collective values, such as public responsibility for the environment and preserving it for posterity. But because our individualistic culture impedes our ability to address issues in such terms—because we have become more comfortable with "rights talk" than with discussions of the public interest—proponents of an issue try to formulate it in terms of a right. They know such formulations gain more serious consideration from individualists used to thinking in "rights" terms. Sadly, such trivialization of rights also serves to reinforce our radical individualism and undermines our capacity to think about the public interest. To assert rights in regard to every political want fuels a circular process in which a radically individualistic outlook encourages rights claims validating, in turn, an even more individualistic orientation.

Along with trivializing a basic democratic concept, the privatization of rights has led to the assertion of rights without consideration of the responsibilities that must accompany them. Because American individualists have tended to see their rights as a kind of private property, rights have become individual claims on government and on the rest of society that convey no reciprocal claim on the individual citizen to participate in the provision or protection of such rights. For example, Americans demand the right to a trial by a jury of their peers, but few are willing to serve on juries.[50] Yet no right can exist unless citizens take responsibility for securing it.

Failure to perceive the relationship between rights and responsibilities seems to characterize Americans' understanding of their role as citizens. In a recent study, when college students were asked to describe what being a citizen means, most immediately mentioned rights, but few believed that having those rights required political participation on their part. As one young man said, "Being a citizen is your God-given right. Politics doesn't have anything to do with being a citizen."[51] Without taking responsibility for participating politically to protect citizenship rights, this young student certainly will need God's assistance if his rights are to last long.

Demanding rights without accepting the responsibilities that go with them has affected how individuals perceive their relation to government. By understanding citizenship as merely the possession of a bundle of individual rights, people begin to think of themselves solely as clients whose rights must be serviced. They do not feel any more responsible for producing these services than they would for producing the programs they watch on television. Government is perceived as an institution totally independent of themselves that must provide services to which their rights entitle them. A lone rights-bearing citizen does not perceive it her or his role as a democratic citizen to take responsibility for these rights and participate in their provision.[52] The extent to which people have come to misunderstand their connection to government is illustrated by the comment of a participant in a television talk show on the savings and loan crisis; she argued that *taxpayers* should not have to pay for the S&L bailout, the *government* should![53] For this citizen, all sense of democratic participation in and responsibility for government has vanished. This citizen may still believe in government *for* the people, but *of* and *by* the people have become no more relevant than if she were referring to McDonald's hamburgers.

To conceive of democratic government as merely a servicer of rights creates severe obstacles to identifying what the *public* interest is in a particular problem. One obstacle is the tendency to assert individual rights in such absolute terms that weighing broader public concerns in regard to an issue becomes impossible. The politics of gun control provides a dramatic example of such rights absolutism.

Interpreting in totally individualist terms the Second Amendment "right to bear arms"—which many constitutional scholars construe as a right to form public militias—the National Rifle Association (NRA) has deployed this right to resist enactment of any restrictions on the individual ownership and use of firearms. It has opposed regulation of even the most dangerous forms of weaponry, such as semiautomatic assault rifles, on the grounds that an absolute individual right to bear arms overrules any concern for the danger to public safety posed by the easy availability of these weapons. For the NRA, the purported right to possess guns takes precedence over any other public consideration—even the thousands of deaths and injuries caused by firearms each year and the mounting insecurity most citizens feel about the burgeoning arsenals of weapons on the nation's streets. The success of the NRA in blocking more effective gun control reflects its lobbying skills and its strategic use of legislative campaign contributions. But it reflects, as well, the resonance of rights talk in our political culture, which tends to privilege any claim of an individual right when public policy problems are addressed. A more balanced, less rights-oriented, less individualist approach to the issue of gun ownership would seek to balance legitimate individual interest in access to guns, for legitimate purposes in sports and recreation, with important broader concerns such as public safety. But our radically individualist culture tends to privilege absolutist rights claims and inhibits our ability to formulate reasonable balances between individual and public interests.

Rights talk also impedes efforts to identify the public interest because of our propensity to formulate nearly all political conflicts in terms of conflicting rights. Resolving conflict becomes impossible when one absolute, irreconcilable individual right is deployed against another. This has been the reason why formulating public policy regarding abortion has been so frustrating and disruptive in the United States. Americans have framed the issue in terms of a woman's right to privacy versus an unborn fetus's right to life, neither of which can be acknowledged without violating the other or denying the legitimacy of the other.[54] Rather than focusing simply on these logically irreconcilable "rights," a more useful approach might be to examine the social context within which abortions occur. What are the financial, personal, and psychological conditions that make pregnancies "unwanted"? What public policies might relieve women of the individual burden our society imposes on them for child rearing? Attention to such questions might lead to the formulation of policies for birth-control education, pregnancy and child care support, facilitation of adoption, and family nurturing, which would reduce the number of abortions while preserving women's legitimate concern for control over their lives. Such an approach is not likely to solve the many complex moral conflicts that the abortion issue raises, but it would offer both pro-life and pro-choice proponents the means of addressing many social issues surrounding the abortion issue on which they could agree.[55] Unfortunately, our radically individualist rights talk often gets in the way of discussing such matters.

One side effect of American rights discourse is excessive judicial involvement in policy making, as discussed in the previous chapter. Because policy issues are framed in terms of recognition of individual rights, partisans on one side of a conflict often go to court to win policy victories, rather than debating the issue in the legislature. Even when Americans do avoid rights discourse and turn to legislative assemblies to address public policy issues, however, the contentious manner in which their representatives do so leaves much to be desired from a democratic point of view. The American radical-individualist culture encourages most Americans to think primarily in terms of their individual self-interest, rather than the public interest, when thinking about public policy. "Looking out for No. 1" seems to have become many Americans' only orientation to political issues. Whenever public policy proposals are raised, the automatic reaction is to ask, How am I helped or hurt by this proposal? Not, Is this proposal good for the country (or town or state)? Legislative representatives face overwhelming pressure both from their constituents and from organized special interests to protect individual and group self-interests when considering legislation; any orientation to the broader public good is a matter of relatively minor concern.

Our recent political history is replete with examples of the politics of self-interest overwhelming attempts to deal with public problems. US Representative (and political scientist) David Price tells of his chagrin in the face of self-interested reaction to his support for catastrophic health insurance in 1988.[56] In that year, Congress enacted major legislation to expand Medicare coverage to include long-term nursing home care for the elderly. Although senior citizens' groups had been major proponents of the legislation, when Congress imposed increased Medicare premiums to pay for the expanded coverage, the same groups were outraged. Price tells of his frustration with the reaction of some of his constituents who, in meetings in his district, would express strong support for catastrophic coverage but also oppose any method of paying for the program. One constituent, in fact, told the congressman that, as a citizen, he felt no obligation to consider alternative ways to pay for the program—that was the congressman's job! It seems this constituent presumed his role as citizen to involve only looking out for his own self-interest.

Given the pervasiveness of radical individualism, the attitude of Price's constituent seems to be widely shared in contemporary American politics. Many Americans are quick to consider how public policies affect their individual rights and interests but are unable to think of themselves as responsible members of the sovereign people with an obligation to be concerned with the public interest. According to the political theorist Joseph Tussman, "The citizen, in his political capacity . . . is asked public, not private questions: 'Do we need more public schools?' not 'Would I like to pay more taxes?' He must, in this capacity, be concerned with the public interest, not with his private goods."[57] When citizens lose the capacity to think about public issues in the terms Tussman describes, solving public problems becomes extremely difficult, if not impossible. Any proposal to solve a public problem is not evaluated or discussed in terms of its capacity to address the overall problem; it is subjected only to self-interested scrutiny by various groups to see how their interest is affected. The "politics of special interests" familiar in any day-to-day account of national politics in Washington reflects this orientation. The existence in the national capital of thousands of organizations and lobbyists whose sole purpose is to monitor how legislation affects their narrow interests seems quite normal once one assumes politics to be solely about self-interest. Political success, in this context, is a matter of what you can get for your group, without any consideration of how the broader public interest is affected. Hesitating to defend one's own interest could bring disaster, as other self-interested groups would move to take advantage of such hesitation. Politics, overall, becomes a matter of all groups fighting for themselves, like sharks feeding on a carcass, while the public interest is left to take care of itself.

Because of the largely self-interested orientation of most citizens and groups to politics, the burden of looking out for the broader public interest is placed on elected officials. Their ability to do so is limited, however, because there are few rewards for doing so. Failure to respond to self-interested demands will result in loss of political support, and attempts to pursue the public interest are likely only to draw suspicion. In a self-interested political culture, all political actions or proposals are assumed to be selfishly motivated. This phenomenon is evident in the cynical approach of most journalistic commentary on politics. Little attention is given to the substance of policy proposals or the consequences of the actions of political figures. Reporters and pundits tend to focus instead on how the proposals of political figures support their political ambitions and presume a self-interested motivation behind them.[58] In the face of special interest pressures, self-interested constituent demands, and a cynical press, it is not surprising that few politicians today consider pursuit of the public interest to be their main concern. A successful political career is more likely to be had by serving a particular interest and watching out for its concerns than by attending to the broader public interest. Politicians who set aside the narrow concerns of their constituents for the broader good of the country, who turn aside offers of special-interest political action committee (PAC) funds, or who devote their time to pushing public-spirited ideas are not apt to last long in office. This does not mean that skillful, public-spirited politicians never put the public interest ahead of selfish interests but that such public-interested behavior is likely to be rare. A political system that expects—and privileges—self-interested political behavior will usually get it.

Our pathological politics of rights and interests follows from the radical individualism of the political culture. As long as Americans understand their relationship to political life primarily in terms of the pursuit of individual goals, they will turn to politics and government only to protect what they consider a right or to promote a selfish interest. The growing radical individualism that Bellah, Gans, and others have documented encourages a politics of rights deadlock and unbridled pursuit of self-interest. As Tocqueville would have expected, citizens who have lost the "habits of the heart" that tie them to the broader community will think of public policy solely in terms of how their individual, selfish interest is affected. They will demand services from government while refusing to support taxes to pay for them and be unable to perceive the contradiction between the two positions. That an astronomical national debt, decaying roads and bridges, and squalid public schools seem to be permanent conditions in the United States naturally follows. Democratic citizens who are "shut up in the solitude of their own hearts" may have some success for a time in watching out for their rights and interests, but unless the broader public sphere is attended to, eventually even individual interests will be ignored, and rights will vanish.

The Failed Opportunity to Build Community After 9/11

The shock of the September 2001 terrorist attacks on the World Trade Center and the Pentagon seemed to stimulate a shift away from radical individualism among Americans. In times of tragedy and loss, people realize their need for others, exposing the limits of the libertarian vision of complete individual self-reliance. The sense of vulnerability and insecurity that the attacks created led most Americans to look to public officials and public institutions for relief. A grateful nation marveled at the self-sacrifice and dedication of the thousands of public servants—firefighters, police, emergency medical technicians—who responded to the disaster, many giving their lives in the effort to help their fellow citizens. The magnitude of the destruction called forth a national communal response, under the leadership of President Bush and other government officials, to find ways to mourn our tragedy and to mobilize a response to prevent a recurrence. The slogan "United We Stand" pushed to the side the "looking out for No. 1" mentality of previous decades.

In the immediate aftermath of the attacks, there were signs of a fundamental change in public attitudes away from the distrustful, selfish perspectives of radical individualism toward a more communitarian spirit. A few weeks after 9/11, a *Washington Post* survey reported that citizens' "trust in government" had risen to a level (64 percent) not seen since the mid-1960s.[59] Robert Putnam and his colleagues found a similar shift in a survey conducted later in the fall of 2001. On a variety of measures of civic commitment, trust in others, and trust in government, Putnam's respondents gave much more positive answers than they had given only a few months previously.[60] These surveys suggested that the terrorist attacks and the newfound sense of vulnerability had the potential to reverse the drift toward radical individualism of the previous two decades. Yet Putnam's data also showed signs that the new communitarian spirit had not penetrated very deeply among Americans. At the time of his survey, when memory of 9/11 was fresh, Putnam found that the shift toward more communitarian attitudes had not been matched by significant changes in *behavior*. Even though people trusted their government and one another more, those feelings had not made them much more inclined to attend meetings, join an organization, or volunteer.[61] To support a permanent alteration of the radical-individualist culture would require specific policies and the creation of institutional structures to encourage civic engagement.

Unfortunately, the leadership needed to forge such a new spirit of solidarity, which had also appeared in previous eras of crisis, did not materialize. As President Bush dispatched America's professional soldiers to war, first in Afghanistan and then in Iraq, he asked no particular sacrifice of ordinary Americans and instituted no public campaign to urge ordinary citizens to do their part in the "war on terror." In fact, his only suggestion was that Americans get on with their lives despite the national emergency—as he admonished them, "Fly and enjoy America's great destination spots. Get down to Disney World in Florida. Take your families and enjoy life."[62] Although Bush often characterized the challenges facing Americans after 9/11 as comparable to those of the World War II generation, he never sought any home-front measures equivalent to the War Bond and conservation drives that President Franklin Roosevelt had instituted in that era. To the contrary, Bush continued with his pre-9/11 plans for massive tax cuts benefiting primarily the richest Americans, despite an escalating deficit and war expenditures. Instead of promoting energy conservation efforts that might reduce American dependence on foreign oil (and reduce any need for military intervention in the Mideast), he supported tax breaks for SUV owners and an energy policy geared toward increased oil consumption. Americans were asked to commit more time to individual volunteer service, but the administration failed to support a national service bill proposed in Congress to expand Americorps.[63] Rather than calling on Americans for sacrifice and commitment to a shared effort, the president seemed intent on relying solely on the professional military and his cabinet officials to defend America. In reference to Bush's policy of cutting taxes while fighting two expensive land wars, Robert Putnam remarked, "The unstated message was that we were not all in this together."[64] As journalist Lawrence Kaplan summed up Bush's post-9/11 leadership, "It is as if the Bush administration, sensing the birth of common purpose after September 11, consciously squashed it."[65]

Not surprisingly, absent any leadership calling them to a united effort, Americans soon fell back into their individual pursuits. Within a year after 9/11, public opinion polls showed that the increase in communitarian attitudes that Putnam and others noted in the fall of 2001 had vanished.[66] Thereafter, while more than 5,000 American soldiers lost their lives fighting in Iraq and Afghanistan and thousands of others suffered severe wounds, most Americans felt little direct involvement in their nation's endeavors and were only mildly inconvenienced—mainly by waiting in long lines for airport security checks—by the challenges the country faced. The post-9/11 period featured instead the rise of "reality TV" programs pitting individuals against one another on desert islands or in Donald Trump's boardroom to see who would emerge as "No. 1." In the end, radical individualism triumphed over "United We Stand."

During the 2008 campaign, when former New York Mayor Rudolph Giuliani and Republican vice presidential candidate Sarah Palin mocked Democratic presidential candidate Barack Obama's experience as a community organizer in Chicago, they implicitly reflected the anticommunitarian spirit of Bush's post-9/11 outlook. Obama's decisive victory a few weeks later signified a repudiation of that outlook and presented new possibilities for bringing Americans together for common purposes. In his election night speech, Obama made the call to service and community commitment that Bush had failed to make during the previous seven years. After referring to the sacrifice American service personnel were making in Iraq and Afghanistan, Obama called on a "new spirit of service, a new spirit of sacrifice" from all Americans. He said, "So let us summon a new spirit of patriotism, of service and responsibility where each of us resolves to pitch in and work harder and look after not only ourselves, but each other."[67] Unfortunately, Obama was unable to instill this spirit in practice as his administration soon faced rabid hostility to his attempts to revive the economy and reform health care. The contentious and polarized conflict that ensued after 2008 reflected the radical individualistic right talk and pursuit of economic interest described in this chapter. Obama's appeals to sacrifice for the common good seemed to fall on largely deaf ears.

Meeting the Challenge: Balancing Rights With Responsibilities

Bringing about a better balance between community and the individual in the United States requires a more communitarian approach to politics.[68] Such an approach challenges the libertarian view that individuals are completely autonomous authors of their own existence; instead, it regards people as products of the many communities—from their families and neighborhoods to the national community—in which they live. Unlike the libertarians, who recognize only freedom from community-imposed constraints, communitarians understand that human freedom and dignity require the support of a network of social institutions. A communitarian approach would seek to nurture and protect such institutions, rather than letting them decay as libertarians have. Instead of a libertarian preoccupation with rights, communitarianism emphasizes the need to balance rights with responsibilities, if rights are to be preserved.

Encouraging a more communitarian political culture requires building a communitarian movement, and in recent years a number of Americans have begun to do that. Communitarians, including the movement's leader, sociologist Amitai Etzioni, seek to renew communities and the sense of individual civic obligation in ways that enhance democracy. In the words of "The Responsive

Community Platform," a communitarian perspective "recognizes both individual human dignity and the social dimension of human existence . . . [and] that the preservation of individual liberty depends on the active maintenance of the institutions of civil society."[69] Since the issuance of their platform in 1991, communitarians have received much attention and have begun to have an impact on both public policy and national politics. They were a force in the Clinton administration, advocating passage of community-support legislation such as the Family and Medical Leave Act and the Americorps national service program. Etzioni hopes that the communitarian movement will have a reforming impact—moderating excessive individualism and promoting community-regarding policies—equivalent to the widespread policy results of the Progressive movement.[70]

Inspiring young people to acquire an understanding of the importance of community through performing public service, as in the Americorps program, is a key part of the communitarian agenda. In addition to that national program, a number of colleges and universities around the country have begun to include requirements for public service as part of their curriculums. At Providence College, for example, the Feinstein Institute for Public Service offers an academic major in public and community service studies that integrates student community service with specific courses on citizenship and the nature of political community. Similar programs have sprung up or are under consideration elsewhere, making it possible for students to address the problem of radical individualism directly on their campuses by getting involved in service-learning programs or, where such programs do not exist, working with faculty and administrators to create them. Service learning reflects a sense that radical individualism in the United States has gone too far and that understanding the value of community needs to be part of a liberal education.[71] The enthusiasm that young people seem to have for service suggests that the time may have arrived for a program of mandatory universal service, including military service, to meet the nation's needs. In chapter 8, I propose such a program as a means of restoring a true citizen army for meeting our national security challenges and reestablishing the notion that all citizens have a duty to serve their country.

A stronger communitarian influence in American democracy will not be easy to establish. Radical individualism pervades our culture, and it has strong historical roots. Also, careful balancing will be necessary to prevent a pendulum swing toward community from going too far. Authoritarians have often used preservation of the community as an excuse to abolish individual liberty and impose a single set of community values and norms. Even when democratic institutions are maintained, too much concern for community solidarity can be as great a threat to democracy as excessive individualism. Whereas too much individualism may be a challenge to American democracy, too much community and too little individualism can also be major challenges, as seen in Japan, where overbearing social conformity seems to stifle individual creativity and self-expression.[72] Balancing American individualism with a greater concern for community and the public good must be accompanied by a judicious concern for preserving the virtues of individualism.

American radical individualism challenges democracy in several ways. Most fundamentally, it erodes the habits of the heart that tie democratic citizens to one another and promote civic virtue. The relationship between radical individualism and civic-minded habits is circular. The more individuals see themselves as isolated and the more they are preoccupied with their own individual goals, the less they participate in public affairs or support the public sphere. As participation declines and the public sphere atrophies, individual isolation grows and individuals understand less about their interdependence with others. In short order, the society becomes merely an aggregation of isolated individuals whose limited perspective cannot encompass a larger society outside themselves. In this infertile ground, as Tocqueville understood, democracy is in peril.

Thought Questions

1. To what extent might the "radical individualism" decried in this chapter be simply a reflection of a self-interested human nature? Or is a self-interested outlook itself a social product—a consequence of a radical-individualist culture?

2. Is it realistic to expect people to approach public issues in the disinterested way advocated by Joseph Tussman? Can you identify examples from history, news accounts, or your own experience in which people seem to have placed the broader public good ahead of their individual self-interest?

3. In discussing the pathology of "rights talk," this chapter makes a distinction between "trivial" and "fundamental" rights (e.g., the right to smoke versus the right to due process). What seems to be the basis for this distinction? How would we distinguish a claim to a fundamental right from a claim that is trivial? What criteria are implied in this chapter? Do you agree that this distinction is possible?

4. Do you find anything attractive in the outlook of Brian Palmer, the middle-class exemplar interviewed in *Habits of the Heart*? What advantages might there be to a society made up of Brian Palmers? Do those advantages possibly offset the disadvantages emphasized in this chapter?

5. If radical individualism is as pervasive in modern America as this chapter argues, can anything be done to counteract it? Are there practical reforms that might encourage Americans to adopt a more communitarian outlook? Or do we need to find ways to adjust our conception of democracy somehow to accommodate radical individualism?

Suggestions for Further Reading

Bellah, Robert N., Richard Madsen, William M. Sullivan, Ann Swidler, and Steven M. Tipton. *Habits of the Heart: Individualism and Commitment in American Life.* Berkeley: University of California Press, 2007. This classic diagnosis of American radical individualism, first published in 1985, is must reading for anyone interested in understanding contemporary American life. *Habits of the Heart* came out in a new edition in 2007.

Ehrenhalt, Alan. *The Lost City: The Forgotten Virtues of Community in America.* New York: Basic Books, 1995. A description of life in Chicago in the 1950s, emphasizing not nostalgia but the advantages and disadvantages of a more communitarian time and place.

Elshtain, Jean Bethke. *Democracy on Trial.* New York: Basic Books, 1995. An analysis of the weakening of democratic civil society and civility in America today.

Etzioni, Amitai. *The Spirit of Community: Rights, Responsibilities, and the Communitarian Agenda.* New York: Crown, 1993. One of the founders of the communitarian movement, which seeks to balance excessive American individualism with more concern for community values, sets out the movement's principles. Communitarians publish a quarterly journal titled *The Responsive Community.*

Glendon, Mary Ann. *Rights Talk: The Impoverishment of Political Discourse.* New York: Free Press, 1991. A thorough analysis of the political consequences of the American preoccupation with individual rights and the simultaneous neglect of community responsibilities. Included are many comparisons of American rights talk with how other democracies address rights issues.

*Hayek, Friedrich A. von. *The Road to Serfdom.* Chicago: University of Chicago Press, 1944. Hayek's works provide a systematic and persuasively argued case for the libertarian position.

*———. *The Constitution of Liberty.* Chicago: University of Chicago Press, 1978.

Hudson, William E. *The Libertarian Illusion: Ideology, Public Policy, and the Assault on the Common Good.* Washington, DC: CQ Press, 2008. A critique of libertarian policy stances on issues ranging from taxation to stem cell research that emphasizes the need for a more communitarian outlook.

Putnam, Robert. *Bowling Alone: The Collapse and Revival of American Community.* New York: Simon & Schuster, 2000. Putnam makes his case that Americans do not involve themselves in the civic realm as they once did and provides some concrete suggestions for bringing them back in.

*Schudson, Michael. *The Good Citizen: A History of American Civic Life.* New York: Free Press, 1998. A thoughtful history of differing American conceptions of citizenship since colonial times. Schudson sees the current preoccupation with rights not as a corruption of civic life but as the latest enriching layer in America's continually evolving understanding of democratic citizenship.

Slater, Phillip. *The Pursuit of Loneliness.* Boston: Beacon Press, 1990. Originally published in 1970, this is one of the most thoughtful analyses of American culture to emerge from the turmoil of the 1960s. Slater believes that individualism provides the key to understanding all of America's ills—from militarism abroad to dysfunctional families at home.

Tocqueville, Alexis de. *Democracy in America,* ed. and abr., Richard D. Heffner. New York: Mentor Books, 1956. This shortened version of Tocqueville's classic provides a good introduction to his work.

*Presents a point of view that disagrees with the arguments presented in this chapter.

Selected Websites

http://communitariannetwork.org/. The Communitarian Network, sponsored by Amitai Etzioni, puts one in touch with the latest communitarian thinking.

http://www.hks.harvard.edu/saguaro/. This is Robert Putnam's project for exploring how civic participation can be renewed.

www.cato.org. The leading libertarian think tank provides a reasoned defense of the libertarian point of view as well as practical policy proposals.

www.cpn.org. The Civic Practices Network website focuses on the Civic Renewal Movement, including articles from several publications such as the *Kettering Review, Change Magazine,* and the *American Civic Forum.*

CHAPTER 4

The Fourth Challenge: Citizen Participation

> *The political activity that pervades the United States must be seen in order to be understood. No sooner do you set foot on American ground than you are stunned by a kind of tumult.*
>
> —ALEXIS DE TOCQUEVILLE

DO WE AMERICAN CITIZENS participate too much or too little for the good of our democracy? To many readers, this may seem a silly question. Of course there is too little participation! As hundreds of editorials have reminded us after recent presidential elections, nearly half of all Americans of voting age fail to go to the polls; in midterm congressional elections, only about one-third of citizens show up; and in many local elections, turnouts of less than 10 percent are not uncommon. Citizen apathy goes beyond just (not) voting. Political scientists have documented citizen disengagement from a whole host of civic institutions and practices that affect our collective well-being.[1] Ordinary Americans have less and less desire to join fraternal associations, talk about politics, read newspapers, watch television news programs, or show up for public meetings. If fewer and fewer citizens participate in civic organization or attend to basic political duties such as voting, those who worry about civic disengagement ask, how can our democracy remain healthy?

While many political observers worry about civic disengagement, others are concerned about *too much* citizen activism. From the perspective of elected lawmakers, the citizen participation issue has two faces. On one side, fewer ordinary citizens seem interested in showing up to vote representatives into office or in following public issues. On the other side, elected representatives are beleaguered by citizen activists monitoring every vote and ready with vociferous demands on

Opposite: *Democracy requires that more citizens participate like these voters lined up to vote in the 2008 election.*

Photo courtesy of Scott Olson/Getty Images.

every conceivable issue. In the past three decades, the number of citizen and advocacy groups seems to have exploded. At the national level, groups concerned about such important national issues as environmental protection, consumer protection, abortion, taxes, and civil rights place tremendous pressure on elected representatives at all levels of government. At the local level, citizen groups with colorful acronyms such as ACORN, COPS, and BUILD press demands for better local services. Political activists are able to raise money, mobilize their supporters, and bombard the media with talking points on a host of issues, both profound and trivial. Advocacy overload has made it impossible for elected representatives to deliberate calmly and devise good policies for the entire society. In addition, not content simply to lobby their representatives, citizens have used voter initiatives and referendums to vote directly on issues in steadily increasing numbers over the past three decades. From the point of view of "overload" on elected representatives, too much participation may be the larger problem for our democracy.

To sort out these contradictory features of citizen participation in American politics, it is necessary to examine how they are affecting the ability of the system to satisfy the prescriptions of democratic theory. How does the nature of participation in contemporary American politics affect our ability to achieve the fundamental values of political equality, liberty, and popular sovereignty? Before proceeding to summarize what political scientists know about the nature and extent of political participation and civic engagement in the United States, let us begin with a brief review of the contradictions within democratic theory regarding the appropriate role of citizen participation in a democracy.

Citizen Participation and Democratic Theory

As we discussed in the introduction, a major disagreement among democratic theorists revolves around the citizen's role in a democracy. The Developmental/Participatory variants of democratic theory assert the need for an active citizenry to participate fully in all aspects of government if democracy is to be healthy. This view contrasts sharply with the more passive citizen role prescribed by the Protective and Pluralist theorists, in which low levels of citizen participation and participation restricted to limited roles are signs of democratic health. What is the basis for this disagreement over the impact of citizen participation on democracy?

Democratic theorists who say that high rates of participation are needed believe that participation promotes healthy democracy in two ways. First, widespread participation ensures that public policy will reflect the good of all and not just the interests of a few. According to the Developmental/Participatory theorists, if democracy is to produce government policies reflecting the interests, preferences, and concerns of everyone—which is the goal of popular sovereignty—then everyone needs to participate in influencing those policies. Participation, in other words, is an instrument for getting what one wants from government; those who fail to use the instrument will be ignored.[2] A healthy democracy involves all in determining government policy because only then will a public good encompassing all be achieved. This participation must involve voting in elections, but it must also include vigorous citizen activity between elections to ensure that representatives pay attention to everyone. It also encompasses participation in a variety of civic associations whereby collective needs can be identified and addressed either directly or by petitioning government officials.

Second, through civic engagement in both political and civic associations, people learn how to be good democratic citizens who are capable of understanding what is in the public interest. According to this view, one learns democracy by practicing it. The process of participation allows people to learn about public issues, to become more aware of public needs and the needs of their fellow citizens. In sum, participation is a way of acquiring "civic virtue." As John Stuart Mill put it, "Among the foremost benefits of free government is that education of the intelligence and of the sentiments which is carried down to the very lowest ranks of the people when they are called to take part in acts which directly affect the great interests of the country."[3] These democratic lessons are learned both through explicitly political involvement, such as working on a political campaign, and through participation in civic associations concerned with improving the community.

Alexis de Tocqueville also believed that political participation was most effective in training people in the necessary values of democracy when it involved them in shared responsibility for making public policy. That is why he admired New England townships in his visit to the United States.[4] Through direct participation in governing their towns, Tocqueville thought, New Englanders acquired the "republican spirit" needed for governing the nation as a whole. Citizens deliberating on matters of local concern, such as building roads, learned how to listen and understand the needs of their fellow citizens and how to reach a consensus on the broad needs of the community. Like Tocqueville, Participatory theorists look to local institutions that involve citizens directly, such as town meetings, as important arenas for learning how to be good democratic citizens. When representation is needed, Participatory democrats insist on the importance of direct citizen monitoring of representatives to make sure that they respond to citizen preferences. A citizenry that participates only by voting occasionally in elections will not learn completely the democratic lessons that participation should provide. Only direct engagement in debating, and to some extent deciding, public issues will teach the civic virtue that all citizens of a democracy can and must possess. The key aspect of that virtue is for citizens to look beyond their individual self-interest to the larger needs of the community.

Proponents of the Protective/Pluralist models are much more skeptical about the capacity of all citizens to acquire civic virtue. They believe that democracies must rely primarily on the civic virtue of representatives, with most citizens confined to the role of participating in the selection of good leaders. In *Federalist* No. 10, James Madison argues that one of the advantages of representative democracy over direct democracy, as it existed in ancient Athens, is that "the public voice, pronounced by the representatives of the people, will be more consonant to the public good, than if pronounced by the people themselves."[5] This greater emphasis on representatives as responsible for healthy democratic politics leads to a very different outlook on the proper level of participation needed in a good democracy.

According to this alternative view, the lack of participation by even a large proportion of citizens in politics is not a problem for democracy. Protective/ Pluralist theorists regard nonparticipation as a sign of stability in democratic regimes—evidence that citizens are content with the policies their representatives have decided for them. Elections are, of course, important for establishing the legitimacy of representatives' decisions, and all citizens in a democracy must have an equal right to participate, but if some citizens opt not to exercise that right, democracy is in no way diminished. As long as democratic rights to participation are assured, those citizens, even if only a minority, with intense interest in public issues will make their concerns known to representatives at the ballot box and between elections. If large numbers of citizens remain quiescent in response to the policies that their representatives enact, it must be because the nonparticipants are generally satisfied with those policies.

For the Protective/Pluralist theorists, dangers to democracy arise when too many citizens become active. If nonparticipation is a sign of citizen contentment and regime stability, sharp increases in participation indicate that something is wrong. These theorists worry that high levels of participation will lead to more conflict than democratic politics can handle. This conflict will interfere with the ability of representatives to work out reasonable compromises to solve societal problems. Moreover, Protective/Pluralists worry that citizens who choose not to participate in normal times may not possess a sufficient commitment to democratic values, and so, when aroused, they will be prone to support authoritarian solutions to public problems. The increase in protest and participation that preceded the rise of the Nazis to power in Germany in the 1930s is often cited as evidence to support this claim.[6] In sum, too much democracy creates more conflict than representatives can easily resolve, and it brings into democratic politics authoritarian elements of the population who are intolerant of democratic compromises.

The division among democratic theorists about the appropriate role of citizen participation in a democracy suggests competing criteria for evaluating the amount of participation in contemporary America. Later in this chapter, I use these criteria to assess whether the state of American political participation is or is not a challenge to democracy. Before that can be done, we need to look at some empirical information about how much Americans participate and why.

Citizen Political Participation

We start our examination of civic disengagement with a look at the most fundamental form of civic involvement for most people—voting. The ballot is the principal mechanism of popular sovereignty in a representative democracy; by voting in elections, individual citizens participate in the exercise of their sovereignty. Universal suffrage and a "one person, one vote" system ensure that participation is distributed equally among all citizens. Whatever other inequalities may exist in society, the equal right to the ballot is supposed to provide all citizens with the capacity to influence their representatives. When some citizens fail to exercise their right to vote, thoughtful observers must question the degree to which government by the people can exist.

If voting in elections were the principal criterion for measuring the health of democracies, the United States would be on the critical list. Among industrialized democracies, the United States ranks next-to-last in average voter turnout in recent elections. Most European democracies have turnouts well over 75 percent of their voting-age populations—a level the United States has not reached since the nineteenth century.[7] Even in 2008, which saw the highest turnout of voters since 1960, only 57 percent of the citizens of voting age actually cast ballots (see Figure 4.1).[8] That meant that nearly 99 million potential voters chose to stay home on Election Day—more people than voted for Barack Obama (Obama received 66,882,230 votes).[9] Nevertheless, the 2008 election was the third presidential election in a row in which voting turnout increased, marking a significant change in what had been a fairly steady decline since 1960. As recently as 1996, turnout had dipped to 49 percent of the voting-age population—the lowest turnout in a presidential election since 1924. The past three elections, particularly the significant increase in turnout in 2008, may be the beginning of a new trend toward higher voter turnout. It is too early to know whether we are experiencing an end to the long-term decline or only a temporary blip. A rise in turnout in the 1992 presidential election—to 55.2 percent of eligible voters—was followed by dismal figures in 1996. Turnout in midterm congressional elections averages about one-third of eligible voters in recent years although it has trended upward recently to close to 37 percent in 2010; nevertheless, this still is down from about one-half of the eligible electorate in the early 1960s (see Figure 4.1). Thus, even if the higher turnout of the last few election cycles represents a permanent end to the steady decline of the past forty years, the level of voting participation remains a serious problem when such large percentages of those eligible fail to vote even in presidential election years. Contemporary American voting participation hardly suggests the "tumult" that Tocqueville observed in the 1830s.

Often when I present these statistics to my students—many of whom have recently turned eighteen and are looking forward to their first opportunity to exercise the right of suffrage—they are amazed that so many of their fellow citizens decline to vote. They ask why so many people seem unable to devote a few minutes every few years to such a simple form of participation. Nonvoting, for my students, is an unambiguous indicator of a lazy and apathetic citizenry. But as I explain to them, before drawing a hasty conclusion that all nonvoters are lazy and apathetic, one needs to think more carefully about the costs and benefits of voting to the individual. We are all acquainted, especially those of us who have taken Economics 101, with how cost-benefit calculations affect one's willingness to engage in a particular activity. I hate to get up early and I detest exercise, but every morning I pay the significant cost, to me, of getting up for an early-morning jog because I value the anticipated benefits of long-term good health and a slimmer waistline. Some students may view reading a political science textbook in these terms—as a costly chore that may pay off in the benefit of a good grade. Although we do not often think of political participation in this way, analyzing the costs and benefits of voting is a good approach to understanding why many people do not vote.

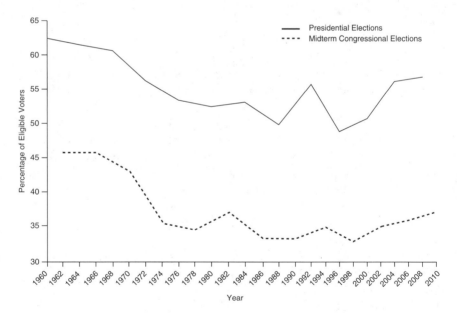

FIGURE 4.1   Voter Turnout in US Presidential and Midterm Congressional Elections, 1960–2010

Source: US Department of Commerce, Bureau of the Census, *Statistical Abstract of the United States: 2012* (Washington, DC: Government Printing Office, 2011), 244, http://www.census.gov/compendia/statab/2012/tables/12s0397.pdf.

At first glance, voting appears to be a cost-free activity; it involves nothing more than showing up at the polling booth for a few minutes every year. Surely the benefits of such a simple act will always outweigh the costs. But if we think carefully about the costs and benefits of voting, we can begin to understand why that may not always be the case. First, although the costs of voting are not usually very high (unless you live on a ranch in Nebraska fifty miles from your polling place), voting is not a cost-free activity. Some time must be found on Election Day to go to the polls. For college professors (and students) with flexible schedules, this may be fairly easy, but for many people—for example, those juggling two jobs, with kids to fetch at the day care center and dinner groceries to pick up—voting can involve considerable schedule rearrangement. Even if they vote only once every four years, busy people may have to consider whether what they gain from voting is worth disrupting their normal routine. In addition, intelligent voting—surely the goal of a democracy—involves much more than simply showing up at the polls. Learning about the candidates and election issues and forming one's own opinion will require at least some time reading newspapers and watching television news shows to acquire the necessary information on which to base one's vote. Again, for busy people this may be a considerable cost.

Even taking into account its costs, voting still is a relatively low-cost activity, especially in comparison to other activities that many people seem to find time for, such as participating in church services, going to movies, or attending rock concerts. Nevertheless, the cost-benefit perspective demands evaluating costs in relation to the benefits of voting, and when we think about voting benefits, we can begin to see how some people may decide that they are not worth even the relatively low voting costs.

One benefit an individual might expect from voting is the opportunity to influence an election outcome, and ultimately public policy, in the direction of her or his preference. Democratic theory assumes that this sort of benefit exists when it connects individual suffrage with popular sovereignty. But what is the probability that my individual vote will, in fact, determine an election outcome? In a national presidential election in which millions of other voters participate, the probability is clearly minuscule. Whether or not I show up on Election Day will not likely make a difference in the outcome of such an election. If the benefit I am seeking from voting is a chance to determine an election outcome and thus see that my individual preferences are taken into account when the election is over, the value of this benefit is extremely low. In fact, it will almost never equal even the low costs of voting.

The value of voting benefits in relation to voting costs becomes even lower if we take into account what political scientists call the "paradox of collective action." This paradox is rooted in the peculiar way the cost-benefit calculation is affected when benefits are collective rather than individual. When I take my morning exercise, the benefits I earn are mainly individual—they contribute to my good health and my slim waist (although my family and friends may also derive some pleasure from seeing me fit and healthy). If I want the benefits of exercise, I can get them only by paying the costs; if I pay the costs, I know I will personally gain the benefits. The benefits I gain from voting are quite different, however, for election outcomes provide collective benefits rather than individual ones. The benefits I may derive from the victory of candidate A over candidate B will be shared with everyone else in society who benefits from such an outcome. If I benefit from the tax cut candidate A promises, so will all other taxpayers. Moreover, I benefit from the tax cut whether or not I pay the cost of voting. Unlike the benefits of my exercise, which I get only if I pay the costs, failing to show up to vote for my favored candidate A does not prevent me from enjoying the tax cut if candidate A wins. Likewise, if I show up and vote for candidate A but a majority of voters choose candidate B instead, I must suffer with high taxes even though I did my bit to get them cut.

The collective nature of election outcomes should affect how I calculate the costs and benefits of voting. Since the probability that my individual vote will determine an election outcome is so small, and since I must live with the outcome whatever it is, I am always better off not paying the low costs of voting—even, paradoxically, when I highly value the benefits I might derive from an election outcome. From my individual point of view, if I do not vote but my candidate wins, I get the benefits of the election outcome without paying any cost. If I do vote, but my candidate happens to lose, I have paid the costs of voting but have not gained any benefits. Given this situation, nonvoting is, from a purely individual, cost-benefit perspective, always more reasonable than voting. Understanding the logic of the "paradox of collective action" leads one to ask not why so many people do not vote, but why so many do!

The reason many of us do vote, of course, is that we do not calculate the costs and benefits of voting precisely in the way I have described them. Although some of us may pretend sometimes that our one vote makes a difference in an election outcome, most voters are realistic enough to know that an individual vote is not going to determine who wins or loses. But people do not necessarily value the benefit of voting in terms of their individual impact on the outcome or the concrete ways a particular outcome will affect their self-interest.

For most of us, the benefits of voting are symbolic and expressive. I vote in every election because I believe that voting is a duty of citizenship in a democratic society. My vote symbolizes my participation in a crucial process that I value very highly. In addition, I usually feel strongly about the competing candidates in a particular election, and voting is a way for me to express my support for the candidate I favor. My vote is an expression of solidarity with my preferred candidate and with the millions of other people who support that candidate. To vote for my preferred candidate is a way of saying, I am the sort of person who believes in the things my candidate represents. Satisfaction from such solidarity comes whether one's candidate wins or loses and may continue to provide expressive satisfaction long after the election is over—as is revealed in the bumper stickers that often appear in the middle of the term of an unpopular incumbent: "Don't Blame Me, I Voted for [the incumbent's previous election opponent]!" For most voters, going to the polls means more than just influencing the election in a way that serves their interest. It is also a way to feel part of a central symbolic ritual of democracy and to express support for a particular political orientation.

Symbolic and expressive benefits, unlike the effects of an election outcome on the public, are individual rather than collective benefits. I derive the benefit simply by showing up at the polls, no matter what the election result. We can now see how, even from a cost-benefit standpoint, some people might calculate their costs of voting in relation to the individual expressive and symbolic benefits and therefore decide to vote. If the benefits to be derived from voting are individual and not collective, there is no paradox of collective action, and reasonable people will sometimes value the benefits of voting more than its costs. The puzzle posed a few paragraphs ago as to why people bother to vote is largely solved. It is also reasonable to assume that many voters, especially in the face of the powerful symbolic and expressive incentives to vote, do not always think clearly about their potential individual impact on election outcomes. The paradox of collective action is not typically part of a civics curriculum and is not a concept most voters think about. Consequently, many voters may calculate incorrectly how their vote relates to how they may benefit from election outcomes. This collective benefit illusion, added to the individual benefits of voting, suggests that many voters may presume that benefits exceed costs when it comes to voting.

To sum up, then, because many voters will not weigh benefits as they should if they understood clearly the voting paradox, and because voting provides individual benefits, many people will weigh the costs of voting against its benefits and decide to go to the polls. At the same time, if we think of voting as a cost-benefit decision, we can understand that some citizens may decide that the benefits of voting are not worth the costs and stay home on Election Day. This understanding, however, leads to another puzzle: Why do voters and nonvoters sum the costs and benefits of voting in a given election differently? In other words, what determines who votes and who does not?

Individual Influences on Citizen Participation

Political scientists identify both individual and systemic factors as important in determining voter turnout.[10] Individual factors include a voter's social status, personal characteristics, and attitudes. Systemic factors include the legal rules and processes associated with voting, the governmental and political institutions that organize elections, and the political culture. The interaction among these factors determines how individuals weigh the costs and benefits of voting.

Among the individual factors, the socioeconomic status (SES) of the individual voter has an enormous impact on that person's propensity to vote. People with high SES—which is usually measured by income, level of education, and occupational status—are much more likely to vote than those with lower SES. Of the components that define socioeconomic status, education is most strongly related to voting. This is not terribly surprising, considering that education is likely to affect the costs and benefits of voting in various ways. The acquisition of election information—who the candidates are, what their stances on issues are, how their positions relate to one's own ideology and interests—becomes easier as one becomes more educated. A college graduate will not have to devote much time to following an election campaign to assimilate the information needed to cast a vote because he or she will know where to look for it. Thus, information acquisition costs will be low. People with very little education will have much higher costs because it will likely take them more time to learn what is needed to make an informed decision. And even without searching for specific information, more educated people possess greater knowledge about politics—a personal characteristic that is itself positively associated with voting. Also, because more highly educated people are more likely to hold higher-status jobs, which provide more autonomy, they will find getting a few minutes off from work to go to the polls much simpler than an assembly-line worker will.

But it is in the area of voting benefits that educational level probably plays the more important role. Schooling exposes a person to indoctrination regarding the duties of citizenship. Moreover, educated people are apt to read newspaper editorials and magazines promoting the importance of voting and so are more likely to develop an expectation that voting is beneficial. Education also provides people with confidence that their ideas matter; thus, they are likely to obtain satisfaction from the expressive benefits of voting. Numerous studies show a strong relationship between the propensity to vote and a series of attitudes that are associated with high levels of education—such as an interest in politics, feelings of involvement with political affairs (demonstrated by reading about politics in newspapers and news magazines or watching television news), feelings of political efficacy ("what I think and do make a difference"), and partisan attachments.[11] Educated people are more likely to vote because education contributes to holding positive political attitudes, lowers information costs, and promotes symbolic and expressive satisfaction.

Education level, political knowledge and interest, and sense of political efficacy are strongly associated with one another and seem to follow from access to economic advantages.[12] The wealthier one's family, the more likely it is that one will be highly educated. Education leads to higher incomes and better jobs and the capacity to educate one's own children. Along with a good education and high status, one picks up positive attitudes toward politics and a strong interest in following public affairs. A person with such experiences will weigh the costs and benefits of voting differently than will an economically disadvantaged citizen. Consequently, the overall or aggregate impact of individual factors on each individual's propensity to vote is to produce an electorate that is more affluent than the general citizenry. Although the right to vote is equally distributed in the United States, the actual practice of voting is unequal. (Chapter 7 explores the implications of this inequality for our democracy in greater detail.)

In addition to these education-related factors, it is a fact that people become more likely to vote as they grow older. Like many other aspects of life, voting is a habit. Nothing lowers the cost of voting like having done it in the past. As an individual experiences additional elections over time, the probability increases that he or she will take advantage of an opportunity to exercise the franchise. As people age, they also tend to develop more ties to their communities, such as property ownership and children in school, that are conducive to an interest in public affairs. So, over the course of the life cycle, voting participation tends to increase until extreme old age.[13]

Systemic Influences on Citizen Participation

Systemic factors of several kinds—legal, organizational, and cultural—establish the context in which voting takes place and tend to raise the costs of voting for most voters. Whereas many other democracies schedule elections on holidays or require that workers be given time off for voting, American elections almost invariably occur on workdays, so that voters must schedule their visit to the polls around their work obligations. Unlike all other democracies, the United States makes voter registration an individual rather than a governmental responsibility.[14] In other democracies, government bureaucracies are charged with the task of identifying, prior to election time, who is eligible to vote. In many countries, governments issue all residents identity cards that indicate voter eligibility; on Election Day, citizens simply show their identity cards to be admitted to the polling booth. Democracies without identity cards, such as Great Britain and Canada, conduct canvasses before each election to determine voter lists.[15] Thus, unlike the practice in other democracies, the United States makes registration subject to the same individual cost-benefit calculations as are involved in voting.

For years, many political scientists—including me—viewed reducing registration barriers as the magic bullet for increasing voter turnout.[16] Yet, both the federal and state governments have reduced barriers to registration in recent years without producing a clear increase in turnout. Many states have modified registration laws—for example, allowing Election Day registration at polling places—to make registration easier. In 1993, Congress enacted the National Voter Registration Act, or "motor voter" law, aimed at simplifying registration by requiring states to provide opportunities to register to vote by mail and at motor vehicle bureaus and other state offices that citizens regularly visit. Since the passage of motor voter, registration rates have fluctuated from election to election (turning higher in 2008, for example), but there appears to be no clear trend toward higher registration rates, which remain at about two-thirds of the voting-age population.[17] However, the law does seem to have increased the proportion of poor voters registering in those states that have implemented it aggressively. As of now, the overall and long-term impact of simplified registration procedures remains to be seen.

Even with simplified procedures, other aspects of the registration process tend to depress voting participation. Most states require proof of legal residence through presentation of a paycheck, utility bill, or bank statement indicating the address of the person seeking to register. While most people would find it easy to meet this requirement, it bars from registering very poor people who may not have a bank account, paycheck, or even a permanent residence—such as the homeless. In effect, proof of residence constitutes a means test, something most history books claim was abolished with the advent of universal male suffrage in the 1830s, restricting the vote to those with sufficient resources to have a stable place to live.[18] Registration forms also must be filled out correctly, signed, and dated to qualify someone to vote. Many times newly registered voters show up at the polls only to be told they are disqualified because of an error on their registration form.[19] In addition, most states require voters to be registered for a certain period prior to the election, a requirement that discourages people who are especially mobile—such as those who have changed jobs or college students—from voting. College and university towns are notorious for the use of residency requirements to prevent students from voting in local elections.[20]

A disturbing trend in recent years has been organized efforts to actively disenfranchise voters. Routine purges of voters lists, ostensibly aimed at removing from the rolls voters who have relocated or died, are manipulated to eliminate poor and minority voters. An egregious example was the removal from the Florida registration rolls of thousands of African American voters prior to the 2000 election in an ostensible purge of "felons" from the lists. Subsequently, the list of alleged felons used proved to be full of errors including names mainly of law-abiding citizens.[21] Since such purges tend to drop poorer and minority voters, who tend to vote Democratic, Republican state officials, as was the case in Florida, have used the tactic repeatedly for partisan gain.[22] Republican politicians, also, have been at the forefront of another tactic of voter suppression—voter ID requirements. Presently, about twenty-seven states have laws, usually pushed by Republican legislators, requiring voters to present a valid voter ID in order to vote. Supposedly aimed a preventing voter fraud (although little evidence of such fraud exists), the laws actually impose another obstacle for poor, elderly, and minority voters who may not have driver's licenses or other "valid" identification. In Georgia, for example, the law requires voters to pay a substantial fee to obtain an approved voter ID, equivalent, in effect, to a poll tax.[23] After the 2010 election, when Republicans captured control of state governments in many states, they enacted new laws requiring photo IDs and restricting early voting.[24] These developments point to a disturbing trend in a return to the era of poll taxes, literacy tests, and voter harassment aimed at disenfranchising poor and minority citizens.[25]

Another important systemic factor affecting voting participation is the presence of organizations that actively mobilize voters and get them to the polls. Many people vote because someone they respect—a neighbor, a public official, or another member of a group they belong to—asks them to vote. Traditionally, political parties have been important institutions for bringing people to the polls. In European democracies, such party mobilization, particularly on the part of labor and social democratic parties, is a major factor in raising voter turnout overall and especially among lower-SES voters. In the late nineteenth century, American political party organizations were equally effective in mobilizing voters, routinely producing turnouts in the 75 to 85 percent range.[26] Progressive reformers, however, in their zeal to stamp out political party corruption in the early twentieth century, introduced various reforms, such as party primaries and civil service reform, that greatly weakened the organizational strength of political parties and their capacity to mobilize voters. The party organizations declined gradually, at varied rates, throughout the country; as recently as the 1960s, many cities still had well-organized parties that routinely generated high rates of voter participation. Yet the continued spread of Progressive-style reform and new methods of campaigning, such as the use of television and Internet advertising, and the rise of candidate-centered campaigns (matters explored in more detail in the next chapter) have effectively undermined the capacity of political party organizations to mobilize voters.[27] At the same time, other organizations that once mobilized voters, such as labor unions and mass membership organizations, have also declined—a development taken up in the next section.

The improved voter turnout of 2008 proved the value of grassroots mobilization for getting people to the polls. Beginning with the primaries, Barack Obama's campaign devoted significant campaign resources to voter mobilization rather than relying on the methods that have come to dominate modern electioneering, such as TV advertising. His grassroots mobilization efforts clearly had an impact on overall turnout and significantly increased turnout among African Americans and young people.[28] The campaign combined the Internet and electronic forms of communication such as text messaging with traditional voter mobilization tools, such as phone banks and door-to-door canvassing. Obama's success proved also that mobilization works best when tied to a partisan cause that can inspire people.[29] In 2010, partisan mobilization in favor of the Republican Party, thanks to the "Tea Party" movement, helped to drive up turnout somewhat in the midterm elections. The impact proved much smaller than the Obama efforts in 2008, since the older white voters the Tea Party mobilized included many people who were likely to vote anyway.[30] Nevertheless, the small increase in turnout suggested that partisan mobilization from both the left and right can raise overall turnout.

Given what we know about general determinants of voting participation, one might have expected participation to have increased significantly over the past forty years—well beyond the higher turnout of 2008. Potential voters are better educated now, and the Voting Rights Act of 1965 eliminated significant barriers to voting by blacks in the South, among whom turnout has increased. Yet rather than exhibiting a dramatic increase, voter turnout declined over most of this period. Lower turnouts in the 1970s were often attributed to the effect of the Twenty-Sixth Amendment, which lowered the voting age from twenty-one to eighteen in 1972—remember that younger citizens are less apt to vote than older ones—bringing into the electorate the large baby boom generation. But when the trend continued even as boomers reached middle age in the 1990s, political scientists had to search for other explanations.

One systematic study attributes most of the decline in voting to a decline in citizens' confidence in their ability to influence government (political efficacy), less interest in political campaigns, and less political partisanship.[31] All of those factors suggest that voting decline is rooted in people's decreasing sense of connection to the political system. More Americans are choosing not to vote because they do not consider politics to be especially relevant to their lives. Although today's Americans overall are more educated than earlier generations, studies suggest that they actually know less about politics. According to one analysis, the level of political knowledge of the average college graduate today is equivalent to what a high school graduate knew in 1960.[32] The continuing decline in political parties as voter mobilization institutions also contributes to the feelings of disaffection. And as is discussed more fully in the next chapter, citizens' disgust with the increasing triviality of election campaigns turns them away from politics. One careful study has found convincing evidence that negative media coverage of politics has fostered public cynicism that has suppressed participation.[33] Not only is media election coverage more negative, but major news organizations devote much less time to election coverage, contributing to the decline in knowledge and interest among voters.[34] This combination of factors has produced citizens who participate less in the most fundamental act of citizenship, the vote.

The factors that affect voting participation influence other forms of electoral participation as well, except that even fewer citizens engage in those activities than vote. Only about one-third of citizens report discussing elections and trying to persuade others how to vote during presidential election campaigns.[35] Other, more intense activities, such as working in campaigns, attending meetings, and giving money, engage even fewer citizens. As with voting, Americans are participating less in these other types of political behavior.[36] At the same time, the more active forms of participation are even more likely than voting to engage the more affluent. Based on their study of all forms of voluntary political participation in

America, political scientists Sidney Verba, Kay Schlozman, and Henry Brady concluded that "the public's voice is often loud, sometimes clear, but rarely equal."[37]

Signs of Civic Disengagement

As we saw in chapter 3, the studies by Robert Putnam and others of declining American involvement in membership organizations such as bowling leagues reinforce the perception that Americans participate less in public life than they once did. If people are "bowling alone" rather than collectively, in leagues—that is, they are less likely to join with other individuals for civic purposes—then declines in voting and other forms of political participation are just part of a broader trend of civic and social disengagement. Such a development strikes at the heart of how Americans perceive themselves as a civically engaged people. Turning once again to Tocqueville, we find that he describes 1830s America as a place "where they have taken most advantage of association. . . . An obstacle comes up on the public highway, passage is interrupted, traffic stops; neighbors immediately establish themselves in a deliberating body; from this improvised assembly will issue an executive power that will remedy the ill. . . ."[38] Most Americans see themselves as people who will join together to address a need, whether to help a neighbor in distress or to raise funds for a faraway disaster, usually through civic organizations such as the PTA, Kiwanis Clubs, Knights of Columbus, or the Red Cross. Putnam's claim that these very organizations are failing to attract members suggests a dramatic change in a fundamental aspect of American life. At the same time, Putnam documents a change that many Americans sense in their own lives: in their preoccupation with career, family, and individual pursuits, they are finding little time to attend the meetings or to serve as the officers of such civic groups.

Through careful analysis of a wide variety of ways in which people connect to one another, and using a variety of data sources, Putnam found that whereas civic engagement rose steadily in the first two-thirds of the twentieth century, beginning in the 1960s people "began to join less, trust less, give less, vote less, and schmooze less."[39] He documents fewer Americans engaging in a wide variety of social and civic activities, including less political participation, lower church attendance, less support for unions and professional associations, and even fewer informal connections. Along with joining fewer bowling leagues, Americans visited less with friends, talked less with neighbors, made fewer stops at the neighborhood bar or coffee shop, played cards less, and even sat down to family dinners less often.[40] In sum, Putnam paints a picture of an American people who no longer get together for civic and social purposes in the ways that Tocqueville observed in the 1830s, or even as they were doing as recently as the 1960s.

Of all the different ways that people have become disengaged in the past few years, one of the most significant for democracy has been the decline of chapter-based mass membership federations. A wide range of such organizations dotted the social landscape of mid-twentieth-century America; they claimed millions of Americans as their members. Many were largely social, such as the Elks, Kiwanis, Masons, or Odd Fellows, although each of these groups also supported service projects in their communities. Some fraternal organizations, such as the Knights of Columbus (Roman Catholic men) or Hadassah (Jewish women), served particular religious communities. Other chapter-based organizations performed specialized community roles, such as the Parent-Teacher Association (PTA) in a public school district or the League of Women Voters, which provided voter education. Many others were made up of particular population groups, such as veterans (the American Legion and the Veterans of Foreign Wars) or farmers (the Grange and 4-H clubs).

Although these groups were organized for many different purposes, they had certain common characteristics. First, each depended on ordinary members to organize and run local chapters on a volunteer basis. Each elected local chapter officers and formed committees to organize meetings and programs, manage chapter finances, and provide community service. Chapter activities were financed through dues paid by the members. Second, most were connected to other local chapters through federations that mirrored the US federal structure, with state and national organizations.[41] Leadership at the state and national levels usually came from members elected by local chapters or their representatives, although they were sometimes assisted by paid staff, particularly at the national level. National policies typically were set through elaborate consultation with local chapters and ratified at annual national conventions. Finally, although most groups throughout most of the twentieth century recruited members from particular ethnic, religious, or occupational groups, and most were racially segregated, they generally were cross-class organizations—that is, they brought together members from different social, economic, and occupational backgrounds.[42] In fact, in fraternal organizations especially, lower- and working-class members had opportunities to exercise leadership along with their wealthier and higher-status "brothers" or "sisters."

Most of these chapter-based groups still exist, but the percentage of the American population involved in them is much lower than it was forty years ago. Putnam traces the percentage of the relevant population (such as Jewish women for Hadassah) enrolled in each of thirty-two national, chapter-based organizations over the past century. After growing steadily for most of the century, the percentages have declined precipitously since the 1960s. As an example, membership in the PTA—the most common community organization—rose steadily among parents with children in school until 1960, when nearly half of all such parents belonged.[43] That figure represented a doubling of the membership rate in 1945.

But by the 1990s, PTA membership had returned to the 1945 level. In all thirty-two national organizations that Putnam examined, average membership rates dropped from a peak in 1960 to 1990s levels comparable to what they had been in the depths of the Great Depression. Chapter-based organizations ranging from the American Legion and the Federation of American Women's Clubs to the Odd Fellows and the Masons have seen membership declines ranging from 40 to 70 percent since the 1950s.[44] Why are these declines, and civic disengagement generally, a problem for democracy?

First, many citizens have learned important democratic skills and habits through their participation in associations. In the 1940s, the noted historian Arthur Schlesinger Sr. praised associations as providing Americans "their greatest school of self-government. . . . In mastering the associative way they mastered the democratic way."[45] Within an association, members must discuss issues affecting the organization, thereby learning how to speak in public, formulate persuasive arguments, and comply with formal rules of debate, such as those set forth in *Robert's Rules of Order*. Less formally, members gain experience in disagreeing with one another yet resolving conflicts in a civil manner based on mutual respect. Through such experiences, members are likely to improve their capacity to understand different points of view, to find common ground acceptable to most members, and even to accept being on the losing side of an issue while maintaining commitment to the organization. These skills, although developed in debating the mundane concerns of the association—whether determining team matchups in a bowling league or deciding on the site of the annual banquet—are transferable to debating weightier public issues. When citizens enter the broader political arena—at city council meetings, lobbying the state legislature, or as members of Congress—these very skills are needed if democracy is to function smoothly.

Association membership allows, as well, many leadership opportunities that can be transferred to the broader political system. The classic, chapter-based membership association typically needs to fill many positions of responsibility if it is to thrive. As noted earlier, these leadership opportunities are important, especially for lower-status individuals, many of whom have held such positions in the typical chapter-based organization. In a study of the leadership of voluntary associations in the New Haven, Connecticut, area in 1913, Douglas Rae found that "a majority of civic organizations were headed by regular folks [blue-collar and white-collar workers] for whom high office was not the routine expectation of life."[46] For most of the twentieth century, leadership positions in associations often served as stepping-stones toward public office, and most politicians proudly listed membership in the Elks, Masons, Grange, or Knights of Columbus on their political résumés. Their backgrounds in these associations also indicated that political leaders, whether city councilors, state legislators, members of Congress, or presidents, interacted regularly with ordinary citizens at the local lodge.

Second, associations have taken on public tasks and responsibilities that improve the broader community, reducing the burden on government and supplementing governmental capacity to meet public needs. Organizing food drives for the needy, raising money for college scholarships, or mentoring local schoolchildren are types of volunteer service that many associations provided. Very often, chapter-based organizations would pool resources of their members to build and maintain public facilities such as orphanages, libraries, or schools. Most associations typically made their meeting halls available for public events such as concerts, meetings, or lectures.[47]

And finally, associations have been significant arenas through which citizens have been mobilized around important public issues. Most associations went to great lengths to emphasize their nonpartisan character, but that did not mean that they avoided political participation. In fact, organizing discussions of important public issues, whether local or national, was a key activity for many associations. Association meetings often featured speakers from within or from outside the community on topical public policy issues. Some groups made member discussion of public issues a regular feature of their meetings. For example, among the topics discussed at the biweekly meetings of the Women's Progressive Study Club of Henry, South Dakota, in 1916 were "Needful Legislation for Married Women," "Our National Defenses Today," and "America's Policy in Regard to Contraband Goods."[48] Members of the Providence Chapter of the League of Women Voters in the 1950s monitored every meeting of the Providence City Council, providing summary reports to chapter members at their regular meetings. Members then typically went on to discuss national issues such as civil rights legislation or America's role in the United Nations.[49] For many Americans during the first two-thirds of the twentieth century, membership in such associations provided a political education and access to political information that was useful to them as citizens.

Often associations played a more direct role in promoting national public policy. Because most chapter-based organizations were structured as federations, with connections among chapters throughout the country, they were excellent vehicles for organizing on behalf of a policy in every congressional district. Because of their broad-based membership, associations brought nonelite opinions to policy debates on important public issues—which proved to be crucial, for example, to the enactment of the GI Bill after World War II.[50] Initial discussions within the Franklin Roosevelt administration and in Congress envisioned much more modest support for demobilized servicemen than was eventually enacted. Many college and university presidents opposed providing returning GIs with a higher education benefit, fearing that their institutions would be swamped with "unqualified" students. To counter these elitist views, the American Legion mobilized its members throughout the country to demand generous benefits, including support for higher education for every returning vet, unemployment benefits for up to a year after demobilization, and VA loans for home purchases. The legislation that resulted had a profound effect on American life, as millions of returning GIs took advantage of the education and housing loan benefits to lift themselves into the middle class. Along with benefiting many individual Americans and their families, the GI Bill is credited with helping to fuel American prosperity over the next two decades. Without the involvement of the American Legion, the bill would not have been as generous or helpful to ordinary Americans, nor would it have benefited the country as it did.

Civic disengagement, then, especially the decline of chapter-based membership organizations in recent decades, means "diminished democracy." Without involvement in civic associations, Americans will have less opportunity to acquire the skills needed for effective citizenship; many important public tasks in their communities will not be accomplished; and public policies will be enacted without broad-based and nonelite input. Before we take a look at the arguments of scholars who question whether civic disengagement is in fact widespread in America, we need to ask what explains the civic disengagement of recent years.

As shown in Figure 4.2, Putnam guesses that about half of the decline in civic engagement is due to the passing of the civic torch from the generation of

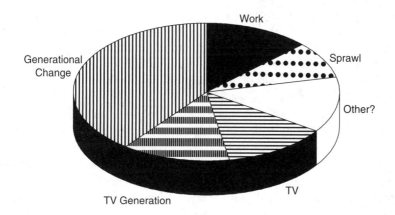

FIGURE 4.2   Guesstimated Explanation for Civic Disengagement, 1965–2000

Source: Robert Putnam, *Bowling Alone: The Collapse and Revival of American Community* (New York: Simon & Schuster, 2000), 284.

Americans who came of age during the Great Depression and World War II to younger generations.[51] From coping with those traumatic experiences, this "greatest generation" seemed to acquire habits that raised rates of civic participation to their peak in the 1950s and early 1960s. Younger generations simply have not shown comparable commitment to civic involvement, so overall participation rates have declined. In addition to the generational factor, Putnam traces reduced civic engagement to a variety of social trends that limit the time available to people for social interaction. They include the advent of new forms of electronic entertainment, such as television and computers, which are typically experienced alone and have reduced engagement by both the older and younger generations (represented as the "TV Generation" in the figure), as well as the longer working hours necessitated by stagnant wages and suburban sprawl, which requires more time commuting and separates people from one another. Finally, part of the "Other" in Putnam's guesstimated explanation is surely a shift in public attitudes away from patriotism and commitment to community and toward more concern for individual wealth and self-fulfillment.

The New Citizen Activism

Not all social scientists agree with Putnam and the other scholars who perceive widespread civic disengagement. Those who worry about Americans "bowling alone," they say, focus too much on the ways Americans got together in the past and ignore the new ways citizens are engaging in civic affairs. The Putnam critics see new forms of activism, advocacy, and social interaction replacing the chapter-based organizations of the past. Some regard these new forms of civic engagement as an improvement over those of the past; others see them as promoting excessive citizen mobilization that itself may endanger democracy. Examining the very post-1960s period that Putnam presents as one of civic decline, his critics point to five countertrends suggesting that the period may have been one of change, rather than decline, in civic engagement.

The first trend is the explosion of citizen advocacy groups that have become such important players in national politics. A look at the growth in the number of voluntary associations since about 1960 suggests not massive civic disengagement in America but hyperparticipation, as the number of civic organizations listed in the *Encyclopedia of Associations* quadrupled from just under 6,000 groups in 1959 to nearly 24,000 by the mid-1990s.[52] Many of these groups can be called "citizen" or "public interest" or "advocacy" groups because they organize citizens to promote positions on particular public policy issues. Although some of the groups—such as the Sierra Club—are quite old, many others—among them, Common Cause, the Children's Defense Fund, the Concord Coalition, and the Environmental Defense Fund—were created during that period of group proliferation. To some extent, the rise in citizen activism is a legacy of the protest movements of the 1960s, which included the civil rights and antiwar movements. Experiences with those movements provided Americans with models for mobilizing ordinary individuals to influence political events. Although most of us associate the citizen mobilizations of the 1960s with liberal causes, their spirit and tactics have inspired conservative activism as well, for example, the Right-to-Life movement, which consciously models itself on the civil rights movement.

Organizationally, citizen advocacy groups look quite different from chapter-based federations. The typical structure of citizen groups comprises a paid national staff, funding from a mixture of membership dues and grants from foundations and wealthy individuals, and sometimes a mass membership base. The size of the membership base varies widely, from groups with millions of members nationwide, such as the American Association of Retired Persons (AARP), to others that have no individual dues paying members at all, such as Families USA or the National Consumers League. One study found average membership to be about 10,000.[53] Most of those with mass memberships have seen their numbers grow significantly since the 1960s. Membership in environmental groups has grown especially, with leading groups experiencing five- to tenfold membership increases since 1970.[54] Although some citizen groups have local chapters, most national organizations connect directly with individual members through mailings, e-mail, social media, and publications. The main focus of citizen group activity is lobbying on national public policy issues of concern to the group.

Second, citizens have been coming together locally in nonprofit organizations, through volunteering and in self-help groups, to serve each other and their communities. One recent study estimated the number of nonprofit organizations in the United States today, including educational, health, cultural, religious, and social service organizations, at about 1.2 million, about one-third of which are churches or other religious congregations.[55] The number of nonprofits providing education and health and social services grew substantially beginning in the 1960s, as federal, state, and local governments increased spending in these areas and used nonprofit organizations to implement programs. This growth leveled off and then began to decline in the 1980s, as government social services spending was reduced under the Reagan administration. So whereas the nonprofit sector has expanded since the 1960s, it has faced growing challenges in recent years, as government spending has decreased and more private, profit-making organizations have competed to provide social services.[56]

To provide social services, nonprofits recruit large numbers of individual volunteers who are managed and coordinated by a small number of paid staff members. This is a very different pattern of volunteerism than existed when fraternal organization members both organized and delivered social services, but it does succeed in generating many volunteer opportunities. The number of individuals volunteering in one-to-one direct service has risen steadily since the 1970s, with senior citizens providing the bulk of the increase.[57] Young people under twenty-five also have increased their rate of volunteering—in striking contrast to the decline in political participation among this age cohort. The rising numbers of youth volunteers include college students participating in campus-based community service and service learning. More Americans also seem to be participating in a broad spectrum of small groups, mostly self-help support groups formed to address various addictions, mental illness, and other personal problems.[58]

Third, citizens are participating more through institutions of direct democracy, such as the initiative and referendum. During the Progressive Era, at the beginning of the twentieth century, some states began enacting constitutional procedures permitting citizens to initiate proposals for new laws through circulating petitions and then voting directly in elections to enact the proposals. At present, about half the states permit the initiative and referendum.[59] This form of direct democracy allows citizens to bypass their elected legislators and seize for themselves the right to pass laws. Citizen use of the initiative and referendum is more common today than it was even a few years ago; it is now typical for more than two hundred referenda to appear on ballots throughout the United States in an election year.[60] Referenda take in a range of political concerns, from seat belt laws to prayer in schools to property tax and term limits. Both liberals and conservatives have used the referendum to enact measures of interest to them. The picture of citizen apathy that appears when we look at voter turnout statistics is at odds with the willingness of some citizens to be more active than ever in asserting their rights to direct democracy.

Fourth, a "backyard revolution" of local activist groups has grown to mobilize people to address local and neighborhood issues, such as preventing crime, improving schools, protecting consumer rights, and forcing toxic waste cleanup.[61] Sometimes these efforts lead to the formation of permanent organizations in which ordinary citizens participate to produce far-ranging changes in their communities. One such organization is Communities Organized for Public Service (COPS) in San Antonio, Texas. Formed in 1974 by community organizer Ernie Cortes in San Antonio's Mexican American barrios, COPS brought together citizen leaders from church parishes, PTAs, Boy Scout and Girl Scout groups, and women's clubs to find ways to influence local government.[62] Cortes had been trained in the tradition of the Industrial Areas Foundation (IAF), founded in Chicago in the 1930s by the famous community organizer Saul Alinsky. Adapting the Alinsky organizing methods to the conditions Cortes found in San Antonio, COPS concentrated initially on such mundane but important neighborhood issues as pressuring the local government to pave streets and install streetlights in the poor neighborhoods of San Antonio's west side. Soon, however, the organization's clout was deployed in behalf of broader issues. By the early 1980s, the citizen activists had changed the city charter to permit more adequate representation of all citizens, elected a majority on the city council (formerly dominated by local business interests), and elected San Antonio's first Mexican American mayor.[63] By the 1990s, IAF organizations had been established throughout the country, producing a nationwide network linking grassroots organizations with colorful acronyms: CAP in Chicago, UNO in Los Angeles, OCO in Oakland, and BUILD in Baltimore.[64]

And finally, the Internet has given rise to a world of new connections among people, producing novel forms of political participation. As an instrument of political campaigns, the Internet came of age during the 2004 presidential campaign, when by one estimate about 75 million Americans went online for political purposes: e-mailing, blogging, giving money, gathering political news, or accessing candidates' websites.[65] Prior to the campaign, certain issue advocacy groups, such as MoveOn.org, had developed techniques for mobilizing supporters and raising money online. Electronic participation exploded in 2008, largely through Obama's effective use of new social media and technologies to support his campaign. Since then, politicians of all stripes have made use of social media, such as Facebook, to communicate with their followers and mobilize them for political events. Sarah Palin, for example, used Facebook routinely to communicate her reactions to political events, making comments that often were picked up and disseminated widely through the mainstream media. Independent of the campaign, more Americans than ever before accessed blogs and politically oriented sites such as Politico and RealClearPolitics for campaign information. Internet organizing has also become a standard tool for political protest, one used first and most effectively by antiglobalization activists.[66] Both the Tea Party on the right and the Occupy Wall Street movement on the left have made use of the new social media central to how they mobilize their supporters. According to some Internet observers, people are forming virtual communities, a new form of association that brings together people committed to particular issues and also accommodates debates among people holding different points of view.[67]

Participation as a Challenge to Democracy

What sort of challenge does this rather contradictory picture of citizen participation in the United States pose for our democracy? Do Americans participate too much or too little for the good of democracy? Have citizens become disengaged from civic life, as Putnam and others argue, or have new forms of citizen activism mobilized Americans as never before? Some observers charge that the new citizen activism poses a real threat to democracy in undermining representative institutions and placing too much pressure on democratic processes. Others lament that the new citizen activism, while laudable in some respects, has not really made up for the broader trends of civic disengagement that remain the true challenge to our democracy.

A number of commentators on recent US political history have expressed concern that pressures from an active citizenry prevent elected government officials from making the "hard choices" and "imposing the necessary medicine" to solve our problems. A Harvard University political scientist, Samuel Huntington,

The Occupy Wall Street movement made extensive use of social media to organize their protests in the fall of 2011, including this media area in their encampment in New York City's Zuccotti Park.

AP Photo/John Minchillo.

made such an argument in a now-famous essay that was published in a report of the Trilateral Commission in 1975.[68] According to Huntington, the "democratic surge" of participation that began in the 1960s was threatening the "governability of democracy" in the United States. Protest demonstrations, social movements, and the rise of citizen advocacy groups were generating adverse consequences for stable democratic politics. Politicians were forced to respond to this citizen participation by increasing the scale of government activities, leading especially to higher levels of expenditure for social programs. At the same time, increased participation constituted a challenge to government authority, preventing politicians from imposing the hard decisions necessary to make government effective in solving problems. Huntington feared that this "democratic distemper" prevented the country from addressing such difficult issues as growing deficits or imposing sacrifices such as a military draft or higher taxes in wartime. Government was thus "overloaded" with democratic demands from all sides, leaving it no capacity to formulate effective policy to address domestic and foreign policy challenges. The only solution, said Huntington, was "a greater degree of moderation in democracy."[69]

As the first section of this chapter shows, Huntington's analysis is grounded in the Protective/Pluralist orientation to democracy, which warns that citizens participating too actively in making demands on their representatives will inter-fere with effective elite policy making. Echoing Madison's belief, overload theo-rists expect representatives, not the public at large, to be the guardians of the public good. If one believes that responsibility for the public good lies with elected elites rather than with the people, keeping the people away from too direct an involvement in policy making becomes, ironically, a requisite for healthy democracy.[70] When popular pressures are too great, representatives are unable to forge the compromises needed for the public good.

Thirty years after Huntington first formulated the overload thesis, many political observers continue to see too much pressure from citizen groups as a source of policy gridlock. The journalist Jonathan Rauch describes a malady he calls "demosclerosis," whereby elected representatives are constrained from ever eliminating a government program yet, at the same time, are pressed to cut taxes.[71] A "hyperpluralism" of citizen groups prevents elected officials from addressing real problems such as the future of Social Security and Medicare. *Newsweek* columnist Fareed Zakaria describes America as caught up in an unrea-soned populism, which leaves Congress surrounded by and beholden to lobbyists representing various activist groups and encourages the citizens of California to pass referenda both limiting taxation and mandating government spending—and then to blame the governor and state legislature for not balancing the budget![72] Like Huntington, these authors favor less participation to free representative elites to govern effectively.

In contrast, for theorists of civic disengagement, the problem with the "new citizen activism" is not that it overloads elected officials but that it is largely illusory. Rather than involving millions of Americans in civic affairs at the grassroots as chapter-based mass membership federations once did, the new citi-zen advocacy groups are vehicles for paid professional activists with letterheads and mass mailing lists.[73] The new groups are incapable of fulfilling the demo-cratic functions of chapter-based associations, in which group members them-selves managed group activities and held leadership posts. The typical member in a contemporary activist group needs to devote little time or effort to its activities, other than responding to funding solicitations or reading the group's literature. Nor do these groups provide the face-to-face interaction that nurtures the civic skills and "social capital" celebrated by Tocqueville and Putnam. Although the minimal membership commitment that they demand may fit bet-ter with contemporary lifestyles, these citizen advocacy groups fail to provide the kind of participatory experience of chapter-based federations. Likewise, most of the increased volunteerism in America today is conducted under the auspices of professionally led nonprofit organizations rather than initiated by the volunteers themselves. Individual volunteer efforts tend to be one-shot, direct service activities, such as serving in a soup kitchen or a mentoring program under the supervision of paid staff. The new civic America, as political scientist Theda

Skocpol points out, has replaced *membership*—"representatively governed, nation-spanning volunteer membership federations"—with *management*— "professionally managed advocacy groups."[74]

In the new civic America, where the bulk of the citizenry remains civically disengaged, those who are involved with activist groups tend to be much more affluent than most Americans.[75] Also, as stated in the earlier cost-benefit analysis of voting behavior, affluent citizens are better able to pay the costs of participation than are the less affluent. Despite the inclusion of "backyard" groups of poorer people, what citizen activism does exist is skewed even more in the direction of the highly educated and affluent than are less costly forms of participation, such as voting.[76] Not surprisingly, national citizen advocacy organizations tend to focus on issues of concern to more affluent Americans—including "postmaterial" causes such as protecting the environment or expanding individual rights, matters of lifestyle and identity, and such social controversies as abortion—rather than on the bread-and-butter concerns of the less affluent, such as stagnant wages, the declining minimum wage, union busting, and the general rise in economic inequality in the country. As the mass membership organizations, usually labor unions, that once raised such issues have declined—in the 1950s about 35 percent of workers belonged to a union, whereas today only 8 percent do—no citizen group has taken their place. Furthermore, the cross-class contact that was typical of many chapter-based fraternal organizations no longer brings elites into regular social contact with the less affluent. The new civic America is increasingly well-to-do.

Moreover, what appear to be citizen groups representing ordinary Americans are often fronts for elite special interests. As is discussed in chapter 6, some powerful, well-funded elite groups, particularly business corporations, have developed sophisticated techniques to use both direct democracy and the appearance of genuine citizen activism on behalf of their special interest goals. In states where referenda are common, such as California, corporate interests routinely hire professional signature gatherers to place initiatives on the ballot and then fund advertising campaigns to pass them. For example, the cigarette company Philip Morris funded a campaign a few years ago to pass what appeared to be an antismoking initiative, but whose small-print provisions actually weakened the state's existing antismoking legislation.[77] Similarly, citizens who attempt to use referenda as a tool to regulate corporate interests must be prepared to counter expensive opposition advertising. Rather than empowering ordinary citizens as the Progressives hoped, the referendum, in an era of sophisticated mass media communication, has become instead a tool for wealthy special interests.

Finally, although both the "backyard revolution" of groups such as COPS and the innovative use of Internet technology have the potential for mobilizing more citizen participation, so far they have fallen far short of countering mass civic disengagement. The backyard revolution still affects only a small number of cities and has had little impact on the broader political system. Even as it has achieved key neighborhood improvements in some Texas cities, COPS and its sister organizations have had little impact on Texas state politics, which conservative business interests still dominate. And whereas the Internet can be used for political mobilization and creating community among diverse people, so far most people tend to go online for individual entertainment rather than communal activities.[78] Even when people chat and blog, they tend to interact with others much like themselves rather than engaging in dialogue with people of differing views. Many social scientists still fear that the Internet may actually be increasing the segmentation and radical individualism of its users rather than connecting them in virtual communities.

Civic disengagement, combined with the rise of new-style national activist groups, coincides with a conservative shift in American politics. Beginning in the late 1970s, federal policymakers have been altering government policy in favor of business interests and more affluent Americans. Deregulation of business, a less-progressive tax code, anti-union labor policies, and cutbacks in social programs for the poor have been the staples of US public policy making for many years now.[79] President Clinton's remark that the "era of big government is over" signaled an admission that both major parties endorsed these policy trends. Of course, ending big government came at the expense of the less affluent, while middle-class but expensive programs, such as Medicare and Social Security, and business subsidies have remained largely untouched. Since the late 1970s, government seems to have been quite capable of imposing hard decisions on poor and working-class Americans, while the more affluent have benefited greatly from government programs.[80]

For some observers, this conservative policy shift was possible only because of widespread civic disengagement and the underrepresentation of workers and the poor among the electorate and the politically active. Richard Cloward and Frances Fox Piven, for example, point to the lack of support in public opinion for most of the conservative agenda.[81] Politicians can safely ignore poor and working-class citizens when enacting policies because they know that these segments of the population are not among the politically active. At the same time, activist groups promoting policies favorable to the very rich, such as massive tax cuts and elimination of the estate tax, gain in influence.[82] Successful campaigns to increase broad social benefits, such as health insurance or higher wages, that were supported by the labor movement in the past, or mass support for a new social benefit, such as the American Legion provided for the GI Bill, is inconceivable given the current level of civic disengagement. Without political party mobilization of working-class and lower-income citizens—like that provided by labor and social democratic parties in Europe—more generous social welfare policies cannot be enacted.[83] Interestingly, the citizens who do not participate politically in the United States have precisely the social and economic characteristics as those who support left-wing European parties. More political participation by, and better representation of, low-income Americans would provide political support for such social programs as universal health insurance, which public opinion polls show a majority of Americans favor and which has existed for years in all other industrial democracies.[84] The long-term conservative bias of American public policy is a reflection of the strongly skewed class bias of contemporary civic engagement. Reversal of the conservative bias of the past few decades and a revitalized American liberalism requires sustained attention to mobilizing citizens on behalf of such a shift. History shows that civic engagement and progressive change go hand in hand.

Declining civic engagement, especially active involvement in chapter-based associations, has meant fewer real deliberative opportunities for citizens. Deliberation involves discussing public issues, listening to alternative points of view, arguing one's position, and through this process forming a consensus, or at least a majority outlook, on what is good for the community. For most Americans today, political participation usually consists of an isolated individual act that is largely disconnected from interaction with others, particularly those who might think differently about issues. The lack of opportunities for deliberation in the election of representatives is duplicated in other forms of participation: voting on referenda, supporting interest or advocacy groups, and even responding to public opinion polls. Polling expert Daniel Yankelovich calls this deliberative shortfall the "missing concept" in American democracy.[85] Deliberation on public issues has ceased to be part of the citizen's role; only experts and elites—elected officials or professional advocates—participate in shaping actual policy decisions. Without appropriate deliberative institutions, citizen opinion on issues becomes an aggregation of individual snap judgments without the thoughtfulness, weighing of alternatives, and genuine engagement with an issue that democracy requires.[86] This explains why public opinion polls reveal seeming contradictions, such as overwhelming support for expenditures for public services along with overwhelming opposition to the taxes needed to pay for them. As long as citizens are not actively engaged with public issues, they do not have to face the trade-offs necessary to cope with them.

At the same time, governing elites exploit contradictions in public opinion on behalf of their own policy agendas. Missing in American democracy are civic institutions through which citizens can deliberate on public issues and form considered judgments. Without them, elites will disregard public preferences when actually formulating policy, even while selectively using public opinion to legitimize their own agenda. This missing concept in American democracy leads to the growing alienation of many Americans from the political system. The feeling that political decisions are made without regard for the concerns of ordinary people is common in the United States today, and many citizens link it to the absence of mechanisms for deliberating on public issues.

Americans' frustration with the absence of meaningful structures for deliberation and participation was the central finding of a Kettering Foundation study
conducted in the early 1990s.[87] Far from being apathetic, the Kettering study
participants were anxious to participate in a constructive way in public life, but
to their chagrin, they felt "pushed out" of a political process dominated by politicians and special interest lobbyists. Sound bites and negative attacks were perceived as dominating public discourse.[88] Most important, debate on public issues
did not address citizens' actual policy concerns because there was little or no
opportunity for citizen involvement. As one participant said, "I'm never aware of
an opportunity to go somewhere and express my opinion and have someone hear
what I have to say."[89] Ordinary citizens seem to share the democratic theorists'
concern that our democracy does not offer structures for citizen deliberation and
involvement in public decisions.

Participants in the Kettering study would surely find the preoccupation of
Huntington, Rauch, and Zakaria with participatory overload in American politics
bizarre. Instead of feeling involved in pressuring elected representatives, the
Kettering respondents perceived representatives as remote figures imposing
choices over which the ordinary citizen had no control. Analysts who emphasize
the class bias of voting participation would also take issue with overload theorists.
To what extent, they would ask, are the pressures on representatives and policy
gridlock really the consequence of democratic pressures? Perhaps the problems
that overload theorists are concerned about, particularly the failure of elected
elites to address problems effectively, are a consequence of the overactive factions
of the privileged few who have ready access to policymakers.

I believe that overload theorists fail to make a sound case that our contemporary policy problems stem from an excess of democratic participation. First,
they do not show that policy failures, such as the inability to reduce government
debt or ensure the financial health of Social Security, are caused by popular
pressure rather than by the demands of privileged elites. In fact, the tax cuts and
increases in military spending that are largely responsible for massive deficits
result from the demands of business interests and conservative ideologues, not
the public.[90] Congressional gridlock over debt reduction or reviving the economy stems from the ability of elites, such as wealthy hedge fund managers who
do not want their taxes increased, to block compromise solutions. Such failures
to address pressing public problems seem the result less of democratic overload
than of the influence of the privileged. Second, over the past decade, policymakers have been able to make the hard choices and impose sacrifices that the
overload theorists thought impossible—but only in regard to programs that
benefit the poor and the working class. Social welfare cutbacks and economic
policies have diminished the standard of living of less affluent Americans while
enormously benefiting the rich (see chapter 7). Instead of being constrained by
participatory pressures, elected elites have felt free in recent years to impose

sacrifice on those segments of the population that are unable to participate effectively on their own behalf.

Finally, the overload theorists, in my opinion, only partially accept the democratic ideal; their outlook has more in common with that of authoritarian critics of democracy than with the mainstream of democratic theorists. Their focus on the need to limit popular interference with elite decision making assigns ordinary citizens too limited a role. Like authoritarian critics of democracy, overload theorists distrust the majority of citizens; they want them to participate only in legitimizing elite decisions, not in forming those decisions. Even in a representative democracy, this is too restricted a role for citizens. A core value of democracy is the equal capacity of all people to govern themselves. As the Kettering study participants understand better than the overload theorists, the future health of our democracy lies not in keeping citizens out of governmental decision making but in finding practical mechanisms for improving their ability to participate.

Meeting the Challenge: More Participation, Not Less

A first step in organizing more effective citizen participation in our democracy must be to reduce the strong class bias in participation. Reform of the one mode of participating most easily available to all people—voting—is surely the place to begin. Students who sense that a little over 50 percent participation in presidential elections cannot be good for democracy are correct. Because nonvoters and voters are different, a restricted electorate cannot reflect the range of preferences and concerns needed in a democracy. Reduction of the barriers to voting, such as further simplifying registration procedures or holding elections on work holidays, are needed to make elections more representative. States also must do more to facilitate ballot access, educate voters, and introduce modern vote-counting machinery. The controversy over counting votes in Florida after the 2000 election revealed the consequences of antiquated and inaccurate voting machines, but sadly, Florida's problematic voting rules and machines are not exceptional. Unfortunately, despite passage of the 2002 Help America Vote Act, which provided grants to states to update voting procedures, problems with election administration and faulty voting machines bedeviled the 2008 election.[91] Although many states have sought to increase participation through "convenience voting"—mail-in ballots, early voting, and unlimited absentee voting—none of these seems to be effective in increasing participation.[92] Simply opening up more voting sites and training poll workers better to speed the voting process and reduce long lines on Election Day would be more effective in increasing turnout.

Second, this chapter describes the emergence of grassroots citizen organizations inspired by the IAF, such as the COPS program in San Antonio and BUILD in Baltimore. These organizations are based on a premise that was familiar to such political theorists as Tocqueville and John Stuart Mill: People learn to be democratic citizens through involvement in solving local problems together. We should build on this "backyard revolution," as political theorist Benjamin Barber advocates, by institutionalizing these grassroots movements in a system of neighborhood assemblies.[93] Such assemblies would serve neighborhoods from 1,000 to 5,000 people and would be both arenas for collective action on local problems and places for deliberation about local and national political issues. No longer dependent on petitioning sometimes-remote representatives, every citizen, according to Barber's vision, could go directly to his or her neighborhood assembly to voice concerns and to work with neighbors to lobby legislatures or city councils for neighborhood needs. Although Barber envisions these assemblies initially as arenas for discussion, deliberation, and lobbying of existing representative bodies, he foresees that they could evolve into institutions with decision-making authority of their own on neighborhood matters. Like the New England town meeting, the Athenian Assembly, or the chapter meetings of a fraternal association, neighborhood assemblies could be places where direct democracy would be integrated as a component of representative democracy.

A comprehensive system of neighborhood assemblies is far from a reality throughout the United States, but similar systems are germinating in many cities. In places as diverse as Birmingham, Portland (Oregon), Dayton, and St. Paul, structures of neighborhood organizations linked to city governing bodies have taken on a powerful role in affecting municipal decisions and promoting citizen participation.[94] None of these experiments precisely fits Barber's model of citizen neighborhood assemblies, but all involve mechanisms that empower neighborhood residents and increase citizen efficacy. In Portland, for example, autonomous neighborhood associations encompassing the entire city are linked by seven District Coalition Boards.[95] Each board has its own budget and staff and works with the neighborhood groups to address local needs, organize crime prevention teams, undertake neighborhood-based planning, and organize discussion of city-wide issues. A major study of structures of neighborhood democracy in five cities, including Portland, found them to be successful in empowering citizens, increasing their sense of efficacy, and affecting municipal decision making.[96] Just as the Developmental and Participatory models predict, citizen participation in governance itself has created, in these cities, a more democratically capable and less-apathetic citizenry. The spread of such urban experiments to other cities would be an important step toward reducing American democracy's peril.

A third step toward enhancing the quality of political participation would be employing the Internet revolution to create more political connections among people and so build social capital. Twitter, Facebook, and other social media sites are being used in the United States and abroad to connect people for political purposes. Observers of the multiple revolts in the Middle East, particularly in

Egypt, in 2011 noted the way activists employed social media to organize protest. In the United States, Scott Heiferman created Meetup.com after reading *Bowling Alone* and in the wake of the 9/11 terrorist attacks as a conscious effort to replace the chapter-based associations of old.[97] At the site, one can join groups involved in a wide variety of activities ranging from reading and knitting circles to religious discussion. Through the Internet, individuals connect with others with similar interests, exchange ideas in blogs, and most important, schedule meetings at community sites. Thus, joining a group goes beyond interacting in cyberspace; the point is to arrange face-to-face meetings in a community to discuss issues or engage in activities centering on the group's shared interests. According to its website, Meetup.com currently has more than 100,000 clubs with 4.7 million members, involving an average of 80,000 monthly meetings. Among the options offered are more than 8,000 explicitly political groups representing all varieties of political opinion. Interestingly, political candidates in 2004 and 2008 found the "meetup" idea an effective way of advancing their candidacies and mobilizing supporters. Meetup groups of both Tea Party and Occupy movement supporters now exist in hundreds of cities across the country.[98] At Meetup.com and similar sites, such as Facebook, the Internet is the means to connect people, but the end is the formation of interpersonal relationships like those fostered in the chapter-based associations of the past.

The Kettering Foundation has also developed a method of bringing people together in face-to-face discussions of public issues.[99] The Kettering National Issues Forums link about 3,000 civic and educational groups in the discussion of important public issues. Each local group is provided with well-prepared issue booklets containing background information and alternative solutions to a given public policy problem. After studying the issue booklets, group members get together to discuss what solution to adopt. An interesting feature of this process is the use of pre- and postforum ballots on the issue under discussion, gauging how deliberation forms and alters a group's outlook on the issue. The foundation collates the results of the forums and distributes them to public officials. Kettering provides National Issues Forums guides on more than twenty issues, among them health care reform, abortion, the federal budget, and terrorism. (Information about how to set up or participate in a National Issues Forum can be obtained at the NIF website, www.nifi.org.) Such forums are an example of how citizens can be brought into democratic deliberation. Structuring similar opportunities for more citizens and integrating them into our formal governmental institutions would be a major step toward reducing democracy's peril.

The underlying theme of this chapter has been the need for a democratic system that does more than merely guarantee its citizens the right to participate. In the past two hundred years, providing this right to all has been a serious challenge to our democracy—only in the past century, for example, did women and black Americans win participation rights. Over the past few decades, such laws as the 1965 Voting Rights Act, when properly implemented, have helped to ensure participation rights. While remaining vigilant about protecting the right to participate, partisans of democracy now need to shift their attention to creating structures for making the participation of all effective in determining government policy. Until we find ways to encourage all citizens to be active participants in deliberating and controlling the decisions that affect their lives, democracy in the United States will remain incomplete.

Thought Questions

1. If, as this chapter shows, nonvoters are less educated, less interested in public affairs, and less knowledgeable about politics than actual voters, would increased participation necessarily enhance the quality of American democracy?

2. The chapter's conclusion describes how Meetup.com attempts to replace the role chapter-based federations once played in our democracy. Do you think this is likely? Can you think of other ways that the goals of learning democratic skills, recruiting democratic leaders, and mobilizing ordinary citizens around public issues might be accomplished?

3. Political parties play an important role in mobilizing voter participation in other democracies and once did so in the United States. Do you think public policies to encourage political parties to play this role again are desirable? Or do you think nonpartisan organizations are more appropriate settings for encouraging citizen participation?

4. Would you favor, as this chapter implies, the government assuming responsibility for automatically registering all eligible voters, as occurs in some other democracies? Should other measures to simplify ballot access, such as voting on holidays, be adopted?

5. As we saw in the introduction to this book, the Pluralist model sees nonparticipation as potentially positive and even as indicative of citizen satisfaction and contentment with the political process. Based on what you learned in this chapter, what do you think of this argument?

Suggestions for Further Reading

*Berry, Jeffrey M. *The New Liberalism: The Rising Power of Citizen Groups.* Washington, DC: Brookings Institution Press, 1999. A thorough study of the rising influence of citizen advocacy groups in American politics described in largely positive terms.

Broder, David S. *Democracy Derailed: Initiative Campaigns and the Power of Money.* Orlando, FL: Harcourt, 2000. The dean of American journalists condemns the initiative and referendum for undermining representative democracy.

Conway, M. Margaret. *Political Participation in the United States.* 3rd ed. Washington, DC: CQ Press, 2000. A leading textbook that reviews the existing political science literature on why and how citizens participate in politics.

*Crozier, Michel, et al. *The Crisis of Democracy.* New York: New York University Press, 1975. A publication of the Trilateral Commission that articulates the thesis of participatory "overload."

Dalton, Russell J. *The Good Citizen: How a Younger Generation Is Reshaping American Politics.* Washington, DC: CQ Press, 2009. Charts how young Americans are creating new norms of citizenship and engagement, including evidence from the 2008 election.

Macedo, Stephen, et al. *Democracy at Risk: Toward a Political Science of Citizenship.* Washington, DC: Brookings Institution Press, 2005. Report of an American Political Science Association task force on declining civic engagement and what to do about it.

Putnam, Robert C. *Bowling Alone: The Collapse and Revival of American Community.* New York: Simon & Schuster, 2000. The classic study of civic disengagement in America.

Rimmerman, Craig A. *The New Citizenship: Unconventional Politics, Activism, and Service.* 3rd ed. Boulder, CO: Westview Press, 2005. A review of the varieties of new citizen activism of the past two decades and an analysis of its implications for American democracy.

Scher, Richard K. *The Politics of Disenfranchisement: Why Is It So Hard to Vote in America?* Armonk, NY: M. E. Sharpe, 2011. A thorough review of the legal and procedural obstacles to voting participation.

Skocpol, Theda. *Diminished Democracy: From Membership to Management in American Civic Life.* Tulsa: University of Oklahoma Press, 2003. Like Putnam, Skocpol documents the decline in associational life in America, with special attention to the history of national, chapter-based federations.

Verba, Sidney, Kay Lehman Schlozman, and Henry E. Brady. *Voice and Equality: Civic Voluntarism in American Politics.* Cambridge, MA: Harvard University Press, 1995. A detailed study based on an extensive survey of Americans about their political participation, documenting the extent to which political participation is skewed on behalf of more affluent Americans. But it also confirms Tocqueville's insight that involvement in associations, particularly churches, teaches citizens crucial civic skills.

Warren, Mark R. *Dry Bones Rattling: Community Building to Revitalize American Democracy.* Princeton, NJ: Princeton University Press, 2001. A detailed study of the successes and failures of IAF community organizations in Texas and elsewhere.

* Presents a point of view that disagrees with the arguments presented in this chapter.

Selected Websites

www.idea.int/vt. The International Institute for Democracy and Electoral Assistance provides detailed information about electoral participation around the world, including the latest turnout statistics.

www.kettering.org. An organization that seeks novel ways to involve citizens in political life.

www.meetup.com. The site of an intriguing effort to promote association building.

www.rockthevote.com. The MTV-inspired organization that seeks to involve young people in politics.

CHAPTER 5

The Fifth Challenge: Elections Without the People's Voice

The key to democracy is a system of government by discussion. A good discussion can draw out wisdom which is attainable in no other way.
— A. D. LINDSAY

ELECTIONS ARE CONSIDERED the essential institution in the modern conception of democracy. Today, scholars, journalists, and ordinary people tend to identify democratic political regimes by the presence or absence of competitive elections to fill government offices.[1] The Schumpeterian definition of democracy as "a competitive struggle for the people's vote" has come to dominate the conventional classification of which countries have democratic governments and which do not. Rarely do knowledgeable commentators delve beyond the mere presence of elections to examine other aspects of society that might bear on the extent of a country's democracy. As long as there seems to be free and open electoral competition in a given country, the existence of elections equals democracy.

The ancient Greeks would have regarded this modern equation of democracy with elections as very strange. In democratic Athens, most officials were selected by lot, not election. The Athenians thought selection by lot superior to election as a democratic device because it gave every male citizen—the Athenians excluded women, slaves, and foreigners from their democracy—an equal chance and right to serve in office and reflected the equal capacity of all men to carry out state policy.[2] According to Aristotle, elections were *aristocratic* institutions because they allowed electors to choose the "best" people (*aristoi*) for public office, rather than the ordinary citizen who would be chosen in a lottery.[3]

Opposite: *Modern presidential candidates pretend to be just ordinary folks, even when they are in reality a multimillionaire businessman or the president of the United States.*

© T.J. Kirkpatrick/Corbis; AP Photo/J. Scott Applewhite.

This concept of elections as aristocratic devices is revealed in an important exception to the selection-by-lot rule in ancient Athens: the election of generals. Because nearly all citizens were also soldiers with combat experience, the Athenians were keenly aware of the need for talent and experience in military leaders. This was one area of government where the efforts of amateurs could not be tolerated, so the Athenians elected their generals. Yet it is important to note that Athenian democrats regarded elections even in this instance as a *deviation* from democratic practice, and it was one that made them nervous. They worried that elected generals would use the popularity shown by their election to claim power for themselves. To prevent such abuse, the Athenian Assembly elected generals for short terms of office and punished them severely if they ignored the wishes of the Assembly. For the ancient Greeks, elections were dangerous to democracy.

The difference between the Greek concept of elections as nondemocratic devices and the modern assumption of their importance derives, obviously, from the difference between Athenian *direct* democracy and modern *representative* democracy. In ancient Athens, the essential democratic institution was the assembly of all citizens. The Assembly discussed, debated, deliberated, and made all public policy decisions; it reflected directly, through its own actions, the will of the people. Public officials were merely instruments for carrying out Assembly decisions, and though they often had discretion in implementing policy—just as modern bureaucrats have discretion—they had to answer directly to the Assembly for their actions. In modern representative democracy, elected officials are chosen not to carry out policy but to debate, discuss, deliberate, and make public policy. Given this very different role of the public official in a representative democracy, elections have a different and important *democratic* function.

Under the logic of representative democracy, the responsibility for public decision making—which in classical Athens was lodged in the Assembly—is shared between citizen voters and their representatives. Election is the mechanism that makes the system democratic—that is, it ensures rule by the people. Whereas Athenian citizens could rule directly by attending the Assembly, citizens of a representative democracy must use the tool of a democratic election to exercise their rule. If government is to be truly democratic, not only must elections occur, but they must be able to serve the democratic purpose of involving all citizens in the policy deliberations of their representatives. In terms of A. D. Lindsay's idea, quoted at the beginning of this chapter, elections must contribute to the "government by discussion" that is the essence of democracy.

In this respect, elections must take on the characteristics of the classic Athenian Assembly if they are to be effective democratic institutions. Because elected officials are not mere civil servants but representatives with actual decision-making power, elections provide the crucial link between citizens and representatives in democratic governance. Elections in which governing officials are chosen are not necessarily, then, in themselves indicators of democracy. Truly democratic elections must provide citizens a chance to join the public policy discussion and guide their representatives' public policy decisions.

In this chapter, I argue that for elections to be democratic, they must meet three essential criteria. First, democratic elections in a representative democracy must provide the opportunity for the *equal representation* of all citizens. To the extent that certain citizens or groups are advantaged in their ability to influence the outcomes, elections are less than fully democratic. Furthermore, for elections to be truly representative, voters need to be able to make a clear choice between alternative candidates. Second, elections must be mechanisms for *deliberation* about public policy issues. Citizens in a modern, representative democracy cannot deliberate and make policy directly, as the citizens of Athens did, but must rely on their representatives to make the ultimate decisions. However, this does not mean that citizens cannot share in democratic deliberation. Well-designed and well-run elections can be occasions for deliberating about what policies government should pursue. To the extent that they do so, they are democratic. And third, if elections are to be democratic, they must *control* what government does. There must be a link between election outcomes and the policies government eventually enacts. If elections cease to determine what happens, the people no longer govern.

Unfortunately, elections in the United States fall short of meeting these criteria. First, our elections do not provide equal representation. Institutional design—the malapportioned Senate, the Electoral College, and single-member plurality elections—operate to give the votes of some more weight than others. Also, the need for candidates to raise large sums to win office gives extra influence to those wealthy individuals and special interests that contribute to campaigns. Second, deliberation about public policy issues facing the country has become impossible, as the sound bite, entertainment-oriented media coverage, and candidate manipulation of symbols have come to dominate campaigns. And finally, elections fail to provide electoral majorities the ability to control government decisions. Political parties that ought to do so do not effectively perform this task today. As a result, much of the power to make important decisions has been ceded to unelected officials, such as members of the Federal Reserve Board, the judiciary, and the bureaucracy. Although the United States satisfies well the simple criterion of selecting thousands of public officials through competitive election, the more demanding criteria of truly democratic elections are far from being achieved. In the United States, elections have become a major challenge to our democracy rather than an indicator of it.

Equal Representation

In ancient Athens, political equality was guaranteed to every citizen not through the right to vote but through the right to speak to the Assembly—a right the

Greeks called the *isegoria*. When matters of public policy were debated, each citizen could be sure that his preferences were given consideration because he could stand up and state them directly to his fellow citizens. Of course, not all citizens spoke on each issue; prominent Athenian orators tended to dominate debates and articulate positions to which large numbers of their fellows would give assent. But every citizen knew that if no one expressed how he felt on an issue, he had direct recourse—to stand up and say what he believed. In addition, debate on matters of public concern took place outside the Assembly—in shops, the public square, and marketplaces—as well as within it.[4] Undoubtedly, arguments put forth in these areas carried over into the Assembly and enhanced the equal representation of citizen views when public decisions were taken. In the small-scale democracy of Athens, equal recognition of the right to be heard was sufficient to ensure democratic outcomes. Simply by speaking up, the Athenian citizen could seek to influence political outcomes.

In modern representative democracies, the equivalent to the Athenian *isegoria* is the equal right to vote. Voting rights are a political resource distributed equally to all citizens, irrespective of wealth or social status, and, according to the theory of representative democracy, they provide each citizen with the capacity to influence public decisions. In a large society without elections, people would be able to influence government only through private actions, whether bribery, flattery, or private petition. The ability to influence government in such a non-democratic setting would be grossly unequal, reflecting inequality in political resources. Elections under universal suffrage, by contrast, are a public institution for influencing the conduct of government officials within which everyone has the same power: one vote. If elections are conducted fairly and if they control the actions of public officials, they give every citizen an equal chance to determine what government does. According to one analysis, "elections, by introducing a formal, public means of influencing official conduct, can compensate for private inequalities in political resources."[5] To do so, however, elections must provide equal representation.

Unlike the direct debate that was possible in ancient Athens, the vote cast in a mass representative democracy, involving millions of voters, vastly complicates the achievement of equal representation. While individual male Athenians could make their preferences known and influence public debate in the marketplace and the Assembly, individual citizens of representative democracies can only mark their ballots and hope that they translate into an expression of their preferences. Clearly, if the right to vote is to lead to equal representation, more is required than simply millions of citizens voting in isolation. There must be some mechanism to lend coherence to these millions of votes and structure them to provide majority control of government. Individual voters must be able to act in concert with other, like-minded citizens to send clear signals about their policy preferences as they vote for their representatives. Voters organized to act in concert are the functional equivalent of hundreds of Athenian citizens responding with their applause in the Assembly to the convincing argument of a fellow citizen. The equal right to vote alone cannot provide equal representation; it must be exercised through an election process that provides meaningful choices and channels for translating votes into the expression of political influence.

One Person, One Vote

Since the 1960s, in several cases regarding representation in both state legislatures and the US House of Representatives, the US Supreme Court has established a standard for equal representation in a democracy. That standard of "one person, one vote" means in the words of Justice Hugo Black that "one man's vote . . . is to be worth as much as another's."[6] While the Court has applied this standard to the drawing of state legislative districts and for the House of Representatives, there remain many ways in which the structure of representation in the United States violates it. The most egregious violations can be found in the requirement for the election of two senators from each state irrespective of state population and how the Electoral College distorts the standard in the election of presidents. The single-member district system for choosing representatives in most legislative bodies also operates to undermine the standard as does the role gerrymandering plays in creating noncompetitive congressional districts.

The scheme of representation in the Senate did not reflect any "constitutional theory, high principle, or grand design" on the part of the Constitution's framers; rather, it was a consequence of a practical political bargain.[7] Representatives at the Constitutional Convention from small states such as Delaware and New Jersey demanded equal state representation in the Senate as a condition for approving the document, despite strong opposition from some of the Convention's most distinguished members, such as James Madison and Alexander Hamilton. This bargain required by the political realities of 1787 produces grave distortions in equal representation in contemporary America. Voters who happen to live in less populous states have more clout in the Senate than those from larger states. The 4.8 million voters who happen to live the seven least populous states (Alaska, Delaware, Montana, North Dakota, South Dakota, Vermont, and Wyoming) have, with their two senators per state, fourteen representatives in the US Senate. An equivalent number of voters living in a single state, the 4.9 million residents of Minnesota, in comparison, have only their constitutionally mandated two votes.[8] When one adds to the seven least populous states the next five slightly larger states, these twelve states contain less than 5 percent of the US population but control a full quarter of all the votes in the US Senate! The political bargain of 1787 has created a situation in which the "worth" of a person's vote, in Justice Black's terms, depends very much on where a person happens to live.

This malapportionment has quite practical consequences for legislative outcomes. In the past century, the Senate "majority" party has often consisted of states containing a minority of the population, in clear violation of any notion of one person, one vote.[9] Also, senators from smaller states are well positioned to demand that benefits be directed to their states as a condition for their votes on legislation. As a consequence, residents of smaller states benefit more from federal expenditures than those residing in large ones. One study found that the smallest states receive $120 per capita in overall federal expenditures compared to $82 for large states.[10] Someone living in Wyoming, for example, receives seven times the per capita funding of someone living in New York. After the 9/11 terror attacks, many commentators seemed surprised to learn that per capita allocations of Homeland Security funding favored smaller states more than large ones, such as New York or California, where terror attacks were more likely to occur. One only needed to look at Senate malapportionment for an explanation.

As we have seen, equal representation of voters is not part of the Senate's constitutional design, so its deviation from the one person, one vote principle comes as no surprise. The House of Representatives, by contrast, is apportioned according to population, suggesting the intent that it reflect one person, one vote. In practice, however, the House—despite districts apportioned by population—fails to provide equal representation. The reason it does not is the single-member plurality (SMP) electoral system employed in nearly all elections in the United States.

SMP electoral systems give the victory in an election to the candidate that wins a plurality of votes in a district. Only those voters who choose the winning candidate actually get represented; those who voted for the loser have no one to speak for them. In a district where only two candidates are running, the victory will go to the candidate that wins the majority of votes cast. The situation changes, however, if more than two candidates run. Then a candidate winning the plurality of votes likely will represent only a minority of people in the district while the majority will go unrepresented. Whether there are only two, or more candidates, SMP systems provide representation only to supporters of the victors in legislative contests. In the United States, we find it perfectly normal for a single Republican or Democrat to represent an entire district in Congress even when a large proportion or even a majority of people in a district voted for another party. The fact that these supporters of losing candidates will be "represented" by someone they opposed produces little or no protest.

Citizens of most of the world's democracies find the loss of representation inherent in SMP systems unacceptable, choosing instead to elect their legislatures by proportional representation (PR).[11] In this system, legislative seats are awarded according to the percentage of votes parties win in an election district. For example, a district might have ten seats in a legislature. If one party wins 60 percent of the vote, it earns six seats, while a party earning the remaining 40 percent of votes receives four. PR systems offer more complete and equal representation because they assure that legislative representation reflects the actual distribution of partisan support in legislative districts. In democracies with PR systems, citizens are less likely to feel disenfranchised because they happen to live in a geographical region where they are part of a minority. Every party gets represented to the degree it has support among voters. No one's vote gets wasted even if one supports a minority party in one's electoral district.

One only need look to the sad fate of a Massachusetts Republican voter to see how unequal representation works in the SMP system.[12] Despite its reputation as a Democratic state, Republican candidates have managed in recent years to win statewide races for governor and senator. Even in congressional races, Republican candidates consistently win about 30 percent of the vote statewide. Yet for many years, the Democrats have controlled all ten Massachusetts House seats. Because of the distribution of Republican voters across the state and the drawing of congressional districts, Republicans constitute a minority in each district, thus receiving no representation in the House. Routinely, about one-third of Massachusetts residents endorse Republican congressional candidates but go unrepresented in Congress. Under a PR system, Republicans would win three House seats and Democrats seven, providing a more accurate and equal representation of the preferences of Massachusetts voters.

The situation in Massachusetts is not unusual. Most congressional districts nationwide tend to be noncompetitive, with voters of one party dominating. This fact explains much of the power of incumbency and the lack of turnover in Congress. SMP also provides the rationale and incentive for partisan gerrymandering to assure one-party-dominant districts—a routine practice in both parties. Since only one party can win a given district, SMP allows state legislatures to draw district lines to pick the desired ratio of voters in elections and assure which party will win. As one North Carolina state legislator described the practice, "We are in the business of rigging elections."[13] SMP also contributes to partisan polarization. Since most members of Congress can safely ignore the preferences, interests, and concerns of the minority party in their district, they have little incentive to pursue compromise and craft legislation that might cross party lines. In a PR system, parties would have an incentive to appeal to voters outside their partisan base to peel off voters from competing parties and increase their legislative seats. In Massachusetts, Republicans might craft policies designed to attract moderate Democrats in order to gain one or two more seats. Unlike under SMP, voters would find themselves neither ignored nor taken for granted—a formula for more responsive representation.

The Electoral College

The Electoral College system for electing presidents combines the worst features of both the malapportionment of the Senate and the SMP system to undermine equal representation and the democratic character of American presidential elections. The remarkable 2000 presidential election, which placed in the White House for the first time since 1888 a candidate who had earned fewer votes than his opponent, demonstrated the need to change this flawed method of choosing the president. The Electoral College is the procedure set out in the US Constitution for selection of the president. Article II gives states the power to "appoint," in a manner determined by the state legislature, electors who then cast their votes for president. The size of each state's total congressional delegation—the number of its members in the House of Representatives plus its two senators—determines the number of its electors. This method of allocating electors to the states embeds into the Electoral College both schemes of representation that the founders devised for Congress: the equal representation of states in the Senate and the proportional representation in the House. Prior to Election Day, political parties in each state designate a list of people who will serve as electors if their presidential candidate wins the most votes in the state. Under this winner-take-all SMP system, the victorious candidate in each state, no matter how small the margin of victory, receives all of the state's electoral votes.[14]

The Electoral College system is undemocratic in two ways. First, because the apportionment of electoral votes is not made in proportion to population—every state is allocated two of its electors irrespective of population—the votes of citizens who happen to live in more populous states count for less than those who live in smaller states; in the smaller states, a vote can have double or triple the value of a vote counted in a large state. Such a disparity is a gross violation of the principle of "one person, one vote." Why should the vote of someone living in Rhode Island count more than that of someone living in California?

Second, the winner-take-all principle used in most states means that a candidate may win many states by very small margins—thereby accumulating a majority of electoral votes—even as his opponent, who may win by large margins in fewer states, gains a majority of votes nationwide. That is what happened in the election of 2000, when the Supreme Court awarded Florida's twenty-five electoral votes to George W. Bush, giving him a bare majority of 271 electoral votes, while Al Gore captured a 500,000-vote majority of the nationwide popular vote. That result made Bush the legal winner of the presidential election but not the democratic choice of the electorate, in violation of the deeply rooted expectations of most citizens. American citizens are probably the world's strongest supporters of the idea that political leaders should attain office by earning the votes of most of their constituents. This is the view of elections propounded in civics classes and evoked in the traditional exhortations at election time that "every vote counts." In reality, just like the SMP system used in voting for Congress, those who vote for a presidential candidate other than the one that captures the plurality of votes in the state find that their votes are wasted, since the plurality winner in most states gains all the state's electoral votes, and their votes do not count toward determining who becomes president.

Prior to 2000, political scientists sometimes referred to the Electoral College as "an accident waiting to happen." Actually, the accident had happened several times before, but the historical remoteness of the experience—the last time had been 1888—made a modern accident seem unlikely. That was the case even though those who have studied this aspect of presidential elections have demonstrated clearly that the probability of a candidate's winning an electoral vote majority while losing the popular vote is quite high in a close election. A careful analysis of recent elections should have alerted us to the high probability of a recurrence. Of the thirteen presidential elections between the end of World War II and 1996, four (1948, 1960, 1968, and 1976)—nearly one-third—were close enough that a switch of only a few thousand votes in a handful of states would have produced a result like the one in 2000. That a divided outcome was avoided in those earlier elections was due primarily to luck. Given this record, Americans should not have been surprised that it happened in the close and hotly contested election of 2000. Nor should we be surprised if it happens again in the near future, as the sharp partisan division of the current electorate seems likely to persist over the next few election cycles. In 2004, a shift of only 118,000 votes in Ohio—about 1 percent of the votes cast—would have given Kerry an Electoral College victory, even though he trailed Bush by about three million popular votes nationally.[15] The Electoral College stands, then, as a permanent challenge to the notion that Americans will be able to choose their presidents democratically.

Defenders of the Electoral College system sometimes claim that because of the bias toward smaller states, it provides a guarantee that residents of the less populous states will not be ignored in presidential campaigns. This argument assumes that if presidents were elected by popular vote, they would focus most of their attention where the most voters are—in the most populous states. The principal flaw in this argument is that it ignores the way that presidential campaigns are actually conducted. Under the Electoral College system, the presidential election actually involves fifty separate state-level elections. Because candidates begin each contest with apparently solid leads—which modern polling techniques allow them to measure with confidence—in most states, the presidential campaigns focus on a handful of "swing states" in which the election outcome is in doubt. In the last three presidential elections, most Americans— even those living in populous states such as California, Texas, and New York— neither watched a presidential campaign commercial nor saw one of the candidates in their community, whereas residents in swing states such as Michigan, Pennsylvania, Florida, and Ohio were inundated with commercials day and night and received repeated visits from both campaigns.

Under a system of direct election, every vote would matter to candidates, no matter where the voter lived. More campaign resources would be directed toward communicating candidate messages to nationwide audiences, either through campaign commercials or through more events targeting broad audiences, such as nationally televised debates. Candidates would focus on issues of national concern, rather than zeroing in on local concerns to gain votes in the few battleground areas. In recent elections, Democratic presidential candidates have opted not to challenge Republican opposition to gun control, although national polls show that most Americans would have been receptive to such an appeal, because they have been worried about alienating National Rifle Association members in the key battleground states of Michigan, Ohio, and Pennsylvania. The Electoral College system gives premium leverage to pockets of special interest voters in swing states. In a direct popular vote system, national majorities spread throughout the country would have greater sway.

The Money Election: Campaign Funding and Unequal Representation

Modern campaigns are expensive. Candidates for elective office must spend large amounts of money on the campaign staffs and advertising needed to run credible election campaigns. This means that, except for candidates wealthy enough to finance campaigns from their own fortunes, most candidates must turn to that small group of Americans who contribute to political campaigns. These few wealthy individuals and special interests gain unequal power because politicians depend on their contributions to gain office. So along with the regular election in which all citizens cast their one vote, there exists a money election in which some citizens gain the equivalent of extra votes for themselves with the dollars they contribute. Not surprisingly, elected officials are quite attentive to those who contribute to their campaigns and the policy issues that concern them. Few will dare to take positions or advocate policies that might anger campaign contributors no matter how popular those policies might be among ordinary voters.[16] The money election creates unequal representation in American democracy in favor of the wealthy few who fund political campaigns.

For candidates seeking office, attracting campaign cash gains them credibility as viable candidates. This factor plays an especially important role in presidential primary campaigns where candidates need to stand out in what is usually a large field of candidates. The campaign for the cash of wealthy donors effectively amounts to a "hidden election" for office that determines the actual electoral choices voters will have.[17] Before any polls are taken or any votes are cast, wealthy individuals and interest groups determine who the credible candidates for office will be. Relative success in raising cash drives news coverage because the news media decide which candidates to cover largely on the basis of how much money they have raised.[18] Thus, early fund-raising success can be crucial to later electoral success as the media provides more exposure for the better-funded candidates, assisting them in rising in the polls, further enhancing their credibility. In the

2008 Democratic presidential primaries, in a field of nine candidates, Hillary Clinton and Barack Obama emerged early as the top contenders for the Democratic nomination because of their fund-raising machines. As the campaign developed in 2007, several of Clinton and Obama's opponents were forced out of the race because of inadequate campaign funds. An ample campaign war chest can also help a candidate overcome mistakes and unfavorable publicity that would drive less well funded candidates from the field. For example, Bill Clinton's lead in the campaign for funds before the Democratic presidential primaries in 1992 was a critical factor in his ability to survive setbacks early in the process—such as the bad publicity over alleged extramarital affairs, his draft record, and his defeat in the New Hampshire primary.[19] Prowess in raising money also can serve to deter opponents from entering the race. In 2000, both Vice President Al Gore and Texas Governor George W. Bush faced only negligible competition in their respective primaries because they had overwhelming financial advantage over potential competitors.[20] The hidden campaign for cash in presidential elections winnows the field of choices early to those individuals whom well-heeled donors find acceptable.

As in presidential primaries, electoral success in congressional elections and in state and local races depends largely on whether a candidate can raise enough money to mount a credible campaign. Contributions often can be especially important in winning elections to the US House of Representatives—in 2004, the candidate for Congress who spent the most won in 96 percent of the races.[21] Understandably, the highest expenditures were in the most competitive races, but even incumbents in the 343 districts considered "safe" in that year spent an average of a million dollars—about five times the average expenditure of their competitors. Why would candidates with only negligible opposition spend so much? In most cases, high expenditures in even noncompetitive districts are signals to discourage potential challengers from even attempting to raise the big campaign war chest needed to fund a serious campaign. In the only five races in which an incumbent was defeated in 2004, challengers were able to match the incumbents in spending. In 2008, incumbent senators outspent challengers eight to one, on average; in House elections, incumbents had an average four-to-one spending advantage over challengers.[22] The money election essentially determines which incumbents can assure themselves of reelection and which candidates can mount credible challenges.

Campaign contributions from the rich and powerful continue to produce unequal representation in American elections despite thirty years of campaign finance reform. In the wake of the Watergate scandals, which featured revelations of fat-cat contributors giving suitcases full of cash to the 1972 Nixon reelection campaign, Congress passed the Federal Election Campaign Act (FECA) of 1974, which created a comprehensive regulatory framework for the financing of all campaigns for national elective office. The legislation had three basic goals: mitigating the influence of big money contributions in presidential elections through a system of public funding for presidential campaigns, limiting the amounts individuals could contribute to any one candidate in presidential or congressional races, and containing the overall cost of elections by imposing ceilings on the amounts candidates could spend in national election campaigns.

To achieve the first goal, a new Federal Election Commission (FEC) would administer a fund, raised by means of a voluntary one-dollar contribution from taxpayers, to partially subsidize the campaigns of all presidential candidates. In the primaries, candidates would receive public funds to match what their campaigns had raised, while in the general election campaign, the two major-party candidates would receive full public funding. In exchange for public funds, however, candidates had to agree to limit their overall expenditures to FEC-determined amounts. The second goal required all candidates for the presidency, House, and Senate to submit detailed reports of all campaign receipts and expenditures and to limit how much they accepted from any individual contributor, political party, or political action committee (PAC). (A PAC is a group—usually representing a corporate or special interest—established to pool funds from individual contributors and funnel them to various candidates the PAC wishes to support.) A ceiling would limit the amount of donations by individual contributors, PACs, and parties to individual candidates in a single election. Finally, FECA set limits on how much total spending could occur in an election campaign. FECA's drafters thought this mechanism would serve both to reduce the cost of election campaigns and to prevent wealthy contributors from gaining special access to elected officials. Over the next thirty years, however, both candidates and contributors found ways to get around the legislation's goals. Today's elections are even more expensive than those before the legislation was enacted and just as open to fat-cat contributors as when Nixon received their money in suitcases.

Limitations on individual, interest group, and party contributions to individual candidates were intended to reduce candidate dependence on any one donor or small group of contributors. Under FECA, candidates can obtain funds for their campaigns with the following limits: contributions of no more than $2,500 (in 2012) each from individuals and no more than $5,000 each from PACs in a single election cycle.[23] Although the legislation prohibits corporations from making direct contributions to campaigns, corporate executives may contribute to a PAC formed to promote corporate interests. Every member of a PAC may contribute up to $5,000 per year to it, and each PAC can give up to $2,500 to a single candidate. In addition to corporate PACs, there are PACs representing professional groups, such as doctors and lawyers, labor unions, and even individual politicians. Many politicians today follow the example Ronald Reagan set in the 1970s when he promoted his presidential candidacy through his own personal PAC, called "Citizens for the Republic," which contributed to the campaigns of Republican members of Congress and state and local candidates.[24]

House and Senate candidates also may receive limited direct contributions to their campaigns from political parties. More important, party committees and the House and Senate campaign committees can make more substantial contributions to their respective party candidates in "coordinated" expenditures for polling, fund-raising advice, advertising, and issue research.[25] In addition, political parties may spend an unrestricted amount to support the election of their parties' candidates through "independent" activities not undertaken in coordination with individual candidates' campaigns. Political parties raise funds from individuals and PACs to support these campaign activities subject to contribution limitations similar to those for contributions to individual candidates and PACs.[26] As a result of FECA, a complex system of campaign regulation evolved regulating how candidates received funds and providing limits on how much could be received from individuals and interest groups but one that did little to stifle the flow of large amounts of cash into elections.

Only two years after FECA's passage, the Supreme Court declared the third goal of the legislation—limiting campaign expenditures—unconstitutional. In *Buckley v. Valeo,* a challenge brought by a Senate candidate seeking to spend an unlimited amount of his own fortune on his campaign, the Court found that limits on campaign expenditures violated the free speech clause of the First Amendment. Campaign expenditures, the Court said, whether from a candidate's own pocket or funds he or she raised, are a form of free political speech and cannot be limited. At the same time, the Court upheld the contribution limits as reasonable efforts to prevent the "corruption" of candidates for office. An immediate effect of the decision was to facilitate the candidacies of wealthy individuals, like Buckley, who could spend freely from their own fortunes to promote their campaigns, an opportunity many such wealthy people have embraced including, for example, billionaire New York Mayor Michael Bloomberg, former New Jersey senator and governor and Goldman Sachs executive John Corzine, Florida Governor Rick Scott, and many others. More important, the decision, in declaring campaign expenditures to be free speech under the First Amendment, prevented any restrictions on the amount individuals, groups, or candidates might spend in elections. Without the ability to limit expenditures, campaign regulation lost the ability to constrain the ever-expanding election cash arms race and enhanced candidates' dependence on wealthy contributors to gain office. In addition, in declaring campaign spending to be free speech, the Court decision suggested that future efforts to "level the playing field" in elections by making candidate access to campaign resources more equal might be held unconstitutional.[27] In future decisions, as we shall see, the Court would indeed deploy the campaign cash as free speech doctrine to open the door for well-heeled interests to bias the electoral process in their favor.

In the forty years since FECA attempted to limit the corrupting influence of money in campaigns, those who seek to use their campaign contributions to influence elected officials have devised creative ways to exploit loopholes in campaign regulation. In the early years, PACs proved an effective way for special interests and corporations to target their contributions to candidates they wished to influence. More recently, industry lobbyists have devised the strategy of "bundling," or coordinating, individual contributions from numerous individual executives in a given industry to get around the $5,000 limitation on PAC contributions to a single campaign. Candidates also can turn to a relatively small number of wealthy donors to bundle contributions from their network of wealthy friends and associates. These bundlers and their ability to raise large sums from their friends become special resources for candidates and gain the access needed to make sure the candidate is responsive to their issue concerns and interests in a special way. George W. Bush and his campaign adviser Karl Rove perfected the use of bundlers in the 2000 presidential campaign. In both the Bush presidential campaigns, bundlers who raised $100,000 were named "Pioneers," and those who raised $200,000 named "Rangers," designations that provided special access to presidential events.[28] In 2008, bundlers raised substantial amounts for both candidates, although McCain relied on them more, receiving $207 million to Obama's $63 million.[29] Even so, Obama's bundlers provided about one-third of his funds.[30] As the 2012 campaign approached, Obama turned to bundlers on Wall Street to gain an early lead among his potential opponents in accumulating campaign cash.[31] The use of bundlers means that despite the limits FECA imposes on what any one individual can contribute to a campaign, those who bundle large packets of cash gain special attention from candidates and the influence that goes with it.

So-called "independent expenditures" constitute the other major loophole campaign contributors use to evade the contribution limits in campaign law.[32] These are expenditures for television ads, mass mailings, or other electoral activities of organizations deemed independent of a candidate's campaign. For example, an organization might run a TV ad favorable to a candidate in a race, say praising a vote on an issue, but as long as the organization does not collaborate with the candidate directly in producing the ad the cost of the ad is considered an independent expenditure. Groups making these expenditures, because they are defined as "issue advocacy" rather than support for the election of a particular candidate—even if they have that effect—are not subject to the same contribution restrictions candidates are for their expenditures.

In the 1990s, political parties paved the way for such independent expenditures through the use of what came to be called "soft money." Congress amended FECA in 1979 to allow political party organizations to raise funds from any source without any restrictions on the amount of contributions for the purpose of "party-building" activities such as voter registration drives, get-out-the-vote activities, and voter education; the money was not supposed to finance the campaigns of individual candidates.[33] Since this money was totally unregulated, the parties were free to ask corporations and other fat-cat donors to contribute any amount they wished, which opened up the prospect that a small number of contributors could gain a corrupting influence over a single campaign by making large donations. Slowly, over the next few years, however, candidates found that "party-building" funds could be directed to activities such as television commercials that supported their campaigns—as long as those activities were labeled "educational." This "soft money," as it was now called, could support a commercial attacking a candidate's opponent as long as the commercial did not specifically advocate voting for the candidate by saying, "Vote for candidate *X*." By the mid-1990s, both Supreme Court rulings and favorable decisions by the Federal Election Commission had interpreted the legislation so broadly as to allow support for virtually any campaign activity, and by the end of that decade soft money had become a major source of funding in presidential and congressional campaigns. As political party soft money for campaigns grew, so too did independent expenditures from a variety of "issue advocacy" groups that raised unlimited amounts of unregulated funds.[34] These groups often are identified as 527 or 501(c) nonprofit organizations labeled according to the section of the tax code under which they are organized. Section 527 groups are identified as primarily political groups and must disclose the identity of contributors giving over $200; section 501(c) groups are not considered primarily political groups and do not have to disclose contributor identities but they still can spend some of their funds for issue advocacy in elections.[35] By 2000, such unregulated independent expenditures rather than the regulated expenditures of candidates came to be a major part of election campaigns.

To rein in these unregulated independent expenditures, Congress passed the 2002 Bipartisan Campaign Reform Act (BCRA), the first major reform of campaign law since 1974. The new law expressly prohibited the use of political party "soft money" in elections. In addition, it sought to regulate "electioneering communications"—advertisements broadcast within a few weeks of elections that featured a candidate—of independent groups by requiring them to disclose the identity of contributors and prohibiting labor unions or corporations from contributing. With access to soft money denied them, political parties simply redoubled their efforts to raise "hard" money from individuals and PACs—now under new, higher contribution limits permitted under BCRA—and again they enjoyed enormous success. In practice, BCRA seemed to do little to restrict political parties' access to large amounts of campaign funds or restrict their activities on behalf of candidates. And the legislation's attempt to regulate the electioneering communications of independent groups soon ran afoul of the Supreme Court's concern that campaign finance regulation violated free speech. First, in *Federal Election Commission v. Wisconsin Right to Life, Inc.* in 2007, the Court defined a test of what constituted "electioneering communication" that severely restricted the ability of regulators to apply the law. Then, in a far-reaching decision in 2009,

Karl Rove, Republican strategist and former senior political adviser to US President George W. Bush, established the well-funded Crossroads Super PAC to raise money for Republican candidates in 2010 and 2012.

Jay Premack/Bloomberg via Getty Images.

Citizens United v. Federal Election Commission found the BCRA's provision for regulating "electioneering communication" an unconstitutional violation of free speech. This decision opened the door for groups to collect unlimited amounts of money from any source, including labor unions and corporations, for unlimited expenditure of funds to advocate the election or defeat of candidates in elections. Not content merely to overturn the electioneering provision of BCRA, the Court used the *Citizens United* ruling to overturn prohibitions in federal law of direct corporate expenditures in federal elections dating back to the 1907 Tillman Act. The Court majority ruled that corporations had the same right of political speech that individuals had and therefore were free to spend, from their own treasuries, any amount they wished on behalf or against any candidate in any federal election. Now, for the first time in over a century, giant corporations can open their coffers to support directly candidates they consider favorable to their interests.

The *Citizens United* decision has opened the door for virtually unlimited and largely unregulated spending by independent groups in campaigns. Ostensibly independent, many of these shadowy groups have close ties to political parties, political operatives, and individual candidates and can raise funds from secret contributors to be spent on behalf of their favored candidates. An example of such group, Americans for Job Security, titles itself in a manner typical of such groups in that it reveals nothing of its political leanings nor anything about whom it represents or who funds it. Organized as a 501(c) nonprofit group, it has spent tens of millions of dollars since 1997 on negative advertisements against

Democratic candidates.[36] FEC decisions and lower court rulings, following the *Citizens United* precedent, soon made possible a new form of independent campaign group: the *super PAC*. Free of the contribution restrictions of regular PACs, the super PAC can raise unlimited funds from individuals and corporations, although unlike 501(c) organizations they must disclose the identity of their contributors. But they also are free to expressly advocate the election or defeat of particular candidates. Super PACs proved quite popular with both contributors and political operatives with seventy-two up and running by the 2010 congressional races contributing $83.7 million overall.[37] In the 2010 midterms, the first election since the *Citizens United* decision, spending of independent groups, 501(c), 527, and super PACs combined increased 130 percent over the 2008 election.[38] As the 2012 presidential elections unfolded, super PACS were formed to support all the major candidates and became a major source of funding for campaigns. In some cases, such as the campaign of Republican presidential contender Newt Gingrich, only a handful of wealthy donors provided all of the money for the candidate's supporting super PAC.[39] Under the existing campaign finance law as interpreted by the Supreme Court, wealthy individuals and corporations have expanded opportunities to deploy their wealth in a variety of ways to influence elections.

Attempts at campaign finance regulation have failed to restrain the growth of campaign expenditures. As shown in Figure 5.1, spending on the presidential campaigns actually doubled from 2000 to 2004 and doubled again in 2008. Compared to 1976, the first presidential election conducted under federal campaign finance regulation, the 2008 election cost more than twenty times as much. The growing cost of presidential campaigns probably has brought to an end the attempt at public financing of presidential campaigns established by FECA in 1974. George W. Bush began the walk away from public financing in 2000 when he declined to take any public money, which allowed him to raise and spend unlimited amounts for the primaries.[40] In 2004, Senator John Kerry and Vermont Governor Howard Dean joined President Bush in refusing public funds for their primary campaigns. Their success using this strategy boded ill for the future of publicly funded campaigns. In 2008, the leading presidential contenders, Hillary Clinton, John McCain, and Barack Obama, all refused public funding in the primaries. Then Obama took the next step. Fearing that Republican-leaning independent groups would spend huge amounts on their candidate not subject to the public financing limits, Obama also opted to refuse public financing for the general election, freeing him from any limits for the entire campaign. Obama justified his decision in part by pointing to his success in using the Internet to raise a large amount of funds (about 52 percent of his total) from small contributors giving under $1,000.[41] His success in both raising campaign funds in record amounts and winning the election may be the death knell for public financing of presidential campaigns. Given his success, future candidates of both parties may follow his example. The advent of super PACs and the new ease with which independent groups can raise large amounts of money has meant huge expenditures on behalf of 2012 presidential candidates. The death knell for public funding of the presidential race and limiting its rising costs has sounded.

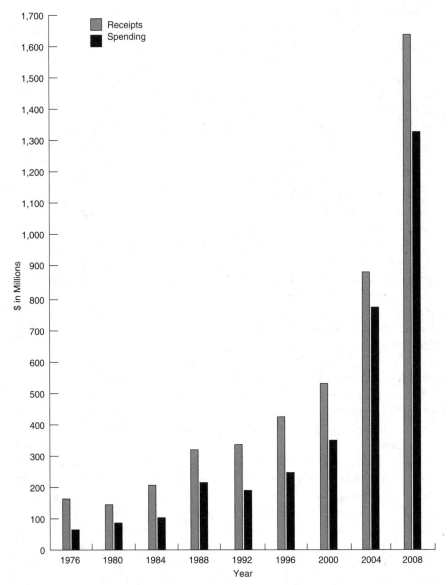

FIGURE 5.1   Total Receipts and Spending in Presidential Elections, 1976–2008

Source: Center for Responsive Politics, www.opensecrets.org/pres08/totals.php?cycle=2008.

We are now in an era when money counts in American political campaigns as much if not more than it has ever counted in our history. Historians once looked to the Gilded Age of the 1890s, when famed political operative Mark Hanna described money as the "mother's milk of politics," as the time when wealthy interests dominated American politics. The current era of super PACS, bundling, and anonymously funded 501(c) groups all funneling mountains of cash to favored candidates has created a new Gilded Age of political spending. From the perspective of equal representation, the money election sharply biases the election process in favor of the very small and wealthy portion of the electorate that contributes to political campaigns. The one-tenth of 1 percent of citizens that provides the bulk of the funds for political campaigns buys unequal influence over elected officials.[42] This influence undermines the fundamental promise of representative democracy that the vote empowers all citizens equally. In elections today, before ordinary citizens cast their votes, the money election has already restricted their choices to candidates who have passed muster with the rich and the special interests.

Deliberation

From what we know of life in ancient Athens, political discussion was lively, intense, and constant. In a society in which citizens made decisions directly in the Assembly, debates and arguments about public decisions were at the center of public life, and no decision was taken without extensive deliberations both within and outside the Assembly. These deliberations were face-to-face affairs, as persons with various points of view confronted one another directly. Various participants also knew one another personally and could weigh arguments according to the personal reputations for wisdom and intelligence of those who made them.[43] Because Athens was a predominantly oral culture, without the equivalent of modern newspapers or other media, political deliberations were unmediated—that is, people received communication directly from the participants instead of learning about it through written reports. The purpose of the deliberations was reaching a public decision, which would be taken by majority vote in the Assembly. Constructive debate and talk leading to democratic decisions on public issues were a natural part of small-scale, direct, face-to-face democracy in Athens.

Obviously, no large-scale representative democracy can come close to re-creating the intense public deliberation of ancient Athens. From the point of view of the typical citizen of a representative democracy, political arguments, by necessity, must be made at a distance; they must be mediated by either written or electronic means; and participants are not likely to be intimately acquainted. Nevertheless, election campaigns in representative democracies do offer citizens the potential to observe and participate in public deliberations. If campaigns illuminate alternative points of view on serious issues and feature debates among those views, they can provide a context for public deliberation in which citizens can participate by means of their votes. For this to happen, the discourse of election campaigns has to provide real contention among various viewpoints on public issues: Candidates must articulate issue positions clearly and address directly the views of their opponents, and the media must report extensively on these contending views in a manner that assists voters in making judgments about them.

According to this ideal, elections are institutions for peaceful conflict over public issues that are resolved at the ballot box after careful deliberation about alternative courses of action. The candidates running for office represent in their platforms and position papers the concrete policy alternatives under deliberation. When a majority of voters choose one set of candidates over another, they are using the election to confer a majority decision about what courses of action the newly constituted government should take. In a representative democracy, the directions given in an election—in contrast to the decisions of the Athenian Assembly—do not provide detailed instructions to elected representatives; the responsibility for actual legislation lies with the representatives. If open, reasoned debate and deliberation occur during the election, however, the outcome resolves fundamental political conflicts and renders a decision regarding the overall direction of government policy. Unfortunately, the contemporary reality of campaign discourse and electoral politics in the United States deviates dramatically from this ideal. In fact, many election observers believe that campaign discourse has become useless as a means for public deliberation on important issues. Consequently, elections provide no resolution of public conflicts and contribute little to the capacity of election winners to govern.

Mediated Information in Political Campaigns

In modern election campaigns, unlike ancient Athens, access to information relevant to politics and election campaigns is mediated. Rather than rely on information they gather directly, citizens must depend on information provided from others. They must look to two main sources for the information they need for democratic deliberation, the news media and the campaigns of the candidates themselves, but neither source sees promoting democratic deliberation as its primary goal. Commercial interests drive nearly all media coverage of campaigns. Newspapers, television networks, and Internet sites for the most part are profit-making businesses. They cover election campaigns and provide information relevant to deliberation in ways that promote their commercial concerns. While these commercial goals sometimes are consistent with providing citizens the information they need for effective deliberation, often they are not and commercial concerns always influence what gets reported and how. Campaigns, as one might expect, concern themselves with winning. To promote this goal, they disseminate large amounts of information through advertising, at campaign events, and through the news media. In many campaigns, particularly for less visible offices that the news media ignore, the candidates' campaign commercials are citizens' main source of information about the campaign. As with the news media, some of the information from candidates' campaigns can be helpful for democratic deliberation, but most distorts and spins information in ways that undermine constructive deliberation. Both media coverage and candidate campaign strategies have evolved in recent years in ways that have diminished the capacity of elections to promote effective citizen deliberation.

The News Media

Over the past few decades, citizens have had access to an increasing variety of media sources for campaign news, yet, despite this increase in news sources, information conducive to deliberation has become rarer.

Table 5.1 shows the main sources of campaign news in recent presidential campaigns. Broadcast television remains citizens' main source of news, although cable channels now provide a growing share of coverage. In 2008, about a third of voters reported accessing information on the Internet, a rapid rise in just a decade, while newspapers offered a declining source of information (although some Internet access may be to newspaper sites). Although citizens have available a variety of media where campaign information might be found, only a small proportion of information disseminated from any of these media relates to elections. Only about 15 percent of TV news political coverage and about 13 percent of newspaper political coverage during presidential election years is devoted to covering the national campaign, and the percentage has shrunk over time.[44] In 2008 many commentators noted that strong voter interest in the Obama/McCain race caused the broadcast networks to pay more attention to the election than in previous years; nevertheless, the three networks combined, in all their news programs from August to November—including convention and debate coverage—averaged only twenty-two minutes per day on election news.[45] Television, the main source of news for most citizens, largely ignores contests for lesser offices, such as campaigns for the House of Representatives and for state and local positions. One 2004 survey of local news coverage found that, even just a few weeks prior to the election, local half-hour news programs devoted only about three minutes, on average, to election coverage, and only 5 percent of the stories dealt with local races.[46] And, while the Internet offers a wealth of election information for political junkies who want to access it, only a small percentage of voters use the Internet to access political news.[47] Despite the wide variety of sources of information, most studies show the information and style of election coverage to be remarkably similar whatever the venue.[48] Whatever the source of election news, the information one finds about elections is remarkably similar and, as we shall see, not very useful for democratic deliberation.

TABLE 5.1   Voters' Main Sources of Campaign News, 2000, 2004, and 2008 (in Percentages)

News Source	2000	2004	2008
Broadcast	70	76	72
Cable	36	42	46
Network	22	33	24
Local	21	12	13
Newspapers	39	46	29
Radio	15	22	21
Internet	11	21	33
Magazines	4	6	3

Source: Doris Graber, *Mass Media and American Politics,* 8th ed. (Washington, DC: CQ Press), 195.

The commercial pressure on journalists to attract as many viewers, readers, or web "hits" as possible leads them to emphasize drama and "breezy infotainment" in their election coverage over substantive issues.[49] For most, covering the campaign "horse race"—that is, whom the polls show to be ahead and competing campaign strategies—overwhelms issue discussion. In 2008, the Project for Excellence in Journalism found that, of the 25,000 stories studied, 71 percent involved the campaign "horse race" and only 13 percent policy issues.[50] This journalistic "schema" or "frame" of an election as a strategic game between opposing campaign teams not only diminishes discussion of issues but also distorts such discussion at the rare times when issues are raised. Rather than portraying the candidates' issue statements as serious proposals for addressing the country's problems, the strategic game frame treats such statements merely as positions taken to attract the support of particular constituencies.[51] Although it is true that candidates seek political support based on their issue positions, campaign speeches and policy positions also give voters information about what the candidates intend to accomplish if elected. Studies show that voters are intensely interested in learning about candidates' issue positions as a way of evaluating their capacity to address real problems, even though the journalists' strategic frame lets little of that information get through to them.[52] Moreover, the phenomenon of the "incredible shrinking sound bite"—the ever-more-strictly compressed time slots that television news programs provide for candidates to state their positions on issues—gives candidates little chance to communicate serious issue positions. In 1968, television evening newscasts allowed candidates an average of 42 seconds of uninterrupted time to communicate their views; by 1988, the sound bite had shrunk to 9 seconds; in recent presidential elections, it had dropped to 7.8 seconds.[53] Consequently, as a study of the 2008 election has documented, voters know little about candidates' issue positions.[54]

When journalists do report on issues, moreover, little information is conveyed that would contribute to constructive deliberation. The media, especially television, tend to ignore broad social and economic policy issues because their complexity makes it difficult to simplify and dramatize them.[55] Longer stories that place issues in context and provide information for evaluating the positions of candidates are rarely seen because producers fear they will not hold the attention of viewers. Instead, narrow, controversial issues such as gun control or abortion are preferred because they invite a focus on dramatic conflict between the opposing candidates. Also, because television news producers have discovered that viewers find fast-paced programs more entertaining, they have devised programs that move quickly through shorter stories; shrinking sound bites are one result. The same need to entertain forces reporters to seek out dramatic stories—hence the emphasis on personality and gaffes instead of issues. In the 2008 campaign, both McCain and Obama found their responses to comments made at town hall forums distorted in media sound bites, so that they had to devote days afterward to clarifying their true positions.[56] In one incident at a Virginia campaign rally, Obama happened to use the clichéd phrase "You can put lipstick on a pig. It's still a pig," in criticizing one of his opponent's policy positions. Journalists seized on the comment, ignoring of course Obama's substantive policy point, to speculate on whether it was meant as an insult directed at Republican vice-presidential candidate Sarah Palin, who had described herself as "a pit bull with lipstick." The controversy dominated election coverage for days at the expense of more substantive coverage.[57] With election coverage steeped in such manufactured controversy, little serious information sifts through to voters to assist them in deliberating about how to address the country's problems. According to some media critics, the fast-paced, entertainment-oriented news coverage of television has conditioned viewers to expect this superficial kind of news. Neil Postman, a leading media analyst, argues that television "has made entertainment itself the natural format for the representation of all experience . . . [because] all subject matter is presented as entertaining."[58]

The proliferation of cable TV channels in the 1990s increased the competition for audience share among all media and also increased pressure to entertain rather than inform. As all-news cable channels such as FOX News, MSNBC, and CNN perfected their technique of nonstop reports on the latest scandal rather than on political substance, all telecast outlets—including venerable morning news programs such as the *Today* show and even the flagship evening newscasts—faced competitive pressure to adopt the same strategy to attract viewers and altered their coverage accordingly. During summer 2001, for example, Americans were inundated with endless stories about shark attacks and California Congressman Gary Condit's alleged relationship with missing intern Chandra Levy. The shock of the 9/11 terrorist attacks brought more serious coverage to the airwaves for a time, but within a few months television news had returned to its accustomed focus on sensationalist schlock.[59] Even when they cover more serious political issues, cable channels do so in formats that promote confrontation and simplistic emotional exchanges, as on FOX's *The O'Reilly Factor* or MSNBC's *Hardball with Chris Matthews,* rather than discussions of substance. Given the superficiality of these supposedly hard news programs, many viewers found Jon Stewart's *The Daily Show,* a satiric "fake news" program, just as reliable a guide to election issues in 2004 and 2008. Stewart himself made this point to *Crossfire* hosts Tucker Carlson and Paul Begala when he appeared on their show during the 2004 campaign, telling them, "You have a responsibility to the public discourse and you fail miserably."[60] Local news programs also are caught in a downward spiral of competition with cable TV and with one another to present sensational, entertaining stories, so that important public issues—unless they relate to political scandal—are ignored. During election campaigns, voters find very little information on television that is useful for deliberating about public issues.

Entertainment venues like Jon Stewart's The Daily Show *have become must stops for political candidates seeking votes.*

© ROGER L. WOLLENBERG/POOL/epa/Corbis.

Unfortunately, the production values of broadcast and cable TV news programs have carried over in recent years to the print media. The creation of *USA Today* was a watershed in the conscious attempt to imitate television news in its design. The paper prints extremely short news stories providing basic information that is much like what one would hear in a televised news report. The use of color and graphics likewise reflects a desire to make the news entertaining and appealing, often at the expense of substantive information. Following the appearance and popular success of *USA Today,* even such prestigious mainstream newspapers as the *New York Times* and the *Washington Post* have experimented with similar formats. Although these changes may be necessary to attract readers in an electronic age, they have undermined the political discourse of campaigns and the possibility of useful deliberation.[61] The bits of information that voters receive from both print and electronic media are simply insufficient for constructive political discourse.

Some observers suggest that the Internet provides an opportunity for improving public deliberation in elections. The number and diversity of news sources available on the web provide an alternative to mainstream news coverage. Through personal websites and blogs, ordinary citizens can participate directly in discussing issues and exchanging information. During the 2008 elections, many more citizens took advantage of the Internet to access campaign deliberations than had done so in previous elections. Blogs, in particular, played an important role by allowing more substantive and interactive discussion of issues and even influenced mainstream media coverage, as the major newspapers and networks disseminated stories that first circulated in the "blogosphere."[62] Politically oriented websites like the *Drudge Report* and *Huffington Post* have devised the capacity to attract attention to stories and issues that the mainstream media then disseminate more broadly. Such sites have spurred a new brand of "citizen journalism" where non-journalists can submit news scoops, often via cell phone, that then appear in blogs or in You Tube videos. One such citizen reporter, for example, embarrassed the Obama primary campaign when she recorded a remark Obama made at a fund-raiser that the jobless often "get bitter, they cling to their guns and religion."[63] Posted first at *Huffington Post,* the mainstream media soon picked it up and made it the centerpiece of coverage of the Democratic primary campaign for days.

While the new citizen journalism has potential to be a democratizing element within the media, so far, much, like the example above, simply feeds the media appetite for sensation and gaffes rather than more substantive policy discussion. Sometimes blogs, free from the restraints of sourcing and factual verification of mainstream journalism, promote false or distorted stories that can have destructive effects. Such an attack from right-wing bloggers led to the demise of ACORN, a nationwide community-organizing group.[64] ACORN's mission was to organize the participation of poor people in local communities on behalf of community objectives like the groups described in chapter 4. Like most of those groups, ACORN sought to expand voter participation of its poor constituents through voter registration drives. During the 2008 election campaign, right-wing bloggers, including well-known provocateur Andrew Breitbart, seized upon reports that a handful of ACORN employees (later fired by the organization) had falsified signatures on some voter registration cards.[65] The blogs exaggerated the incident to claim that ACORN was promoting widespread voter fraud on behalf of the Obama campaign. Soon conservative talk show hosts and media personalities, such as Glenn Beck, began promoting the story on their shows. At this point, mainstream media organizations reported on the accusations as part of their election coverage, repeating the claims of voter fraud, but devoting little time or independent reporting to documenting that ACORN had in fact never been found to promote fraudulent voting and that the supposed "voter fraud" consisted of a few falsified voter registration cards. After the election, polls found that 26 percent of Americans, including 52 percent of Republicans, believed ACORN had stolen the election for Obama. In 2009, Breitbart would continue his campaign against ACORN in posting videos on his website of two conservative activists posing as a pimp and prostitute visiting ACORN offices asking for tax advice. The edited videos gave the impression that ACORN volunteers were eager to help the pair and soon were all over conservative websites and featured on *The Glenn Beck Show.* After weeks of relentless and distorted coverage, ACORN lost most of its private and public funding and was forced to close. In this case, "citizen journalism" had led to the propagation of a distracting, false story during the 2008 campaign and the loss to poor communities around the country of an organization that worked on their behalf.

It remains to be seen whether the Internet will improve deliberation over the long run. Despite the blogosphere's rising influence, conventional media conglomerates—the major networks and newspapers—continue to dominate web hits but also, as we saw in Table 5.1, remain the main sources of citizen election information. One disturbing aspect of Internet usage is the tendency toward segmentation of the electorate, as people tend to access the sites most sympathetic to their own views rather than to learn what those they disagree with are saying. As political scientist Doris Graber puts it, "people tend to choose venues in tune with their existing political orientation."[66] Such segmentation may make deliberation among those with different points of view—a key requirement of democratic elections—even more difficult.

Campaigns and Democratic Deliberation

Not surprisingly, candidates for office have adjusted their campaigning methods in response to tabloid-style media coverage. They attempt to manipulate the coverage to their advantage by using techniques that, while effective in winning votes, do nothing to advance coherent deliberation on public policy. Instead of direct debates between opponents on what policies the country needs, modern campaigns are exercises in image manipulation. Campaign managers strive to manufacture favorable images of their candidates and, by means of negative advertising, unfavorable images of opponents. The basic approach is to strike a "responsive chord"—that is, to convey a message that resonates with concerns already present in the electorate to stimulate a positive or negative reaction.[67] Nothing in this strategy relates to raising or discussing serious policy issues; the point is to stimulate an emotional response that will help in obtaining votes.

Candidates today employ professional campaign managers and media consultants to organize their campaigns and create the image of the candidate to be promoted to the electorate. Although the use of campaign consultants employing modern public relations methods to market candidates dates back to the 1930s, only since the 1970s have these professionals come to dominate campaigning at all levels. Before the era of professional campaign consultants, a candidate for office would turn to a friend or associate with experience working in previous campaigns in the particular locality to handle campaign organization. Often, these individuals would be party officials, or they would have close ties to the local party organization. Their loyalty was shared between the individual candidate they were supporting and the broader political community of which they were a part. In the early 1960s, only a handful of consultants worked in campaigns; now there are thousands.[68] These consultants are responsible solely to the candidate who employs them and focus exclusively on the goal of getting the candidate elected. Today, professional consultants are standard participants in nearly all congressional campaigns and many state and local ones.

Campaign advertising provides the most direct way for candidates to communicate with the electorate. As mentioned earlier, for many campaigns for less visible offices, including the US House, advertising is the major source of information citizens have about candidates. Even in higher-profile races, ads provide candidates and their managers the ability to address voters directly and define the image they want to convey. Campaign ads employ certain stock images to elicit emotional responses rather than reasoned reflection. As one consultant described the technique, "When you want to signify that your candidate is good on jobs, you shoot him in a hard hat, pointing at a steel beam. That's the universal code for jobs. When you want to reach seniors, you shoot him in a nursing home, smiling gently at older folks."[69] Consultants use campaign ads for image manipulation, not for serious democratic deliberation, simply as packages "of stimuli whose sole purpose [is] to win the elections."[70]

Much of the work of campaign consultants involves manipulating the way the media cover the candidate. During a campaign, much of the candidate's day involves attending events and greeting supporters in order to gain media attention, especially television cameras, to convey favorable images of the candidate. In campaigns, favorable images—"good visuals"—count for more than content. During the 1984 presidential campaign in a now legendary incident, CBS reporter Leslie Stahl broadcast a hard-hitting commentary criticizing the vacuity of President Reagan's campaign.[71] To her surprise, a presidential campaign assistant phoned her thanking her for showing great pictures of the president during four and a half minutes of the evening news. While making her critical comments, Stahl had shown a montage of Reagan at various campaign events, including one where he stood among a crowd of flag-waving supporters. From the Reagan campaign's point of view, the favorable images of Reagan overwhelmed anything negative that Stahl said.

In recent years, campaign consultants have developed the art of crafting campaign commercials for the express purpose of attracting media coverage. They devise commercials that create controversy so the media will cover the controversy the commercial creates and in the process broadcast the commercial.[72] One of the first and most effective uses of the technique was devised by George H. W. Bush's campaign manager, Lee Atwater, in the 1988 presidential campaign. The ad featured a black criminal named Willie Horton, shown in a mug shot. During Michael Dukakis's tenure as Massachusetts governor, Horton had raped a woman while on a weekend furlough from a Massachusetts state prison. Although Dukakis did not make the decision to furlough Horton, Atwater discovered in precampaign focus groups that people reacted strongly against Dukakis when they heard the Horton story. The ad ran only once and was sponsored by an independent group, not the Bush campaign itself. Nevertheless, the TV news shows reported the controversy around the racist tone of the ad and how it exploited voters' fears about violent crime.[73] Network coverage not only showed the Horton ad repeatedly but reinforced the Bush campaign theme that Dukakis was a "liberal" who coddled criminals.

Since the Horton ad, campaigns have routinely sought attention through provocative ads. Often these ads are developed by "independent groups" and gain attention because of their distortions and inaccuracies, but in the process promote a favored campaign theme. In 2004, a group called "Swift Boat Veterans for Truth," financed by billionaire oilman T. Boone Pickens, broadcast an ad, full of distortions and outright falsehoods, in a small West Virginia media market claiming that Democratic presidential candidate John Kerry had not earned his Vietnam War medals.[74] Both the TV networks and major newspapers soon ran stories about the ad, most of which pointed out its falsehoods, but in the process rebroadcast much of it. One study found there were more news reports on the ad during the campaign than on the war then raging in Iraq.[75] By 2008, the presidential campaigns posting ads on campaign websites aimed at attracting media coverage, even if they were never broadcast, had become the norm. In 2011, candidates were again employing the tactic in the run-up to the 2012 election. In June of 2011, Republican candidate Mitt Romney gained considerable mainstream media attention with an ad attacking President Obama's record on unemployment.[76]

Not only in advertising but in all campaign events and communications, consultants have perfected the art of using particular words or phrases to strike the responsive chord. Legislative proposals and campaign promises are designed and worded to maximize positive voter response.[77] Bill Clinton's 1996 campaign consultant, Dick Morris, provided daily polling reports to identify the precise themes and words that Clinton should use to elicit a positive voter response. According to campaign insiders, Morris's polling analysis influenced nearly everything Clinton did prior to the election, including where he spent his summer vacation![78] Unfortunately for democratic deliberation, these packages of stimuli have come to dominate contemporary campaigns, as candidates and their professional consultants manufacture series of images to be presented in the media. Campaign staffs huddle in "war rooms" to devise responses to the campaigns of opponents and concoct endless efforts to "spin" events in ways favorable to their candidate. Rather than composing speeches to advance reasoned arguments about public policy, professional speechwriters build them around pithy phrases and slogans that can provide sound bites for the television news programs. Media events—such as the Clinton/Gore bus tours in 1992 and 1996, Gore's postconvention Mississippi River boat tour in 2000, George W. Bush's innumerable inner-city school visits to convey his "compassionate conservatism," or Obama's massive campaign rallies—are staged to attract media coverage and strike a responsive chord with voters. Promises are made—such as "No new taxes"—that the candidates know are unrealistic.

Even the televised candidate debates are primarily regarded as opportunities to project images and strike poses rather than to discuss public policy issues seriously. Afterwards, both candidates and the media focus on who "won" the debate rather than on what was said, and winning or losing is defined in terms of candidate appearance and style rather than substance. In the first 2000 presidential debate, much more was made of Al Gore's stiffness and his loud sighs in response to George W. Bush's remarks than of the issues they discussed. Bush received the same treatment in 2004, when he scowled and appeared petulant in his first debate with John Kerry, and McCain was derided in the same way when he seemed to glower with anger at Obama in their first debate. Debate foibles feature in the jokes on late-night comedy shows, *Saturday Night Live* skits, and *Daily Show* satire—some of it later rebroadcast on news programs. Voters thus gain from the debates little information about where the candidates stand on policy issues; instead, they are offered superficial impressions of candidate personalities as filtered through news stories and comedy shows.[79]

Entertainment media provide candidates many opportunities to obtain the favorable media coverage that they seek. Candidate appearances on entertainment shows such as Letterman and Leno, Oprah, *The View,* and above all *Saturday*

Night Live (SNL) have become staples of presidential campaigns. These shows offer candidates the chance to engage in light banter, trade jokes with their hosts, and cultivate a congenial image rather than face hard questions from traditional journalists.[80] In 2008, Tina Fey's impersonation of Sarah Palin on SNL became one of the most-commented-upon incidents of the campaign. Palin was able to capitalize on the focus the SNL skits, even their less-than-flattering aspects, gave to her presence in the campaign and had no difficulty participating in the joke herself in joint appearances with Fey on the show. Her participation showed her as a good sport and helped to soften her image. In contrast, the harsh grilling she received from Katie Couric on *Sixty Minutes* that showed her as ill informed and inarticulate proved a serious problem to her candidacy throughout the campaign. Small wonder that Palin and other candidates prefer the image-enhancing opportunities of an appearance on an entertainment show, like Jay Leno, to responding to substantive questions from journalists.

With campaign advisers seeking only to strike the responsive chord and the media seeking more to entertain than to inform, voters have found little in recent presidential campaigns either to inspire them or to help them deliberate about important issues. Instead, much of the media's focus has been on attempts to identify elements of each candidate's "character" to be presented as a central campaign issue. In popular "gotcha" journalism, however, examining character seems to begin and end with checking for embarrassing incidents in a candidate's background or anything inconsistent in a candidate's past public statements. Rarely do journalists delve very deeply into how candidates have conducted themselves in office as an indication of character. In the 2000 election, for example, candidate Al Gore was pilloried for supposedly claiming to have been the "inventor of the Internet." Gallons of ink were spilled and much airtime spent examining, in detail, whether or not Gore actually had made such a statement (he had not) and in discussing the implications for his character ("Is Gore a serial exaggerator?"). Meanwhile, little attention was devoted to Gore's actual role in the Senate in the late 1980s in promoting legislation that had, in fact, laid the foundation for the Internet.[81] Coverage of George W. Bush also tended to focus on the trivial rather than the substantive. Much attention was given to his malapropisms and mispronunciations, but there was little exploration of his business background. In 2004, both campaigns and the media focused in minute detail on Kerry's and Bush's military records, which were portrayed as somehow relevant to political leadership, although presidential scholars find little connection between prior military experience and the national security responsibilities of a president.[82] The slight acquaintance in Chicago that Barack Obama had with former 1960s radical Bill Ayers received intense media scrutiny as a character problem yet quickly was ignored once Obama was elected. For all their supposed emphasis on "character," neither the media nor the campaigns provide reliable insight into the actual background, experience, or personalities of the candidates.

New social media like YouTube, Twitter, and Facebook now offer candidates the opportunity to overcome the limitations of mainstream media coverage and bypass journalistic filters—thereby creating an unmediated campaign. These media, plus candidate e-mails and websites, also create new opportunities to promote favorable images of the candidate directly to voters. Such unmediated campaigning proved a centerpiece of Obama's 2008 campaign. Early on, the campaign used its website, Twitter, and Facebook to connect supporters to the campaign and raise campaign contributions. It produced nearly 2,000 online videos posted to its site and to YouTube, obtaining about 900 million hits over the course of the campaign.[83] While social media opened many opportunities to candidates to polish their images, little of this material did much to advance issue deliberation. The "Obama Girl" video featuring a model describing her "crush" on Obama, developed by a nonaffiliated group, proved one of the most popular and spawned imitations extolling John McCain, Rudolph Giuliani, and Ron Paul.[84] Yet, despite the prevalence of such frivolous material, the new media did offer candidates the opportunity to communicate substantive ideas at length, free from the sound bite constraints of conventional media. For example, Obama responded to the criticism of his affiliation with his controversial minister Jeremiah Wright in a 37-minute video posted on YouTube that received more than five million hits (about half the number for "Obama Girl," however).[85] In sum, as with the Internet and new media technology generally, social media offer an opportunity for improving campaign deliberation and make available to the discerning voter much new information about candidates and campaign issues. The problem remains filtering through the vast amount of this material, much of it frivolous and self-serving, to the useful substance.

The campaign manipulations and vacuous media coverage described so far suggest that American elections provide little opportunity for democratic deliberation. At election time, citizens are mere observers of a spectacle that is designed to entertain them in order to attract their votes but offers no opportunity for them to engage in debate about policy directions.[86] Political communication during elections makes no effort to create coalitions behind "governing ideas." According to the political scientist Lance Bennett, "Missing almost entirely is any sort of give and take exchange through which social groups, parties, and candidates might develop mutual commitments to a broad political agenda."[87] By abandoning substantive exchanges on policy issues that matter, our trivialized political campaigns have diminished the value of elections as a democratic device. Voting may remain the means by which Americans choose the individuals who govern them, but because of the dearth of deliberation, election outcomes provide little indication of how the voters expect to be governed. Small wonder, then, that elections have ceased to be effective instruments for democratic control of government.

Control

Because of the poverty of electoral discourse in American elections and the absence of deliberation about important issues, the meaning of electoral outcomes is always in doubt. Neither winners nor losers are required to draw specific policy lessons from election outcomes. In this situation, elections have begun to lose their capacity to control what happens in government. Elections decided on the basis of sound bites, debate gaffes, and campaign image manipulation fail to resolve the political conflicts going on in society. All sides to fundamental conflicts can easily point to the irrelevance of what went on in the election to their particular concerns. Nor do elections empower anyone's governing agenda when they have ceased to play the role of building a governing coalition behind a specific agenda. Elections that fail to send clear direction to those holding government office permit those officials to set the direction themselves, independent of the democratic electorate's control.

To cite the example of Athenian democracy once again, the contemporary American situation contrasts sharply with the control Athenian citizens exercised over public action through the Assembly, when public deliberations conveyed precise directives of the citizenry's will to officials charged with carrying it out. As participants in those deliberations, officials knew from direct experience what decisions they were to execute. They were also subject to direct intervention by the Assembly if their actions deviated from what was intended. In addition, the Athenians provided for annual audits of official actions to evaluate whether they conformed to Assembly intent.[88] Punishment was immediate and severe if official misconduct was discovered. During the period of democratic rule in Athens, there was no question that democratic institutions were in control of public policy. Unfortunately, the same cannot be said of the foremost American democratic institution—elections.

Political Parties and Democracy

Since the beginning of representative democracy, political parties have provided the means of putting democratic majorities in control of government. As the political scientist E. E. Schattschneider once put it, "Modern democracy is unthinkable save in terms of parties."[89] It is unthinkable because some way has to be found in a mass democracy to bring together millions of voters with diverse concerns and interests to form a broad governing majority that can control what government does. Individuals are represented and gain control when they have the potential of contributing to that majority, and parties have been the traditional mechanism through which such majorities are brought to life. In addition, by organizing government, parties can make the electoral majority they represent effective in formulating policies that reflect the preferences of the individuals and groups who support the party in elections.

Ideally, parties perform three vital functions that promote democratic governance.[90] First, they select candidates for office and mobilize voters to create a link between individual citizens and government. Political parties exist to win control of government offices and, in a democracy, can win office only by attracting the votes of a majority of citizens. This gives parties an incentive to seek candidates who can represent the preferences of a majority and appeal to voters around policy issues that address broad public needs. Since every vote can be of value in contributing to winning a majority, democratic political parties will compete to attract votes by supporting policies that address the preferences, needs, and concerns of all voters, regardless of wealth or social status. Second, on winning office, the political party provides the structure around which government can be organized to implement a winning party's campaign promises. As shown in chapter 1, this is a particular challenge for the American separation of powers system, but as was also argued earlier, overcoming the institutional barriers to the implementation of majority preferences has always involved the use of parties, as in the Jeffersonian governing model. In all representative democracies throughout the world, political parties remain the universal mechanism for organizing governments to enact the will of electoral majorities. Third, when parties are in charge of what happens in government, they can be held responsible for what happens. Again, as discussed in chapter 1, this accountability empowers voters. Through the use of the party label, citizen voters can pass judgment on the performance of elected officials, rewarding them with continuance in office if they have addressed majority concerns or throwing them out of office in favor of an alternative party if they have failed. According to the ideal of party government, if all these functions are performed, the right to vote can lead to equal representation.

Of course, no political parties in actual representative democracies have satisfied perfectly this ideal vision of party government. The American historical experience with the bossism of urban political machines and political party corruption has deviated often from the ideal vision sketched in the previous paragraph. Nevertheless, no other mechanism besides parties has been developed anywhere that structures the votes of millions of individual citizens to provide fair and equitable representation. As I argue here, without strong political parties, alternative means of structuring votes are likely to develop that bias representation in the direction of the rich and powerful much more than parties do.

For all their potential faults, the democratic virtue of political parties is that they are mechanisms for collecting votes; their power depends on the number of votes they gather. The fact that each citizen in a representative democracy has a vote makes her or him, because of that fact alone, worthy of attention from party leaders. Whatever other attributes or resources a citizen may have—wealth, education, status—the possession of a vote alone gives even the poorest and weakest a measure of influence through a political party. That is why, in the United States in the nineteenth and early twentieth centuries, political party workers stood on the docks to organize arriving immigrants. It is also why, in the evolution of nearly all democracies, vigorous party competition has resulted in the expansion of suffrage, as parties in power have granted the vote to additional groups of voters in hopes of enlisting them as party supporters. According to political scientist Walter Dean Burnham, political parties "generate countervailing collective power on behalf of the many individually powerless against the relatively few who are individually—or organizationally—powerful."[91]

Over the past one hundred years, a number of factors have diminished the ability of political parties to provide this countervailing power of the powerless against the powerful. The mass-based political party was invented in the United States in the 1830s, when it became the world's first mass representative democracy under universal white male suffrage. Throughout the balance of the nineteenth century, the dominant Democratic and Republican Parties organized voters and competed to control government. Urban party machines integrated millions of immigrants into American political life and, along with their rural counterparts, oversaw the emergence of an industrial society. Elections were well-organized affairs in which tightly structured precinct and ward organizations kept in contact with individual voters and turned them out to vote in massive numbers. This method of organizing elections prevailed through the middle of the last century.

Beginning with the Progressives' attacks on machine bossism and corruption early in the twentieth century, the dominant role of political parties in organizing elections steadily diminished. First, civil service reform and the government bureaucracy's assumption of traditional party functions—such as running elections (printing ballots, setting up voting booths, and so on) and providing social welfare—eliminated patronage resources that nineteenth-century parties had used to reward supporters. The ability of parties to mobilize an army of party loyalists to work on behalf of party candidates diminished. Second, the direct primary took away from party officials, party conventions, and party caucuses the crucial power to choose who ran under the party label. Although primaries were first introduced in some states at the beginning of the twentieth century, they only gradually became the dominant means of selecting party nominees. As recently as 1968, Hubert Humphrey gained the Democratic nomination for president without entering a single presidential primary; he accumulated sufficient support from delegates chosen at state party conventions and caucuses to win. By 1972, this campaign strategy had become impossible for presidential aspirants in either political party, as most states enacted comprehensive primary laws, and by the end of the 1970s, nomination to nearly all elective offices in the country required winning primaries. Finally, by the 1960s, ambitious individual politicians began to create their own personal campaign machines independent of political party organizations. Utilizing the advice of expert political consultants and advertising on television, candidates were able to organize their campaigns and mobilize voter support without the need for party-controlled resources. In response, political parties changed from organizations that directly mobilized voters and controlled politicians elected as a result to ones that served the needs of politicians as they sought to gain office.[92]

Balancing these changes that seemed to undercut the democratic function of political parties have been more recent ones that offer the possibility of rein-vigorated parties and party competition. First, the Democratic and Republican Parties now present voters with distinct choices as to what each has to offer in terms of ideology and policy preferences.[93] An ideological sorting has occurred between the parties as conservative Democrats have moved to the Republican Party and liberal Republicans to the Democratic. The shift of the once Solid Democratic South to Republican political allegiance during the 1970s and 1980s represents the most obvious indicator of this phenomenon. But a similar but opposing shift occurred in the North and Far West where states and districts that routinely elected liberal Republicans to office in the middle decades of the twentieth century now send Democrats to Washington. Today, both the office-holders and voters of each party hold more internally consistent views on political issues and diverge clearly from each other. The days of "there's not a dime's worth of difference" between the parties is definitely over. Second, con-gressional partisans are now more unified. Both parties in both houses of Con-gress can mobilize voting blocs on behalf of party issue positions on most votes. Party label thus gives voters in districts throughout the country a fairly clear indication of what a candidate stands for and with whom she will associate once elected to Congress. Third, congressional elections have become more national-ized. While many voters still vote based on local concerns, the most important of which is familiarity with the incumbent, several recent elections have pro-duced shifts in congressional control reflecting shifts in national mood. Perhaps the first of these recent "wave" elections occurred in 1994, when the Republi-cans gained a majority in the House of Representatives for the first time in forty years based on discontent with President Clinton. A similar wave swept the Democrats to power in 2006 in response to voter discontent with Bush, which would be reinforced in 2008 along with the election of Barack Obama. In 2010, the wave switched in the opposite direction, putting the Republican majority back in control in the House. What all these waves show is many voters perceiving their choices for representatives in terms of partisan evaluations of national government performance.

Some observers decry these developments as evidence of growing "partisan polarization." Yet from the point of view of democratic party theory, they are evidence that American political parties now clearly stand for principles, ideas, and policies that allow voters to distinguish between them. According to political scientists John H. Aldrich and John D. Griffin, this is the first condition that must be met for political party competition in elections to control government.[94] The second two conditions—that a party gain control of government and that voters can hold a party accountable for that control—are not met. We now come back to the defects in the separation of powers structure of government described in chapter 1. The institutional structure of American government and antimajoritarian procedures like the filibuster prevent parties from being instruments of either responsiveness or accountability. With these institutional barriers in place, political party competition cannot be a mechanism for a democratic electorate to control government.

Without the capacity for partisan control of government and for voters to clearly hold parties accountable for government actions, partisanship that ought to facilitate democratic control has become destructive in modern America. Normally, partisanship provides the means for parties to articulate alternative solutions to public problems and represent competing interests affected by them. Political party competition structures political conflict within society peacefully and addresses problems in ways that accommodate diverse interests. Both Edmund Burke and J. S. Mill, neither a huge fan of political parties, understood the value of partisan competition for resolving political conflict.[95] Parties in control of government and accountable to voters need to devise policies responsive to the wishes of its partisan supporters but also capable of maintaining support from a majority of the electorate. Too much partisan zeal can risk losing support from more moderate voters and the opposing political party always will be vigilant to convert those moderates to its policy agenda. The failure of one party's partisan solutions results in their replacement or modification when the other party comes to power. This sort of partisanship defines choices for voters but also leads to moderate and practical policy solutions. What happens if partisanship becomes unfettered by the responsibility for government action and from accountability?

The answer can be seen in irresponsible hyper-partisanship that seems to prevail in America today. Numerous studies have documented the rising partisan polarization in American politics.[96] Political elites, including officeholders, in both the Democratic and Republican Parties are more ideological and divide more sharply from one another on major issues than they did a few decades ago. Partisan division among the mass public also has grown with Democratic and Republican identifiers differing more on policy issues, but the public at large remains less divided and more moderate than political elites. Some political scientists, in fact, argue that polarization is primarily an elite phenomenon marking a sharp division between governing elites and a more moderate public. Others argue that the partisan divide goes beyond narrow elites and also characterizes the most active and attentive portion of the mass electorate. All sides, however, document the extent to which the issue positions elected officials take in public debates diverge sharply from the more moderate positions reflected in public opinion polls.

Political scientist Paul J. Quirk uses the term "polarized populism" to describe this partisan divide. He argues that elected officials must adhere to hard right or hard left positions to appease their most ideologically motivated constituents who dominate primary elections.[97] Given the relatively small turnout in primaries, informal political organizations, financial contributors, and the voters they mobilize control election outcomes. Since many congressional districts are noncompetitive in general elections—due to partisan gerrymandering and other factors—winning a primary, or for an incumbent, avoiding a primary challenge, are essential to winning or remaining in office. Ideologically motivated activists in primaries also affect presidential races, as candidates must stake out positions in primary contests that bind presidents once in office. Although presidential nominees tend to moderate partisan rhetoric to win the votes of more moderate voters in the general election, the commitments made to their more ideological primary supporters cannot be ignored if they want to mobilize their "base" and, more important, if they want to prevent a primary challenge when they seek reelection.

While Quirk and others argue that polarized populism binds elected officials in both parties, the phenomenon has pushed the Republican Party, especially, far to the right. The growing clout of the "Tea Party" in the 2010 elections and after drew attention to the pressure hard-right activists exert on Republican representatives, but the Tea Party is the latest manifestation of the hold right-wing Republican activists hold on the party.[98] Anti-tax activists, in particular, such as the libertarian Club for Growth and Grover Norquist's Americans for Tax Reform have for years demanded that all Republican office seekers pledge not to vote for any tax increases. Terrified of the financial power of the backers of both groups and their ability to finance primary challengers, Republican lawmakers refused to support reasonable compromises to include tax increases along with spending cuts to reduce the nation's budget deficit even though public opinion polls, even among rank-and-file Republican voters, show public support for raising taxes to reduce the deficit.[99]

Polarized pluralism combined with the lack of responsiveness and accountability of the separation of powers system stymies the ability of the party system to place electoral majorities in control of government policy. It promotes the gridlock inherent in the system and undermines the ability to reach any bipartisan compromise needed to bridge divided institutions. Members of Congress, in particular, find themselves free of collective responsibility for policy outcomes and thus the need to formulate practical solutions. Instead, they stake out extreme positions, like no new taxes, that satisfy their political "base" regardless of how widely shared these views are among their constituents as a whole. Rather than clarifying choices for voters and promoting moderate policies reflective of an electoral majority, partisanship in contemporary America serves to obscure choices and promote extreme policies far from what most citizens want.[100] The consequence has been ongoing policy gridlock with electoral institutions unable to devise solutions to national problems. The failure of elected officials to formulate effective policies has meant giving control over key policies to nonelected officials.

One area in which much policy responsibility has been ceded to nonelected bureaucrats is the making of national economic policy. Since the 1970s, several presidents and Congresses have been unable to formulate coherent policies to manage the national economy. Because of the ambiguity of election outcomes, elected representatives have not had a political mandate to deal with major economic problems, whether the spiraling inflation of the 1970s, the sluggish economy of the early 1990s, or the financial crisis of fall 2008. Candidates have sought election based on promises to address these issues, but once in office they find themselves unable to agree on specific policies.

In the absence of effective action by elected officials, the Federal Reserve Board, an appointed body designed to be insulated from electoral pressures, took control of much of the responsibility for economic policy. When Congress and the president failed to come up with an effective policy to stem inflation in the late 1970s, the board's chairman, Paul Volcker, stepped in to impose stringent controls on the nation's money supply, which restricted the availability of credit and pushed up interest rates. While that approach proved effective in bringing down inflation in the 1980s, it did so at the cost of precipitating a massive recession and unemployment for millions of Americans. Alternative approaches to inflation control or strategies that might have balanced controlling inflation with other policy goals, such as maintaining high employment, could not be implemented because elected officeholders did not possess the electoral mandate to enact them. Chairman Volcker stepped into a policy vacuum, but not with the policies that a democratic citizenry would have chosen.

In 1990, a similar policy deadlock, this time over how to bring the country out of a recession, again left the problem in the hands of the Federal Reserve. With Congress and the president unable to agree on how to stimulate the economy or deal with the huge budget deficit—itself a consequence of electoral and institutional deadlock that inhibited enactment of stimulative spending programs—the Federal Reserve attempted to stimulate the economy by lowering interest rates. Only when the new president and Congress agreed, beginning in 1993, on a fiscal policy aimed at balancing the budget did the economy begin to revive. Interestingly, as the economic boom of the 1990s became the longest sustained period of economic growth since World War II, many observers credited Federal Reserve chairman Alan Greenspan, rather than elected officials, and looked to him to maintain prosperity.

Yet Greenspan's genius for economic management became tarnished as the Fed, under his direction, turned a blind eye to the risky loan practices of banks in the early 2000s that brought on the subprime loan crisis of 2008 and the massive recession of 2009. Because the Fed was responsive to the banking industry and its desire for huge profits, it failed to exercise adequate oversight of bank lending practices or regulate the exotic investments banks were using to package mortgage securities. In this case, the Fed's insulation from political pressure from elected officials enhanced its responsiveness to the special interests of Wall Street. In the wake of the crisis and the ensuing recession, the Obama administration managed to push a stimulus package through Congress (as described in chapter 1), but congressional gridlock prevented any follow-up stimulus, when the first proved inadequate to revive robust economic growth. With fiscal policy stymied, once again Americans looked to the Federal Reserve and chair Ben Bernanke to revive the economy. The Fed did approve monetary expansion to stimulate the economy in 2010 and 2011, but limited its actions out of fear that it might ignite inflation. As a result, unemployment remained at high levels. When faced with a choice of sustained high employment or the risk of inflation, the Fed opted to respond to investors' and bankers' fear of inflation rather than the pain of the unemployed.

The increasing use of the judiciary to make important policy decisions (as was examined in depth in chapter 2) also reflects the decline in electoral control. As elections fail to bring closure to serious social conflicts over issues such as abortion, the status of minorities and women and gays, or the need to protect the environment, the parties to these conflicts, as we saw, turn to the courts. Thus, many significant public policy choices are made without any discussion in election campaigns. In the early 1980s, for example, a federal judge supervised one of the most significant economic and business developments of the decade—the breakup of the AT&T telephone monopoly. That decision, which went well beyond merely dividing AT&T into several "Baby Bells," dictated much of American telecommunication policy well into the present century, including regulation of the development of such new technologies as fiber optic networks.[101] Amazingly, in a representative democracy in which elections are supposed to be controlling, these momentous decisions were made without the participation of any elected officials and with virtually no discussion during election campaigns.

The failure of elections to control what government does derives both from the inequality of representation and from the absence of meaningful deliberation in contemporary elections. As argued earlier, elections are a mechanism to "compensate for private inequalities in political resources."[102] When public officials are truly subject to the will of the electorate, they are under the control of a mandate that each voter has had an equal hand in producing. In the absence of electoral authority, powerful private interests will find some way, whether through bribery or flattery, to influence government officials. As special interests have come to undermine equal representation in elections, they have increased their capacity to influence officials independent of elections. Contributions to election campaigns are means to ensure access to the bureaucracy more than to influence legislation.

The powerful interests that provide money for modern campaigns do so primarily to prevent elections from controlling what government does. As long as elected officials are constrained by promises made in the hidden election not to enact legislation adverse to the interests of their big contributors, they have an incentive to delegate decision making to the bureaucracy and then to intervene selectively on behalf of wealthy and powerful contributors. In much the same way, meaningless campaign rhetoric keeps discussion of major issues out of election campaigns. When important issues eventually are dealt with—in congressional committees, the bureaucracy, or the courts—their resolution is left to powerful, well-placed interests with access to those arenas. Keeping deliberation on important issues out of the public arena of electoral politics empowers those with access to the less visible arenas where the final decisions are made. In this way, the absence of meaningful campaign deliberation reinforces biased representation, and both undermine electoral control over government policy.

Meeting the Challenge: Reform Electoral Institutions, Promote Democratic Deliberation

For all our celebration of elections as the touchstone of representative democracy, the practice of electoral politics in the contemporary United States falls far short of what democratic theory requires. Contemporary practice meets none of the three criteria for democratic elections listed earlier in the chapter. The money election, faulty apportionment of the Senate, single-member districts, and the Electoral College all undermine equal representation in elections. By the time the ordinary voter pulls the voting lever, the powerful special interests that have structured the ballot have left him or her with very little meaningful representation. To compound this flawed representation, the trivial rhetoric of modern elections obscures the relevance of important issues. Elections decided on the basis of sound bites, negative campaign commercials, and sensationalized exposure of character flaws provides no meaningful direction for government. As long as candidates can be elected without discussing what truly matters to voters, they need not pay any attention to the electorate when governing. As a result, elections make less and less difference to what government does. Decisions on important issues are increasingly made out of public view, in legislative committees, the bureaucracy, and the courts. In a representative democracy, the degree to which elections fall short of satisfying the criteria for genuinely democratic elections defines the extent to which government fails to be truly democratic.

The criteria of equal representation, deliberation, and control are demanding ones. Elections in the United States have never satisfied them completely, nor do elections in other representative democracies. The failure to satisfy those criteria is not in itself the challenge facing American democracy today. Making elections democratic institutions is a continual struggle in democracies, one that can never be fully won. The true challenge that current electoral practice poses for American democracy is that the struggle to make elections democratic institutions seems to have been largely abandoned. Democrats should hope that however short of the democratic ideal elections may fall, they are at least evolving toward it. Unfortunately, Americans' recent experience with elections suggests that we are regressing from the democratic ideal. The challenge to our democracy is to reform our electoral institutions so that they once again evolve in a democratic direction.

Institutional reforms to assure more equal representation are a crucial first step to more democratic elections. Altering the constitutional design for Senate representation would be a good place to begin. The best solution, from the standpoint of one person, one vote, would be apportionment of Senate seats purely on the basis of population as is the case for the House of Representatives. Such a reform probably would require enlargement of the Senate so that the least populous states could have, at minimum one senator, with the additional senators given to more populous ones. Larry Sabato has proposed a reform that, falling short of pure apportionment by population, would give additional Senate seats to more populous states. In his plan, each state would retain at least two senators, but the ten largest states would receive two additional seats and the next fifteen largest one seat.[103] This plan also would serve to make the Electoral College more representative than it now is, but a better approach more consistent with equal representation would be simply to abolish the Electoral College and elect presidents by popular vote. Democracy requires that a majority of voters determine who is to be president. As regards House elections, a proportional representation system offers a more democratic alternative to the single-member plurality system. To shift to proportional representation in the US House, state delegations could be elected from multi-member districts. In small states with only a few representatives, the district could encompass the whole state, while larger states could be divided into several multi-member districts. A state with a delegation of fifteen, for example, could be divided into three districts each electing five House members.[104] Seats within each district would be allocated according to the proportional vote of the parties in the district. While the changes in Senate representation and the Electoral College would require constitutional amendments, state legislatures could enact the switch to proportional representation since they now have the constitutional authority to determine how House members are chosen.

The ideal approach to the problem of the money election would be public financing of election campaigns. Campaign funding biases our entire political system in favor of the wealthy and makes a mockery of any notion of equal representation. None of the challenges to democracy discussed in this book will be addressed unless we can end the dominance of big money in our electoral system. The best solution would be an expanded system of public financing of elections, combined with provision of free broadcast airtime for candidates for office. As long as candidates are dependent on private funding for their campaigns, wealthy special interests will find loopholes to get around even the best-crafted regulations and will remain a major source of contributions to most candidates. Only full public funding of national campaigns eliminates the money election and permits equal representation. The most logical way to reduce campaign costs would be to provide free media access to major candidates, eliminating the biggest expense of campaigning.[105] Elections are a *public* institution for ensuring democratic governance; they can succeed as such only with *public* funding and free candidate access to the public airwaves. Regrettably, the demise of public funding of presidential campaigns demands a more vigorous effort for more comprehensive public funding.

Devising a fair and democratic system for allocating public campaign funds and determining who obtains media access would be complex, but many European democracies and some state and local governments already have such systems.[106] Maine, Vermont, Arizona, and Massachusetts have passed laws providing public funding of campaigns. Maine's Clean Election Act now funds about one-third of the state's candidates. Except for a small amount to be raised from fifty small donors to qualify for public funding, candidates cannot spend any privately raised funds or their own fortunes on their campaigns, and their overall spending is limited to 75 percent of the average spending on campaigns for a particular office in the previous two election cycles. So far, Maine's law has increased the competitiveness of state legislative offices and increased the number of contested primaries by 40 percent.[107] In Tucson, Arizona, according to political scientist and former mayor Thomas Volgy, public funding has combined with spending limits to increase the competitiveness of local races, stimulated more grassroots as opposed to media campaigns, and reduced total spending on campaigns.[108] Regrettably, recent Supreme Court decisions, enforcing its doctrine that campaign spending constitutes free speech, have put limits on such state experiments. In a 2011 decision regarding the Arizona law, the Court declared a provision unconstitutional that allowed a candidate whose opponent opted out of the public funding and spent private funds over the law's expenditure limits to receive additional public funds to match the private funding. While a system of comprehensive public funding would be ideal, the barriers to achieving such a system are enormous. As long as the Supreme Court continues to equate campaign spending with free speech, as it did in the Arizona case, privately financed candidates have the potential of overwhelming any publicly financed one. In the face of adverse Supreme Court decisions and other obstacles, a comprehensive public funding system may be out of reach for some time.

In the meantime, a second-best approach would be to make the mass of voters the primary source of campaign cash, given in small amounts, in place of big money donations from the wealthy. As an alternative to full-scale public funding, several Washington think tanks have proposed such a small donor approach.[109] Building upon the recent ability of Obama and other candidates to raise substantial amounts from small donors using social media, the proposal recommends public matching funds for small contributions without any limits on overall spending limits. Current contribution limits on larger donors would be maintained with mandated disclosure. The public matching combined with the limits on larger contributors would provide incentives for candidates to make small contributions a larger proportion of their campaign chests. It would widen the involvement of ordinary citizens in supporting campaigns while diminishing candidates' dependence on big donors. In this same vein, Yale law professors Ian Ayres and Bruce Ackerman have developed a more radical and most ingenious idea for public funding of campaigns: They would allot to every citizen an equal amount of "Patriot Dollars"—in effect, campaign vouchers—to spend in support of the candidates of his or her choice.[110] Under this system, instead of hitting up fat cats for campaign donations, candidates would have to convince ordinary voters to support their campaigns with their Patriot Dollars. Ayres and Ackerman's proposal offers a potentially attractive way to apply the principle of one person, one vote, to the realm of campaign finance.

In the near future, neither the commercial media nor candidates themselves can be expected to promote effective deliberation on issues at election time. Providing effective deliberation will require specific public institutions dedicated to this aim. The existing Public Broadcasting System, including the fine programming on National Public Radio, offers much of the best coverage of issues in campaigns today. Better funding of these efforts, from both public and philanthropic sources, and more time dedicated to issue deliberation could enhance the quality of elections. In addition, political theorist James S. Fishkin has suggested an intriguing way to improve public deliberation in presidential election campaigns.[111] He proposes bringing a random sample of voters to a single spot, perhaps a university campus, early in the presidential nominating process to meet with prospective candidates. Over a period of several days, the voters would meet the candidates, hear their campaign speeches, and have an opportunity to question them. All these events would be broadcast to a national television audience. In addition to meeting the candidates, the group would hear from experts on various issues affecting the country and, most important, would have an opportunity to discuss and debate among themselves. At the end of the period, the voters would be polled on their opinions of the presidential candidates. Fishkin calls this a "deliberative opinion poll" because, unlike conventional polls, which are mere aggregations of responses that isolated individuals make to questions, this poll would come after the sample of citizens had listened to, and talked among themselves about, the candidates and the issues. Fishkin hopes that this event, if well publicized, could be a major factor influencing the presidential campaign and could bring an element of deliberation to the process. Similar deliberative polls could be used in congressional, state, and local elections.

The best mechanism for giving electoral majorities better control of government policy would be to improve the ability of political parties to perform this key function. As long as the separation of parties prevents effective governmental responsiveness and accountability as detailed in chapter 1, parties will be impeded in working effectively to empower democratic majorities. So, improving the party system depends on accomplishing the institutional reforms recommended earlier. Even without such comprehensive reform of the separation of powers, modifications of the system for nominating party candidates could end the primary system's tendency to make candidates beholden to the most extreme and zealous partisans. One approach would be to return control of nominations to political party organizations and the party officials who lead them. While the era of the party bosses often is decried, they did have an ability to select candidates who could appeal to the moderate middle of the ideological spectrum. More concerned with winning elections and governing effectively to stay in office, party professionals dampen the pressures of extreme ideologues. Yet given how well entrenched the primary system now is in the political system, a more realistic approach to ending "polarized populism" might be to reform the dominant closed primary system in which each party's nominees are chosen in separate elections. In an open primary system, candidates from all parties compete in a single election. The two candidates winning the most votes in the primary then compete in the general election to win office. Open primary advocates claim that this system, because the electorate comprises both Republican and Democratic partisans as well as independents, rewards candidates who moderate their appeals to attract support beyond their partisan base. California recently adopted the open primary, creating a natural experiment to see if it can truly create less polarized politics.

Innovative ideas for making elections more democratic cannot succeed, however, unless citizens become more aware of why and how our elections are deficient. Citizen discontent with election processes has been well documented in recent years and is reflected in the popularity of "anti-politicians" such as Ross Perot, Jesse Ventura, and Arnold Schwarzenegger. But making elections more effective instruments of democracy will require more than voting for folksy demagogues or glitzy entertainers. As this chapter argues, effective democratic reform must begin with an understanding of what makes elections democratic instruments—equal representation, citizen deliberation, and control of government policy through elections. To meet this challenge to democracy, we must remember that elections alone do not guarantee democratic government. Only elections organized to empower ordinary voters can satisfy democracy's promise.

Thought Questions

1. Would you favor a shift from single-member plurality districts (SMP) in electing members of the House of Representatives to a proportional representation (PR) system? Many political scientists argue that PR systems encourage multiparty systems. Assuming that this would be a consequence of PR in the United States, would you consider that a positive or a negative? Why?

2. One way to enhance party control of election campaigns would be to eliminate primary elections and allow party organizations to choose their candidates. Would you favor such a reform? What are the pluses and minuses of choosing candidates for office through primary elections?

3. In the landmark 1976 case *Buckley v. Valeo,* the Supreme Court ruled that campaign expenditures were a form of free speech and thus protected by the First Amendment—thereby overturning any mandatory controls on the amount of money spent in campaigns. Do you agree with the Court that campaign expenditures deserve protection under the First Amendment? Can you think of reasons why limits on spending might be justified?

4. This chapter argues that democratic elections need to provide opportunities for citizen deliberation on public issues. Is this a realistic expectation in modern America? Can you come up with any suggestions for how deliberation might be successfully integrated into modern election campaigns?

5. The intervention of the judiciary in setting policy in a variety of areas such as civil rights, the environment, abortion, and business regulation is presented in this chapter as undermining electoral control of these policy areas. Is diminishing electoral control in these areas necessarily undemocratic? Think about this issue from the point of view of a member of a racial or ethnic minority, a gay person, a pregnant woman, or an environmental activist.

Suggestions for Further Reading

Amy, Douglas J. *Real Choices/New Voices.* New York: Columbia University Press, 2002. A detailed analysis of the advantages of proportional representation.

Ayres, Ian, and Bruce A. Ackerman. *Voting With Dollars: A New Paradigm for Campaign Finance.* New Haven, CT: Yale University Press, 2002. An intriguing proposal to give every American an equal stake in financing campaigns to match their equal vote.

Corrado, Anthony, et al. *The New Campaign Finance Sourcebook.* Washington, DC: Brookings Institution Press, 2005. Brookings Institution experts explain how our complex system of campaign financing works, including analysis of various reform

proposals. There is a linked website at www.brookings.edu/press/Books/2005/
campaign_finance_sourcebook.aspx.

Edelman, Murray. *Constructing the Political Spectacle.* Chicago: University of Chicago
Press, 1988. According to this book, all the political world's a stage and citizens are
mere spectators, especially at election time.

Fishkin, James S. *Democracy and Deliberation: New Directions for Political Reform.* New
Haven, CT: Yale University Press, 1991. A critique of American elections as deliberative institutions, with intriguing proposals for reform.

*Morris, Dick. *Behind the Oval Office: Winning the Presidency in the Nineties.* New York:
Random House, 1997. Bill Clinton's 1996 campaign strategist provides a professional's perspective on American elections.

Nelson, Michael, ed. *The Elections of 2008.* Washington, DC: CQ Press, 2009. The best
among several anthologies analyzing the 2008 elections, with thoughtful essays on
every aspect of the process.

*Polsby, Nelson W., Aaron Wildavsky, and David A. Hopkins. *Presidential Elections.* 12th ed.
New York: Rowman & Littlefield, 2008. While not uncritical of American elections,
these leading political scientists see them as fairly effective democratic institutions.

Rosenblum, Nancy. *On the Side of Angels.* Princeton, NJ: Princeton University Press, 2008.
A leading political theorist defends both political parties and partisanship and the role
of both in democratic politics.

Vote for Me: Politics in America. Produced by Louis Alvarez, Andrew Kolker, and Paul
Stekler. Film distributed by the Center for New American Media, 524 Broadway, 2nd
Floor, New York, NY 10012. This entertaining and educational film documents how
elections, at all levels, are conducted in America today.

White, John Kenneth, and Daniel M. Shea. *New Party Politics: From Jefferson and
Hamilton to the Information Age.* 2nd ed. New York: Wadsworth, 2003. A comprehensive review of the important role parties have played in the history of American
democracy, with keen insights into renewing them as democratic institutions.

*Presents a point of view that disagrees with the arguments presented in this chapter.

Selected Websites

http://cdd.stanford.edu. Site of James Fishkin's Center for Deliberative Democracy provides the latest information on deliberative polling experiments.

www.campaignlegalcenter.org. The Media Policy Program of the Campaign Legal Center
monitors news coverage of campaigns and advocates for improved public debate.

www.commoncause.org. Information about campaign finance expenditures and the latest news on attempts at reform.

www.opensecrets.org. The Center for Responsive Politics provides detailed and up-to-date information on campaign contributions and lobbying. Look up your congressperson!

www.publicampaign.org. Public Campaign is a nonprofit, nonpartisan organization working to reform the campaign finance system.

www.votesmart.org. Election news plus specific information on candidates for office. Look up your congressperson here, too!

CHAPTER 6

The Sixth Challenge:
The "Privileged Position" of Business

The flaw in the pluralist heaven is that the heavenly chorus sings with a strong upper-class accent.

—E. E. SCHATTSCHNEIDER

The large private corporation fits oddly into democratic theory and vision. Indeed, it does not fit.

—CHARLES E. LINDBLOM

THE PLURALIST MODEL OF DEMOCRACY, described in the introduction to this book, has been influential as an interpretation of American democracy. In fact, many of the political scientists who developed the model in the middle of the twentieth century considered it a concrete description of democracy as actually practiced in the United States. American politics was widely viewed as group politics, in which a wide variety of interests interacted to influence government policy. In both textbooks and journalistic accounts, interest groups were portrayed positively as vehicles of democratic representation. As groups competed with one another to influence election outcomes or lobby for the passage of legislation, they represented the interests and concerns of virtually all Americans. No one group held a dominant position in American society.

This chapter offers a critique of that central assumption of the Pluralist description of American politics. I argue that one can indeed identify a dominant group in our politics: business. More specifically, I present evidence that the

---

Opposite: *Bank CEOs, despite causing the 2008 financial crisis by irresponsible lending policies, demonstrated business privilege in obtaining a massive government bailout. Pictured here testifying before Congress is Bank of America's Ken Lewis.*

Photo courtesy of Chip Somodevilla/Getty Images.

people who control large business corporations dominate our political processes and largely control the public policy outcomes. Although the United States is a highly diverse society with a lively variety of groups—some even organized as "interest groups" to influence government—Big Business is a special group. Unlike other groups, it has a "privileged position" in US politics.[1] This chapter describes the nature of that privileged position and how this situation impedes democratic politics.

Before I develop that argument, however, we need to revisit the Pluralist model and see how political scientists deployed it in the 1950s and 1960s as a description of how American politics worked.

American Politics as Pluralist Heaven

Many political scientists writing in the post–World War II period considered the Pluralist model a realistic description of how American democracy works. Books such as David Truman's *The Governmental Process* (published in 1951) focused on the activities of interest groups as the key to understanding how American public policies were actually formulated.[2] The starting point for that analysis of American democracy was the diversity of American society and the lively associational life of Americans—a phenomenon that Tocqueville had remarked on as early as the 1830s. Certainly, little empirical investigation was required to demonstrate that American society contained lots of different groups with varying preferences on public policy issues. Farmers, businessmen, workers, fishermen, retailers, manufacturers, poor people and rich people, pro-lifers and pro-choicers, environmentalists and those opposed to excessive environmental regulation—this is just the beginning of what would be an extremely long list of politically relevant groups in America. And as the Pluralists could easily document, many of them organized into formal interest groups for the purpose of influencing government. A brief perusal of the Washington, DC, telephone book (or that of any state capital) would yield the names of many such groups. Through careful observation of the actual process of government, Pluralists documented the important role of these organized interest groups in influencing the day-to-day formulation of legislation.[3]

Whereas earlier observers of American politics had often characterized such influence as the undemocratic activity of "special interests," political scientists such as David Truman celebrated group politics as the essence of American democracy. Truman formulated three key concepts to demonstrate the democratic character of American politics: rules of the game, potential groups, and points of access.

By "rules of the game," Truman meant the variety of procedures, formal and informal, that ensure that a wide variety of societal interests will be able to influence government. Elections, free speech, the rights to assemble and to petition, press scrutiny, and politicians' sense of fair play create a context in which many different groups can form, promote their points of view, and receive a fair hearing from government. In such a context, no one group in society will be able to develop a privileged position in government because opposing groups will quickly form to counter it. There can be no "special" interests when the rules of the game make government responsive to any and all interests. Truman argued that the group process itself protects the rules of the game and ensures governmental openness. Any attempt to undermine the rules of the game on behalf of a special interest will produce retaliation from other groups, the general citizenry, and such government officials as the president, congressional leaders, and judges. In the view of the Pluralists, public officials have a special responsibility to protect the rules of the game.[4]

Clearly, elections are a crucial part of the rules of the game because they provide for the continuing responsiveness of government officials to a wide variety of interest groups. Pluralist descriptions of American politics characterize politicians as brokers who make deals among various conflicting groups because they want the widest possible support at election time. Given the openness of the political process, a strategy favoring the preferences of one special interest over others will be too risky for most politicians. Instead, in formulating public policy, they will attempt to craft compromises that reflect as much as possible the preferences and interests of a wide variety of groups. Such a strategy is most likely to gain a politician reelection and ensures the democratic character of public policy.

According to Truman, the influence of what he called "potential groups" also enhances politicians' incentives to craft democratic policies. As a realistic observer, Truman understood that groups differ in the degree to which they are effectively organized. On any given policy issue, it is possible that some affected interests may be too weak and disorganized to be represented directly in the negotiation of policy compromises. But even though potential groups are not directly represented, policy compromises will take their interests into account because, given the openness of the system, "if [potential groups] are too flagrantly ignored, they may be stimulated to organize for aggressive counteraction."[5] Over the long run, government policy will democratically represent not only all the formally organized groups lobbying directly on issues but also the relatively unorganized ones.

Contributing further to the widely representative character of American democracy is the nature of our government structure and the many "points of access" it provides. Truman praised the separation of powers and federalism, as well as political parties and the bureaucracy, as offering different groups multiple opportunities to be represented in decision making. This diversity of access points allows different groups with different political resources to be represented in different parts of the government structure. Some groups will find political party leaders responsive to their needs; others may find parties uninterested but can turn to the courts. Multiple points of access ensure that almost any group can find a way to have its interest represented.

In the years since Truman and others formulated it, this Pluralist description of American democracy has been subjected to thorough criticism from a wide variety of viewpoints, but a complete review of those arguments would divert us from the central concern of this chapter.[6] I mention only two of them, which I think undermine significantly the Pluralists' claim that group politics results in democratic politics. First, Pluralists have never been able to substantiate their theory that interest group politics in the United States is actually representative of all citizens, yet a demonstration is required if we are to accept the claim that such politics is inherently democratic. In fact, careful empirical studies, examined in more detail later, show that interest groups represent only a small proportion of Americans. In the everyday policy-making process, the play of group pressures leaves out many citizens.

Of course, Truman realized this problem and tried to get around it with the concept of potential groups, but that is an inadequate solution. Responsiveness to potential groups cannot be empirically tested because, by definition, the demands of those interests remain unarticulated. If no potential group rises up in reaction to a policy, does that mean, as the Pluralists claim, that the interests of that potential group have been addressed or, as a skeptic might argue, that the group lacks the capacity to organize even in the face of action adverse to its interests? The absence of response could support either interpretation. Also, even if we were to concede that politicians sometimes anticipate the objections of potential groups and may therefore respect their interests when making policy, it seems unlikely that this would be a frequent occurrence. In the face of direct and sometimes conflicting pressures from *organized* interests, it seems more plausible that policy-makers will usually be too preoccupied with these interests to give much thought to the unorganized ones. But merely occasional attention to the needs of potential groups falls far short of satisfying the standards of democratic theory.

A second major flaw in the Pluralist description is that it underestimates the significance of inequalities in political resources available even to organized groups. Pluralists do not deny that political resources—for example, money, organizational leadership, group cohesiveness, and size—affect the ability of groups to influence policy. Instead, they argue that these resources are widely distributed among different groups and that no systematic bias exists in favor of a particular group or set of groups. Some groups may have lots of money, but others can balance that resource by the size of their membership. Small groups with few members can gain attention by the cohesiveness of their membership and the skills of their leaders.

This chapter challenges this assertion of group equality. Its argument is that one group in society does monopolize political resources and can exact a response from the political system in a way that no other group can. The political power of business in American society provides convincing refutation of Pluralist descriptions of democratic group politics. Furthermore, business power, although always a decisive influence in American politics, seems to have been increasing in recent years, and its increase constitutes a major challenge to the future of American democracy.

Business: The Privileged Group

The position of political privilege accorded to business has two faces in American society. The first face is the more familiar one. It involves businesses and groups that represent business, actively manipulating the political system through lobbying, elections, and media propagandizing to attain their political objectives. As I later show, business has overwhelming political resources that make it virtually unbeatable whenever it mobilizes decisively to move government on its behalf. The second face of business power is subtler; it is one that most of us rarely think about. It involves the power that business wields over society and the political system without needing to seek actively to influence them. This is the privileged position we give to business when we opt, in a capitalist market economy, to give business leaders autonomous power to make society's crucial economic decisions.

Face I: Access to Political Resources

The first face of business power—the predominant role of business groups within the governmental process—has received thorough documentation by political scientists and journalists.[7] In this chapter, I can provide only a brief summary of that literature, focusing on three aspects of this open face of business power: the predominance of business in lobbying policymakers; the role of business in financing elections; and the propagation of ideas and messages favorable to business in the news media, schools, and universities.

Group theorists were correct in describing the day-to-day politics of public policy making, both in Congress and in the bureaucracy, as a politics of group pressures. A wide variety of groups actively seek to influence legislation and regulations.[8] What is significant about these group pressures, however, is not, as Pluralist group theorists would have us believe, the groups' representativeness; instead, it is the extent to which they represent one societal interest: business. An overwhelming majority of these pressure groups represent business. A first level of such representation includes the groups that represent the broad, general interests of all businesses and are especially active on legislation dealing with issues that affect the entire business community, such as general tax legislation, labor laws, and overall business regulation. The three most powerful groups in this category are the US Chamber of Commerce, representing federations of about 250,000 business members nationwide; the National Association of Manufacturers

(NAM), representing the nation's largest industrial firms; and the Business Roundtable, made up of the CEOs of the two hundred largest US corporations. Although these groups have distinct policy agendas, they usually unite to coordinate their activities when it comes to matters affecting business as a whole. Over the past three decades, these groups have worked effectively to enhance business dominance in Washington and to promote the business-friendly policies of tax cuts, reduced business regulation, globalization, and barriers to unions that have defined the era.[9] When it comes to empowering business as a whole, these separate groups speak with one voice.

Second, about a thousand trade and commodity organizations represent different segments of the business community. These narrower interests include groups such as the American Bankers' Association, the National Association of Home Builders, and the National Association of Wheat Growers. The last sounds as if it should be classified as a farmers' group, but like most commodity organizations, it represents agribusiness and food-processing firms along with some family farmers. Trade associations concentrate on policies aimed specifically at their particular segment of industry, as when the American Bankers' Association organized a massive grassroots lobbying campaign in the early 1980s to defeat a congressional attempt to institute tax withholding from stock dividends and savings accounts, as occurs with wages. This classic effort involved widespread advertising in the mass media and the distribution of postage-paid postcards in banks across the country that bank depositors could mail to their members of Congress. The proposed legislation was defeated in short order.

A third and increasingly important form of business representation is the direct Washington presence of individual corporations. Sometimes—in the case of the five hundred largest corporations—this presence involves corporations with Washington offices employing large staffs that lobby full-time on legislation affecting corporate interests. More often, such representation involves the retention of one of the many Washington law firms specializing in lobbying or of specialized consultants with Washington experience and connections. With their deep pockets, large corporations can hire the most skilled and well-connected lobbying experts. Microsoft's $3.7 million lobbying budget in 1998 brought to its lobbying team the services of Michael Deaver, Ronald Reagan's renowned campaign adman; Haley Barbour, former Republican National Committee chair; Ralph Reed, former Christian Coalition director; Mark Penn, a top pollster to the Gore presidential campaign; two former staffers to House Majority Leader Dick Armey; and former Democratic congressmen Vic Fazio and Tom Downey.[10] Notice that Microsoft's lobbying team spanned the political and ideological spectrum, including well-known Republican conservatives such as Reed and Deaver and Democratic liberals such as Downey and Fazio. Corporations seeking influence cover all political bases in buying support.

These three kinds of business groups account for most of the interest group activity in Washington, DC. Political scientists have found that, in studies since the 1980s, corporations, trade associations, and general business organizations (including foreign business) account for about three-quarters of all groups with Washington representation.[11] In sheer numbers, business groups outnumber labor unions, public interest groups, and citizen groups that often are their issue adversaries. When it comes to financial resources, business has an overwhelming advantage, routinely spending twice what labor spends on lobbying and five times more than citizen groups.[12] Business groups, also, are much more likely than other groups to employ Washington insiders like former members of Congress, congressional staff, and executive branch employees as lobbyists, providing enhanced access for business concerns. Not surprisingly, when business opposes either labor or citizen groups on issues it usually prevails.[13]

Businesses have become quite sophisticated in linking their Washington lobbying activities with efforts to generate the appearance of grassroots support for their concerns.[14] In recent years, business and trade associations have fine-tuned their procedures for influencing individual members of Congress.[15] Businesses employ sophisticated "astroturf" campaigns (so-called because they mimic genuine grassroots activity) to generate e-mail, phone calls, and letters favorable to their concerns. In 1993, the National Restaurant Association defeated an attempt to reduce the tax deduction allowed for business meals by mounting a television advertising campaign that included a toll-free telephone number to patch calls directly to Senate offices. Such a process allows consultants to screen the calls to make sure that only opinions favorable to business interests get through.[16]

Business advantage in the world of political lobbying depends, of course, on the receptivity of those being lobbied—elected officials. Election campaign contributions are one way in which business groups can make sure of a friendly reception when they come calling to influence legislation. Obviously, business is not the sole source of campaign contributions in the United States, but just as business dominates congressional lobbying, it also predominates in campaign contributions. As discussed in chapter 5, in the past, corporations could fund campaigns by means of PACs or by bundling individual contributions. In the 2008 election cycle, for example, business groups provided over 70 percent of all contributions of both these types.[17] As Figure 6.1 shows, business groups spent nearly $2 billion to influence the 2008 election—about two-and-one-half times as much as all other kinds of groups. Individual contributions, usually bundled, from corporate executives and PAC contributions remain an important means by which business dominates the world of campaign finance. In the 2010 congressional elections, for example, business-connected individuals provided about 74 percent of individual contributions and business PACs provided about 70 percent of all PAC contributions.[18]

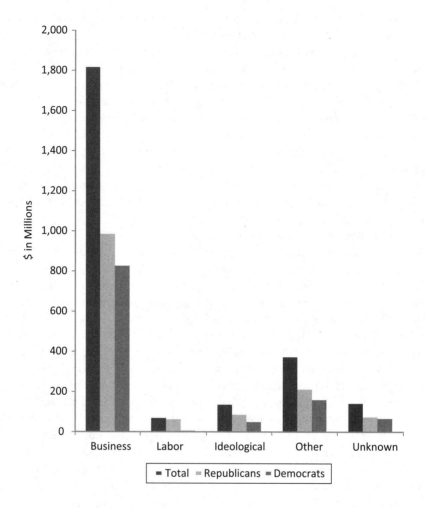

FIGURE 6.1   Business, Labor, and Ideological Contributions to Presidential and
Congressional Election Campaigns, 2008

Source: Center for Responsive Politics, www.opensecrets.org/overview/blio.php.

With the *Citizens United* decision (discussed in chapter 5), the Supreme
Court opened a new world of possibilities for business campaign contributions
when it struck down prohibitions on direct corporate contributions to campaigns
as unconstitutional. Corporate funds, in unlimited amounts, can now be used
directly to fund campaign ads supporting particular candidates. There are also no
limits on how much a corporation can contribute to new super PACs set up to
take advantage of the relaxation of campaign contribution limits. For the first

time in 2010, these groups became major sources of campaign funds and seemed to be dominating the 2012 campaign funding, as well.[19] Corporations also now have the ability to make unlimited, secret contributions to 501(c) nonprofit groups that also can fund campaign advertising. In striking a blow on behalf of corporate "free speech," the Supreme Court enhanced business privilege, giving it unlimited power to use its financial resources to influence election campaigns.

Key questions relating to business influence are, What does all this money buy? and To what extent do campaign contributions ensure public policies favorable to business? The answers are complex, for concern about the interests of campaign contributors is only one of several factors—among them ideology and personal experience—that influence an elected official's stance on an issue. Studies by political scientists have not been able, for example, to establish a direct relationship between the flow of PAC money and roll-call votes in Congress.[20] Nevertheless, most studies show that contributions provide contributors with *access* to elected officials, and as political scientist Larry Sabato states, "Political analysts have long agreed that access is the principal goal of most interest groups, and lobbyists have always recognized that access is the key to influence."[21] Business campaign contributions, then, buy business representatives the ability to be heard when public policy is formulated and ensure that their concerns are at the forefront of the policy-making agenda. This access and agenda setting does not guarantee that business groups can dictate decisions, but it ensures that business preferences will be taken into consideration—insurance that many other groups in society do not have. As Senator Robert Dole put it when asked to explain why the Reagan budget cuts of the 1980s seemed to fall most heavily on the poor, "There aren't any Poor PACs or Food Stamp PACs or Nutrition PACs or Medicare PACs."[22] In the first three months of 2011, for example, Congress devoted more time to a major concern of the banking industry—debit card swipe fees—than on the deficit, the Iraq War, or unemployment.[23] In this case, the bankers' massive contributions assured that the congressional recipients of their largess would pay attention to the banks' priorities. Unlike the poor and other interests, business can be sure that government officials will listen to its concerns because business provides the campaign contributions officials need.

Although access is probably the primary benefit that business buys with its campaign dollars, considerable anecdotal evidence suggests that it often gets more. In 1999, after a massive lobbying campaign by the banking, insurance, and securities industries, Congress repealed the Depression-era Glass-Steagall Act, which had protected consumers by keeping those three industries distinct from one another.[24] Under the new legislation, firms in the three industries would be allowed to merge, allowing an acceleration of the growth of megabanks that could provide one-stop shopping for stock trading, insurance, and traditional banking services; it also reduced their obligation to invest in poor communities under the Community Reinvestment Act. To obtain these policy changes, the three affected industries invested, according to the Center for Responsive Politics, $175 million in federal campaigns between 1997 and 1999. The money was carefully targeted to key members on the congressional banking committees, such as Texas Republican Senator Phil Gramm, chairman of the Senate Banking Committee, who received a total of $2.07 million from the three industries between 1993 and 1998. In addition, these industries collectively spent $163 million on direct lobbying for the legislative changes. The repeal of Glass-Steagall would be followed by additional legislation, such as the Commodity Futures Modernization Act of 2000, and favorable deregulation decisions by the US Securities and Exchange Commission, which gave the financial industry all the freedom it needed to create new, exotic financial instruments and make risky investments. When the financial system collapsed in fall 2008, critics pointed to the legislative and administrative deregulation that the industry itself had demanded as a primary cause.[25]

The banking and financial services industry, already a major source of campaign cash, ramped up its contributions in the wake of the financial crisis. The concern clearly was to ward off any new financial regulations being proposed to prevent a future repeat of the crisis that might interfere with industry profits. In 2008, industry contributions jumped 80 percent over contributions in the previous two years.[26] In 2010, as Congress was considering the Dodd-Frank financial regulation legislation, the finance industry contributed an all-time record of $300 million for midterm congressional campaigns.[27] Not only was the industry concerned with financial regulation; it also sought to influence the debate over the national deficit to protect tax provisions favoring financial services. In particular, hedge fund managers and private equity firms wanted to maintain low taxation of capital gains and their ability to have their income taxed at the lower capital gains rate. As part of their effort, they targeted contributions to the Republican leadership who stood fast against any changes to these favorable provisions in the 2011 debt ceiling negotiations with the Democrats. In fact, House Majority Leader Eric Cantor, whose contributions from the financial industry doubled in 2010 to $2 million, walked out of negotiations over the debt ceiling with Vice President Joseph Biden over these issues.[28] With well-aimed contributions, business can make sure that its interests are well defended when policy is made.

The pharmaceutical industry deployed its political resources with similar finesse to make sure that the Medicare prescription drug bill enacted in 2004 would serve its needs. The industry favored passage of a bill because it would increase drug sales, but it wanted to prevent any regulation of the prices its members could charge. In the four years prior to the bill's passage, the industry had steadily ramped up its campaign contributions. In the 2002 congressional elections, in particular, "Big Pharma" was among the largest donors, giving about $20 million to House and Senate candidates, with special attention to the chairs of the committees writing the Medicare prescription drug legislation.[29] As work on the bill approached completion, the industry shifted its focus, joining with the rest of the health care industry to spend more on lobbying than any other industry sector in 2004.[30] Like those of the bankers, these investments paid off handsomely, when the bill enacted in November 2004 specifically prohibited the federal government from negotiating price reductions in the Medicare prescription drug program. The result is a program that will protect the profits of the drug industry while imposing huge costs on taxpayers and seniors.

Big Business also uses its resources to influence public opinion. The most direct approach is advertising in print, on the Internet, and through television advertising to promote probusiness views and cast doubt on opposition arguments. Systematic print advertising can be used to target advocacy ads in publications read mainly by policy elites in Washington, such as the *National Journal* and *Congressional Quarterly Weekly*.[31] The Business Roundtable found the Capitol Hill newspaper *Roll Call* to be an effective vehicle for an ad directed at the congressional community as part of its effort to prevent expansion of mental health care benefits.[32] Whether the audience is the general public or key policy elites, business uses its resources to shape opinion to meet its concerns. Many industries advertise routinely to promote their image and create an atmosphere supportive of probusiness policies. In the wake of the huge oil spill off the coast of Louisiana in 2010, BP carried out a massive ad campaign to give its version of events. Usually, these ads exhort viewers to contact their congressional representatives, generating the appearance of a spontaneous grassroots uprising on a particular issue.[33] Without the resources to mount a countercampaign, those opposing the industry position on an issue are unable to present an alternative view to the public.

Along with direct promotion of business interests through advertising, corporations try to influence the country's public policy agenda by supporting public policy think tanks—private research establishments employing hundreds of scholars who write books and articles on public policy issues. Although think tanks come with a variety of ideological agendas, the overwhelming number of them are business funded and churn out policy proposals that are, not surprisingly, favorable to business. Organizations such as the Heritage Foundation, the American Enterprise Institute, the Hoover Institution, the Cato Institute, and the Manhattan Institute receive their funding from big corporate donors and produce scholarly studies that promote ideas advantageous to business.[34] Even the Brookings Institution, one of the oldest think tanks—and traditionally one with a reputation for supporting liberal scholars—has shifted in a more conservative direction in recent years in response to corporate funding. Sometimes businesses seek to generate favorable studies related to immediate concerns, as Microsoft did in early 1999 by contributing to the Hudson Institute and the Heritage Foundation, both of which published analyses of antitrust law that were supportive of Microsoft's position in the Justice Department's antitrust suit against it.[35] Through support of think tanks, business buys intellectual support for and research favorable to probusiness policies and a probusiness ideological climate.

In addition to dominating the production of information about public policy, business controls citizen access to information by means of its ownership of the news media. Newspapers, magazines, television and radio networks, and publishing houses are themselves businesses, and not surprisingly, most of them project probusiness views. Moreover, the wave of business mergers and acquisitions in the 1980s and 1990s tended to concentrate control of the mass media in the hands of a small number of large business conglomerates. Only about ten multinational corporations dominate the mass media today.[36] Some of these media giants, such as Disney and Viacom, own diverse properties, including broadcast and cable networks, newspapers, book publishers, and production companies. One such media conglomerate, Rupert Murdoch's News Corporation (the parent company of FOX News), specializes in promoting its owner's personal conservative political views. Even when the political bias is not as pronounced as in Murdoch's empire, those employed by these media conglomerates—in the business of "informing the public"—must be mindful of the political interests of their owners.[37] When in 2011 the *New York Times* reported that General Electric Corporation, which owns NBC, had paid no federal taxes in the previous year, the story received wide media attention—except on the NBC *Nightly News,* which ignored the story.[38] Avoiding stories embarrassing to its parent corporation has not been a rarity at NBC, which has a history of downplaying such news, according to Fairness and Accuracy in Reporting, a media watchdog group. Corporate ownership of the media gives business a privileged ability to influence what the public learns about the world that no other group possesses.

Face II: Authority Over Society's Resources

So far this discussion has outlined various aspects of only one face of business power—political resources. Lobbying power, electoral influence, and media manipulation are direct and obvious ways in which business exercises its power in society. The second face of power, emphasized by such analysts as Charles Lindblom, is subtler and sometimes goes unnoticed, but it is essential to business's privileged position. This subtler aspect is the power that business gains from our society's view of private property and its willingness to interpret control by giant business corporations as merely the exercise of property rights.

According to Lindblom, to understand how property rights lead to the "privileged position" of business one must understand that the laws that confer and protect property rights amount to a grant of public authority.[39] They give to business owners and managers "authority over society's resources"—authority they exercise without any democratic control. This authority is exercised in two arenas: within the business enterprise itself and outside it, over society.

Viewers should always keep in mind that NBC News Anchor Brian Williams is an employee of one of America's largest industrial corporations: General Electric, which owns the NBC network.

Virginia Sherwood/NBC/NBCU Photo Bank via Getty Images.

American business enterprises are not normally organized democratically. Our legal system and business managers assume that managers have the right to decide how work will be organized and what rules workers will follow. For the minority of workers protected by union contracts, there are sometimes limits placed on the authoritarian control by management, but the range of unrestrained management power remains wide even in unionized firms and is nearly absolute in nonunion ones. Authoritarian control of the internal operations of business is usually justified as necessary for the sake of efficiency, but however it is justified, it removes from democratic control many decisions that directly affect the daily lives of most citizens.

Outside the firm, business managers also make numerous decisions that greatly affect the lives of citizens, independent of any control by democratic processes. They have virtually autonomous authority to determine how production will be organized and where it will occur. Will products be manufactured on assembly lines or by small groups of workers who complete an entire product? What technologies will be employed? Will robots replace workers? Will the factory be located in Indiana, Georgia, or Mexico? Business managers are not required to seek the approval or advice of either government officials or citizens when they make these decisions. The same applies to decisions about the social consequences of production and the use of products. Within some constraints imposed by government regulation—which business seeks to keep at a minimum through deployment of its political power—its decisions about what to produce and how to produce it have far-reaching consequences for society. Pollution levels, along with health and safety hazards resulting from products, are to a great extent determined by business managers. Will automobiles have airbags? Will guns be sold? Will hamburgers be wrapped in Styrofoam? These decisions are left, in the main, to business.

More fundamentally, the doctrines of private property and the free market leave it to private business managers to decide how society's resources will be allocated among alternative investment options. Should resources invested in transportation emphasize mass transit or private automobiles? Since the 1920s, American business has directed most investment into the automobile industry and away from mass transit. In fact, the auto and tire industries went so far as to buy up existing trolley car systems in many cities and destroy them, thereby encouraging the sale of cars and buses.[40] In the United States, government has left the development of much of our current system of transportation to "the market"—which means, in effect, to business.

Leaving important societal decisions to the market means dividing authority for important social decisions between two sets of rulers. In any capitalist market system, the question, Who rules? has to be answered: government officials *and* business executives.[41] The decisions of government officials may be subject to the control of democratic processes, such as elections; those of business executives are not. Yet in many respects, the decisions left to business have more direct significance for most of us than those made by government. This significance gives business tremendous leverage, in turn, over governmental decisions. The result is a privileged position for business.

The federal government's response to the financial crisis of 2008 provides a classic illustration of how the second face of business privilege works. In our capitalist economy, the allocation of investment capital to various economic activities is left to large private banking and financial institutions. Large banks and Wall Street financial firms such as Bank of America, Goldman Sacks, and Citigroup and various hedge funds, venture capital, and private equity firms such as the Blackstone Group or Bain Capital provide the capital for corporate investments in new products and services, housing construction, loans to state and local governments for public works, and consumer credit. In brief, the smooth operation of the entire economy relies on the private investor-owned financial industry to allocate capital efficiently and responsibly to productive economic enterprise.

In the years prior to 2008, the lords of high finance used their control of the nation's capital markets in an extremely irresponsible manner as they sought spectacular profits from exotic investment instruments based on home mortgages.[42]

Taking advantage of the deregulated financial environment that their own lobbying had made possible over the previous thirty years, Wall Street financial firms developed a huge business in buying and selling mortgage securities based on increasingly risky "subprime mortgages"—mortgages held by homeowners with poor credit ratings. As long as housing prices continued to rise, these investments remained quite lucrative for investors and seemed to have little risk. When housing prices began to fall in 2007 and homeowners began to default on their mortgages, the value of mortgage-based securities plummeted, placing the entire financial industry at risk. The bankruptcy of Lehman Brothers, an old, renowned Wall Street firm, in the summer of 2008 triggered a financial panic that threatened to bring down the entire economy. To prevent this, the Bush administration Secretary of the Treasury Henry Paulson proposed in late September a $700 billion bailout of the financial industry—the Troubled Asset Relief Program (TARP). Although Congress initially balked, rejecting the plan in a vote on September 29, a subsequent stock market crash in the wake of its vote caused it to reverse course and approve TARP on October 3.[43]

What is remarkable about the enactment of TARP was the speed with which government officials and institutions moved in response to business need and provided taxpayer-funded relief. Our normally glacial political process, as described in chapter 1, worked like lightning when the interests of the financial industry were at stake. We now also know that the TARP bailout was only the tip of the iceberg of the financial assistance the government provided. For several months in late 2008 and early 2009, the Federal Reserve made trillions of dollars of secret loans to the major Wall Street banks to shore up their balance sheets. While these loans, made at quite favorable interest rates, were eventually paid back (as most of the TARP money would be as well), the banks eventually made a $13 billion overall profit on the loans.[44] The reason for the quick decisive action to bail out the banks is understandable. A failure or delay in saving the financial institutions would have led to the collapse of the entire economy. Given the economic structure that depended on these institutions' support, those who ran them understood they could call on the government to save them from their irresponsible behavior. And they could do so on very favorable terms. Despite grumbling from politicians about the unfairness of taxpayers paying for the mistakes of Wall Street bankers, the federal government had to come to the rescue of the financial industry to prevent an economic collapse. Business privilege meant giving Wall Street investors autonomy in investing the bulk of the country's financial capital and making the whole economy dependent on their decisions. When those decisions failed, Wall Street could use that very dependence to demand that government officials come to its rescue. Even after the rescue, bankers successfully resisted effective government oversight of how banks used the bailout money, as they dragged their feet on issuing new loans to stimulate economic activity and spent a portion of government largesse on bonuses for their top executives.[45] Nor were any major financial executives prosecuted in the wake of the crisis despite considerable evidence of deceptive and fraudulent behavior in promoting risky mortgage securities.[46] Business privilege means that taxpayers pay for business mistakes but possess no democratic control over business decisions.

The recent history of General Motors Corporation provides another example of how face two of business privilege works. In the early 1990s, General Motors Corporation announced a major reorganization affecting many communities and thousands of people across the country. Citing GM's poor economic performance and the need to improve the company's competitiveness in the global market, corporate executives closed twelve plants in the United States and Canada—a move that affected 16,300 workers—as the first phase in a decade-long process that shut down a total of twenty-one plants.[47] A relatively small number of GM executives made these decisions in secret, without any participation by GM workers, national government officials, citizens, or local governments in the communities where the plants were located. Although these decisions were made in private by "private sector" executives, one can imagine no government official's decision in recent years that would have as far-reaching an impact on American society. Beyond the nearly 17,000 workers directly affected, thousands of other workers in the communities where the plants were located would lose their jobs as the plants ceased purchasing supplies and would no longer have wages to spend. Local communities would lose millions of dollars in tax revenues, forcing them to close schools and cut back public services. Ultimately, the quality of life of millions of people would be lowered as a consequence of these supposedly private decisions. As this illustration shows, people who are able to make decisions that will have vast impact on society exercise a large share of authority in society. No decision taken by any of the mayors in the various towns hurt by the GM decision could possibly have affected their communities more. Yet our "democratic" society gives to business executives complete autonomy to make such decisions without even informing anyone of the basis for doing so.

In making these reorganization decisions and others over the next two decades, GM executives did not have to be accountable for their decisions to the broader public affected. Business privilege freed them from any requirement to divulge any of the facts and analyses that had convinced GM management to close plants as a way to address competitiveness problems or to explain why particular plants had been chosen for closing. Nothing was revealed about what alternatives had been considered or whether some other way—possibly less devastating to the well-being of the workers and communities involved—might have been found to make the corporation more competitive. There was also no attempt to explain how or why GM had become so noncompetitive, or whether previous decisions by GM executives might be responsible for creating a situation necessitating such drastic action. Nor was there any mechanism to hold GM executives accountable for how they would go about improving GM competitiveness, such

U.S. GOVT.
1. EXECUTIVE
2. LEGISLATIVE
3. JUDICIAL

SIPRESS

"What about business—which branch is that?"

© David Sipress/The New Yorker Collection/www.cartoonbank.com.

as the type of vehicles they would produce or long-term planning for keeping the corporation viable. Any notion that such democratic values as responsiveness or accountability might, in any way, be relevant to decisions with such a broad public impact were absent from corporate statements and from media discussion of the GM action. The company's executives decided what would happen, and so it did.

In fact, the decisions that GM executives made in its various restructurings in the 1990s and after proved disastrous for the long-term health of GM and its workers. As did other American auto producers, GM opted to carve a market niche for itself in the sale of gas-guzzling SUVs and trucks. Rather than compete with Japanese and other foreign automakers in marketing a wide range of products, including developing more fuel-efficient models, GM sought short-term gains based on the low cost of gasoline. When oil prices spiked in 2008, the gas-guzzler strategy proved a failure and GM faced bankruptcy. Rather than suffer any consequences for their failed strategy, GM executives turned to the federal government for a taxpayer bailout, citing the disastrous consequences a GM collapse would have for the nation's economy.[48] Once again executives engineered plant closings, union givebacks, and layoffs to restore the company. Business privilege meant that corporate executives were not democratically accountable for the decisions they made, but when those decisions proved wrong, society's dependence on business gave the executives leverage to induce government to salvage their business.

The economic bailouts of 2008 and 2009 offer dramatic examples of a commonplace phenomenon brought about by business privilege—the necessity that public officials respond continually to business needs. Whenever public officials consider policies involving taxation or public services, they must be very attentive to the effect of those decisions on business. Because the community's well-being is so dependent on the willingness of business decision makers to invest in the community, public officials must make sure that nothing they do will alienate business and lead to community disinvestment. In fact, realizing their situation, most astute public servants devise various inducements, such as tax breaks and subsidies, to encourage business to invest in their communities. They avoid raising taxes to finance generous social services, so that businesses will not consider moving to communities with lower taxes. No business lobbying is necessary to produce these favorable decisions. Intelligent public officials know without being told what they must do: Keep business happy. If, perchance, citizens somewhere elect to office people who are resistant to automatic probusiness policies, a corporate threat to move a local firm elsewhere suffices to change the "business climate."[49]

Such threats to extort taxpayer subsidies are a routine part of the American business playbook. Every year, state and local governments spend about $70 billion to attract businesses to their communities.[50] Ostensibly, these subsidies are meant to create jobs, but many subsidy programs provide few guarantees that jobs will be created. Corporations are quite adept at demanding subsidies even when only a small number of jobs are promised. In 2001, Boeing Corporation, which had been based in Seattle, Washington, for seventy-five years, announced it was considering moving its corporate headquarters, which accounted for only 500 jobs.[51] It set up a competition among three cities that Chicago, Illinois, won with a state-financed subsidy of $53 million—about $100,000 per job. Suitably chastened and fearful that Boeing might move some of its manufacturing out of Washington, Washington's governor put together a $2.3 billion package of tax breaks over twenty years to subsidize production of the Boeing 7E7 Dreamliner. Despite this huge subsidy, Boeing opted to spread some of the production to a new plant in South Carolina in return, of course, for an additional $900 million subsidy from that state. Thanks to such tax subsidies, many Fortune 500 companies pay no state income taxes.[52]

Hyundai Motor Company's ability to induce competition between the states of Alabama and Kentucky to attract the construction of its new US manufacturing plant in 2002 provides a classic case study of business privilege and its consequences. Early in the year, the company announced that it was considering sites in both Hardin County, Kentucky, and Montgomery, Alabama, for its new plant; then it sat back and waited for the best offer. Both state legislatures mobilized to pass, in record time, sweet packages to lure the Korean automaker. The Kentucky legislature went so far as to abolish a Farmland Advisory Committee it had created a few years earlier to monitor economic development that eliminated farmland. The governor feared that the mere existence of this committee, which had not met since 1989, might deter Hyundai from accepting Kentucky's package. Such extreme measures were to no avail, however, as Alabama won the plant with a $318 million incentive package that included a new highway, acquisition of the plant site, and a worker training program.[53]

Such interstate competition for manufacturing plants reveals the essence of business's political privilege. Most citizens and groups must bring their cases to elected officials to influence public policy. Nonprivileged actors must compete against other groups for limited resources and try to persuade elected representatives—and often the public at large—of the wisdom of their position on an issue. In Kentucky and Alabama, for example, both of which are near the bottom nationally in per capita state expenditure for schools, educators and parents must fight for every dollar for education. Business is different. It can sidestep the process of group interaction and competition that Pluralists describe, merely announcing its decisions regarding the disposition of its economic resources. Such an announcement, by itself, will cause public officials to act on business's behalf, sometimes tripping over themselves as in the cases described here to devise public policy inducements to attract business to their community. Business does not have to plead or cajole elected officials to win favorable public policies; it gets to choose among competing offers. No other group in the "pluralist heaven" has such a privilege.

Economic globalization has served to increase business leverage over politicians to extract policies favorable to its interests. Free trade arrangements, such as the North American Free Trade Agreement (NAFTA) and the World Trade Organization (WTO), have facilitated the movement of business production to anywhere in the world. NAFTA, which took effect in 1994, is a pact among the United States, Mexico, and Canada to guarantee free movement of goods, services, and investment capital throughout North America. The WTO was established in 1995 as the culmination of several decades of negotiation among more than one hundred nations to liberalize trade worldwide. The International Monetary Fund (IMF) and the World Bank, both established after World War II to rebuild war-ravaged Europe, also have evolved into institutions that seek to encourage favorable business climates in the developing world. As the price for receiving IMF loans or World Bank development assistance, national governments must agree to enact free-market policies to facilitate business investment and trade, including cutbacks in government programs that benefit their citizens. Thanks to these international arrangements, business investment capital is free to travel around the globe in search of such conditions as low wages, government subsidies, and policies discouraging labor unions, all of which maximize profit opportunities. In the new global marketplace, American workers in places such as Birmingham and Louisville find themselves competing not only with each other but with workers in Monterrey, São Paulo, and Shanghai. Not only governors and mayors, but presidents and prime ministers must be mindful of business interests if their people are to prosper.

Trade agreements, such as NAFTA, and international trade enforcement institutions, such as the WTO, the IMF, and the World Bank, constitute a supranational governing system that favors business interests and is not accountable to any democratic electorate.[54] Nobel Prize–winning economist Joseph Stiglitz labels this a system of "global governance without global government."[55] The bureaucrats who work for such international organizations interact with the trade, finance, and commerce ministries of member countries and with business and financial interests in their areas of operation. This structure of global organizations—which is in no way accountable to the world's ordinary citizens—has been a conscious creation of the world's business elites to facilitate their ability to invest around the world and protect the profits they derive from their investments. Through mechanisms such as the World Economic Forum in Davos, Switzerland, business executives from around the world have collaborated to shape global trade and investment policies, and then pressured their national governments to negotiate agreements favorable to business. The result is a structure of rules that facilitate investment and corporate profits but overlook environmental concerns, workers' rights, and consumer protection.

Why Business Privilege Is a Threat to Democracy

Business's position of privilege in American society threatens our democracy in at least four ways. First, and most obvious from the preceding discussion, business privilege means that, contrary to the claims of the Pluralists, the full range of political interests in society are *not* equally represented. Second, business power restricts the agenda of policy alternatives that are seriously debated and discussed when public policy is formulated. Third, business power undermines the development of an effective democratic citizenry. And fourth, business privilege results in substantive policies that are contrary to the needs and interests of a majority of Americans and many others throughout the world.

Political equality is a central value of all the models of democracy presented in this book's introduction. The strength of the Pluralist model is its argument regarding the representative role of groups. Because, as the Pluralists claim, no group is privileged, the opportunity of all groups to influence public policy satisfies the democratic value of political equality. The reality of business privilege refutes this depiction of American group politics. Business can deploy its political resources and exploit its position in the economic structure to ensure itself an unequal position in the group universe. Given its position, no policy can be made democratically, with the concerns and interests of all citizens given equal weight. In sum, the demonstration of business privilege, in itself, shows how the unequal representation of interests prevents the achievement of political equality when American public policy is made.

But the incompatibility of business privilege with democracy goes beyond its advantage in influencing the outcome of public policy debates. A more fundamental threat is the ability of business to bias the policy agenda so that only alternatives that take into account its interests are ever seriously considered. Even before debate on any public policy begins, the discussion is biased so that business privilege is assured. Lindblom identifies two mechanisms through which business structures the agenda to its advantage: circularity and "the market as prison."

Even in its position of privilege, one could imagine a situation in which business in a democratic society would occasionally face challenges to its goals. In the United States, nonbusiness groups and citizens in general are free to formulate or support political positions contrary to the interests or even the privileged position of business. One might expect, then, considerable conflict when policies bearing on business privilege are considered or when the preferences of business are opposed to those of other groups. Sometimes business leaders might need to deflect the preferences of a democratic majority to ensure governmental response to their particular needs. Imagine, however, a different sort of situation for business—one in which nearly everyone in society seems to prefer policies that favor the interests and preferences of business. In this case, business would rarely face political opposition because what it wanted was what everyone else in society wanted. When government leaders formulated policy, they would seem to respond to popular preferences, but in doing so, they would be serving the interests of business.

According to Lindblom, this latter situation is often the case in capitalist market societies such as the United States. But the genuine coincidence of citizen policy preferences and business preferences does not arise from the coincidence of citizen *interests* and those of business. It occurs because of the ability of business to indoctrinate the rest of society into wanting what business wants. The result is a circular process in which "people are indoctrinated to demand . . . nothing other than what a decision-making elite [government and business leaders] are disposed to grant them. The volitions that are supposed to guide leaders are formed by the same leaders."[56] Business control of media messages and their influence over other opinion-molding institutions, such as schools, permit such indoctrination.

The most important indoctrination, from business's point of view, is that which serves to preserve its privileged position.[57] This goal is accomplished in two ways. First, business persuades citizens to overlook business's privileged position by equating that position with the preservation of democracy. This is the aim of messages in the media, in schools, and from business and government elites that associate the preservation of private enterprise with personal liberty, national sovereignty, and democracy. In newspaper articles, publicity, and school curricula, Americans are taught that democracy means "our free enterprise system." Any challenge to business autonomy is equated with a challenge to the liberty of all Americans.

Second, business molds public opinion to keep any challenge to its privileged position off the political agenda. It promotes silence on major issues of politico-economic organization that might raise questions in people's minds about the appropriateness of business privilege. Such issues as how much autonomy corporations should have, what is an appropriate distribution of income and wealth, the role of labor unions, and worker participation in enterprise decision making are deemed too radical to merit serious discussion. And the absence of any serious discussion of them on television, in newspapers, or in college courses suggests that they are unimportant to society. Corporate ownership of the media ensures that journalists who inquire too deeply into issues that raise questions about business's position in society will not see their stories in print and soon learn that "their jobs depend in part on keeping their corporate parents happy."[58] With such control over cultural production in our society, business ensures the absence of inquiry into ideas, issues, or even history that might challenge its dominance.

Subtler even than this circularity, the market system itself provides a built-in bias in favor of business preferences. This bias grows directly out of the privileged position business holds. Since in a private market system we give to business executives the responsibility for most economic decisions, any attempt to enact a reform or impose any cost on business will have an immediate negative impact on the economy. If, for example, a community seeks to reduce pollution by requiring local businesses to clean up their emissions, some businesses may decide to move their local production facilities to communities with less-stringent pollution controls, producing unemployment in the more environmentally conscious community. The immediate and direct economic pain of increased unemployment will deter most communities from serious democratic deliberation about pollution controls. In this example, the market acts as a sort of prison that restricts the range of democratic deliberation and control to those policies that will not adversely affect business.

Thoughtful readers might object that the situation just described represents not a limitation of democracy or the "market as prison" but merely the reality of trade-offs between competing social goals. Any society, whether it has a market economy or not, must cope with the trade-off between the desire for a clean environment and the need for economic production. Some kinds of production will always produce pollution; communities must decide what they value more—jobs or a pristine environment. Is not the need for a local community to consider the adverse economic effect of environmental regulation merely a reflection of a natural reality?

This question indicates the subtle way in which the market imprisons policy making. It assumes that communities control democratically the full range of decisions related to trade-offs between competing social goals, such as the one between a clean environment and economic productivity. In a fully democratic society, this assumption would be valid. But given the privileged position of business in a market society, business managers control the economic side of the trade-off. How a community might respond to the adverse effect of environmental controls on productivity is outside the control of democratically chosen government officials. In their deliberations, government officials can only anticipate and cope with the response of business to attempts to regulate. Because a whole range of reforms—from raising business taxes to support needed public services to environmental regulation—may elicit immediate negative economic consequences, prudent government officials avoid them.

In addition to unequally representing political interests and restricting the policy agenda and policy formulation, a third way in which business power undermines democracy relates to the "developmental" aspect of democracy. As discussed in the introduction, many democratic theorists, especially those advocating the Developmental and Participatory models, have valued democracy because they believe it promotes the development of good, fully human people. Through participation with their fellow citizens in collectively solving community problems, people have an opportunity to develop their capacity to deliberate, communicate, form critical judgments, and control their lives. According to Participatory theorists, only democratic participation allows people "to realize . . . their dignity and powers as responsible agents and judges."[59]

This concern is related to the discussion in chapter 3 of Tocqueville's comment on the necessity for the proper "habits of the heart," or political culture, for democracy to succeed. That account describes the challenge that American individualism poses for democracy. Tocqueville believed that in such an individualist culture, political participation was an important means of promoting good citizenship values. Through direct experience with self-government in town governments, Tocqueville thought, Americans honed the active, nondeferential skills that promoted effective democracy throughout the system. If Tocqueville was correct that the practice of democracy is needed to promote a democratic outlook in citizens, then the lack of participation permitted by authoritarian structures in society may undermine this outlook. This is the danger that the privileged position of business poses for democracy.

The authoritarian structure of business is a serious impediment to democracy, given the extent to which the workplace dominates the lives of most Americans.[60] Most of us spend our working days in a tightly structured environment where we are usually required to follow orders uncritically. From the point of view of the Developmental and Participatory models, this experience can only undermine our capacity to be effective democratic citizens after we leave the workplace. Much of

246 AMERICAN DEMOCRACY IN PERIL

our lives goes on within the confines of authoritarian business institutions that actively discourage participatory discussion, independent thinking, critical analysis, and skepticism regarding authority. As long as business is organized in this authoritarian manner, its workers' opportunities to develop the character that democratic theorists associate with a democratic citizenry will be severely restricted and perhaps undermined.[61]

Finally, business power is a threat to contemporary American democracy because of a new divergence between the substantive economic interests of business elites and those of a majority of Americans. In the past few decades, in response to an increasingly competitive international economy and a business-friendly global trade regime, American corporations have developed strategies that enrich top corporate managers and wealthy stockholders but tend to lower the standard of living of most American workers. American business elites have opted to shore up corporate profits in a competitive marketplace by lowering wage costs, shifting much industrial production abroad to low-wage countries, downsizing corporate employment, and avoiding taxation.

Over most of the past century, the success of US corporations and a rising standard of living were tied together. The large business corporations that emerged at the beginning of the century both produced and sold their products largely in the domestic economy. As Henry Ford realized when he raised the wages of his workers to the unheard-of level of $5 a day, corporations would not earn profits unless higher wages allowed the workers themselves to buy mass-produced industrial products. When some of his business friends criticized Ford for bidding up wages and raising their costs of production, Ford replied with a subtle truth about the interdependency at the heart of a mass consumption economy: If he kept costs low by not raising wages, he said, "Who would buy my cars?"[62] As long as business elites understood this reality, there was no fundamental conflict between the economic interests of business and those of most American citizens. A rising standard of living meant growing corporate profits, and vice versa; this linkage was a key reality of American prosperity in the two decades following World War II. A few hundred core corporations—giants such as General Motors, General Electric, and U.S. Steel—dominated the US economy and that of the world.[63] Although these corporations sold their products throughout the world, their principal market was the United States. Business leaders readily identified corporate success with the success of the whole nation. This identification was reflected in corporate slogans such as U.S. Steel's "As steel goes, so goes the Nation," and in the remark of GM president C. E. ("Engine Charlie") Wilson: "For years I thought what was good for our country was good for General Motors, and vice versa. The difference did not exist."[64]

In many respects, Wilson and U.S. Steel were correct: Rising corporate profits coexisted with steadily rising living standards. Between 1945 and the early 1970s, the US standard of living doubled.[65] This impressive growth was based on rising worker productivity, which grew at 2.7 percent annually.[66] Corporate profits kept pace, providing an after-tax rate of return on investment of about 10 percent.[67] During this period, managers of the largest corporations readily accepted the presence of well-organized labor unions and endorsed contracts providing steadily increasing benefits and wages. These contracts added a stimulus to higher wages and benefits throughout the economy, distributing a portion of the gains from economic productivity to nearly all Americans. Although economic inequality persisted, and many of the poorest Americans were left out of the overall prosperity, the trend was in the direction of lessening income inequality until the mid-1970s (for more discussion of income inequality, see chapter 7).

In recent decades, this happy identification between American corporate success and a rising standard of living has broken down. The principal cause has been a decline in corporate profits, brought on by greater international competition. By 1979, the rate of return on corporate investments had dropped from 10 percent to about 5 percent.[68] In both domestic and international markets, US corporations faced vigorous competition from their Japanese and European counterparts. Most businesses responded to the situation by adopting a strategy that was beneficial to the balance sheets of individual firms but has undermined the rising standard of living of many American workers.

Economists Bennett Harrison and Barry Bluestone have identified two basic elements of corporate strategy to cope with international competition since the late 1970s.[69] The first they call "zapping labor"—that is, reducing worker wages and benefits to lower production costs. This strategy involves transferring manufacturing plants abroad to low-wage countries instead of investing in domestic manufacturing. In the shadow of shuttered American factories, American workers can be made to accept contract concessions under the threat of permanent loss of their jobs to foreign workers. Central to this element of corporate strategy has been an aggressive campaign against labor unions that has radically reduced the proportion of organized workers in the workforce. Weak oversight by the National Labor Relations Board has allowed corporations to blatantly impede union organizing efforts through illegal tactics such as firing workers supporting unionization.[70] Trade agreements such as NAFTA and the WTO have given corporate bosses tremendous leverage to keep wages low and prevent labor organizing because workers now know that companies can easily transfer their jobs to workers anywhere in the world.

The second element in the corporate coping strategy involves financial manipulations in what is sometimes called the "casino economy." These manipulations turn corporate investors into gamblers, treating the economy as a high-stakes casino in which they seek high profits through high-risk investments. Rather than investing in new plants and equipment, corporations have used their capital to buy and sell one another or to earn paper profits through exotic investment schemes. Mergers and acquisitions, encouraged by favorable tax laws, and the invention of novel financial instruments, such as "junk bonds" and "credit default swaps," have delivered enormous paper profits to corporate elites without contributing to future economic productivity. The mania for investments in securities based on subprime mortgage loans after 2000, described earlier in this chapter, was the perfect example of the casino economy in action. Wall Street investment banks found they could earn high profits and gain big bonuses for top executives through the repackaging of subprime mortgages as "collateralized debt obligations" (CDOs).[71] While ostensibly these mortgage securities made low-cost financing available for homeowners, their ultimate effect was to fuel a massive housing price bubble that burst with devastating consequences for the overall economy. The high stakes bets of the Wall Street financiers, while enriching their portfolios, brought disaster to Main Street. Business privilege came into play, however, as Wall Street bankers turned to the federal government for a $700 billion bailout, described earlier, to compensate for their disastrous financial gambles.[72] Foreclosed homeowners and those unemployed in the ensuing recession suffered the consequences without any prospect for a bailout.

Another feature of the casino economy was the "virtual corporation"—an entity that managed nothing directly but produced profits for its stockholders, or sometimes simply compensation for its executives, by continually acquiring and selling assets of other companies. The now-infamous Enron Corporation evolved in the 1990s into an entity comparable to such a virtual corporation. Beginning with a natural gas pipeline company in 1985, CEO Kenneth Lay turned Enron into a worldwide trader in energy commodities: natural gas, electricity, and oil. Taking advantage of newly deregulated energy markets—which its political lobbying and contributions had encouraged—the company specialized in making deals to buy and sell energy in complex arrangements that earned it a profit. Soon its success in energy trading led Enron to expand into trading a wide variety of other commodities and devising complicated financial techniques to manage its deals.[73] The object of most of these deals was not necessarily to make a profit, but to create the appearance of a profit on the company's balance sheet that would drive up its stock price and thus the value of the stock options awarded to its executives. For example, in 1999 Enron managers negotiated a sham energy deal with the company's banker, Merrill Lynch, so as to be able to record on its books a figure that met a year-end profit target. As a result, Enron stock prices soared, increasing the value of the options of its top executives, who cashed out to the tune of $82.6 million. No actual profit materialized from the deal.[74] When similar accounting manipulations eventually caught up with Enron in 2001, most of the same executives managed to earn additional millions for themselves by selling their stock before revelation of the company's true profit picture produced a collapse of the stock's value. At the same time, most of the company's rank-and-file employees saw their retirement savings, invested by the company's 401(k) plan in Enron stock, simply vanish when the stock price collapsed.

Enron executives were not the only ones who prospered as their corporations crumbled, nor did their manipulations contribute to improving Americans' standard of living. In fact, they had just the opposite effect. To make its brand of energy trading possible, Enron had been a major advocate of electricity deregulation in the nineties, arguing that efficiencies from deregulation would provide consumers with cheaper electricity. Seeking such efficiencies, the state of California deregulated in 1998, only to experience, two years later, soaring electricity prices and supply shortages that produced blackouts throughout the state. As subsequent investigation showed, deregulation had provided Enron and other energy companies the ability to manipulate the supply of electricity in the state to drive up prices and the company's profits.[75] A *Financial Times* of London investigation found that in the twenty-five largest corporate bankruptcies of 2001, sixty-one executives or directors managed to walk away with $10 million or more apiece in compensation, a total of $3.3 billion.[76] In the world of paper entrepreneurs and virtual corporations, top corporate executives can get rich even as the companies they run are failing. Within the corporations of the "new" economy, such old-fashioned notions as benefiting stockholders, providing good jobs, or serving the public are swept away in the mania of top corporate executives to enrich themselves.

The paper profits and financial manipulations in the contemporary global economy come at the expense of American factory workers, who lose their jobs and retirement benefits when the paper entrepreneurs acquire their factories, close them, sell off the assets, and take away huge profits for themselves. Such corporate restructuring, in combination with the transfer of manufacturing abroad, has resulted in the loss of millions of the high-wage blue-collar manufacturing jobs that once delivered the high living standards of the post–World War II generation. The priorities of the current corporate elite are far different from those of the "Engine Charlie" Wilson era. Rather than seeking compatibility between business profit and the well-being of the nation as a whole, contemporary business leaders have pressed for policies that enhance their incomes at the expense of other citizens. The entire mix of policies characteristic of the past two decades, even under the Democratic Clinton administration—tight monetary policies, lower taxes on corporations and the wealthy, economic and social deregulation, lower social spending, privatization, and relaxed labor laws—has served to enhance business income without benefiting most Americans. These government policies and corporate strategies have produced the growing inequalities of income and wealth that are described in the next chapter.

Even in the aftermath of the national crisis created by the 9/11 terrorist attacks, some American businesses were relocating their corporate headquarters "offshore" in tax havens such as Bermuda to avoid paying federal income taxes.[77] No sense of patriotic duty to help pay for the new war on terrorism seemed to concern the executives of modern multinational corporations. In the international marketplace, the traditional link between corporate success and the nation as a whole no longer exists. As the political economist Robert Reich writes,

> Neither the profitability of a nation's corporations nor the success of its investors necessarily improves the standard of living of most of the nation's citizens. Corporations and investors now scour the world for profitable opportunities. They are becoming disconnected from their home nations.[78]

The danger to democracy deriving from business privilege in this new context can now be clearly seen. Although business privilege in the United States has always been a threat that undermined our democracy, until recently the exercise of that privilege, however objectionable on theoretical grounds, was consistent with substantial material benefits for most Americans. In pursuing their own interests, business elites supported policies that improved living standards for nearly all. Now the disparity between what business wants and the needs of most citizens highlights the danger of people trusting their fate to the benign rule of an elite. As long as business maintains its political privilege, it appears more and more likely that public policies will continue to benefit that elite at the expense of the majority. Perhaps at no time in American history have elite interests and those of a democratic majority been as sharply at odds as in the current era. If business elites continue to exercise their traditional political privileges, policies conducive to providing a high standard of living for all are not likely to be enacted. Only a truly democratic movement organized to counter the privileged position of business can restore the American dream.

Objections to the Privileged-Position-of-Business Thesis

Not all political scientists accept that this description of a privileged position is an accurate portrayal of business's political role, and many, writing from a Pluralist perspective, disagree that business has abused the power of privilege in recent times.[79] Those who disagree generally raise two objections to the thesis. First, they point out that Big Business does not always win—sometimes legislation and policies that business vociferously opposes are enacted and adopted. And they ask, How can this be, if business has such a privileged position? Second, some object to the implication of the thesis that business is a monolithic interest. They argue that on many important public policy issues, businesspeople and corporations are often divided and seek alliances with nonbusiness groups. Conflict over policy, they argue, usually involves opposing coalitions, each containing business and nonbusiness groups.

In *Fluctuating Fortunes: The Political Power of Business in America,* David Vogel makes both of these arguments, basing them on a history of the political power of business between 1960 and the 1980s.[80] Vogel sees in that period major fluctuations in business power rather than consistent business privilege. The early 1960s, he agrees, can be characterized as a period of business privilege, but by the late 1960s, the mobilization of labor, consumer, civil rights, and other liberal groups overwhelmed organized business. Vogel focuses particularly on the enactment of a series of laws between 1969 and 1972, over strenuous business opposition. The laws included the creation of the Environmental Protection Agency (EPA), the Occupational Safety and Health Administration, and the Consumer Product Safety Commission; the enactment of progressive tax legislation; a reduction in the oil depletion allowance and price controls on oil and gas; a ban on some cigarette advertising; and the enactment of auto safety standards.[81] Vogel portrays the mobilization and resurgence of business power in the late 1970s, which some analysts use to document business privilege (as I do), as merely a defensive action on business's part in response to the serious setbacks of the previous period. According to Vogel, business, as does any interest group in a pluralist system, succeeds when it organizes and promotes its agenda effectively but loses when its opponents mobilize more effectively.

In my opinion, there are a number of serious flaws in Vogel's analysis. First, he assumes that occasional legislative defeats for business interests somehow refute the privileged-position thesis, and yet those who advocate the thesis readily admit that extraordinary public mobilization can sometimes overcome business privilege. Since the emergence of truly *big* business as part of the industrialization in the late nineteenth century, there have been a number of periods when mass movements have succeeded in enacting restraints on business power: The Populists in the 1880s promoted railroad regulation and antitrust laws; the Progressives enacted food, drug, and fair trade regulations in the early twentieth century; laws legitimized labor union organizing during the New Deal; and new social regulations emerged in the late 1960s. Yet what all those periods have in common is how rare and extraordinary they have been in comparison to the norm of business dominance. Even Vogel himself admits that "during [the twentieth] century the years when business has been relatively powerful have been more numerous than those when it has not."[82] Over the nearly thirty-year period he studies, Vogel focuses on a brief three years during which business suffered legislative defeats. The perception of the privileged power of business is supported by much longer and more constant periods of business dominance.

Even when business suffers a major legislative defeat, evidence of its overall power can be revealed. In response to revelations of the ways that Enron and other companies collaborated with their accounting firms to manufacture phony profit statements, Congress passed new legislation in 2002, the Sarbanes-Oxley Act, tightening regulation of the accounting industry, despite opposition from the industry and the Business Roundtable.[83] Although the legislation was passed in the face of business opposition, the extraordinary circumstances required to overcome that opposition demonstrate how politically formidable business is. The bill was first proposed in late fall 2001, after the Enron/Arthur Andersen debacle had called attention both to the accounting industry's failure to regulate itself and to the laxity of government regulation. Over the next few months, however, business groups mounted a successful campaign to stall the legislation and by June 2002 seemed to have succeeded in killing it.[84] Then, new revelations of similar manipulations at other corporations—in particular, the collapse of WorldCom and Adelphia Communications—demolished investor confidence in corporate profit statements, and the stock market tumbled. Most worrisome, foreign investors began withdrawing from the American market. Faced with panic in the financial markets, many in Congress began to argue once again for accounting reform and Sarbanes-Oxley was passed. The public outcry over corporate malfeasance in this case was enough to overcome business power. Even so, business still managed to prevent Congress from including in the legislation the elements it most feared, such as restrictions on the use of stock options to compensate executives.

Even in the face of legislative defeats, business has the capacity to undermine the implementation of legislation it opposes. After the passage of the Sarbanes-Oxley Act, the accounting industry made sure that members sympathetic to its interests were appointed to the new accounting oversight board that is required under the act. Likewise, after the passage of the Dodd-Frank Act in 2010—intended to end the abuses that led to the financial crisis of 2008—the financial industry mobilized to impair its implementation. First, as described earlier in this chapter, the industry upped its contributions in the midterm elections, which succeeded in bringing in a Congress more favorable to financial interests.[85] Republican friends of the industry then worked to place roadblocks to the implementation of its provisions. For example, Senate Republicans blocked the Obama administration appointment of consumer advocate Elizabeth Warren to head the new Consumer Financial Protection Bureau (CFPB), meant to prevent abuses like those that led to defaults on subprime mortgages and, then, also refused to endorse the administration's second choice.[86] The clear aim was to prevent the new bureau from carrying out its powers under Dodd-Frank. The Republican House further undermined implementation through cuts to the budgets of the CFPB and other agencies like the SEC, meant to regulate the financial industry. While the Dodd-Frank bill had given these agencies new powers, they were unable to add the staff resources needed to exercise them.[87] Not surprisingly, without serious oversight as required by the new law, financial traders were seeking to engage in the same kinds of derivatives transactions that led to the 2008 crisis.[88] So, even when high-profile scandals like Enron in 2001 or the financial abuses prior to 2008 bring about business defeat on major legislation, business still can pour its resources into modifying and delaying implementation to soften the reforms' impacts on its interests.

A second problem with Vogel's critique arises when one examines the so-called defeats business suffered during the 1969–1972 period of liberal mobilization.

Some of the legislation passed during that period actually received business support. As Vogel admits, the creation of the EPA received strong business backing because business saw the environmental movement as a benign alternative to the demands of the then-burgeoning youth, civil rights, and antiwar movements—a view shared within the Nixon White House, which sponsored the legislation.[89] Besides, the creation of the EPA was a consolidation of existing agencies and imposed no new mandates on business; corporations trusted the Republican administration to be sensitive to their interests when environmental laws were implemented.

Finally, a close look at the antibusiness victories of the 1969–1972 period shows no fundamental losses in relation to the central concerns of business—those relating to its continued privileged position in the economy. Business could easily absorb increased government oversight in the areas of environmental, consumer, and worker safety. In fact, increased federal government responsibility in these areas provided certain advantages. It relieved business of the need to comply with highly variable, and in some cases more stringent, state government regulations. It also permitted business to deflect responsibility onto the government for environmental and safety disasters; inept government regulators, rather than corporate managers, could be blamed when disasters occurred. None of the legislation from 1969 to 1972 touched on central business concerns, such as its relations with labor or its control of the economy.

The most powerful refutation of the Vogel thesis was the ability of the business community to mobilize effectively to recoup its privileged position in the face of the minor setbacks of the 1969–1971 period. In 1971, the future Supreme Court Justice Lewis Powell, who at the time was chair of the Chamber of Commerce education committee, wrote a famous memo outlining a strategy to recoup and expand business power. He admonished business leaders that "power must be assiduously cultivated; and that when necessary it must be used aggressively and with determination—without embarrassment."[90] Over the next few years, the business community followed Powell's prescription and vastly expanded its Washington, DC, presence and put additional resources into exerting political influence. The National Association of Manufacturers moved its headquarters from New York to Washington; the Business Roundtable was formed; corporations hired more lobbyists and established public affairs offices in the Capitol; and new business-oriented think tanks, like the CATO Institute, the American Enterprise Institute, and the Heritage Foundation were opened.[91] This new business mobilization had its first major victory in 1977, when liberal and labor groups tried to enact government planning to guarantee jobs (the Humphrey-Hawkins Act) and labor law reform, which were handily defeated.[92] Since then, business has maintained the clear dominance of national policy making as described earlier in this chapter. The speed and decisiveness with which business moved to assert its power leads even Vogel, by the end of his book, to wonder whether the "fluctuations" in business power in the future will be as wide.[93]

Critics of the privileged-position-of-business thesis also misconstrue it when they point out political divisions in the business community. The argument of this chapter does not deny that different firms and segments of industry have different interests and preferences or that business fights over these differences in the political system. In fact, the Pluralist model of group interaction describes fairly well how the political system handles these disputes. Our politics is replete with squabbles within business. For example, in 1996, competing business interests clashed in Pluralist fashion over telecommunications policy.[94] As Congress considered the first major rewrite of telecommunications regulations since the 1930s, all the affected business interests—including the regional Bell operating companies ("Baby Bells"), long-distance providers (such as AT&T), the cable television industry, major broadcast networks, and the computer software industry—lobbied intensively on behalf of their particular concerns. All reinforced their lobbying efforts with record contributions in that year's election campaign. The result was classic Pluralist bargaining over the legislation, with the resulting Telecommunications Act of 1996 reflecting compromises among the conflicting interests of these major industries. Absent from the process was the broader public. Republican Senator John McCain described the bill as "protective of all the interests with the exception of the consumer. That's why we are seeing increasing phone rates, increasing cable rates, consolidations and mergers, and little if any increase in competition."[95] In the year following enactment of the legislation, which substantially loosened government regulation of the cable industry, cable rates rose 8.5 percent, more than four times the rate of inflation.[96] The case of the Telecommunications Act reveals Pluralist politics to be a privileged game for big business, one that ordinary citizens are not able to play.

The need to settle such conflicts among themselves may explain why business elites support the democratic "rules of the game" that are so important to the Pluralist model. These elites do not want any one business interest using governmental power against other business interests. Government brokering among business interests can produce compromises that recognize competing business interests. And businesses may seek out nonbusiness allies for their internecine battles. But these conflicts among businesses and their use of alliances do not mean that nonbusiness interests are brought in on an equal footing. Nonbusiness groups are likely to be temporary allies while businesses pursue their particular agenda. Most important, business conflict ends when it comes to fundamentals. The central insight of the privileged-position-of-business thesis is its recognition that business can prevent the raising of basic questions about its economic role. On questions of government economic planning or labor relations, when fundamental business prerogatives are at stake, business presents a united front. That businesses disagree on peripheral matters does not undermine the central claim of business privilege.

The privileged position of business is at odds with the Pluralist description of American politics. The overwhelming political resources of business, combined with its special economic role, demolish the Pluralist vision of a democracy of group competition. The competition cannot be democratic when the game is biased so decisively in favor of one of the competitors. Moreover, its privileged position relieves business of the need to compete when it comes to business control in the market economy. We turn over to business elites the responsibility for key economic decisions with far-reaching implications for the public good. In making these decisions, business leaders perform a public policy-making role without the need to answer to the broader public. Whereas the Pluralist model pictures interest groups approaching government officials with demands that their interests be considered when policy is made, this picture is reversed with respect to business. Instead of business petitioning government policymakers, elected government officials petition business decision makers with favorable policies that are designed to induce business to act for the good of the community. The flaw in the Pluralist model is its failure to accommodate this privileged position of business.

Meeting the Challenge: Democratic Action to Reduce Business Privilege

The first step toward reining in business power would be to make elections more democratic. The reform agenda outlined in the previous chapter—especially public funding of campaigns—is a prerequisite for reducing business privilege. As long as corporations fund election campaigns, politicians will be beholden to business interests.

Second, in the 1950s economist John Kenneth Galbraith argued that democracy succeeded in America only because of "countervailing" institutions that restrained big business—chief among them big government and big labor.[97] Since Galbraith made this argument, however, both government and labor have grown smaller, diminishing their ability to counteract business power. A key to cutting business down to size is a revitalization of both of these countervailing institutions. Congress needs to amend existing laws and enact new ones to make government regulation of business more effective. The power of the Securities and Exchange Commission, the Federal Trade Commission, and other regulatory agencies needs to be enhanced, and these bodies require an infusion of funds and personnel so that they can watch over business effectively. At the same time, government should take on the role originally envisioned in 1935 in the Wagner Act to protect the right of workers to organize and join labor unions. A shift to a prolabor position would include repeal of the Taft-Hartley Act, which was passed in the late 1940s to impede union organizing, and a ban on state-level efforts, such as so-called right-to-work laws, that are aimed at preventing unions from being formed. Even if government fails to provide a more favorable legal environment for union organizing, the labor movement itself must work harder to show American workers the necessity of joining a union if they are to protect their rights and gain a fair share of the country's economic prosperity. More than anything else, probusiness organizations such as the Business Roundtable fear a revitalized American labor movement. Their fear is well-founded because the counterweight of organized and mobilized workers in a strong labor movement is the classic formula for checking business privilege.

Third, when the World Trade Organization and its Big Business allies met in Seattle in 1999 to discuss the next steps toward a more business-friendly world, they were astonished to find thousands of protesters in the streets. While the corporate elites gathering over sumptuous meals in the city's plushest hotels regarded globalization as the expansion of worldwide economic prosperity—defined mainly as larger corporate profits—the street protests attracted the world's attention to the fact that globalization has not delivered prosperity to all. A wide variety of groups assembled in Seattle to highlight the many ways in which the new global governance institutions have failed to better the lives of most of the people of the world. Environmentalists demonstrated how trade rules not only ignore environmental protection but enhance business's ability to override local and national environmental regulation. Advocates for developing nations demanded an end to the increasing impoverishment of Africa, South America, and parts of Asia, which stand in stark refutation of the claim that globalization will be an engine to end world poverty. Despite increasing world economic growth in the previous decade, the number of the world's people living in poverty was increasing and the inequalities both within and between nations were growing.[98] Labor union representatives from both the developing and developed world protested the increasing worldwide wage competition that undermines the ability of workers everywhere to earn a living. Uniting all the protesters was a commitment to making globalization more democratic, both by forcing changes in substantive policies and by creating mechanisms of democratic accountability. After facing similar protests the next year in Genoa, Italy—this time resulting in the death of a protester—the WTO retreated in 2001 to Doha, Qatar, a remote island in the Persian Gulf, but still it could not escape the realization that a worldwide movement was growing on behalf of democratic accountability.

Although the globalization protesters in Seattle and elsewhere were portrayed in the press as "antiglobalization," in reality they were demanding not that globalization cease but that it be made more democratic. If the world is not to become a place where business privilege reigns unchecked, democratic means must be found to control the new global institutions. Only through more democratic institutions can we be sure that as the world grows closer economically, it does so in a manner that ensures prosperity for all and protects the global environment. To accomplish this goal, citizens must insist that governments amend existing agreements and negotiate new ones that contain specific protections for the environment, workplace standards, prohibitions on child and forced labor, recognition of the unionization rights of workers, and other provisions to enhance the living standards of all people. More important, new mechanisms must be created to ensure that decision processes in the WTO and other international bodies will be open and transparent to press and public scrutiny. These bodies also need to be made more democratically accountable through mandated participation of nongovernmental organizations (NGOs) and labor unions in their decision-making structures. Because many of these issues have been ignored in the formation of the new global economy, a sustained worldwide movement on behalf of democratic globalization is needed.

Finally, the privileged position of business raises fundamental questions about the scope of democratic politics. Americans readily agree on the need for government to be "of the people, by the people, and for the people," but business decisions whose impact on the public good is far beyond that of most governmental decisions are placed outside the sphere of public control. If we are to pay serious attention to democratic ideals, this customary understanding of the proper scope of democratic politics needs to be revised. Demanding public control of government policymakers, but denying the public the right to influence business policymakers, seems increasingly arbitrary from a democratic point of view.

The philosopher Michael Walzer tells an interesting story about the railroad car magnate George Pullman that illustrates the arbitrary nature of the way Americans define the scope of democracy.[99] In 1880, Pullman founded and built a town—Pullman, Illinois—which was designed to be a totally planned community for the workers in Pullman factories. Along with housing for about 8,000 workers, the town contained a hotel, schools, shops, a library, a theater, and a church—all owned and controlled by George Pullman, who ruled his town in an authoritarian manner, just as he ruled his factories. As sole proprietor of the town, the railroad magnate thought it his right to govern the people in the town as he saw fit. He imposed autocratic rules detailing the behavior of town residents and employed a private police force to enforce them. Although the quality of housing was good and the community was a more pleasant place to live than workers of the time were used to, Pullman residents lacked any control over the rules that governed their lives in the community. Their subordinate situation as Pullman town residents was identical to their position as Pullman factory workers, and the peculiar absence of democracy in Pullman soon attracted public attention.

In 1885, an article in a popular magazine of the day, *Harper's Monthly,* described the town as "un-American . . . benevolent, well-wishing feudalism."[100] Pullman's autocracy was deemed at odds with American democratic values. Americans were supposed to be able to govern their communities themselves, not live by the rules of one man. In 1898, the Illinois Supreme Court agreed with this viewpoint and demanded that the Pullman Company divest itself of the town and that it be given a democratic government. Although the court would not have found Pullman's rule over his factories a problem for democracy, it found his rule over the town to be "incompatible with the theory and spirit of our institutions."[101]

Walzer raises a democratically interesting question about this story: "Most observers seem to have agreed that Pullman's ownership of the town was undemocratic. But was his ownership of the company any different?"[102] Both town and company were products of Pullman's entrepreneurial vision; both were built with his capital; both residence in the town and employment in Pullman's factories were voluntary on the part of residents and workers; and in both town and company the residents and workers derived concrete benefits—good housing and wages—in return for submission to Pullman's rules; but only in the town did the arrangement seem at odds with democratic principles. As Walzer's question suggests, our customary expectation that democracy is relevant to the governance of geographic entities but not corporate ones may be arbitrary. If democracy is good for towns, why not for factories?

An understanding of the privileged position of business calls attention to this question, which Americans need to address in an era when Big Business decisions seem at odds with the well-being of the rest of us. Taking democracy seriously in the new century will require ways of reining in corporate power, not only through government regulation but also through direct democratic controls. Ways must be found to provide workers and other citizens with a more direct voice in corporate decision making. Just as the abolition of aristocratic privilege was a prerequisite for democracy in the eighteenth century, twenty-first-century democracy may require the abolition of business privilege.

Thought Questions

1. Businesses often claim that their campaign contributions are meant to ensure that they have access to legislators rather than to influence specific votes. If this is true, and we elect legislators with integrity, is there any reason to be concerned about contributors' seeking opportunities to make their case regarding legislation that affects their interests?

2. Would you favor more community control over business decisions about investing in or leaving a local community? Or should these decisions be left solely to business owners and managers?

3. This chapter's conclusion implies that we should expect to control corporations democratically just as we expect to run a city democratically. How could this be done? Would you favor introducing democratic control of corporations? Who should be represented and how?

4. Lindblom sees business privilege following logically from the decision-making autonomy that businesses are assigned in a capitalist market economy. Is this a reasonable price to pay for the economic advantages of a market economy? Are you willing to limit democracy in exchange for material prosperity?

5. This chapter argues that authoritarian business structures—and those of other social institutions such as schools—undermine our capacity to learn how to be good citizens. Is this argument consistent with your own experience as a student and/or employee? What expectations do you have about your ability to influence decisions where you work?

Suggestions for Further Reading

Kuttner, Robert. *Everything for Sale: The Virtues and Limits of Markets.* New York: Knopf, 1997; and *The Squandering of America: How the Failure of Our Politics Undermines Our Prosperity.* New York: Knopf, 2007. These books together offer clearly written arguments about how the capitalist market system works and contend that it must be regulated if it is both to work well and to provide prosperity to all.

Lindblom, Charles E. *Politics and Markets: The World's Political-Economic Systems.* New York: Basic Books, 1977. An analysis of how market and government command systems differ from one another, detailing the advantages and disadvantages of each. In his analysis of market systems, Lindblom develops the "privileged-position-of-business" thesis. A challenging but rewarding book for students who want to understand how the world works.

McLean, Bethany, and Joe Nocera. *All the Devils Are Here: The Hidden History of the Financial Crisis.* New York: Norton, 2010. An engagingly written history of the 2008 financial crisis and its causes.

Mills, C. Wright. *The Power Elite.* New York: Oxford University Press, 1956. While the Pluralists were celebrating the democratic character of American politics in the 1950s, one of America's most famous sociologists was writing this little book documenting how elites, including business leaders, manipulate our democracy to their advantage. A classic must-read for serious students of politics.

*Novak, Michael. *The Spirit of Democratic Capitalism.* New York: Touchstone, 1982. Unlike this chapter's premise, which questions the compatibility of capitalism and democracy, Novak believes the two are not only compatible but essential to one another.

Ricci, David. *Community Power and Democratic Theory: The Logic of Political Analysis.* New York: Random House, 1971. A clearly written summary of the several variants of Pluralist theory, including a superb critique.

Schattschneider, E. E. *The Semi-Sovereign People: A Realist's View of Democracy in America.* New York: Holt, Rinehart and Winston, 1960. This classic text by a great political scientist presents a theory about the interaction of interest groups and political parties that takes issue with most of the Pluralist description of American politics. Each page is packed with fascinating propositions about politics.

Stiglitz, Joseph E. *Globalization and Its Discontents.* New York: Norton, 2002. The winner of the 2001 Nobel Prize in Economics analyzes how the ideology driving the creation of a global marketplace benefits large financial institutions and large corporations at the expense of the poor.

*Vogel, David. *Fluctuating Fortunes: The Political Power of Business in America.* New York: Basic Books, 1989. Vogel argues that the political power of business is usually exaggerated.

West, Darrell M., and Burdett A. Loomis. *The Sound of Money: How Political Interests Get What They Want.* New York: Norton, 1999. A still-relevant account of the means special interests use to get their way in Washington. Includes detailed case studies of significant legislative battles.

*Presents a point of view that disagrees with the arguments presented in this chapter.

Selected Websites

http://federalreserve.gov. Website of the Federal Reserve Board.

www.aflcio.org. Home page of the AFL-CIO—America's largest labor union organization.

www.businessroundtable.org. Site of the Business Roundtable, a lobbying group of the CEOs of America's largest businesses. Take the pulse of what is on the mind of Big Business.

www.citizenworks.org. A nonprofit, nonpartisan organization that monitors corporate America and how government does and does not regulate it.

www.corporatepolicy.org. The Center for Corporate Policy is a "public interest organization working to curb corporate abuses and make corporations publicly accountable."

www.epi.org. The Economic Policy Institute offers studies and analysis of the impact of globalization on the economy, plus general information on economic issues.

I AM A VETERAN

I AM THE 99%

WE ARE THE 99%

WE ARE THE 99%

WE ARE THE 99%

CHAPTER 7

The Seventh Challenge: Economic Inequality

No novelty in the United States struck me more vividly during my stay there than the equality of conditions.

—ALEXIS DE TOCQUEVILLE

That democracy and extreme economic inequality form, when combined, an unstable compound, is no novel doctrine.

—R. H. TAWNEY

"WE ARE THE 99%." With this slogan a new American social movement was born in the fall of 2011. Beginning as a handful of mostly young protesters camped out in tiny Zuccotti Park in lower Manhattan, the Occupy Wall Street movement soon spread to cities nationwide with "Occupy" protests springing up from Philadelphia to San Francisco. A variety of concerns and issues motivated the occupiers, but at the core of the movement was a concern largely ignored and papered over in the mainstream culture—rising economic inequality in America. For decades more and more of the country's income and wealth had been accumulating in the hands of the 1 percent of wealthiest Americans. The slogan also captured the protesters' awareness that along with this concentration of economic resources at the top of the income distribution went a growing concentration of political power. The 2008 financial crisis brought on by those in the top 1 percent had induced the Great Recession from which most

Opposite: *The Occupy Wall Street movement has raised awareness of rising economic inequality, particularly the growing gap between the richest 1 percent and everyone else.*

of the 99 percent were still suffering in 2011, while the economic and politically powerful had escaped any accountability for the crisis and seemed to have recovered nicely from it. The young people of Occupy Wall Street and the many sister organizations across the country were demanding a democratic restoration in which the 99 percent would hold the 1 percent accountable for America's economic misery and a reversal of the economic inequality that was stealing opportunity from the many.

The contrast of the 99 percent and the 1 percent raised in the protests reflected accurately a reality that economic analysts have amply documented. An astounding feature of the American economy for the past four decades has been the extent to which the very rich have claimed the bulk of the fruits of the economy. In 2008, the top 1 percent took 21 percent of all income, about twice their share back in the 1970s.[1] More recently, between 2002 and 2007, about two-thirds of increases in income have gone to the top 1 percent. Their incomes increased about 10 percent per year while that of 99 percent of Americans rose a paltry 1.3 percent. In terms of wealth—the total assets, such as homes or stocks and bonds one owns—the top 1 percent do even better: They control about one-third of total wealth in the country.[2] Excluding the value of homes, however, which is the main asset of most Americans, the top 1 percent owns about 42 percent of assets. So, the Occupy Wall Street slogan captures nicely the contrast between the excessive concentration of wealth among the very rich and the situation of most Americans.

But statistics on wealth and income distribution alone do little to capture the real impact that income inequality and economic insecurity have on people's lives. Two of the Occupy protestors decided to capture these personal economic struggles with a website, "We Are the 99 Percent," that invited people to post a picture of themselves and a handwritten sign about the toll economic insecurity was taking on their lives.[3] Within a month, the website included thousands of posts and was receiving new ones at a rate of about 100 per day. The site is a chronicle of the impact of the Great Recession, but also of the economic stagnation that many Americans have been experiencing for decades. The tales on it are of the young and old, the newly poor and the always poor, those getting by paycheck to paycheck, those mired in debt and bankruptcy, many ill but without health insurance, students burdened with college loans, and parents fearful for the future of their children. Many are tales of people who worked and studied hard in quest of the American Dream but find they are caught in a nightmare instead. Most despair that anything will improve their economic plight. The site provides evidence of the fruit of not just temporary hard times but decades of rising inequality.

The economic distress of the recent Great Recession and the stagnant economy left in its wake plus the political activism of the Wall Street protestors have drawn new attention to growing economic inequality, but the trend toward greater inequality is now decades old. The economic stresses that have led to the despair expressed on the "We Are the 99 Percent" website have been building for a long time. Yet these developments have only sporadically gained the attention of the mainstream media and politicians. Less than a decade ago, the vivid images of the abandoned poor in New Orleans after Hurricane Katrina drew the attention of the national media to rising poverty and inequality in America. *Newsweek,* on its cover, termed the poverty in New Orleans and America "A National Shame"—although it was, as a *Washington Post* columnist commented, "not exactly a national secret."[4] Even in 2005, growing inequality, persistent poverty, and declining social mobility were, in fact, old news—facts of American life that were transforming the country even as the mainstream press looked the other way.

Americans resist facing this reality because it contrasts so sharply with the myth of America as a land of opportunity and a place where equality rather than social difference defined us. Social inequalities—particularly racial inequality, both in the institution of slavery and then in the practice of racial segregation—have always existed in American society. Nevertheless, from the beginning of the Republic, American egalitarianism seemed to stand out in comparison to other societies. That was the observation of such nineteenth-century European visitors as Alexis de Tocqueville, who made equality the central theme of his classic *Democracy in America.* Moreover, whatever inequalities have existed in our society seemed to diminish over time. The historical experience of many immigrants who arrived in this country penniless, who experienced discrimination and hardship, but who over time acquired wealth and eventually political power, has been, for many, the definition of the American Dream. Even our most troublesome and disruptive inequality, that of race, seemed, as shown with the election of America's first black president, to be diminishing.

The rise in economic inequality, then, poses a challenge both to our image of ourselves and to our democracy. The anger of the Occupy Wall Street protesters derives partly from shock that, in the view of the protesters, a plutocratic elite has hijacked American democracy. The same shock can be seen in public opinion polls showing Americans worrying that their children will live less well than they do—a novel development in our history. That, in comparison to other industrial countries, the United States is no longer the model of social and economic equality seems at odds with the entire American story.[5] In this chapter, we will examine the challenge this rising economic inequality poses for our democracy. In the pages that follow, we will see how economic inequality has grown since the 1970s, examine various explanations as to why this has occurred, look at its destructive impact on other social inequalities such as those of race and gender, and discuss the dangers it poses for political democracy. But to begin, the first section examines the importance of the concept of equality—both political and social—in democratic theory and American tradition.

Equality and Democratic Theory

Political equality, the idea that all people are equally qualified to rule, is the core value of democratic theory and the source of democracy's radicalism. From the time of the ancient Greeks, proponents have justified democracy by pointing to people's shared capacity to make the political and moral judgments that governing requires. They have been skeptical of all formulas for justifying the primacy of an elite or elect group of people because of its allegedly superior wisdom or virtue. That skepticism about elite rule has been a radical position because, for most of humanity's history, an existing governing elite has formulated elaborate doctrines to explain why it alone was qualified to rule and to ridicule the concept of political equality. Belief that ordinary people have the capacity to govern themselves has led ordinary people—whether American farmers in 1776, French *sans culottes* in 1789, or the black residents of the South African township of Soweto in the 1980s—to revolt against those in power. These revolutions have required not only seizing power from ruling elites but also refuting their philosophical claims that they had some right to rule others. What arguments have proponents of elite rule used to justify their power?

Over the centuries, a wide variety of doctrines have been advanced to "prove" why some group of people or some superior individual should rule over others. Divine right, racial superiority, aristocratic blood, or the superior insights of the revolutionary vanguard have been some of the formulations of the underlying notion that some group has special qualities that ordinary people do not that justify its power. All the arguments are based on the assumption that certain people have the special knowledge required to govern the community, whether it be divinely granted, inherited, or derived from the study of revolutionary dogma.[6] All arguments against political equality assume that some special knowledge is needed to govern the polity, and that only certain people are capable of acquiring it. To deny such a political elite the right to rule, according to these arguments, is to accept inferior government.

This argument is central to one of the oldest works of Western political philosophy: Plato's *Republic*. In his description of the best polity, Plato gives complete responsibility for governing to philosophers trained from birth in the art of government. This training would give the philosophers the special knowledge and capacity to make appropriate political judgments and produce justice for all. Just as one would turn to a well-trained shoemaker skilled in the art of shoemaking when seeking a good pair of shoes, one should look to a well-trained philosopher skilled in the art of government when seeking good government. For Plato, people are no more equal in their capacity to govern themselves than they are in their ability to make good shoes.

In a famous passage in the *Republic,* Plato has his protagonist, Socrates, present a parable of a ship to illustrate the folly of political equality. Imagine, says Socrates, a ship in which every sailor claimed equal capacity to take the helm, although none had any special training in navigation.[7] This would produce a long and dangerous quarrel over control of the vessel, resulting in eventual control by an incompetent helmsman. Who would want to sail on such a ship? Plato believes that democracy is like this ship because of the effect of political equality. The lesson of his parable is that no reasonable person would want to live under a condition of political equality, any more than one would want to travel on a democratic ship.

As many democratic theorists have pointed out, the flaw in Plato's reasoning is that the ship parable does not distinguish between technical competence and political competence.[8] Political judgments are concerned primarily with the ends and purposes of government—what we should *do*—rather than with the best way technically to accomplish something. In the parable of the ship, Socrates never mentions where the ship he describes is going, but politics is often about the ends, the destinations of polities, rather than the technical details of getting there. Although special technical expertise may be required in government, as it is in sailing a ship, that technical knowledge is neither required nor especially helpful in determining the destination. Even democratic sailors would be foolish to quarrel over who takes the ship's helm; there is nothing undemocratic in recognizing the need for navigational expertise, which sailors do not possess equally.[9] But in a democracy, political equality means the equal capacity to make judgments about political ends. Democratic sailors, whatever the range of inequality in navigational expertise, are equally capable of debating whether the day's sail should be devoted to whale watching or finding the best spot for snorkeling. When democrats claim that people are *politically* equal, they mean that all people possess roughly equal capacities to evaluate alternative courses of action from their particular perspectives and so make political judgments.

But why are people equal in making political judgments? Might not some people, like Plato's philosopher-kings, possess superior knowledge about the ends of politics as well as the technical details? One way to approach this question is to imagine turning over a contemporary public problem to the philosopher-kings and to think about how they would handle it. Take, for example, the serious issue of the government debt accumulated over the past decades. What would happen if the American Economics Association—surely an appropriate group of philosopher-kings for this issue—were given responsibility for solving that problem? Would they be able to handle it better than democratically elected leaders?

The first difficulty economists would face is deciding whether or not government debt is, in fact, a problem. Perhaps more than most Americans, the economics profession is divided over the degree to which the national debt threatens our economy. Some economists say that trillions of dollars of national debt poses a serious threat to future economic growth; others reply that the debt is not that great in relation to the overall size of our economy and therefore is not a threat. Still others take various positions in between. Knowledge of economic science, in itself, does not provide unambiguous guidance regarding how to evaluate a concrete political issue such as the national debt. Like most social phenomena, the operation of the national economy is very complex, and economics, like all social sciences, offers no certain answers about how it operates. After all the expert opinion is reviewed and evaluated, political judgments about public problems come down to intuitive guesses about which expert prescriptions to choose. Democracy assumes that, given the general uncertainty about how the world works, the intuitive judgment of ordinary people will likely be as good as that of experts.

What is true about identifying public problems is even truer, once problems are identified, about choosing policy solutions. Experts nearly always disagree about policy proposals on complicated issues such as the debt because such proposals involve predictions about the future. Will future economic growth be strong enough that the debt will gradually disappear, or are concrete policy steps—such as allocating a portion of all future budget surpluses to paying down the debt—required to deal with it? Even economists cannot be certain, because of the limitation of their science, how future economic growth will affect the national debt. Because of this uncertainty, there are likely to be different schools of thought within the profession recommending different courses of action.

Besides predictions about the future impact of alternative policy options, any policy solution will always involve value choices. Should we reduce the debt by raising taxes or by cutting spending? The answer rests in part on expert predictions about which course of action is likely to be more effective in reducing debt, but it also requires judgment about what citizens value more: money in their pockets or government services. When we begin to consider alternative spending cuts, the role of value judgments becomes more obvious. Should we cut spending on defense or spending on education? Such a choice involves a decision about what people value more: a high level of security from foreign threats or educating their children. What increase in military insecurity is acceptable in return for better-educated youngsters? The democratic option assumes ordinary people to be equally capable of making such judgments; once they have determined the probable consequences of alternative courses of action, the advice of experts does not help us to choose which set of consequences we are willing to accept. Furthermore, political equality, in contrast to the philosopher-kings theory, assumes that individuals are more competent than any expert to judge for themselves what they want, by exercising the kinds of value choices just described. Equal citizens in a democracy bring to political decision making their individual judgments about what they want—something they know best.[10] Democratic decision making involves a process of discussion among those individuals until a consensus, or at least a majority opinion, is reached on what they collectively want to do. The theory of democracy makes room for the advice of experts, just as the sailors and passengers on a democratic ship need the navigational skills of the captain, but in a democracy, the decision about where we are going requires judgments about the uncertain future and value choices that all people are competent to make.

Although democrats agree on the central value of political equality, the relationship between political and social equality in a democratic society remains controversial. To say that people ought to have equal rights to political participation does not necessarily require that they be equal in any other way. In fact, vast inequalities among citizens—in social status, wealth, and lifestyles—can be found in all countries claiming to be democratic. Can these inequalities safely coexist with political democracy, or do they interfere with the ability of people to govern themselves as equals? To what degree does the democratic ideal of political equality require a measure of social and economic equality?

The response to these questions is usually framed in terms of the debate between *equality of opportunity* and *equality of condition*. Proponents of equality of opportunity argue that democracy may be compatible with social and economic inequalities, depending on the source of those inequalities. If they arise from a political elite's use of its political power to give themselves special economic and social privileges that are denied to others, then they not only are inconsistent with political equality but are the result of its absence. A truly democratic polity would not likely give special privileges to an elite. If, however, some individuals become wealthier than others and acquire higher social status because of their own intelligence, initiative, and luck, there is no conflict with political equality. As long as the political rules of the game are the same for everyone, there is no cause for concern when some are able to succeed better than others, and inequality results. Proponents of equality of opportunity believe that political equality ensures that government will make the rules of economic and social competition fair for all. Unequal success under these rules does not challenge democracy as long as the rules are fair.

Proponents of equality of condition question whether true equality of opportunity can exist when there are large differences in wealth and social status in society. From this point of view, abstract assurances of equal opportunity have little meaning when one compares the actual opportunities that are open to a child growing up in New Orleans's impoverished Lower Ninth Ward with the opportunities available to a child in a wealthy suburb. Existing differences in social and economic status translate automatically into differences in opportunity. And because a society of political equals would seek ways to narrow these differences as part of providing equal opportunity for everyone, the very existence of acute social inequalities is probably an indicator of political inequality. Only a society in which some have less political power than others would accept large socioeconomic inequalities. Proponents of equality of condition also emphasize the ease with which economic and social privilege can erode political equality. They insist that people blessed with such privilege will use it to acquire greater political power and, inevitably, to bias the rules of the game in their favor. Social and economic inequality leads directly to political inequality, and then to inequality of opportunity.

The concepts of equality of opportunity and equality of condition provide different vantage points for evaluating socioeconomic inequalities in a society: The former seeks to evaluate them in terms of their causes, the latter in terms of their effects. A democratic commitment to political equality is consistent with either concept, depending on where one wishes to focus one's attention. Indeed, neither point of view alone is very satisfactory for understanding the relationship between socioeconomic and political equality in actual societies. The theoretical debate assumes a sharper distinction between these two sorts of equality than has actually been true historically when people have struggled to establish democratic government.

In nearly all movements to establish democracy, democrats have seen the struggle for equality as embracing both political and social equality, perceived simultaneously as both equality of opportunity and equality of condition. The historian Gordon Wood argues that that was the case with the American Revolution.[11] "Equality," argues Wood, was "the most radical and powerful ideological force let loose in the Revolution."[12] The American revolutionaries sought to break down the sharp, hierarchical social distinctions of colonial society and replace them with the concept of republican citizenship. This was obviously a political concept—a demand for political equality—but because political and social statutes were so closely related in prerevolutionary America, it implied more social equality as well.

That concern for equality did not mean that the American revolutionaries wanted to "level" society—to make everyone the same economically. According to Wood, equality of opportunity was clearly their aim. At the same time, the revolutionaries thought that eliminating the hierarchical structures obstructing equality of opportunity would lead, over time, to greater equality of condition.[13] A measure of social and economic equality, they thought, would be essential for political equality. Only relative equality of property holding, as in Thomas Jefferson's vision of the independent yeoman farmer, would ensure that no citizen would become dependent on someone else. Economic dependence was thought to be incompatible with the free exercise of citizenship.[14] In addition, equality "made possible natural compassion and affection and . . . bound everyone together in a common humanity"—a condition conducive to equal political participation.[15] As a result of the Revolution, political and social equality were intertwined in American minds, as "ordinary Americans came to believe that no one in a basic down-to-earth and day-in-and-day-out manner was really better than anyone else."[16] By the 1830s, Alexis de Tocqueville found equality of condition to be a distinctive characteristic of the American democratic society.[17]

The interrelationship Wood finds between political and social equality in the American Revolution seems to be characteristic, to some degree, of all "transitions" to democracy.[18] Such transitions usually involve displacing power elites that have used their political privilege to secure their own social privileges. During the democratic revolutions that have occurred since 1989 in Eastern Europe and the former Soviet Union, for example, denunciation of the social privileges of the former Communist Party elite—the dachas, special stores, and vacation retreats—has accompanied the introduction of democratic processes. In some countries, a major concern has been to prevent the former elite from using social privileges obtained under communism to establish a privileged position for itself under democratic capitalism. In democratic revolutions everywhere, the egalitarian sentiment of democracy seems based on a notion of equality that embraces both political and social equality. Equality in a democracy means "no more bowing and scraping."[19]

The relationship between social and political equality in democratic revolutions suggests a need to examine their interrelationship in societies—such as the contemporary United States—that claim to be mature democracies. To what degree does our society retain the revolutionary sentiment that "no one is better than anyone else"? Do we still exhibit the sense of "common humanity" that is characteristic of a society of equals and necessary for a successful democracy? Or have social and economic inequalities grown to such an extent that they threaten our democracy?

Before we can discuss these questions, we need to examine more carefully the extent of social inequality in the United States today. Like many other societies, American society is pervaded by inequalities—based on gender, culture, language, sexual orientation, organizational status, or physical capacity—that undermine political equality. All these social inequalities are important barriers to achieving the level of political equality that is necessary in a democratic society. For example, social structures that place American women in an inferior status in the economy, in the family, and in many organizations impede their ability to participate equally with men as citizens. The significance of this inequality is obvious in the extreme gender imbalance in supposedly representative bodies such as the US Congress, despite women's gains in recent years. Full understanding of how social inequality impedes political equality and democracy requires sensitivity to the wide variety of forms that inequality takes.

In this brief chapter, however, I have chosen to concentrate on two kinds of social inequality that are particularly troubling for the future of American democracy because they appear to have been worsening in recent years. First, the trend toward increasing inequality in wealth and income during the past two decades challenges our central myth about the nature of American society: the

American Dream. Second, racial inequality, the persistent divide between black and white Americans, has deep roots in our history. Of all the social inequalities that challenge American democracy, these two are likely to be the most explosive.

The End of the American Dream?

Our most enduring myth is the American Dream. It is a myth, not in the sense of a fictional story, but in the sense of a symbolic representation of some fundamental expectations that Americans have about the character of their country and their own place in it. The American Dream is a narrative about ordinary people striving for material success and social acceptance in a new kind of society where such striving is actually rewarded. Unlike other societies, where rigid social hierarchies reserve independence, wealth, and power to a select few, the America of the American Dream is a place where no system of social stratification stands in the way of individual success. In one popular variant of the myth, a poor immigrant arrives alone on our shores without resources but in a few short years, through hard work, provides a comfortable living for his family. Within a generation his children become educated professionals, sometimes wealthy, perhaps state governors, or even president. Another variant is simply a mental picture of an entire nation living in neat, well-kept, single-family houses surrounded by equally neat, well-kept lawns, sending their children to cheerful neighborhood public schools, barbecuing on weekends in their backyards when they have not gone on an excursion in one of the family automobiles. The American Dream, in short, is a vision of individual and collective material prosperity.

Like all myths, the American Dream contains different components within the many stories that compose it, but expectations of material prosperity and social mobility are central to all of them. The myth assumes that greater wealth and higher income can be had and can be more widely distributed than has been possible in other societies. Consistent with the individualist bias of our culture, the myth projects individual effort and striving as the source of prosperity, but the absence of social barriers to mobility provides the context in which individuals do, in fact, gain their rewards. Implicit in both expectations is an assumption of social equality in society.

Within the symbolism of the American Dream, social equality does not mean a society of absolute equality and sameness, for the link between individual effort and social mobility requires a system of differential rewards. Nevertheless, the American Dream emphasizes that the potential for material success and social mobility is available to all. In the United States, there are no castes or limits on particular groups' gaining access to even the best opportunities. And it is a vision of society in which material differences between people do not sharply divide them from one another: no snobbism here. The ideal of the comprehensive American high school in which children of the rich and the poor are educated together, rather than the exclusive prep school, epitomizes the American Dream.

The reality of American society has never conformed to the vision presented in the American Dream. Like all myths, although it may be grounded in a basic reality, the vision does not accurately reflect the historical experience of all Americans. Like all societies, American society has had its inequalities, its prejudices, and its own system of stratification. There have always been exclusive prep schools along with the public high schools. Immigrants arriving in the United States have found not just "streets paved with gold," but also discrimination and abuse. The shameful treatment of African Americans forced to dream their American dreams in the cargo holds of slave ships represents the most glaring contrast between myth and reality. Yet for all these failures of reality to live up to the myth, one of the sources of the American Dream's enduring strength is that it has always been a *dream* for the future, not existing reality. Poor immigrants, hardscrabble farmers, and even former slaves could dream the American Dream in filthy, unheated tenements and dirt-floor shacks because its focus was on aspirations for the future. Within the dream, existing social inequalities were seen as

A modest single-family home with a car in the driveway was the fulfillment of the American Dream for many Americans in the 1950s and 1960s.

Photo courtesy of George Marks/Getty Images.

carryovers from the past; the future promised steady progress toward the equal, inclusive society envisioned in the myth.

In sum, the American Dream provides a series of promises about the trajectory of society. Throughout our history, it has promoted expectations that we are moving together toward greater prosperity, greater mobility, and greater equality than can be found today. That people have perceived such a trajectory over the course of their own lives—even when their lives may have fallen short of attaining the dream—has solidified the myth in American consciousness. This central American belief in the inevitability of progress explains why the growing perception, in the past few years, that the trajectory of our society may have shifted from greater social equality to greater social inequality has come as such a profound shock. The prospect of more inequality, rather than less, in the next generation calls our culture's central myth into question and must challenge the future of our democracy. This challenge is all the greater because it comes after a period—the thirty years that followed World War II—when the reality of American life seemed on the verge of securing the American Dream for all.

Moving Toward the American Dream: 1945–1970s

The postwar years in the United States produced the longest and greatest expansion of economic prosperity in the history of humanity. Ordinary Americans were the direct beneficiaries of this prosperity, as the real (inflation-adjusted) median family income doubled between 1945 and 1970.[20] Unlike most families today, the typical family during that period had one breadwinner, whose single income was sufficient to deliver a steadily increasing living standard. A young man—most family breadwinners during the period were men—starting his working life at age twenty-five in 1950 or 1960 could count on doubling his income by the time he reached thirty-five.[21] Not only did income double, but fewer hours of work were required to earn it—average annual hours worked declined during this period, and American workers put in fewer hours than did their European counterparts.[22] Given this explosion of prosperity, the real experience of most families involved moving to a roomy house in the sunny suburbs, with a two-car garage (filled, of course, with two cars), a backyard barbecue (perhaps next to a swimming pool), in a neighborhood filled with similar families—just like the American Dream.

Increasing prosperity spread widely among Americans, producing a dramatic reduction in the level of income inequality. One of the ways in which social scientists analyze income distribution is to look at how total national income is distributed among fifths (quintiles) of the population, ranging from the poorest fifth to the richest. Tracing shifts in this distribution over time shows that between 1947 and 1974, although the overall distribution remained very unequal, the income share going to all but the richest fifth of the population increased

TABLE 7.1   Family Income Distribution, 1947–2009 (in Percentages)

	Poorest Fifth	Second Fifth	Third Fifth	Fourth Fifth	Richest Fifth	Richest 5%
1947	5.0	11.9	17.0	23.1	43.0	17.5
1959	4.9	12.3	17.9	23.8	41.1	15.9
1974	5.7	12.0	17.6	24.1	40.6	14.8
1980	5.3	11.6	17.6	24.4	41.1	14.6
1990	4.6	10.8	16.6	23.8	44.3	17.4
1996	4.2	10.0	15.8	23.1	46.8	20.3
2007	4.1	9.7	15.6	23.3	47.3	20.1
2009	3.9	9.4	15.3	23.2	48.2	20.7

Source: US Census Bureau, *Historical Income Tables—Families,* Table F-2. Share of Aggregate Income Received by Each Fifth and Top 5 Percent of Families (All Races): 1947 to 2010, accessed December 27, 2011, http://www.census.gov/hhes/www/income/data/historical/families/.

(see Table 7.1). Naturally, the gains of the bottom four-fifths of the income distribution came at the expense of the richest fifth, whose share of national income declined by more than 2 percent. This was true, as well, at the very top of the distribution: The overall income share of the richest 5 percent shrank by nearly 3 percent. Meanwhile, even the poorest Americans gradually increased their share of national income by more than half a percentage point.

This shift toward greater income equality is more dramatic if we consider the percentages of families at various levels of income. In 1947, immediately following World War II, 97 percent of Americans earned less than $10,000 per year (in 1984 dollars); about one-third earned less than $2,500.[23] Most Americans were concentrated at the lower end of the income distribution. By the early 1970s, this situation had changed substantially, as most families moved into the middle class. By 1973, the proportion of families earning less than $10,000 (again, in constant 1984 dollars) had been cut to 39 percent, as 42 percent moved into the $10,000 to $20,000 category, and the remaining 20 percent earned more than $20,000. Most dramatically, the proportion at the bottom, earning less than $2,500, had declined to 4 percent—about one-tenth of what it had been in 1947. The family income distribution had shifted from one with most families at the lower end, to one with most concentrated toward the middle. In terms of family income, the American Dream's vision of more people sharing in the general prosperity was the reality of the thirty postwar years.

As economist Frank Levy has shown in his book *The New Dollars and Dreams,* the increase in economic equality between 1947 and 1973 was the result

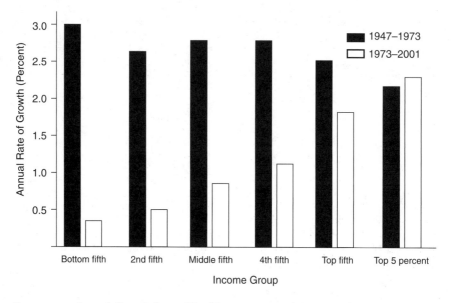

FIGURE 7.1   Annual Growth Rate of Real Income Across the US Family Income Distribution, 1947–2001

Source: Gary Burtless and Christopher Jencks, "American Inequality and Its Consequences," in *Agenda for the Nation,* ed. Henry J. Aaron et al. (Washington, DC: Brookings Institution, 2003), 65.

of broad distribution of the gains of growing economic productivity.[24] During the period, the United States experienced a twenty-seven-year economic boom, with inflation-adjusted wages growing by about 2.5 to 3 percent per year. This era of sustained growth had a direct effect on average family incomes, which grew 30 percent during the 1960s and 1970s. The postwar boom was a classic period of a "rising tide"—overall economic growth—"lifting all boats," improving the standard of living of everyone. The expansion occurred because of increased economic productivity—the economic value produced by each hour of labor—and the distribution of those productivity gains to all workers. During the period, productivity grew each year by an average of 3.3 percent, producing a total gain of 104 percent, which translated into a comparable rise in family incomes across all income categories.[25] As Figure 7.1 shows, between 1947 and 1973 all income groups shared in the benefits of a growing economy, and—surprisingly, in light of more recent times—the poorest Americans saw their incomes grow faster than those of the more affluent. No wonder this was an age of growing equality: The equal distribution of growing prosperity made the American Dream a real possibility for all Americans.

Moving Away From the American Dream: 1970s–2012

The early 1970s brought an end to growing equality, and by the early 1980s the proportion of families at the lowest income levels began to increase—a trend that has continued into the twenty-first century.[26] By 1990, the gains of the poorest Americans had been wiped out (see Table 7.1), and by around 1995 income distribution had become even more unequal than in 1947. By 1996, someone in the top 5 percent of the income distribution earned *twenty-three times* the income of someone in the bottom 5 percent of the distribution.[27] Neither the Clinton economic boom of the 1990s nor the more modest economic growth during the Bush years stemmed growing income inequality. By 2009, the richest quintile of families were closing in on capturing half of all income earned, while the poorest 20 percent had lost more than a full 1 percent share compared to the poorest Americans in 1947. In contrast to the American Dream's picture of a steady march toward widespread prosperity, American reality seemed to be moving backward.

Some of the rising inequality of family incomes in the past four decades seems related to stagnant productivity and wage growth early in the period and to sharp inequalities in the distribution of productivity and wage gains when they finally resumed in the late 1990s. After 1965, the rate of productivity growth began to decline; productivity grew an average of only 1 percent a year between 1973 and 1996.[28] In contrast to the 75 percent growth in real wages between 1947 and 1973, real hourly wages actually fell by 9 percent between 1973 and 1998, producing an inflation-adjusted hourly wage in 1998 that was the same as it had been in 1967.[29] But even when economic productivity revived in the 1990s, only the top of the income distribution benefited. The economic boom of the late 1990s began to push up median wages, but sluggish growth between 2001 and 2007 saw a $500 drop in annual, inflation-adjusted, median family income.[30] Since the recession hit in 2008, this trend has accelerated with median income dropping an additional 9.8 percent.[31] Over the past two decades, only the rich have gotten richer from rising economic productivity.

Rising productivity has not produced higher incomes for most Americans because the gains from higher productivity have gone to capital, not labor, except for those at the top of the income distribution. In sharp contrast to the pre-1973 period, when wages increased across the board, between 1979 and 2001, the poorest 10 percent of workers saw their wages decline by about 4 cents per hour, and median-wage earners experienced a meager 7 percent rise, while the top 10 percent of wage earners earned 23 percent more.[32] Also in contrast to the pre-1973 period, productivity gains have gone to higher dividends and value for stockholders rather than to wages.[33]

Because wages were stagnant after the 1970s, the only way families were able to maintain their income was to work more. In most cases, this necessity pushed more women into the workforce as their families' second breadwinner. In addition, to maintain their standard of living, these dual worker households were putting in more hours—often in two or three different jobs.[34] Whereas Americans had shorter workdays than those in other industrial countries prior to 1970, by the end of the century they were working, on average, more hours than workers in Japan, Britain, France, or Germany.[35] But, in the first decade of the twenty-first century, additional hours of work ceased to be sufficient to maintain living standards, so many Americans turned to easy credit.[36] Rising housing prices and aggressive bank lending practices (as described in chapter 6) led families to borrow against the value of their homes, a practice that maintained aggregate economic demand until the credit bubble burst in 2008. With the resulting recession and faltering economy, more work and easy credit no longer papered over the consequences of decades of growing inequality as American families experienced them in a lowered standard of living.

Figure 7.1 offers a dramatic representation of the contrast between income growth for different income quintiles after 1947 compared to after 1973. In contrast with the relatively even income growth from 1947–1973, income growth from 1973–2001 was distributed in stair-step fashion—with annual growth rates increasing from poorest to richest. Note that among all income groups, only the top 5 percent saw their incomes grow faster in this latter period than before 1973. If one looks at the distribution of income growth between 1979 and 2009, the inequality becomes even greater as the poorest 20 percent of families saw their incomes *decline* while that of the richest fifth more than doubled.[37] While these census statistics comparing growing inequality across population quintiles paint a dramatic picture, to get a more complete image of changes in income inequality, one needs to look at how those at the very top of the income distribution have captured an increasing share of economic prosperity.

In 2003, two French economists, Thomas Piketty and Emmanuel Saez, published a pathbreaking study that delved deeply into precisely who had benefitted most from income inequality.[38] Using income tax data (which they have now updated to 2008), they offered a more detailed look at income distribution within the top 10 percent of the income distribution going back to 1913. Consistent with the history of income inequality recounted in this chapter, they found that the 10 percent of richest Americans saw their share of national income drop from a high of nearly 50 percent of income in 1928, just prior to the Great Depression, to around 35 percent in 1947, a share that remained steady until the early 1980s. At that point, as the reader should expect, these richest Americans claimed increasing shares of income until they had returned by 2007 to the 1928 peak.[39] What was most revealing, however, was Piketty and Saez's discovery that even among the richest 10 percent of Americans there was tremendous inequality. The top one percent (those earning over $368,000 in 2008) accounted for about half of the income of the entire top 10 percent for a total of nearly 25 percent of national income. Moreover, while the entire 10 percent had seen their share of national income grow after 1980, most of the growth went to the fortunate 1 percent who saw their share rocket from 10 percent of national income in 1980 to nearly 25 percent in 2007. As the Occupy Wall Street movement slogan says, the divide between the one and the ninety-nine is real. But digging even deeper, Piketty and Saez learned that even among the 1 percent of the very richest Americans, about half of the average gains went to the top 0.01 percent—a mere 13,000 taxpayers with an average income of $17 million.[40] These fortunate ones draw incomes 300 times that of the average American family, earning as much as the 20 million poorest Americans combined. By 2006, this tiny group of super-rich had seen their share of national income quadruple since 1980, to a share equal to that of the top tenth of the top 1 percent of 1916. We now live in a new Gilded Age, as today's billionaires resume building extravagant mansions and buying yachts in the manner of the Vanderbilts and Rockefellers of the previous Gilded Age (with the addition of a Gulf Stream jet or two).

An important element of the skyrocketing prosperity among the rich is the generosity of American corporations in their compensation of upper-level executives compared to what they pay their average workers. In the 1960s, the average CEO earned about 26 times the salary of the average worker. Despite the decline in overall corporate performance that began in the early 1970s—and just when workers' wages began to stagnate—the ratio of CEO-to-worker compensation began to grow (see Figure 7.2). By 2000, corporate CEOs were earning a mind-boggling 310 times the pay of the average worker. In other words, in 2000 the boss earned in *one day* what many of his workers earned in a whole year.[41] Although the Great Recession brought the ratio of CEO-to-worker compensation down to a mere 185 times the pay of the average worker, by 2011 corporate boards were again ratcheting up executive compensation to restore them to pre-recession levels.[42] Even though it is only part of the story, this dramatic escalation in the compensation of those running corporations, compared to that of their employees, symbolizes the shift toward greater income inequality over the past four decades.

The increasingly unequal distribution of income over this period has led to a comparable increase in inequalities of wealth. Social scientists define *wealth* as the things people own—stocks and bonds, houses and other real estate, bank accounts—minus, of course, their debts, whereas *income* includes the money coming into a household over a fixed period of time in the form of wages and salaries, interest earned, business profits, and dividends. The distribution of wealth is in some ways a better measure of societal inequality than income distribution. Incomes may vary greatly from year to year because they can be affected by short-term events: Someone wins the lottery, another person is unemployed for part of the year, someone else sells a house and retires to Florida. In comparison, wealth distribution tends to be more stable, and because wealth earns future income, it is a good measure of future living standards.

In our new Gilded Age, these possessions are one way the opulent elite divide from the rest of us.

©iStockphoto.com/Bluberries; ©iStockphoto.com/negaprion; ©iStockphoto.com/CT757fan.

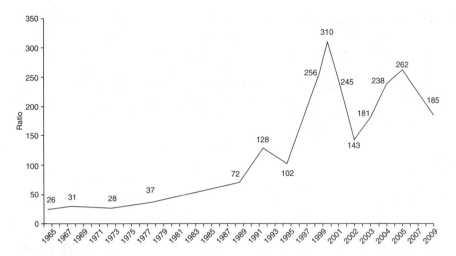

FIGURE 7.2 Ratio of CEO to Average Worker Pay, 1965–2009

Source: Mishel, Bernstein, and Allegretto, Figure 3. *The State of Working America 2006–2007.*
Update for 2009: http://stateofworkingamerica.org/inequality/wages-compensation/.

Toward the end of the past century, wealth became more concentrated in the hands of the richest families. Between 1983 and 1995, only the top 5 percent of the population saw their net worth increase. Everyone else lost ground—especially the bottom 40 percent, who saw nearly an 80 percent decline in wealth. As of 1997, the top 1 percent of the population controlled 40 percent of net wealth, and the next 4 percent about 22 percent, leaving the remaining 95 percent of the population with only a bit over one-third of total national wealth.[43] To gain a sense of the dimensions of this wealth concentration, consider that the assets of a single immensely wealthy individual, Microsoft CEO Bill Gates, are equal to the total assets of 100 million Americans—the least affluent 40 percent of the population.[44] The Great Recession produced widespread destruction of wealth, but that destruction was uneven.[45] The richest quintile saw its share of a shrunken pie grow by 2.2 percent to 87.2 percent while the bottom fourth-fifths saw its share decline to only 12.8 percent of all wealth. The wealthiest 1 percent in 2009 had a net worth 225 times greater than the median household, the highest disparity on record, and the 1 percent owned more than the entire bottom 90 percent.[46] As Figure 7.3 shows, in the late 1990s American wealth was more concentrated than it had been since the 1920s. Whereas in that early decade, wealth was more equally distributed in the United States than in Europe, by the century's end it was less concentrated in major European countries than in the United States.[47] While the wealthiest 1 percent of Americans controlled about 40 percent of US wealth, 26 percent of French wealth, 18 percent of British wealth, and 16 percent of Swedish wealth was in the hands of each of those countries' top 1 percent.[48]

The continuing concentration of wealth in the United States is most significant at the heart of the productive economy. The wealthiest 1 percent of Americans can assure themselves of high future incomes through their ownership of more than 60 percent of business assets and securities: stocks, bonds, and trusts. As a *New York Times* article reporting these findings noted, such a huge concentration of wealth "flies in the face of" Tocqueville's observation, in the United States of the 1830s, about "the general equality of condition among the people."[49]

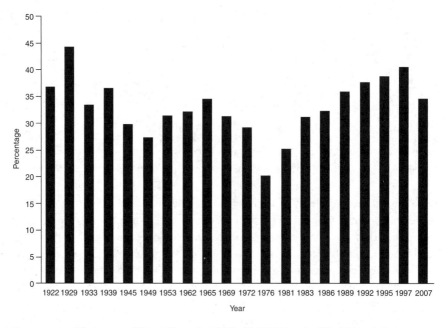

FIGURE 7.3   Percentage of Total Household Wealth Held by the Wealthiest 1 Percent, 1922–2004

Source: Edward Wolff, "Recent Trends in Household Wealth in the United States: Rising Debt and the Middle-Class Squeeze," Levy Economics Institute, 2007, Table 2; 2009 update, Table 2, accessed March 2010, http://www.levyinstitute.org/pubs/wp_589.pdf.

While the rich got richer in recent years, the poor got poorer. As one might expect, the poor suffered serious setbacks in the severe recession of the early 1980s and in the less-severe ones of the early 1990s and 2001. Recessions tend to most affect those at the bottom of the income distribution because unskilled workers earning low pay tend to get laid off sooner during a recession, and in greater numbers, than skilled workers. But the poor suffered especially in the recessions after 1980 because, unlike previous periods of economic growth, the rapid economic expansions in the 1980s and 1990s did little to ameliorate their poverty—they had no gains to cushion the downturns that followed. Fewer than 12 percent of all Americans were poor in 1979, but in 1997, even at the height of an economic boom, 13.3 percent were poor.[50] Although the 1990s boom finally lowered the poverty rate to 11.3 percent in 2000, the ensuing recession and feeble recovery had brought it back up to 12.3 percent by 2006. The Great Recession wiped out these gains as poverty rose to 15.1 percent in 2010.[51] The 46.2 million people in poverty was the highest number of poor in fifty-two years. Unlike the trends of the 1950s and 1960s, when steadily increasing prosperity cut the poverty rate in half, the economic growth since the 1970s has resulted in no reduction in the proportion of Americans living in poverty.

Often commentators claim that continued social mobility in the United States offsets rising inequality and continued high poverty rates. The ideal of equality of opportunity in these accounts trumps equality of condition. Yet evidence is growing that increasing inequality has been undermining the very social mobility championed in the rags-to-riches myth of the American Dream. Recently, a number of economists, using large data sets and the most sophisticated statistical measures, have found the chances that a son or daughter will earn an income similar to that of their parents to be quite strong.[52] According to one of these studies, successful parents convey about 65 percent of their earnings advantage to their children—a statistical correlation that is similar to the heritability of their height.[53] Of course, whereas the inheritance of income potential conveys an advantage in well-off families, it becomes a disadvantage for the poor. Those children born into the poorest quintile of the population have about a 50 percent chance of staying at that level all their lives and only about a 10 percent chance to rise into the top quintile.[54] And while the heritability of income potential is related to a variety of factors, wealth and the educational advantages it provides, rather than genetically related endowments such as IQ or personality traits or an aptitude for economic success, are the most important reasons that wealthier parents can enable their children to do as well as they did.[55] Children of poor parents have only a limited chance to move up the social ladder, no matter how smart or ambitious they may be, because they must compete with children who have benefited from their parents' economic resources. Thus, growing socioeconomic inequality has contributed to declining social mobility, as the privileged improve their ability to pass on their economic advantage to the next generation.[56] More recently, a study by the PEW Economic Mobility project has found more declining mobility in America with about one-third of children born into middle-class families dropping out of the middle class as adults.[57] Finally and most ironically in light of the myth of the American Dream, there now seems to be less social mobility in the United States than in many of the countries from which many immigrants once came to America. A poor child now has a better chance of moving up the economic ladder in places such as Sweden, Germany, Britain, or Finland than in the United States.[58]

Economic Inequality and Race

Rising economic inequality over the past four decades has put a damper on what had been a gradual amelioration of the large racial income inequalities in the United States. The postwar economic boom fueled a reduction of income inequality between blacks and whites—a process that was accelerated by the civil rights movement. After 1963, the difference between the median income of blacks and that of whites dropped steadily, a convergence that was consistent with the American Dream's vision of progress toward equality. Between 1977 and 1990, however, that convergence slowed. Before the 1960s, racial discrimination had denied blacks access to many high-paying manufacturing jobs, which in the post-1945 period offered other Americans the opportunity for social mobility. Just as governmental action to prevent racial discrimination came into force, however, the elimination of these high-paying entry-level jobs again prevented blacks from closing the income gap with whites. In other words, having been denied access by racial discrimination to the pre-1973 growth in life prospects, blacks found that the abolition of that legal discrimination arrived primarily in a period when the struggle for the American Dream had become more difficult for everyone. The booming economy of the late 1990s began to narrow the gap again, partly because of a rise in wages at the bottom of the income distribution, where many black workers are concentrated.[59] By 2000, median black family income had reached about 64 percent of median white income. But during the first decade of the twentieth century, black income relative to whites began to decline and then fell after the recession hit to only 57 percent of median white family income in 2009.[60] Hispanic Americans also saw their income decline relative to whites after 2000 to about 64 percent of white median family income.

Although there are nearly twice as many poor white families as there are poor black or Hispanic families in America today, poverty often has a black or Hispanic face because a minority family is more than four times as likely to be poor as a white family. As with income trends, minority poverty fell considerably in the economic boom of the 1990s but is now on an upward slope. Even before the Great Recession, nearly 22 percent of black families and 20 percent of Hispanic families lived below the poverty line in 2006, compared to just over 6 percent of white families. Since 2008, the recession has raised poverty levels across the board but had a devastating impact on minority communities. By 2010, the black poverty rate had climbed to 27.4 percent and the Hispanic poverty rate to 26.6 percent, more the twice the 9.9 percent poverty rate of whites. If part of the vision of the American Dream has meant less difference in economic status between people with different racial and ethnic backgrounds, rising economic inequality has destroyed that part, too.

Even more alarming for the future of racial equality, black access to educational opportunity began to decline just when the value of education to economic success was increasing. The proportion of black students dropping out of school, many from decaying inner-city schools, increased faster in the 1970s and 1980s than did the proportion of white dropouts. As the difference between the entry-level wages of college graduates and those of high school graduates increased, the proportion of blacks going to college decreased. Between 1977 and 1988, while the percentage of white youths enrolled in college grew from 27.1 percent to 31.3 percent, the percentage of blacks enrolled declined from 22.6 percent to 21.1 percent.[61] This bleak situation began to improve considerably in the 1990s: The gap between black and white high school graduation rates was cut in half, and there was a slight narrowing in the gap between the proportions of blacks and whites graduating from college.[62] Still, despite the positive trend, there remains a sharp contrast between the experience of the vast majority of black students and that of the small number of very talented, middle-class and poor black students. The latter have benefited from the affirmative action programs that attracted them to the country's best universities, but such policies have not prevented other barriers from rising in the path of most blacks' access to college. To a much greater extent than whites, blacks depend for their early education on deteriorating urban public schools that do not provide adequate college preparation. Rising costs at state colleges and universities and diminished higher education grants dispropor-tionately affect working-class blacks who, like all working-class people, depend on them for access to higher education.

The gap between the economic status of blacks and Hispanics and that of whites becomes even wider when we look at wealth accumulation. The major economic consequence of being denied equal access to economic opportunities in America has been the inability of black Americans to gain ownership of wealth. Even before the 2008 recession, the contrast between blacks and whites was stag-gering: The median net worth of black households was $12,124 and Hispanic households $18,359 while that of whites was $134,992 (see Figure 7.4). The Great Recession represented a decline in wealth for everyone but had a devastating impact on the wealth of nonwhites. As Figure 7.4 shows, blacks saw more than one-half of their accumulated wealth destroyed and Hispanics saw a huge decline of two-thirds of their median net worth. The huge declines in minority wealth occurred because of the large decline in housing values that characterized the 2008 recession.[63] For both blacks and Hispanics, their wealth consisted primarily in home ownership. Few owned other assets such as stocks and bonds that declined less in the recession than the value of housing and constitute a larger share of the wealth of whites. In fact, many nonwhites do not own any assets at all. In 2009, with the exception of a vehicle, about one in four nonwhites had no assets compared to only 6 percent of whites.[64] Within the overall disparity of income and wealth in America, the persistent racial gap remains huge and seems to be growing.

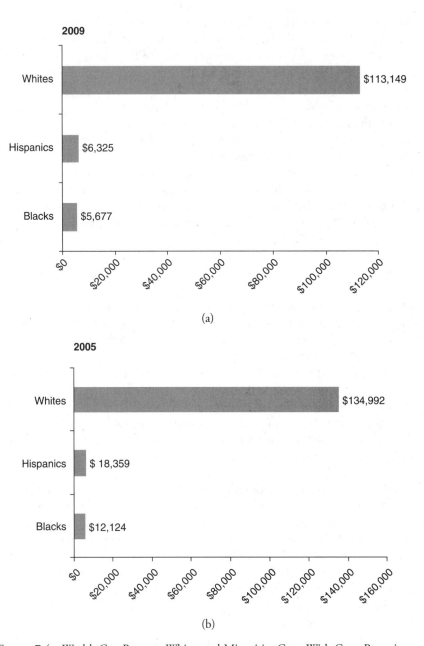

FIGURE 7.4 Wealth Gap Between Whites and Minorities Grew With Great Recession

Source: Rakesh Kochhar, Richard Fry, and Paul Taylor, *Twenty-to-One: Wealth Gaps Rise to Record Highs Between Whites, Blacks and Hispanics* (Washington, DC: PEW Social and Demographic Trends, July 26, 2011).

Two Stories About Growing Economic Inequality

Story #1: Long-Term Structural Economic Change

What accounts for this collapse of the American Dream? How can the phenomena described here—growing economic inequality, prosperity mainly for the rich, declining social mobility, persistent poverty—be explained? In recent years, two distinct but not incompatible stories have been offered to account for rising inequality. The first story points to long-term changes in the structure of the American and world economy. In this story, the protagonists are globalization and technology. In the second story, the plot revolves around politics and public policy choices. Political elites for the past forty years have promoted policies that have exacerbated the trends toward inequality highlighted in the first story, have failed to soften their impacts, and have shaped the political economy in a way that guarantees that the fruits of economic growth move mainly to the top. In this section, we will take up the first story and then look to the second.

The structure of the American economy looks very different today than it did prior to 1973. In the post–World War II period, the United States dominated the world economy, manufacturing most of what its own people and much of the world consumed. Many Americans improved their standard of living by taking jobs in the core manufacturing industries of the economy. These jobs often involved unskilled or low-skilled assembly-line production, but nonetheless they were high-paying, union-backed jobs that allowed workers to acquire suburban homes and put their kids through college. They also provided substantial stimulus to the entire economy, creating more well-paid nonmanufacturing jobs, as workers spent their union-protected wages in their communities. Moreover, most workers could count on relatively stable employment with the same employer for their entire working careers.

By the 1970s, American industry faced growing global competition from rising Asian powers such as Japan and South Korea and from Europe. In response, US corporate leaders responded beginning in the 1980s with systematic "deindustrialization"—closing manufacturing facilities in the United States and moving production to countries where average wages were lower. This process devastated much of the industrial Midwest, which soon became known as the "rust belt." Industrial towns such as Youngstown, Ohio, which had prospered in the 1950s and 1960s as workers found high-paying union jobs in the auto and steel industries, became industrial wastelands with shuttered factories and stores, high levels of unemployment, and declining populations.[65] Between 1973 and 1986, about 1.7 million jobs were lost through this deindustrialization process.[66] Deprived of their high-paying manufacturing jobs, former assembly-line workers found themselves searching for positions in the new "service economy"—often as hamburger flippers or retail sales clerks—at much lower wages. Economists estimate that deindustrialization accounts for much of the depression of wages among blue-collar workers since 1973.[67] Over the same period, these lower-skilled workers have faced increasing competition from immigrants, another consequence of globalization that puts further downward pressure on this group's wages.[68] The end of the Cold War brought new players into the world economy as the former Socialist economies of Eastern Europe adopted free market economies and, even more significantly, China and India opened their former closed economies to capitalist trade and investment. By the turn of the century, American workers were in competition with roughly three billion new workers that had entered the world economy in the previous decade.[69] In the new global economy, workers with lower skills and less education are simply unable to find jobs at the wage levels their parents attained in the post–World War II economy.

Globalization placed downward pressure on white-collar as well as blue-collar workers as corporations sought to reduce costs through "downsizing"—laying off middle managers, professionals, and more-skilled workers and either replacing them with temporary workers, outside contractors, and consultants or requiring those remaining in their jobs to make up for the lost employees by working harder and longer hours.[70] Downsizing introduced a new word into Americans' vocabulary—24/7—as many employees found that keeping their jobs, whether in corporate bureaucracies or with the consulting firms serving them, meant devoting all of their time to work. The impact on income inequality was twofold. Some former middle managers and professionals saw their incomes decline as they moved on to lower-paying positions as temporary workers, with contracting firms, or in the lower-wage service jobs alongside their former blue-collar workers. At the same time, those who had kept their corporate jobs and some downsized employees who had found lucrative work as consultants or in new, creative enterprises experienced dramatic increases in their incomes. In the new, more entrepreneurial, "winner-take-all" economy, a small proportion of highly skilled workers were able to claim much higher rewards than had been available to them in the industrial society of forty years ago.[71] Whereas a corporate middle manager in the 1960s earned a salary modestly higher than the blue-collar workers that manager supervised (but with similar benefits), today's corporate manager commands an astronomical salary in comparison to the assembly-line employees or white-collar employees who work for the firm's contractors, whether they work in South Carolina, Mexico, or China.

Along with globalization, most economists regard technological innovation—the computer, the Internet, and other electronic technologies—as a critical part of the story of rising income inequalities. Those skilled in the development and use of these technologies were rewarded with higher salaries, while the workers the technology displaced coped with falling incomes. To take just one example, the introduction of automatic teller machines has wiped out most of the work of bank tellers—one of the fastest-growing occupations back in the 1970s.[72] Work as a bank teller used to be a decent lower-middle-class job that paid a decent wage requiring no more than a high school degree. Now, not only have most of these jobs vanished, but their diminished supply means a decline in salary for the remaining human tellers. At the same time, as new technologies eliminated jobs for bank tellers, appliance repairmen, and secretaries, they created new jobs for highly skilled workers in software development and web design. In recent years, however, these workers, too, have seen their incomes threatened as the Internet has allowed even their jobs—in specialties ranging from software development to radiology—to be outsourced, or sent abroad, to lower-paid but highly skilled workers in places such as India or the Philippines. This outsourcing means that even technically skilled workers will see their jobs vanish, with declining incomes for those who remain, while increasing the wage premium for those whose skills are not easily outsourced and those of corporate managers who supervise workers in Bangalore and Manila.[73]

Economists use the term "skill-biased technical change" (SBTC) to explain the inequalities that arise from greater economic return to technical skills brought about through this interaction of globalization, technological change, and the new, more entrepreneurial economy.[74] Since the onset of rising income inequality in the 1970s, the correlation between level of education and income—a relationship that has always been strong—has become even more pronounced.[75] Between 1973 and 1999, the average wage of a worker with a high school diploma declined 16 percent, from $16.14 per hour to $13.61 (in 1999 dollars). High school dropouts fared even worse, experiencing a 28 percent decline in wages, from $13.61 to $9.78 per hour.[76] College graduates saw their incomes grow, but by a small amount, while those with advanced degrees enjoyed a 20 percent increase. Children of families toward the top of the income distribution have understood the increasing value of education; they have been enrolling in institutions of higher education in ever-greater numbers. At the same time, college and university attendance by those from lower-income families has been declining—a likely consequence of higher tuition costs.[77] Consequently, the increasing payoff of higher education is benefiting those who are already well-off rather than those striving to rise from the bottom of the income ladder, which bodes ill for future social mobility.

To sum up, substantial inequalities are now embedded in the labor force much more deeply than in the thirty years after World War II. In the 1950s, the typical high school graduate could go to the local factory and find a permanent, blue-collar manufacturing job in which to earn a wage high enough to raise a family in the middle class. The same factory also recruited college graduates, even those with mediocre academic records, for a large number of middle-management supervisory positions. A decade into the twenty-first century, however, both the high school graduate and the middling college graduate are likely to find a

"Moved to China" sign hanging on the factory gates and few opportunities available in downsized corporate suites.

Story #2: Public Policy and Inequality

The interaction of globalization and technology undoubtedly has contributed to growing inequality. The resulting skill-based technological change (SBTC) does seem to have altered significantly income distribution throughout the economy. Yet does the SBTC story alone explain fully the dramatic rise in inequality over the past forty years? Or have conscious policy choices on the part of political elites played an independent role in promoting inequality? This section will present an alternative story that places the blame for rising economic inequality in America on public policymakers. But before we get to that story, we need to look more closely at the logic of the SBTC story. Why is it so attractive to some as an explanation for inequality, and are there reasons for questioning its adequacy?

The SBTC story follows a basic argument in most economic texts that free markets naturally create winners and losers: Individuals with ambition, willingness to work hard, the skills the market requires, and good luck will succeed, while those lacking these attributes will not. Inequality naturally tends to emerge as a by-product of market forces because those who possess more economic resources have an advantage over those who have less, and they can invest those resources for future gains. If changing technology alters the rules for economic success, the market's propensity to provide unequal rewards will be magnified. Just over a century ago, ambitious youngsters who had worked to develop their skills as buggy-whip makers or as blacksmiths saw their economic prospects plunge with the introduction of the automobile. So we should not be surprised that globalization, deindustrialization, and new technologies have made winners of computer geeks and global investors, and losers of assembly-line workers. Our economics text would make the further point that, despite the pain inflicted on the losers, the higher rates of growth and productivity that economic change brings should offer future compensation in a rising standard of living for all. Just as the children and grandchildren of those unfortunate blacksmiths of yore achieved a much higher living standard than their grandfathers, the hope of recent economic changes lies in the potential for rising living standards for all in the long run.

This benign story of growing inequality as a consequence of natural economic forces leading to a better future for all—eventually—has been very attractive to many of those in political power. George W. Bush's Treasury secretary, Henry Paulson, embraced the SBTC explanation for growing inequality in 2006, saying, "Market forces work to provide the greatest rewards to those with the needed skills in the growth areas." Hence, as Paulson went on to say, "This trend . . . is simply an economic reality, and it is neither fair nor useful to blame any political party"—nor, he might have added, is it the responsibility of policymakers such as himself.[78] If more inequality is a natural outgrowth of market forces, then both trying to account for it based on policy choices that have been made and seeking policies to mitigate it are futile exercises. There is no point in raising the trend as a political issue or expecting policymakers to do anything about it.

This benign story, however, misses some interesting facts that suggest policy may have more to do with growing inequality than the SBTC explanation allows. First, if market forces, not public policy, have produced growing inequality in the United States, then one needs to account for the different experience of populations living under different policies abroad. Family income inequality is greater in the United States than in any of the world's other industrial democracies. All of those countries, buffeted by the same global economic forces, have also seen income inequality grow since the 1970s, but inequality has grown much more in the United States than elsewhere.[79] Second, Princeton political scientist Larry Bartels has documented clear differences in the growth of income inequality based on whether Democrats or Republicans control the presidency.[80] Bartels shows that since 1948, the incomes of poor and middle-income Americans grew more rapidly, relative to the wealthy, under Democratic than under Republican presidents. Furthermore, he traces the differences in income growth to the specific policy choices made when different parties were in control. At least some of the growing inequality since the 1970s results from the policy impact of Republican control of the White House for over two-thirds of the past four decades, when inequality has exploded. Third, the SBTC story cannot explain why, if increasing returns to education and skill account for inequality, income growth has skewed so sharply to the benefit of the super-wealthy while leaving the incomes of the bulk of educated workers so far behind. The real incomes of even college-educated workers have risen only 17 percent since 1973, well behind the growth of productivity over that period, while, as shown earlier, CEO salaries have skyrocketed from around thirty times the wage of the average worker in the 1960s to over 300 times today.[81] Fourth, SBTC fails to account for why, even among those with the same years of education, inequality in incomes has grown.[82] For example, many of those in the top 1 percent of income probably have gone to college and beyond, but that alone cannot account for why their incomes are so far above the many other individuals also with professional degrees who earn far less. Finally, the computer revolution of recent decades is not the first such period of SBTC in American history. As my buggy whip example above suggests, the twentieth century saw several waves of new technologies, from automobiles to television, introduced into the economy and that altered the economic fortunes of many particular individuals. But none of those produced a broad increase in aggregate inequality; rather, the opposite tended to occur.[83] Why has new technology produced greater inequality this time?

To answer this question, we need to consider carefully an alternative story about economic inequality that places politics squarely into the narrative. As described in detail in the last chapter, business interests mobilized aggressively beginning in the 1970s to shape public policy in conformity to their needs. Business success in conjunction with right-wing political allies has resulted in a series of public policy shifts that have contributed to growing inequality.[84] First, policymakers have eagerly adopted policies to encourage economic restructuring through globalization, deindustrialization, and downsizing, with little attention on their differential impact on incomes. Second, rather than strengthening the social safety net and institutions supportive of the incomes of those at the bottom of the income distribution, they have pursued a forty-year campaign against them in the name of "reducing the size of government." Third, they have failed to invest adequately in public education to help workers acquire the skills to succeed in the new economy. And, finally, our policymakers have cut tax rates deeply and systematically, benefiting the after-tax incomes of the very rich while depriving governments at all levels of the revenues needed to fund programs to relieve inequality.

The wave of economic deregulation that began in the late 1970s and continued into the twenty-first century assisted businesses in fulfilling their deindustrialization, downsizing, and globalization agendas. With less government oversight, corporations were free to pursue whatever measures they wished to enhance their bottom lines and the salaries of their top executives—irrespective of the impact on employees' incomes. As CEO-appointed executive compensation boards hiked executive compensation to the astronomical levels described earlier, business allies in Congress blocked attempts of the Financial Accounting Standards Board to regulate CEO compensation.[85] Deregulation of the financial industry during this period and the failure to devise new regulations of exotic financial instruments like derivatives and credit default swaps opened the door to investment bankers and hedge fund managers to rake in higher and higher fees and returns to themselves. Public policy choices enabled much of the growth in corporate executive compensation and financial industry income that accounts for the income expansion of the very rich. At the same time, government policy intensified globalization's downward pressure on wages, as the United States entered into agreements such as the North American Free Trade Agreement (NAFTA) and the creation of the World Trade Organization (WTO). While these agreements opened up new opportunities for higher returns to corporate investors, policymakers failed to include provisions to prevent labor exploitation abroad or to guard against job losses at home.

Just as free trade and globalization were placing tremendous downward pressure on wages, the principal institutions for defending workers' living standards and economic justice generally, labor unions, were under attack.[86] Employers across the nation moved aggressively, with the assistance of union-busting consultants, to crush union organizing drives. These efforts received a green light from Washington when President Reagan fired striking air traffic controllers, sending the message that aggressive antiunion tactics would receive federal government support. Reagan and his Republican successors, for twenty of the past thirty years, appointed pro-business members to the National Labor Relations Board, which regulates labor-management disputes, who looked the other way as businesses moved aggressively to eliminate established union representation and prevent union organizing. These management-friendly tactics, combined with the elimination of union jobs as factories have moved offshore, have had a devastating impact on the American labor movement. Unions saw their membership drop precipitously, from nearly a third of the workforce in the 1960s to only 13.5 percent of workers (and only about 7 percent in the private sector) today.[87] The declining power of unions has denied workers the clout to negotiate contracts with their employers, thus freeing corporations to lower production costs by lowering real wages and benefits while reaping larger profits for their shareholders. Because union-protected wages tend to set the standard for the whole economy, the loss of union representation has led to lower wages throughout the economy.

While promoting the economic interests of corporations and the wealthy, conservative Republican policymakers have—in the name of "reducing the size of government"—slashed much of the safety net for the most economically vulnerable Americans. Social welfare programs ranging from food stamps to energy assistance have borne the brunt of cuts in discretionary federal spending since the 1980s. The "welfare reform" legislation enacted in 1996 eliminated the fifty-year-old entitlement of poor women with children to federal assistance but, while removing millions from the welfare roles, has done little to improve the economic circumstances of former welfare recipients. According to one estimate, the percentage by which safety net programs reduced income inequality fell by 25 percent between 1980 and 2003.[88] In addition, government policy, rather than encouraging corporations to provide pension and health care benefits to their employees, has shifted toward allowing them to reduce such guarantees. Since the late 1970s, corporations have replaced guaranteed retirement pensions with 401(k) investment programs that shift the burden and risk of retirement security from the companies themselves to individual employees.[89] At the same time, many corporations have reduced or eliminated health insurance benefits, producing an explosion in the number of Americans without health insurance.

At the same time that unions were losing their ability to push up wages and the safety net was being slashed, the value of the federal minimum wage, which undergirds the wage structure throughout the economy, has lagged far behind inflation. A 1996 increase still left the real value of the minimum wage well below where it had been in 1968, and by 2002, inflation had wiped out the 1996 increase.[90] By 2006, the minimum wage had declined to nearly half the value it had in 1968.[91] Congress voted a series of increases in 2007, raising the minimum to $7.25 per hour, a figure that will restore its inflation-adjusted value to what it had been in 1996, but still well below its value in 1968.[92]

A key factor contributing to rising inequality in a time of rapid technological change has been the failure of public investments in education to prepare the workforce for these new technologies. As Claudia Goldin and Lawrence Katz document, unlike previous periods, the educational system over the past several decades has not provided Americans with the skills needed to keep up with rapid technological change.[93] American high schools, which for most of the twentieth century led the world in preparing workers for work, fail in the critical task of preparing students for higher education, particularly the growing number of young people who drop out. Even as the importance of higher education for economic success has increased in recent years, access to it has become more difficult. College tuition at private, four-year institutions rose 136 percent between 1980 and 1999, and 114 percent for in-state students at public universities.[94] In contrast to the pre-1973 period, when a steady expansion of public community colleges and universities offered low-income residents of many states access to an inexpensive, high-quality education, cash-strapped state legislatures in many states have raised tuition and cut support to higher education. While median incomes have stagnated since 1980, the percentage of median income required to cover tuition costs at both public and private institutions has tripled—at public colleges and universities, now equal to about 12 percent of median income compared to 4 percent in 1980.[95] During this latter period, the federal government shifted from providing grants to students needing help with college costs to offering them low-interest loans instead. The result is a generation of college students who leave school with burdensome debts to repay. Public efforts to provide more equality of opportunity might mitigate rising inequality, but government policies have instead moved steadily in the other direction—diminishing the opportunities of those at the bottom of the economic ladder.

Reducing inequality would require progressive taxation—placing a larger burden on the winners in the new economy—to generate sufficient revenues to help raise the incomes of the losers. But federal tax policy has moved in the opposite direction—shifting the nation's tax burden in reverse–Robin Hood fashion, away from the rich and onto the shoulders of the middle class and the poor. First, regressive payroll taxes have become an ever-growing source of federal government revenue—rising from 18 percent to 40 percent between 1970 and 2010. These taxes come mainly from lower-wage earners, who see their entire paychecks taxed, while high-income earners pay no tax on income over $106,800 (in 2011). Income from investments and savings, of course, is free of these withholding taxes.

At the same time they face a larger payroll tax burden, lower-income workers are made to bear an increasing share of the income tax, as Congress, beginning with the Reagan tax cuts of 1981, has dramatically reduced income tax rates for the wealthiest taxpayers. This process culminated in the Bush tax cuts of 2001, which delivered nearly 40 percent of their benefits to the richest 1 percent of Americans—about the same amount that was to be divided among the 80 percent of the population earning less than $72,000.[96] The 2001 cuts, combined with another tax cut in 2003, saved the top 1 percent of taxpayers an average of $67,000, while middle-income families received only $600 on average, and the lowest 20 percent only $61.[97] The effective tax rates for the top 1 percent were reduced from 48 percent of income in 1970 to 32 percent in 2004. The decline in progressivity at the very top has especially benefitted the richest of the rich. The top 0.01 percent of taxpayers saw their share of after-tax income explode from a mere 1.2 percent in 1970 to 7.3 percent in 2004.[98] Among this fortunate 0.01 percent have been hedge fund managers who benefit from a special tax loophole that allows them to pay the low capital gains tax rate on their incomes rather than the much higher personal income tax rate. When one takes into account both the impact of "safety net" income transfers, which have decreased, and income tax cuts, only the top 1 percent saw an increase in their share of income between 1979 and 2007—it doubled from 8 percent in 1979 to 17 percent in 2007.[99] This increase came at the expense of the bottom 8 percent of the population that saw their share of income decrease. And as if this blatant tilt toward the rich were not enough, Congress also began a phaseout of the estate tax, which affects, at most, only the richest 2 percent of taxpayers. Even after delivering massive tax cuts for the very rich, congressional Republicans and presidential candidates continue to advocate various "flat tax" reforms that would end taxation of virtually all income earned on savings and investments resting the entire tax burden on the shoulders of middle- and lower-income workers, who derive the bulk of their incomes from wages and salaries. Those who benefit most from life in America—the wealthiest, who owe their livelihoods to ownership of the country's assets—would be, in a manner reminiscent of the eighteenth-century French aristocracy, privileged to live tax-free.

Finally, if the claims are correct that inequality is primarily the result of inevitable market forces and SBTC, and everyone may be better off in the long run, can anything be done to mitigate the economic pain and growing inequality these trends have produced in the short run? In the terms of our economics text, the answer lies in "winners compensating losers"—that is, appropriate public policies, devised to distribute some of the economic gains the winners have received through structural economic change to those who have lost out through no fault of their own. Such compensatory public policy would reduce growing inequality and forestall the harm it can do to society. In particular, it would make sure that when economic change delivers unequal rewards, those inequalities do not become permanently embedded in society.

Such compensatory policies would require doing the opposite of what policymakers have chosen to do for the past forty years. First, the existing social safety net, which was devised to relieve the distress of those in dire economic circumstances, would need to be strengthened rather than shredded. Second, support for institutions and programs, such as labor unions and minimum wages, that tend to support wage growth would need to be enhanced, again the opposite of what has happened. Third, major rather than minimal investments—the reality of recent years—in new programs to help workers adjust to economic change would be needed. Finally, progressive taxes on economic winners would be needed, both to compensate for unequal gains in market-produced pretax gains and to provide the revenue to pay for compensatory and safety net programs. If the market is producing unacceptable inequality, the only solution is to institute some redistribution of income and wealth from the rich to the poor. Economic winners should keep much of what they gained from success in the new economy—markets do require incentives if the economy is to grow and prosper—but in the name of the common good, a portion of their winnings should be devoted to helping those left behind. As we have seen, however, policy has moved in the opposite direction, and that is one reason why inequality has grown so much faster in the United States than in other industrial democracies. European and other democracies have used redistributive strategies to counteract the inequalities that structural economic change has produced, while American policymakers have failed to do so.

In spite of the heedlessness of elite policymakers, most ordinary Americans continue to be aware of the growing inequality and blocked social mobility in contemporary America. Myriad issues, from growing consumer debt to family breakdown, reflect the fact that many wage earners cannot keep up financially even in times of overall prosperity. Most people can see the changes described here in their own lives: lower wages, lost jobs, and homeless people in their communities. More important, these changes raise questions about the underlying optimism of the American Dream—that we can expect steady progress toward greater equality and prosperity for all in the future.

Economic Inequality's Challenge to Democracy

Increasing economic inequality challenges democracy's survival in at least three ways. First, it undermines a central democratic value: political equality. A growing body of evidence shows that economic inequality in the United States creates vastly unequal political representation. Second, it becomes a barrier to the sense of community that citizens must have to rule themselves. And finally, inequality undermines the quality of life for everyone in society.

The first point returns us to the basic insight of the American revolutionaries: Social inequality and political inequality are inevitably linked. The most obvious linkage is in the fact that social advantages, especially wealth, are political resources convertible into influence and power. As we saw in earlier chapters, people with high levels of education and income find political participation and representation much less costly than do the poor and less educated. Inequality in their ability to influence government inevitably follows. Such inequality is tolerable in a democracy if it is not extreme and if those who are disadvantaged have access to opportunities to improve their condition. Unfortunately for American democracy, social inequalities seem to be moving beyond tolerable levels. Both the increase in income inequality and the coincidence of differences in wealth, race, and even geographical location have produced tremendous differences in political power and influence.

Recent studies by political scientists document the extent to which rising economic inequality in the United States has increased political inequality.[100] To some extent inequalities in political representation result from differences in political participation between the rich and the non-rich. Whether one looks at voting, involvement in campaigns, contributions, or representation by interest groups, participation in political life skews increasingly toward the more affluent. As an American Political Science Association (APSA) study put it, "Ordinary Americans speak with a whisper while the most advantaged roar."[101] And politicians hear that roar. In a pathbreaking study comparing public policy outputs and public opinion, Martin Gilens found that changes in policy generally reflect the opinions of high-income citizens rather than the population as a whole.[102] In a similar study, Larry Bartels has found that when they vote on legislation, US senators are more responsive to the concerns of their more affluent constituents than to the concerns of the less affluent.[103] Bartels found that senators gave the views of constituents in the top third of the income distribution about 50 percent greater consideration than those in the middle third, and that they disregarded the views of the lowest third altogether.[104] And these disparities were not merely the consequence of lower levels of political participation and information on the part of the less affluent. When Bartels controlled for these differences, there remained substantial disparity in senators' responsiveness to the more affluent compared with poorer constituents.[105] He concludes that senators' greater attentiveness to the concerns of the most affluent stems partly from campaign contributions by that group, but that perhaps more important is the fact that senators themselves are affluent.[106] Their greater responsiveness to the affluent reflects class solidarity with people like themselves, with similar outlooks and concerns, more than anything else.

This disparity in political influence may explain why public policy over the past few years has contributed to economic inequality rather than reduced it. Wealthy taxpayers who seek to lower their taxes receive the attention of policy-makers; the travails of working-class Americans trying to make ends meet on stagnant incomes are ignored. Jeffery Winters and Benjamin Page argue that the wealthy exert critical influence over financial and monetary policies that bear importantly on their wealth.[107] Overall, Winters and Page conclude that the political influence of "a very small number of extremely wealthy individuals [means] it is useful to think about the US political system in terms of oligarchy."[108] Some political scientists fear that political inequality in America has reached such a level that to enact policies to address rising economic inequality has become impossible.[109] More and more, political representation in America suggests a plutocracy rather than a democracy.

The second point about economic inequality's threat to democracy also follows from the American revolutionaries' sense of social equality: If we are to have a society in which all citizens have a say in how they are governed, social disparities cannot grow beyond the point at which people lose that down-to-earth sense that no one is fundamentally better than anyone else. Shared respect between fellow citizens is needed if they are to accept one another as equal participants in governing the community. Only people who hold one another in mutual regard can begin to understand others' problems and needs and then devise mutually acceptable solutions. But continued growth in income inequality must lead eventually to the dissolution of these ties of mutual regard among citizens of different classes, which are necessary for maintaining democratic community. As Americans come to live in radically different social spheres, their capacity to perceive common interests or to deliberate together will vanish.

The country's increasing spatial segregation by class and race increases the likelihood that inequality is leading toward an attenuated democratic community. We are increasingly a geographically divided society, in which the economically successful, mostly white citizens live in suburban communities or exclusive urban residential neighborhoods, apart from and politically independent of the poor, mainly black and other minority residents of central cities. By the 1990s, the gradual suburbanization of American society—a trend that dates to the beginning of that century—had reached the point where a majority of citizens lived in suburbs.[110] Today, suburban communities themselves differ based on the wealth and race of their residents: Some are reserved for the very wealthy, others for the broad middle class, and still others predominantly for the poor. By walling themselves off in their own economically segregated communities, wealthier citizens have been able to avoid the costs of growing social inequality.[111] They are able and willing, according to most studies, to tax themselves for local public services, while they defeat taxes intended to raise revenues for state and federal governments with jurisdiction over central cities and less exclusive suburban towns. The consequence for public services—schools, for example—is that some affluent suburbs enjoy well-funded, quality programs, while those in the inner cities and poorer suburbs deteriorate. The urban poor do not constitute an adequate tax base to support decent schools; at the same time, state and federal governments cannot subsidize those in the cities because the majority of voters living in affluent suburbs resist the taxes needed to do so. Racial imagery promotes this pattern. The poor, often black or Hispanic citizens concentrated in urban communities become largely invisible to wealthier white citizens. Predominantly white suburban voters consider themselves public spirited in supporting their own insular communities, while opposing federal and state taxes to support "big government," which they associate with giveaway programs for undeserving black and minority communities. This divisive formula can only deepen existing inequalities and perpetuate them into future generations—hardly the optimistic vision of the American Dream.

The rise of the super rich 1 percent creates another divide destructive of common life. Their extreme wealth allows them to live in an increasingly insular society of their own divided from the cares and concerns of most Americans.[112] They typically own multiple mansions and apartments scattered across the globe to which they travel in private jets. Their children attend exclusive private schools. For health care, they and their families receive state-of-the-art care in private clinics. Most important, their wealth insulates them from economic downturns and the economic anxieties of most Americans. In this exclusive private world, the top 0.01 percent need not be concerned with crumbling highways and bridges (which they fly over), deteriorating public schools, environmental degradation, or declining job opportunities. As Nobel Prize–winning economist Joseph Stiglitz points out, "The rich don't need to rely on government for parks or education or medical care or personal security—they can buy all these things for themselves."[113] Yet their political power gives them outsized influence over whether government will invest in infrastructure, education, and new technology for the common good. Instead, they support smaller government and lower taxes for themselves.

Finally, inequality threatens democracy because it undermines the social well-being upon which democracy depends. Two British epidemiologists, Richard Wilkinson and Kate Pickett, have reviewed statistical data worldwide and discovered strong correlations between levels of inequality and a long list of social pathologies.[114] When economic inequality rises, societies become sicker and more violent; their citizens also are more obese, less well educated, and less socially mobile, and they commit more crimes. While these pathologies often are associated with poverty, Wilkinson and Pickett argue that inequality has an independent impact. Even in relatively wealthy countries, social well-being declines as inequality increases. Perception of large economic differences seems to make human beings socially anxious, lowers self-esteem, and induces destructive status competition—all of which contribute to destructive behaviors. These social pathologies affect the lives of all. Those with similar levels of income, from the very poor to the very rich, in different countries are uniformly better off on a range of social measures in the more equal societies.[115] Given these findings, the social conditions of mutual trust, reciprocity, and sense of common purpose, which political theorists from Tocqueville to Putnam have found essential for democracy, are lacking. Rising economic inequality leads to less social well-being and produces barren ground for thriving democratic politics.

Without a shared sense of community, not only is democracy impossible, but any sort of common politics is destroyed. Wide social disparities turn politics into a contest between "us" and "them," making politics more divisive. Not surprisingly, political scientists have found the increasing political polarization and partisanship in America strongly associated with rising inequality.[116] When social disparities become extreme and politics highly polarized, the threat of political violence becomes acute. Even if actual violence is avoided, political leaders of varied ideologies may emerge advocating extremist political solutions. In response to crises, when societies are sharply divided, elites are likely to become impatient with democratic niceties and resort to authoritarian measures. As R. H. Tawney and others have pointed out, the progression from inequality to societal division, extremist politics, often violence, and, finally, authoritarian leadership is a classic path to the end of democracy.

Of course, the current era of growing inequality need not result in the end of democracy. In the past, Americans have worked to preserve their democratic community by engaging in periods of social reform that have corrected dangerous inequalities. At the beginning of the twentieth century, for example, the Progressive Era created new institutions of economic reform—the progressive income tax, antitrust prosecutions, health and safety regulation, and expanded education—to correct many of the excesses of the Gilded Age of the 1880s and 1890s. A few decades later, the New Deal introduced further economic regulations and social welfare programs that set the stage for the egalitarian economic expansion of the post–World War II period. These efforts were reinforced by President Lyndon Johnson's Great Society programs in the 1960s. In responding to the economic crisis as he came into office, Obama has the opportunity to be a transformative president like FDR and Johnson and to bring about progressive change. To correct the rising inequality of the past thirty years, America needs to embark on a new era of progressive reform to distribute economic prosperity and reinforce racial equality among all Americans. What specific public policies are needed in a new era of reform to meet the challenges of inequality?

Meeting the Challenge: Policies to Promote Equality

A new progressive era will require a variety of policy innovations to counter the trend of the past few decades toward greater social and economic inequality. Serious attention must be given to more investment in education, expansion of our social welfare state, shifts in public policy to increase the wages of all and raise the incomes of the middle class, and perhaps a major program of asset distribution on the order of the GI Bill.

One of the solutions most commonly recommended to address rising inequality is increased investment in education. Such a solution seems to follow from the growing correlation between education levels and income differentials discussed earlier in this chapter. Certainly, from the point of view of an individual seeking to increase her chances for economic success, access to education is crucial. For this reason, public policies to provide more educational opportunity should be a part of any progressive movement to restore the American Dream. Such policies must include more generous funding of K–12 public schools, especially those in poor communities. State governments must reverse the trend of decreasing support for public colleges and universities while raising tuition and fees. In fact, to promote more individual social mobility for hardworking and talented students, the United States would do well to emulate many other industrialized nations by making state colleges and universities free to the citizens of their states, as California did in the 1950s and 1960s. The federal government should increase its investment in higher education, as well, by making grants more generous and loans more affordable to deserving students. From the point of view of connecting many individuals to the American Dream, increased public investment in education makes good sense.

From a systemic perspective, however, increased education investments alone are not likely to decrease differentials in income and wealth. Even if, as Goldin and Katz argue, increased investment in education helps to improve America's overall ability to reduce the SBTC gaps, substantial individual differences in educational levels will remain. Those who can reach higher educational levels will still stay well ahead in their individual economic gains from education. At the lower end of the income scale, individuals have to spend more time in school just to maintain the income level that people with much less education earned thirty years ago. In the new economy, everyone seems compelled to pursue ever-higher levels of education either to maintain or to increase their individual income level, meaning individual level economic inequality resulting from educational differences will remain a problem. Moreover, as Goldin and Katz acknowledge, globalization diminishes the value of educational investment as a means to reduce inequality.[117] With the advent of instantaneous electronic communication, even the most sophisticated and highly skilled work can be outsourced to any place on the globe. Today, highly educated workers in China and India perform skilled work for much less than comparably skilled American workers. In the future, even the most highly skilled workers—even those performing highly analytical tasks from medical doctors to college professors—will have to compete in the global market. Although high levels of education investment will still be needed to equip individual Americans to compete in this new context, there is less and less chance that those investments alone will diminish the inequalities within our society.

Progressive reform to correct growing inequality cannot shy away from redistributive public policies that direct some of the economy's gains from the top of the income distribution to those at the bottom, by reformulating the economic "rules of the game" more in favor of lower- and middle-income workers. A first step toward more redistributive policies should be restoration of a truly progressive tax system in the United States. Wealthier people ought to make a larger contribution to public revenues than the less wealthy for two reasons: First, they have more discretionary income, more income beyond what is needed for necessities, than do poorer individuals, so a higher rate of taxation will have less impact on their living standard. This is the classic justification of progressive taxation. Second, as the most comfortable and successful members in society, the wealthy benefit the most from the public order and prosperity that public expenditures provide. For these reasons, the wealthy should bear a larger share of the burden for all public programs, from national defense to building highways. Whatever the specific form this more progressive system might take, it would mean reversing the trend, since the 1980s, of shifting more and more of the tax burden to middle- and lower-income wage earners through reliance on payroll taxes while lowering marginal income tax rates. Not only should the Bush era tax cuts be repealed, but a new taxation strategy should be instituted that substantially shifts the tax burden back to the wealthy, who can more easily support it. And, by all means, right-wing proposals for flat taxes that tax labor but not capital should be resisted.

More progressive taxation in itself will begin to reduce inequality by drawing more on the incomes of the rich than on those of the poor to support public programs, but inequality also can be addressed directly by channeling public expenditures toward helping the poor. A wide variety of social programs aimed at improving the lives of the poor—food stamps, housing assistance, energy assistance, and job training—need to be made both more generous and available to more people. While assistance to those most in need (means-tested assistance) needs to be increased, the most effective way to boost the incomes and living standards of all Americans, including the poor, is by fully supporting universal programs such as public schools and Social Security, which are available to all regardless of income. These universal programs provide successful models for reducing social inequality within our individualist political culture. Unlike welfare, Social Security benefits are provided to virtually all American workers on retirement, and people perceive them as a return on their payroll tax contributions, to which they are entitled. At the same time, Social Security is also a very successful redistributive program that has substantially reduced inequality among the elderly.

The United States needs more such universal programs that are available as an entitlement to all citizens but also provide special help to the poorest citizens, who need them the most. Such programs are common in Europe, where they have reduced inequality below American levels. First on the list of such programs would have to be universal health insurance, which would eliminate a substantial source of insecurity in the lives of the poor and would attract widespread political support. Second, a universal system of child allowances could replace welfare, eliminate the stigma attached to receiving aid to support families, and provide resources directly to the poorest group of Americans—children. Third, universal child care, in the form of public day care centers or vouchers for purchasing private care, would ease the anxieties faced by parents in two-earner households and facilitate the integration of poor single mothers into the workforce. Most Americans find such programs consistent with their individualist values, and they would help to bridge the chasm between rich and poor.

Such expansion of the social welfare state should have a substantial impact on inequality, but it would need to be supplemented by shifts in the economy's "rules of the game." To raise the incomes of workers, government must enact policies that make work pay. For a start, macroeconomic policies aimed at sustaining full employment over a long period of time are required if real wages are to rise, especially for the lowest-paid workers. The Federal Reserve Board and other policymakers must prioritize full employment over controlling inflation, so that workers do not see the gains they have made in good economic times wiped out periodically by recessions. Second, Congress should raise the minimum wage—in real, inflation-adjusted terms—to its 1960 level, and it should attach a cost-of-living adjustment (COLA) to the minimum wage, as it has done for other programs such as Social Security. A minimum wage that keeps pace with inflation would serve as a floor for all wages throughout the economy, ensuring that workers can gain a fairer share of economic growth. Third, public policy should revert to promoting unionization rather than assisting corporations in their campaign against unions. Labor law reform to expand the power of labor unions would be one of the most effective means of reducing economic inequality.

Finally, the Earned Income Tax Credit (EITC), which provides the poorest wage earners with an income supplement in the form of a refundable tax credit, should be made more generous. Congress needs to raise the income ceiling so that more workers can participate in the program, increase the supplemental income given to workers at various wage levels, and provide communities with more resources to educate low-income workers about the program. (To receive EITC, low-wage workers must file an income tax return, even if they do not earn enough income to owe any tax. More information about the program's benefits, along with assistance in filing returns, would enable more workers to participate.) Finally, more communities need to enact "living wage" ordinances, requiring businesses that have contracts with the community or benefit from community subsidies to pay their employees not just a minimum wage, but a wage high enough to support a decent life in the community. Living wage ordinances have been enacted in about seventy localities nationwide, ranging from a $6.25 level in Milwaukee to $12 in Santa Cruz, California.[118] The experience of the communities that have enacted them proves that local governments can mandate decent compensation for their citizens without jeopardizing either the business climate or the availability of jobs.

In addition to supporting higher pay for workers, economic policy must address the biases that have allowed the richest 1 percent to gain ever-increasing shares of national income. First, the SEC should use its statutory authority to review the accounting practices of large corporations to end CEO compensation methods that award higher and higher pay to CEOs irrespective of corporate performance. Given the ability of corporate CEOs to handpick board compensation committees, only government regulation has a chance to stop the explosion in CEO compensation. Second, regulation of the finance industry must oversee its practices, including outlandish salaries and bonuses paid to investment bankers. The special tax breaks for hedge fund managers that allow them to pay the lower capital gains tax rate instead of the personal tax rate that everyone else pays on their income from their investment funds should be eliminated.

A new progressive movement that enacted all of these measures would transform the distribution of income and wealth in America. Many observers believe that inequality has become so great in recent years that a major national effort, on the level of the GI Bill or the Homestead Act of the 1800s, is needed to ensure equal opportunity for all. In the spirit of the Homestead Act, which gave away real assets—plots of land—to farmers, some see a major program to distribute financial assets to all Americans as the best solution for restoring the American Dream. One such proposal, by law professors Bruce Ackerman and Anne Alstott, would provide to every American who graduates from high school a wealth account of $80,000 that would constitute a "stake" from which the individual could draw for investment in education, starting a business, and/or accumulating savings.[119] The stakes would be financed initially by a 2 percent "wealth tax" on assets over $80,000 and eventually by means of a revolving account funded by repayments from stakeholders upon their deaths. The economist Richard Freeman has proposed a similar plan, endowing every American at birth with an investment fund that would be sufficient to generate a small lifetime income and would also be repayable at the end of one's life.[120] Advocates of these asset redistribution plans argue that they would be consistent with the traditional American values of individualism and equal opportunity but would significantly level the societal playing field.

All these components of a new progressive era in American politics are paths toward a more equal American society. All deserve more thorough investigation than has been possible in this chapter; students should explore these ideas further in the suggested readings. Mentioning them briefly is intended to show that we do not have to accept as inevitable the trends toward inequality discussed here—or the dire consequences they are likely to bring. Although one could argue that a concern for fairness or a spirit of charity should motivate programs to improve the plight of the poor, this chapter has established that attention to reversing increasing inequality in the United States is a political necessity. If we are to have democratic government in the future, we must act to promote political equality. To increase political equality, we must reduce social inequality. Failure to reverse the trend toward a more unequal America may spell the end of a democratic America.

Thought Questions

1. Do you agree that people are basically equal in their capacity to make political judgments, or are some political decisions best left to the experts?
2. If everyone has an equal vote and equal political rights, what does it matter that some people have more money than others? Do you agree that political equality in a democracy depends on a measure of economic and social equality, as this chapter argues?
3. Would you support some redistribution of wealth, such as that proposed in the Ackerman/Alstott "stakeholder" plan, for the sake of more equality? What are the arguments for and against such an idea?
4. This chapter emphasizes the dangers that economic and racial inequality pose for American democracy. What other sorts of inequalities exist in America, and what relationship do they have to democracy?
5. According to this chapter, geographic segregation according to race and class exacerbates the impact of inequality in undermining democratic community. What might be some ways to reduce such segregation without interfering with a person's freedom to choose where to live?

Suggestions for Further Reading

Ackerman, Bruce A., and Anne Alstott. *The Stakeholder Society.* New Haven, CT: Yale University Press, 1999. A proposal to correct inequality in wealth by providing an $80,000 "stake" to every American high school graduate.

Bartels, Larry M. *Unequal Democracy: The Political Economy of the New Gilded Age.* Princeton, NJ: Princeton University Press, 2008. Traces both the economic and the political roots of the current age of inequality.

Frank, Robert. *Richistan: A Journey Through the American Wealth Boom and the Lives of the New Rich.* New York: Three Rivers Press, 2008. An amusing but also informative look at how the rich are different from you and me.

*Gilder, George. *Wealth and Poverty.* New York: Basic Books, 1980. In contrast to the argument of this chapter, Gilder finds inequality a positive force in American society.

Green, Phillip. *The Pursuit of Inequality.* New York: Pantheon, 1981. A closely argued critique of attempts to justify various forms of social inequality.

Jacobs, Lawrence R., and Theda Skocpol. *Inequality and American Democracy: What We Know and What We Need to Learn.* New York: Russell Sage Foundation, 2005. The published version of an American Political Science Association report on rising economic inequality and its implications for American democracy.

McCarty, Nolan, Keith T. Poole, and Howard Rosenthal. *Polarized America: The Dance of Ideology and Unequal Riches.* Cambridge, MA: MIT Press, 2006. Describes how economic inequality has contributed to partisan political polarization.

Phillips, Kevin. *Wealth and Democracy: A Political History of the American Rich.* New York: Broadway Books, 2002. More than a history of the relationship between democracy and wealth, as Phillips makes a plea for the necessity of reducing inequality if we are not to become a plutocracy.

Walzer, Michael. *Spheres of Justice: A Defense of Pluralism and Equality.* New York: Basic Books, 1983. One of the most distinguished American political philosophers makes a case for creating more equality in democratic societies in a way that also enhances individual freedom.

Wilkinson, Richard, and Kate Pickett. *The Spirit Level: Why Greater Equality Makes Societies Stronger.* New York: Bloomsbury Press, 2010. A comprehensive review of the many ways economic inequality affects overall social well-being.

Wolff, Edward N., and Richard C. Leone. *Top Heavy: The Increasing Inequality of Wealth in America and What Can Be Done About It.* 2nd ed. New York: New Press, 2002. Economists provide a clear and readable analysis of the distribution of wealth in America and suggest how policy changes could make its distribution more equal.

*Presents a point of view that disagrees with the arguments presented in this chapter.

Selected Websites

http://extremeinequality.org. A website devoted to documenting inequality in the United States.

www.faireconomy.org. United for a Fair Economy, an organization dedicated to remedying economic inequality, provides data on this issue and opportunities to get involved.

www.irp.wisc.edu. The Institute for Research on Poverty, at the University of Wisconsin, has developed and evaluated social policy alternatives and analyzed trends in poverty and economic well-being in an attempt to reduce poverty and raise public awareness.

www.naacp.org. America's oldest and most prestigious civil rights organization, the NAACP.

www.trinity.edu/~mkearl/strat.html. "Explorations in Social Inequality" discusses social, political, and economic inequality in the United States, with a huge number of links to other websites and related articles.

CHAPTER 8

The Eighth Challenge: The National Security State

Perhaps it is a universal truth that the loss of liberty at home is to be charged to provisions against danger, real or pretended, from abroad.

—James Madison

The conjunction of an immense military establishment and a huge arms industry is new in the American experience. The total influence—economic, political, and even spiritual—is felt in every city, every state house, and every office of the federal government. . . . In the councils of government, we must guard against the acquisition of unwarranted influence, whether sought or unsought, by the military-industrial complex.

—President Dwight D. Eisenhower,
Farewell Address to the Nation, January 17, 1961

THE END OF THE COLD WAR, symbolized by the tearing down of the Berlin Wall in 1989, was a surprise to the whole world. No one, including American intelligence agencies, foresaw the speed with which America's superpower adversary, the Soviet Union—with all its military might—would collapse. For fifty years, the American people had feared the USSR and the prospect of the horrendous conflict that would result should Americans and Soviets ever come to direct blows. To avoid this confrontation and to defend against the Soviet threat, they had supported the creation of a "national security state"—the conglomeration of agencies,

Opposite: *Visiting the troops at Bagram Air Field in Afghanistan, President Obama reflects the increasingly militarized character of the presidency in the national security state.*

AP Photo/Pablo Martinez Monsivais.

activities, and attitudes put in place since the 1940s to provide for the national defense. This new establishment within the heart of American society had cost trillions of dollars, changed the way the United States related to the rest of the world, and profoundly altered the working of our own political institutions. To meet the Soviet challenge, Americans had acquiesced in the creation within their own country of institutional structures that challenged their democratic ideals. In the midst of the Cold War, many argued that the risks to democracy that the national security state posed were necessary in light of the external threat. The surprising collapse of that Soviet threat opened the possibility that Americans could step down from fifty years of warlike mobilization and dismantle substantial parts of the security machinery that had accompanied it. More than a decade into the post–Cold War era, however, that demobilization had not occurred. The national security state remained as powerful as ever—giving the nation a sense of invulnerability as the world's only superpower.

That sense of invulnerability was shattered on the morning of September 11, 2001—a date that will, as President Franklin Delano Roosevelt said about another historic moment, "live in infamy." America's massive national security state proved helpless to prevent nineteen al Qaeda terrorists from hijacking four airplanes, flying two of them into the World Trade Center towers in New York City, and crashing a third into the Pentagon. The only one that did not reach its target was brought down in a Pennsylvania field, not by elements of the national security state, but by a group of ordinary Americans who were passengers on the plane. In a couple of hours on that morning, more Americans lost their lives to an attack by a foreign aggressor than had been lost at Pearl Harbor. The enemy behind the assault was not a mighty national foe, as the USSR had been, nor even a smaller regional adversary, such as Iraq's Saddam Hussein, but an international terrorist organization under the leadership of Osama bin Laden, a Saudi Arabian exile operating from Afghanistan. The national security state had not been organized to protect us from such a foe, and despite warnings in recent years about the dangers of nonstate terrorism, it had not retooled itself to do so, as the events of 9/11 proved. In the aftermath, nevertheless, the president, Congress, and the American people turned to the national security state to prosecute a novel conflict—a "war on terrorism."

The shock of the 9/11 terrorist attacks focused the attention of most Americans on finding the appropriate means for protecting our country and preventing a repeat of such an event. Many justifiably wonder about the efficacy of the existing national security structure for addressing the threat. Undoubtedly, innovative national security policies, strategies, and approaches are needed. In a democracy, one should expect that deliberation about these issues would involve, and ultimately be resolved by, the people. Yet our experience with the handling of similar national security dilemmas in the past half-century should raise doubts about how democratically the policies governing the new war on terrorism will be reached. The national security state that was created to fight the Cold War—in the name of protecting US democracy from external threats—has also engaged in practices that were destructive of democracy at home, and this experience should caution us that efforts to fight the war on terrorism may present a similar domestic peril. Indeed, as we see in the following discussion, there are strong signs that this latest war may pose even greater challenges to our democracy. The irony of fighting to defend democratic values is that the very means devised to do so are likely to jeopardize those values. This chapter examines how the national security state has posed a challenge to democracy in the past and suggests how it may do so again as the country mobilizes to fight a new kind of war.

The Burgeoning of the National Security State

Before World War II, a distinctive feature of the United States was the small size of its military establishment. Although a standing national army had been maintained since the ratification of the Constitution in 1789, in times of peace that army had always been extremely small. The basic principle informing America's relation to its military was that the armed forces would consist of a token core of military professionals in peacetime, to be augmented by citizen-soldiers mobilized in time of war. As Figure 8.1 shows, the size of the armed forces increased during times of crisis, but it shrank again once each crisis ended. Following World War II, however, the pattern changed significantly. True, by 1950 the size of the military had fallen from its massive wartime peak of more than 12 million men and women, but unlike previous postwar periods, it did not decrease to anything like prewar levels. During the period of the Cold War (after 1945), the United States maintained a peacetime military of about 2 million men and women—a force about ten times the size of the 1930s military. After the end of the Cold War, the active-duty force was reduced to just under 1.5 million, supplemented with about 1 million reserve and National Guard forces.[1] When we take into account the increase in population since the 1930s, there are still about two-and-one-half times as many people in the active-duty armed forces now as there were prior to World War II.

Another change in the character of the American military—a change instituted only since the 1970s—has been the shift from a military dependent on citizen draftees to all-volunteer, or professional, armed forces. All American wars up to and including the Vietnam War had been fought by citizen-soldiers who either volunteered for the duration of a conflict or were drafted for the purpose. Because of the controversy the draft created during that unpopular war, Congress, at the urging of the Defense Department, agreed thereafter to end the draft and to increase military pay and benefits so that the armed forces could attract professional soldiers. By the beginning of the twenty-first century, the United States had not only a peacetime military establishment much larger and more powerful than had been the American tradition, but one that was made up primarily of professional soldiers.

American citizens of earlier times would have been seriously alarmed at the existence of such a large, professional standing army. From the time of the nation's founding, partisans of democracy usually regarded a large standing army as an implicit threat to democratic liberty. The Virginia Declaration of Rights in 1776, for example, pronounced that "standing armies, in time of peace, should be avoided, as dangerous to liberty." Even former generals concurred with this sentiment: At his first presidential inaugural in 1829, General Andrew Jackson promised, "Considering standing armies as dangerous to free governments in time of peace, I shall not seek to enlarge our present establishment." Throughout most of our history, Americans viewed a large military as a feature of foreign autocracies that had no place in the democratic, new nation they were creating. Threats to national security would be met as they arose, by the temporary mobilization of a democratic citizenry under arms.

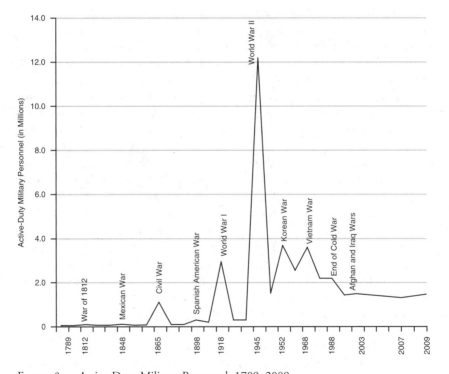

FIGURE 8.1   Active-Duty Military Personnel, 1789–2009

Sources: US Bureau of the Census, *Historical Statistical Abstract of the U.S.* and *U.S. Statistical Abstract* (Washington, DC: Government Printing Office, various years).

The massive mobilization of World War II and that war's outcome dramatically altered this traditional stance. The near-total destruction of other, especially European powers during the war left the United States as the preeminent world power. In what would become known as "the free world," only the United States possessed the economic wealth to support a military force capable of ensuring international stability, and so it took over from such prewar colonial powers as France and Great Britain the responsibility for protecting world commerce. After the war, the only power capable of challenging the United States was the Soviet Union—a nation that most Americans regarded as especially threatening. Fear of the spread of communism, particularly after the establishment of communist governments in Eastern Europe, China, and North Korea, was the primary factor that legitimized the new, larger American military. Americans were convinced that a permanent military establishment was essential to contain expansion of their ideological adversary. The Cold War seemed to require a permanent mobilization to meet an unrelenting threat to freedom.

Two related factors contributed to the new attitude toward a militarized United States. One was the perception that 1930s American isolationism and military weakness had contributed to the growth of German and Japanese power. Americans were told that only constant vigilance would prevent the rise of comparable threats in the future and that America had a special role in defending the world from antidemocratic powers. Reference to this new post–World War II responsibility, in explicit contrast to prewar isolationism, has been a standard justification for such recent conflicts as the 1991 and 2003 wars against Iraq, the interventions in Bosnia and Kosovo in the 1990s, and the ongoing war on terrorism. A second factor supporting the new militarism was the increasing complexity of military technology. The military establishment pointed to new, highly sophisticated weapons—most dramatically nuclear weapons—as proof that temporary mobilization of the citizenry would no longer be adequate to forestall military threats. Advances in military technology meant that the nation had to undertake the permanent support of the means to develop and deploy new weapons. The sophistication of these weapons also required the maintenance of a large standing army that was trained in their use.

The institutional foundation for America's new international role was provided in the National Security Act of 1947, which created a Department of Defense by consolidating the former Departments of War and the Navy.[2] The military services were organized under the Joint Chiefs of Staff, which reported directly to the civilian secretary of defense. Although the National Security Act thus provided for an enhanced political role for the military, civilian control of the Defense Department was supposed to offset any concerns that role might create. The act also formalized the increased importance of national security issues by establishing a National Security Council (NSC), composed of the vice president, the secretaries of defense and state, and other agency heads, to advise the president. In future years, the NSC staff, rather than the council members themselves, came to play an important national defense role. The NSC staff would provide presidents with their closest advisers on foreign affairs—advisers who owed allegiance to no other governmental agency—and the power of national security advisers such as Henry Kissinger, Richard Nixon's powerful NSC chief, would rival that of cabinet secretaries.

A very important feature of the National Security Act of 1947 was the section that created the Central Intelligence Agency (CIA), which was to have overall responsibility for providing to the president "intelligence estimates" drawn from a variety of sources, including covert agents overseas. Many of the new agency's operatives had formerly worked for the wartime spy agency, the Office of Strategic Services (OSS); their temporary, wartime duty to fight Nazis became a permanent career duel with the Soviet spy agency, the KGB. Under pressure from the director of the Federal Bureau of Investigation (FBI), J. Edgar Hoover, Congress explicitly forbade the CIA to perform any domestic counterintelligence work—a restriction that was meant to allay the fears of citizens and elected officials who might have moral qualms about creating an undercover agency. Because it was prohibited from operating within the United States, the chance that the CIA would interfere in domestic democratic politics was supposedly eliminated; CIA dirty work would be directed only against foreigners. In later years, this limitation would prove not to have prevailed.

With the National Security Act, Congress created the core of the national security state, but in the years that followed, other institutions emerged to extend the segment of government concerned with national security.[3] Intelligence gathering became a concern not only of the CIA but also of expanded intelligence components in all the military services, plus a new agency, the National Security Agency (NSA), which was given responsibility for collecting so-called hard intelligence from electronic intercepts and eventually from satellites. Domestically, the FBI expanded its roles in counterintelligence and the surveillance of domestic dissidents. These activities remained the FBI's top priority for thirty years, reflecting J. Edgar Hoover's rather hysterical preoccupation with communist subversion.

Even in those areas of government not obviously associated with the safety of the nation, the demands of the national security state took priority. The Atomic Energy Commission (AEC) was responsible for developing nuclear warheads for the Defense Department, but with the willing cooperation of the nation's largest business firms, it stimulated as well the development of civilian nuclear reactors, and a domestic nuclear industry was thereafter considered a national security requirement. Most of the resources of a new governmental agency created to support scientific research, the National Science Foundation (NSF), were directed toward defense-related projects. In the 1950s, Congress justified new initiatives in building roads and in education—the National Defense Highway Act and the

National Defense Education Act—on national security grounds. Even state and local governments were involved in operating civil defense agencies and military units of the National Guard. Supporting all these government activities were the private-sector businesses, universities, and consultants of what President Eisenhower famously called, in his 1961 farewell address, the "military-industrial complex."

Within a decade after the end of World War II, the national security state had become a massive complex of relationships linking much of government with a large sector of domestic society. The agencies connected with the national security state employed millions of civilian bureaucrats, as well as a clear majority of all federal employees, and spent more than half the federal budget. The areas of government concerned with foreign and defense affairs had grown considerably larger than the foreign policy establishment of the 1930s, when the small Department of State had only a few hundred Foreign Service officers scattered around the globe and the military consisted of only about 250,000 soldiers and sailors. In addition to these expanded governmental agencies, a large defense industry made up of some of the largest American corporations came to depend on contracts for complex and expensive weapons systems to boost their profits and pay the wages of their workers. The military-industrial complex intertwined the national security state with both corporate power and the national economy.

Simply because of the size of its bureaucracy and budget, the rise of the new national security state brought about changes in the operation of American democracy. Even more than in its institutional dimensions, the new national security state represented a potent shift in the psychology of democratic politics. In his famous "garrison state" hypothesis, formulated in the 1930s, political scientist Harold Lasswell predicted the consequences of a perpetual crisis mentality brought on by a "continued expectation of violence."[4] In future garrison states, Lasswell warned, measures sometimes tolerated in democratic societies as temporary, emergency necessities—secrecy, military mobilization, procedural shortcuts, increased power in the hands of military professionals, and repressive measures—would become permanent fixtures of political life and would come to be regarded as normal. Lasswell also wrote that the increasing atmosphere of suspicion fostered in the garrison state would lead citizens to question one another's loyalty.[5] And indeed, in the years following the creation of the national security state, the psychology of fear and distrust outlined in Lasswell's dark vision became a regular feature of American politics.

The end of the Cold War did not diminish America's garrison state mentality, and the current war against terrorism has reinforced it substantially. The United States maintained a remarkably high level of military mobilization even after the collapse of the Soviet Union left it the world's only remaining superpower. In 2009, the most recent year for which complete figures are available, American military expenditures were higher than the next forty-five highest-spending countries combined.[6] The United States spent 5.8 times more than the second-highest spender—China—and ten times more than the third—Russia. The United States now accounts for nearly one-half of all world military spending. Massively increased since 9/11, US military spending in 2011 topped 700 billion dollars and, in inflation-adjusted dollars, now surpasses expenditures at the height of the Cold War (see Figure 8.2).

Even before the post-9/11 expansion, budget increases during the Clinton administration were pushing military spending to Cold War levels. At the time, former Assistant Secretary of Defense Lawrence Korb described the situation as "a Cold War budget without a Cold War."[7] Although the heightened expenditures of more recent years seem a natural response to the war on terror, much of the added costs come not from the demands of fighting terrorism but from renewed spending on Cold War–era weapons systems. According to Korb, the war on terrorism requires strategies and weapons, such as the smart bombs and unmanned surveillance aircraft that proved effective in Afghanistan and Iraq, that should be much less costly than existing ones.[8] Clearly, our national security state remains committed to maintaining the colossally expensive military structures built up during the Cold War—no matter how inappropriate for the threats we now face.

As the Berlin Wall came down, many Americans looked to the dismantling of the national security state as a welcome prospect. There was talk of a "peace dividend" that would allow the reallocation of resources, as in the Bible verse, from "swords into plowshares." The trillions that would have been needed for weaponry had the Cold War continued could now be spent on educating children, repairing roads, building better housing, and bringing prosperity to all. Governmental agencies created to fight the Cold War could be eliminated. The new diplomatic and security environment that now faced the United States seemed to require a complete rethinking of military strategic policy, expenditure requirements, and institutional structure. But post–Cold War demobilization was not a welcome prospect for the military services, defense contractors, national security bureaucrats in the various security agencies, and their friends in Congress, whose concerted resistance has been largely successful in preserving much of the national security infrastructure from which they derive profits, salaries, careers, and power. Even when confronted with the new demands of the war on terrorism, the national security state, in the interest of retaining its power and resources, has prevented a reasoned and democratic reexamination of public priorities. Instead, the national security state has been somewhat reorganized—much as a corporation reorganizes to face new market challenges—but its basic form remains substantially intact.

Political and economic interests whose power derives from the existence of the national security state are well positioned to ensure its continuance for many years to come. Moreover, although policymakers used the Soviet threat to justify the expansion of the national security state during the Cold War, containing

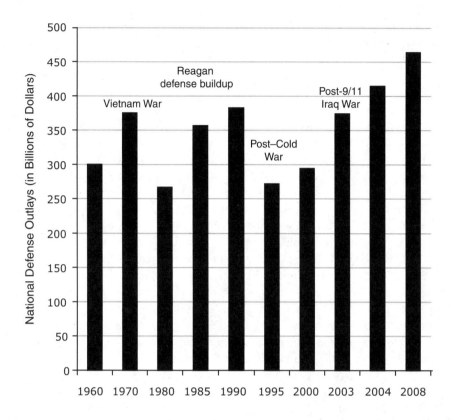

FIGURE 8.2   National Defense Outlays, 1960–2011 (in Billions of Constant 2005 Dollars)

Source: US Census Bureau, *2012 Statistical Abstract,* Table 503. National Defense Outlays and Veterans Benefits: 1960 to 2012, http://www.census.gov/compendia/statab/2012/tables/12s0503.pdf.

communism was never its sole rationale. As early as the late 1940s, American leaders saw expanded military power as necessary to establish a US-dominated international economic order; the Soviet threat provided a convenient way to secure domestic political support for policies thought to be desirable anyway.[9] Thus, when President George H. W. Bush began to speak of a "New World Order" as Soviet might crumbled, he was rearticulating the underlying rationale that had motivated the creation of the national security state from the beginning. International relations specialist Andrew Bacevich calls the American commitment to assuring world order the "American credo" that "summons the United States— and the United States alone—to lead, save, liberate, and ultimately transform the world."[10] Enforcing this credo requires a global US military presence, global power projection, and global interventionism.[11] To accomplish these goals, the national security state maintains a global presence that includes over 300,000 troops stationed abroad at over 761 locations in thirty-nine foreign countries organized in six unified military commands each headed by a four-star general.[12] These commands encompass the entire world including outer space in the "Space Command"!

Both Presidents George W. Bush and Barack Obama embraced the American credo. In September 2002, Bush, in a speech to cadets at West Point, restated it as the so-called Bush Doctrine, declaring that the United States is prepared to act preemptively and unilaterally to defeat regimes it regards as a threat anywhere in the world in order "to bring the hope of democracy, development, free markets, and free trade to every corner of the world."[13] Although President Barack Obama rejected the Bush Doctrine during the 2008 presidential campaign, as president he has behaved largely in conformity to the American credo—expanding the war in Afghanistan, maintaining the American military presence in Iraq, expanding the use of predator drones and Special Forces against terrorist targets in Pakistan, Somalia, and Yemen, and intervening in Libya. In his own speech at West Point in 2009, Obama echoed his predecessors' commitment to underwriting global security.[14] The "war on terror" has given new life to Bacevich's American credo in justifying a vague, endless conflict requiring permanent military mobilization, just as envisioned in Lasswell's garrison state hypothesis.

A new domestic component of the national security state was born in 2002 when President George W. Bush signed legislation creating the Department of Homeland Security.[15] This massive reorganization consolidated twenty-two federal agencies with 177,000 employees into a single department. Among the agencies brought into the new department were the Immigration and Naturalization Service, the Secret Service, the Customs Service, the Federal Emergency Management Administration, and the Border Patrol. With the addition of homeland security to America's national security state, the garrison state seems complete.

The creation of the national security state has been justified as necessary to permit the United States to protect itself and its interests in a hostile world. The specific threats that produced the national security state—the USSR and communism—may be gone, and its energies may now be focused on very different enemies, but its continued existence should be worrisome to democrats. The leaders and institutions that have direct control of the instrumentalities of force and violence pose a special problem for democracies. If the people are to rule, those within the national security state must be willing to acquiesce to the control and direction of the people and the people's representatives. Yet those who wield the weapons and instruments of organized violence clearly have the capacity to resist, defy, and even overturn democratic control. History is replete with examples of popular governments undone when those controlling military power decided to substitute their own will for that of the people. Although democracies, like any other form of government, require military forces and national security states—as the current menace of international terrorism proves—democratic citizens need to be vigilant in demanding that those forces remain subject to democratic control. Unfortunately, America's own recent history provides evidence, some of which is presented in this chapter, of insufficient citizen vigilance in controlling the national security state. As long as the policies and institutions that make up the national security state exist, democrats need to be aware of the challenges they pose.

Proponents of democracy identify several dangers in the practices and attitudes that appear to be inherent in the national security state:

1. *Secrecy.* Information relevant to the enactment of public policy is often kept secret from the public and even from elected officials. Censorship and the classification of information as secret are usually justified as necessary to prevent its use against the nation. But keeping crucial information from enemies also prevents citizens from using that same information to hold government officials accountable for their actions and to participate more effectively in the formulation of policy. Secrecy also is easily abused by public officials who exploit national security as an excuse to insulate themselves from democratic control.

2. *Centralization.* National security is often cited as a justification for limiting the range of actors involved in making public decisions. Democratic procedures are said to be too cumbersome for the swiftness and decisiveness required for defense and foreign policy decision making. Only a small number of officials have access to the secret information and possess the expertise needed for these decisions. In the United States, this restrictive approach has meant concentrating responsibility for such decisions in the president and his close advisers, excluding Congress and the public. Yet decisions of peace and war are among the most important to be made in any society. Can a society long remain a democracy if the people are excluded from such important decisions?

3. *Repression.* National security requirements are often used to justify the suspension of civil liberties to combat domestic enemies. Fear that one's fellow citizens may be in traitorous collusion with a foreign enemy leads to campaigns that stifle dissent and interfere with political expression and participation. Police institutions developed to protect national security can become instruments for interfering with legitimate democratic processes.

4. *Distortion.* National security requirements lead to the creation of societal institutions such as a military and defense industry with a vested interest in high levels of mobilization and defense spending. Such institutions also

acquire significant power that can be used to influence public policy and to undermine the ability of ordinary citizens to make judgments about the nature and level of security threats. The military-industrial complex exaggerates such threats in order to maintain its power and economic well-being. The existence of a large military concentrates and organizes force in a way that can weaken democracy.

Secrecy

A key value of democracy, common in some degree to all the democratic models discussed in this book, is openness. If a society is to operate democratically, citizens must have open and free access to information about public policies and the performance of government officials. Citizens cannot participate effectively in influencing policy unless they know the facts about policy alternatives under discussion. Information that is withheld, or available only to certain participants in public debates, biases those debates and prevents a democratic outcome. For example, scientific studies about the probability of contamination from nuclear power plants are likely to affect the degree of support for such plants. Unless people have access to that information, they cannot know whether nuclear power is in either their interest or the public interest.

Citizens also need information about the activities of public officials so that they can evaluate official behavior. Democratic accountability is impossible unless citizens know what officials have done and what the consequences of those actions have been. Even the Protective and Pluralist models of democracy, which assume that officials have fairly wide discretion, place a high value on the ability of democratic citizens to evaluate the performance of officials. An election cannot function effectively as a means to hold governments accountable if officials can exaggerate their successes and keep their failures secret. In times of crisis—such as the current war against terrorism—citizens need accurate information about both the failures and the successes of military actions and intelligence operations if they are to evaluate how that war is being prosecuted. Openness is needed to facilitate both democratic participation and democratic accountability.

Openness and citizen access to information are in direct conflict with one of the key practices of the national security state: information classification. In 1951, President Truman issued an executive order extending a wartime system of information classification that has since become a permanent feature of American government. Under the system, millions of government documents are routinely classified as either "confidential," "secret," or "top secret" and are kept from public view. Even after a recent, major reform effort, intended to reduce the amount of classified information, nearly a billion pages of documents remained classified.[16]

Not only documents are classified. Over the past fifty years, many major foreign policy initiatives of American governments have involved "covert operations" that are kept secret from the public. Most, though not all of them, have been carried out by the CIA, and many have had far-reaching consequences for the United States. Among the major covert operations we now know about are the overthrow of democratically elected governments in Iran and Guatemala in the 1950s, the funding of pro-US political parties in Europe, the aborted Bay of Pigs invasion of Cuba in 1961, the "destabilization" of Chile that brought to power the dictator Augusto Pinochet in the 1970s, and the secret *contra* war against Nicaragua in the 1980s. None of these operations was discussed or debated in public, and some, as has been disclosed in congressional investigations, were never even revealed to Congress.[17] The budgetary allocations to support them were kept hidden as well, despite an explicit constitutional prohibition against such secret accounting.[18]

During the Cold War, covert operations were justified as necessary to counteract the actions of a ruthless enemy. Yet even a decade after the end of the Cold War, national security agencies refused to reveal information about those operations. In 1997, the CIA was still dragging its feet on declassifying documents from its 1954 coup in Guatemala, the 1953 coup in Iran that installed the shah, and the 1961 Bay of Pigs invasion—years after any justification for keeping those secrets had disappeared.[19] The refusal persists today, despite numerous public promises to declassify historical records. Not only is the size of the CIA's current budget kept secret, but the agency has also denied requests from historians to declassify its budgets from the 1950s and 1960s, although those budgets have little relevance to current CIA activities.[20] This long-standing concealment of intelligence expenditures is in direct violation of the constitutional requirement that "[a] regular Statement and Account of the Receipts and Expenditures of all public Money shall be published from time to time." In this, as in many other aspects of the national security state, the US Constitution is deemed not to apply.

The current war on terrorism has spawned a new wave of government secrecy. In 2004, the government classified approximately 16 million documents, nearly double the number in 2001 and four times as many as in 1996.[21] This escalating effort of concealment should not be at all surprising, given our experience of the Cold War and other national security crises. As the late former senator Daniel Patrick Moynihan pointed out, "Proclamation of a wartime crisis automatically increases the amount of government secrecy."[22] Fifty years of clandestine activity during the Cold War routinized America's secrecy apparatus and inculcated a culture of secretiveness among government officials that has been quickly and easily tapped as the war on terrorism has been used to expand institutional secrecy.[23]

Almost immediately following the 9/11 terrorist attacks, the George W. Bush administration began instituting new secrecy measures. In October 2001, President Bush issued an executive order to federal agencies restricting the information that would be made available to Congress.[24] The USA Patriot Act, passed hastily with little congressional debate, gave the Justice Department new powers to obtain patrons' library records and other private information secretly, to conduct covert electronic surveillance, and to secretly search people's homes with relaxed court oversight.[25] In a 2010 investigative report entitled "Top Secret America," the *Washington Post* documented the huge expansion of the country's secrecy apparatus since 9/11. It describes a vast network of at least 263 government agencies and private contractors devoted to finding, keeping, and managing secret information.[26] Most have seen personnel and budgets expanded, such as the Pentagon's Defense Intelligence Agency, which grew from 7,500 employees in 2001 to 16,500 today, or the doubling of the budget of the National Security Agency.[27]

Late in 2005 it was revealed that, unwilling to comply with the minimal court oversight mandated in current law, the administration had even instituted a secret National Security Agency program called the Terrorist Surveillance Program (TSP) to eavesdrop on the phone calls and electronic communication of American citizens without legal authorization.[28] The TSP bypassed completely the safeguards Congress had enacted in the 1978 Foreign Intelligence Surveillance Act to prevent the NSA from violating Americans' civil liberties. President George W. Bush also gave the heads of the Environmental Protection Agency, the Department of Health and Human Services, and the Department of Agriculture new powers to classify documents—powers that had been formerly restricted to national security agencies.[29] Paradoxically, this embrace of more secrecy occurred despite a key finding of the 9/11 Commission: that excessive secrecy had prevented law enforcement officials from sharing information that might have led to the capture of the 9/11 attackers.[30]

Even democracies sometimes need to keep secrets. Some national security matters—such as the nature of weapons technology, weapons deployment, intelligence methods and sources, military plans, and diplomatic negotiations—must be kept from public view. For example, no one would object to government officials keeping secret the time and place of a wartime military attack, such as the invasion of Normandy in 1944, or the identity of agents planted in a terrorist cell.[31] Unfortunately, very few of the 6 million documents newly classified each year relate to such necessary secrets. More often, secrecy provides a means for government officials to pursue actions that do not have public or congressional support, to deceive the public about the effectiveness of policies, and to protect themselves from legitimate public scrutiny so as to escape future accountability for their actions. As historian Arthur Schlesinger Jr. has written, "Secrecy, carried too far, becomes a means by which the executive branch dissembles its purposes, buries its mistakes, manipulates its citizens, escapes its accountability and maximizes its power."[32]

Since the 1940s, government officials have used the instrumentalities of secrecy to deceive the American public as routinely as they have sought to deceive

The National Security Agency outside Washington, DC, collects a massive amount of information from around the world, including on US citizens.

Greg Mathieson/Mai/Mai/Time Life Pictures/Getty Images or Time & Life Pictures/ Getty Images.

foreign enemies. Government classification and covert actions have been justified as needed to combat our enemies, but government officials have succumbed frequently to the temptation to use secrecy to combat domestic opponents of their policies as well. In a democratic society, disagreement about the wisdom of pursuing a particular policy is supposed to produce discussion and debate about that policy until a majority can agree on a course of action. Pursuing a controversial course of action in secret, so as to avoid such public policy discussion, constitutes the most serious way in which secrecy can undermine democracy. In the Iran-*contra* affair in the 1980s, staff members of the National Security Council, led by marine Lieutenant Colonel Oliver North and with the blessing of CIA director William Casey and NSC director John Poindexter, used secrecy to conceal a policy that lacked democratic support and had been explicitly prohibited by Congress. The Reagan administration saw Central America solely as an arena of superpower confrontation with the Soviet Union. To combat "communist subversion" in the region, it was willing to support brutal military regimes in El Salvador, Honduras, and Guatemala and to oppose the Sandinista regime in Nicaragua, which had come to power in a 1978 popular overthrow of the American-backed military dictator, Anastasio Somoza.[33] In an attempt to topple the Sandinistas, the Reagan administration decided to support the anti-Sandinista rebels known as *contras,* a group made up primarily of supporters of the former dictator. Because a majority of its members regarded the *contra* war as a violation of international law, Congress in 1984 passed the Boland amendment, prohibiting the administration from funding the *contras.* In defiance of the Boland amendment, North organized a scheme to secretly sell arms to Iran (contrary to Reagan's public stance toward that country) and used the money to fund the *contras.*[34] He, Casey, and Poindexter had, in effect, set up a secret government, insulated from any legal or democratic accountability, to pursue their own policy agenda and defy the explicit will of Congress. Later, under congressional investigation, both North and Poindexter would justify their actions by claiming that national security required it. Democrats should question, however, how Poindexter and North arrogated to themselves alone the responsibility for determining what national security required. The current revival of covert operations within the war on terrorism means that latter-day Norths and Poindexters seem to be pursuing equally ill-conceived schemes while avoiding the scrutiny of Congress and the public.

Secrecy not only creates opportunities for deception about what government is doing but also allows deception regarding the effectiveness of public policies. In a secret report on the Vietnam War prepared by the Defense Department in the 1960s—eventually leaked to the *New York Times* and published as *The Pentagon Papers*—repeated instances of this sort of deception are documented.[35] Throughout the war, various officials in the CIA, the military, and the Defense Department had lied and released—to the public, to Congress, and even to their administrative superiors—distorted information about the war's progress. These distortions were intended to maintain support for continuing the war by underestimating the strength of the Vietcong and overestimating the military successes of South Vietnamese and US troops. This manipulation of information contributed to the prolongation of a disastrous policy.[36] Had more Americans, critics and supporters of the war alike, both in and out of government, received less-distorted accounts of what was actually happening in Vietnam, the war might have ended much earlier, saving thousands of American and Vietnamese lives.

As in the Vietnam War, keeping secrets about military operations to impede accurate evaluation of military policies seems habitual within the national security state. Already in the war on terrorism there are clear signs that information about the results of military action and intelligence activities has been manipulated to avoid revealing failures and mistakes. In early 2002, when Afghan sources said that an American missile targeted at al Qaeda terrorists had mistakenly killed innocent villagers instead, the US military blocked access to American reporters who wanted to question survivors directly from the scene of the attack.[37] After the mistreatment of Iraqi prisoners by American soldiers at the notorious Abu Ghraib prison became public in 2004, the George W. Bush administration refused to make public or share with Congress most of the details regarding the extensive system of secret interrogation sites and interrogation procedures it had been employing against terrorist suspects in American custody. These procedures included the use of torture by CIA and military personnel; the "extraordinary rendition" of suspects to third countries, such as Syria, well known for the brutality of their interrogation methods; and holding without trial hundreds of prisoners at Guantanamo Bay, in US prisons, and in secret CIA prisons. While the Bush administration claimed that such methods had produced effective intelligence preventing terrorist attacks, verification of its claims was impossible since the administration classified all the information regarding them.[38] We do know that once questions began to be raised about CIA interrogation techniques, the agency destroyed all tapes of its interrogations to cover up the methods used.[39] Despite his denunciation of Bush secrecy policies during his presidential campaign, President Barack Obama continued some of them once in office, for example, asserting "state secrets" as the basis for dismissal of a lawsuit by former CIA detainees.[40] The Obama administration, even while condemning torture, the use of extraordinary rendition, and incarceration of prisoners at Guantanamo Bay and at "black sites," has fought vigorously and successfully in court to keep secret details of these operations and prevent victims from receiving compensation.[41] For Obama, consistent with the logic of the national security state, protecting state secrets trumps public exposure and evaluation of even the misguided policies of his predecessor.

Not only does secrecy undermine democratic policy making; there is some evidence from our experience with the national security state that secrecy can produce very bad policy. In fact, most serious US foreign policy failures have followed from initiatives taken in secret. By making decisions in secret, policymakers avoid having their plans critically evaluated by observers outside the small circle making the policy. The foolishness of such policy decisions as the Bay of Pigs invasion and the Iran-*contra* arms-for-hostages deal would have been quickly exposed had they not been made in secret. As Senator Moynihan said, "The secrecy system protects intelligence errors, it protects officials from criticism. Even with the best of intentions the lack of public information tends to produce errors; the natural correctives—public debate, academic criticism—are missing."[42] In addition to shielding bad decisions from scrutiny, the deception that often accompanies secret actions can lead to self-deception on the part of policymakers, who come to believe the web of lies they have woven to cover their actions. The political philosopher Hannah Arendt wrote eloquently about how such self-deception led the architects of American policy in Vietnam to make bad decisions again and again.[43] Similar mistakes, such as the use of torture and denial of basic human rights that have undermined America's reputation around the world, seem to have been made in the war on terror. Better and wiser government has always been a chief virtue of democracy; it only follows that by undermining democracy, secrecy also precludes wise government.

Centralization

All presidents since the rise of the national security state have sought to broaden their control over foreign and military policy. They have tended to interpret their constitutional role in such a way as to exclude all but a close circle of advisers from participation in some of the most important decisions affecting the life of the nation. Although the US Constitution provides that Congress and the executive shall share responsibilities for foreign affairs and defense, post–World War II presidents have been successful in asserting their constitutional prerogatives and using their control of the apparatus of the national security state to concentrate practical control of national security decisions in their own hands. Treaty making, which requires Senate participation, has often been replaced by executive agreements, which do not. Although the Constitution grants to Congress—not the president—the specific authority to declare war, presidents have repeatedly asserted their power as commander in chief as justification for military action initiated without congressional or public involvement. Throughout the postwar period, public participation in major foreign policy decisions usually has been limited to receiving notification after the fact of decisions made and actions taken. In the early years of the twenty-first century, presidential autonomy in making major public decisions without consulting anyone has come to be accepted as normal in our government. This is a rather odd state of affairs for a democracy.

Since 1945, numerous military actions, including four major wars resulting in American casualties in the tens of thousands, have been presidentially initiated without public or congressional consultation. The first major assertion of presidential war-making power came in 1950 when President Harry Truman sent American troops to fight in Korea under the auspices of the United Nations. Describing the effort as a "police action," Truman claimed that action under a UN resolution relieved him of the constitutional requirement to seek a congressional declaration of war. Fifteen years later, Presidents John Kennedy and Lyndon Johnson gradually involved American forces in a major war in Vietnam without significant congressional participation.[44] Throughout that war, Presidents Kennedy, Johnson, and then Nixon made all the crucial decisions about its management, expressing mainly contempt for attempts by Congress or the public to influence those decisions. When a sizable antiwar movement developed to oppose those decisions democratically, both Johnson and Nixon denounced the movement as subversive. In addition to these major wars, American presidents have initiated several brief but intense wars in locales as varied as Iraq (in 1991), Panama, and the Dominican Republic, as well as numerous smaller military actions, including "regime changes" in Grenada, Haiti, the Balkans in the 1990s, and Libya in 2011. America's third major undeclared war since 1945 began when George W. Bush ordered the invasion of Iraq and the overthrow of Saddam Hussein in 2003. As of 2011, when the bulk of American forces were scheduled to be withdrawn, more than 4,000 American soldiers had died fighting in Iraq.[45] When President Barack Obama in 2009 expanded the conflict in Afghanistan, originally begun in 2001 in the wake of 9/11, he turned it into America's fourth major war with over 100,000 troops fighting there and resulting in just under 2,000 soldiers killed as of 2011.[46]

Added to these discrete conflicts have been ongoing presidentially directed secret "special operations" around the world involving targeted assassinations—such as that of Osama Bin Laden in 2011 and the overthrow of perceived unfriendly governments (i.e., Guatemala and Iran in 1953). Today, the president commands a growing array of remote-control drones deployed around the world to spy on and direct violence on those he deems national enemies.[47] President Obama has used drone strikes routinely against alleged terrorists in Pakistan, Yemen, Afghanistan, Libya, and, perhaps, elsewhere.[48] For nearly seventy years, Congress and the American public have acquiesced to a state of presidentially directed war and "semi-war" in defiance of constitutional constraints on executive war power.[49]

Until the Vietnam period, most Americans—and especially Congress—registered little objection to presidential dominance of the national security state. The mobilization against communism and an ideology of bipartisanship in foreign affairs made dissent from presidential initiatives difficult. As disaffection with the Vietnam War grew, however, many Americans began to question the wisdom of growing presidential war-making and foreign policy powers. Some, including historian Schlesinger, worried about the growth of an "imperial presidency," at odds with both the Constitution and democratic values.[50] Revelations in the *Pentagon Papers* about presidential deception and manipulation of public opinion during the Vietnam War provided considerable support for those arguments.

In response to these concerns, Congress passed the War Powers Act in 1973, over President Nixon's veto. This legislation was supposed to limit the ability of presidents to involve the nation unilaterally in military conflict without the participation of Congress. The act required the president to consult with Congress before sending troops into hostilities, to inform Congress in writing of the reasons for a military action within forty-eight hours, and to limit involvement to sixty days unless explicit congressional approval was obtained. Although the War Powers Act seemed to represent a restraint on presidential war power, in practice it has not significantly reduced unilateral presidential control in this area. Every president since the act was passed has claimed that it is an unconstitutional infringement on the president's power as commander in chief, despite the absence of any cogent legal justification for that contention.[51] Facilitating this presidential assertion has been Congress's own acquiescence; it has formally initiated provisions of the act only once, when President Reagan sent marines into Lebanon in 1983.[52] Even when they have complied in a formal sense with some of its provisions, however, all presidents have refused to acknowledge the authority of the act to constrain their power to initiate military action.

Although Presidents Ford and Carter used military force with restraint, ordering only small actions to rescue American forces in danger, every president from Reagan to George W. Bush has engaged American forces without congressional authority numerous times. Reagan initiated military actions in Lebanon, Grenada, and Central America. President George H. W. Bush sent troops into battle in Panama and Somalia, and although he eventually received congressional authorization for his war with Iraq, he was prepared to act without it. President Clinton personally authorized military actions in Iraq, Haiti, Bosnia, Yugoslavia, Afghanistan, and Sudan.[53] Clinton claimed that he had no need to seek congressional consent for any of those actions because "the Constitution leaves the President, for good and sufficient reasons, the ultimate decision-making authority"—a claim that is difficult to prove by reference to the Constitution's actual words.[54] Little more than two years after entering the White House, George W. Bush had already launched two wars, in Afghanistan and Iraq. Following in the footsteps of his predecessors, President Obama did not deem congressional authorization needed to expand the Afghan war or intervene in Libya. These four post–Cold War presidencies provide ample evidence that presidential usurpation of the power to make war was no Cold War anomaly. In fact, even before the post-9/11 conflicts, a blue ribbon commission report in 1999 found that the end of the Cold War had produced an increase in American military interventions around the world.[55]

Forty years after its passage, the War Powers Act has not been effective in restraining presidential war power; in fact, the president's power to make war seems instead to have expanded in scope. Whereas earlier presidents sought to justify their actions as necessary to respond to attacks on American forces (as in the Gulf of Tonkin incident), to protect American lives (as in Reagan's invasion of Grenada), or to honor the requirements of international treaty commitments (as in Korea), more recent presidents have articulated a much broader conception of presidential war power—that the president may commit American forces to combat based solely on his individual determination that it is the "right thing to do." George W. Bush's National Security Strategy made preemptive, unilateral war at the president's discretion a matter of official policy, and by the time he opted to invade Iraq in 2003, Americans had come to regard it as the norm.

In retrospect, the highly centralized and presidentially dominated decision-making process that led up to the 1991 Gulf War seems a prelude to the approach that the second President Bush would take in initiating his own attack on Iraq twelve years later. In response to Saddam Hussein's 1990 invasion of Kuwait,

President George H. W. Bush and a very small circle of advisers made all the critical decisions about the initiation and conduct of the war.[56] When Iraq invaded Kuwait in August, Bush immediately dispatched a large force to defend Saudi Arabia, without informing Congress or seeking its approval. In a conscious allusion to the Korean War precedent, the administration did obtain a UN Security Council resolution condemning Iraq and authorizing military action to liberate Kuwait, but unlike the Korean situation, the administration never acknowledged any UN authority over the conduct of the war. Throughout the conflict, Bush's team emphasized that an international coalition supported the action, although American forces dominated. Bush eventually decided to ask Congress for a resolution authorizing military action, but he never acknowledged that he would be bound by a congressional decision.[57] In fact, Bush later wrote, "even had Congress not passed the resolutions I would have acted and ordered our troops into combat. I know it would have caused an outcry, but it was the right thing to do." In this president's mind, neither the Constitution nor the views of Congress, but only his own judgment about the "right thing to do," should matter in committing the country to war.[58]

George W. Bush went well beyond his predecessors—even his own father—in asserting a monarchical conception of his authority to wage war. After the 9/11 terrorist attacks, he characterized the decisions regarding military action as his alone to make, without any need to seek authorization from either Congress or the broader public. Although Congress itself initiated a resolution authorizing military action in Afghanistan, Bush explicitly denied the legal necessity of the resolution he signed, asserting "the authority of the President under the Constitution to take action to deter and prevent acts of terrorism against the United States."[59] After the success of the military campaign that overthrew the Taliban government in Afghanistan, the administration turned its attention to the possibility of an attack on Bush's father's old nemesis, Iraq's Saddam Hussein. In an August 2002 statement, the president again asserted that he had the authority to initiate military action on his own:

> Listen, it's a healthy debate for people to express their opinion. People should be allowed to express their opinion. But America needs to know, I'll be making up my mind based upon the latest intelligence and how best to protect our own country plus our friends and allies.[60]

In this statement, Bush graciously permits a public discussion of the pros and cons of war with Iraq but makes it clear that he does not expect it to be in any way binding upon him. Nor does he see the decision to go to war as subject to any external control—the decision is all his. With the war on terrorism, the US president seems to have gained truly absolute power to commit the nation to war, based on his sole discretion—at any time, in any place, and for any reason.

Bush advisers developed elaborate legal arguments to justify virtually unlimited presidential war power.[61] Based on a controversial legal theory of "the unitary executive," which articulates an expansive view of presidential power, administration lawyers such as David Addington, Vice President Cheney's chief of staff, and John Yoo, of the Justice Department's Office of Legal Counsel, advised Bush that the constitutional power of commander in chief allowed him to do whatever he thought necessary to conduct the war on terror. In a series of secret memos, Yoo advanced dubious legal arguments asserting that the president could authorize any military action, whether an invasion, imprisoning suspects—including American citizens—without access to the courts, eavesdropping, or brutal interrogation techniques, that he thought necessary to protect national security. Yoo claimed that Congress had no legal right to interfere with Bush's actions.[62] Republican legal activist Bruce Fein found such theories alarming and warned, "If you used the President's reasoning, you could shut down Congress for leaking too much. His war powers allow him to declare anyone an illegal combatant. All the world's a battlefield—according to this view, he could kill someone in Lafayette park if he wants! It's got the sense of Louis XIV: 'I am the state.'"[63]

The months leading up to the 2003 invasion of Iraq revealed Bush's conception of his unconstrained war power, including disregard for many of the ancillary constraints and rationales his predecessors had used to justify their actions. Although the administration claimed that its concern about Saddam Hussein was a response to the 9/11 attacks, many of Bush's advisers had been ardent proponents of invading Iraq, as a means of altering the strategic situation in the Middle East, long before the terrorist attacks.[64] Bush himself seems to have made up his mind as early as July 2002 to invade Iraq; the only task thereafter was to organize a public relations campaign to sell the war to the public.[65] As his father had done before him, Bush denied any constitutional obligation to seek congressional approval of military action, but then sought a congressional resolution of support when it was clear that it would be granted. In contrast to the sharp debate in Congress in 1990, both houses now quickly passed, with only perfunctory debate, a resolution giving the president authority as broad as the 1964 Tonkin Gulf Resolution that President Johnson used to justify escalation of the war in Vietnam.[66] Also reminiscent of the Tonkin Gulf Resolution, which was passed in response to later-discredited administration claims about a North Vietnamese attack on an American destroyer, was that many in Congress in 2002 based their votes on the Iraq resolution on administration reports that later proved to be false, that Saddam Hussein had been plotting to use "weapons of mass destruction."[67]

In stark contrast to the emphasis placed on the support of allies and international institutions such as the UN and NATO in the 1991 Iraq War, the younger Bush's administration sought to remain "unfettered" by such relationships.[68]

America's overwhelming military dominance now meant that US forces could go it alone against Iraq, without concern for support from allies, most of whom were not inclined to provide support in this case anyway. After several months of trying to convince a skeptical UN Security Council of the threat of Iraq's weapons of mass destruction, Bush proceeded to war without UN sanction and with meaningful military support only from Britain. In thus pressing forward with his invasion of Iraq, Bush signaled clearly that his new strategic doctrine meant that in the absence of any concrete aggressive action, and without legitimization by any international body, an American president could rely solely upon his own judgment about a potential threat to the United States in choosing to send the mighty American war machine into action anywhere in the world. The concentration of war-making power in the hands of the American president alone, begun after World War II, was now complete. Such quaint anachronisms as congressional declaration of war or United Nations sanction for use of military force are now consigned to the past.

Despite his own opposition to the Iraq War and his denunciation of the Bush administration's expansive claims of presidential war power, including the theory of the "unitary executive," President Obama has exercised presidential war power, in practice, in a manner little different from his predecessor. Early in his term, he expanded American troop levels in Afghanistan and, by 2010, agreed to a "surge" of 30,000 additional troops modeled on a similar surge Bush had employed in 2007 in Iraq that candidate Obama had denounced. To lead the now expanded Afghanistan War, Obama tapped the author of Bush's Iraq surge—General David Petraeus. As president, Obama was unable to alter the expectations embedded in the national security state that the president must assert American military control in any region of the world deemed unstable and that his was the unilateral power of the presidency.[69] Obama expanded the use of special forces, such as the US Navy Delta Force used to kill Osama bin Laden, and enlarged the fleet of drone aircraft used to assassinate enemies from the sky.[70] The president exercises unilateral and secret control over both special forces operations and the drone force. When, in 2011, the Obama administration decided to intervene in a revolt against Libyan leader Col. Muammar el-Quaddafi under NATO auspices, he did so without seeking congressional authorization. Although he did inform Congress of military involvement in Libya within forty-eight hours, as required by the War Powers Act, he ignored the sixty-day deadline the act requires for seeking congressional authorization for military action claiming it did not apply because no troops were involved and US forces primarily were supporting NATO actions and not directly involved in "hostilities."[71] In making this claim, Obama overruled the interpretation of the Justice Department Office of Legal Council and relied, instead, on a contrary interpretation of the White House Legal Counsel. This marked a new step toward White House centralization of national security policy making beyond even what the Bush administration had done. The Bush administration, at least, had observed the traditional legal practice of following Office of Legal Council (OLC) interpretations even as it had made sure OLC personnel would support its policies. Now Obama felt free to simply ignore the Justice Department and interpret the War Powers Act any way he wished. Any hope that the War Powers Act might restrain the imperial presidency may have ended with this new assertion of presidential power.[72]

A deplorable consequence of the centralization of national defense policy making in the White House has been the militarization of the presidency itself.[73] This effect can be seen in the way that presidents have transformed the interpretation of their constitutional role as commander in chief. In recent times it has been implied that this designation makes the president the nation's military leader. That implication is reflected in the common mistake of describing the president as "the people's commander in chief"—a locution that turns our elected chief executive into a kind of warlord. But what the Constitution actually says, in initiating a short list of administrative powers, is this: "The President shall be Commander in Chief of the Army and Navy of the United States and of the Militia of the several States when called to the Service of the United States . . ."—a clause clearly placing a civilian in control of the military establishment. The penchant of recent presidents for wearing military garb, such as crisp military jackets and military caps, when they visit the troops only reinforces the popular martial image. President George W. Bush took the symbolism of a militarized presidency to a new level when he landed on the flight deck of the USS *Abraham Lincoln,* dressed in a pilot's flight suit, to declare "Mission Accomplished" after the invasion of Iraq.

Some people argue that foreign policy decisions must be highly centralized because democracies are ill equipped to make the kinds of decisions required in a hostile world.[74] This is a point of view with a long history, originating perhaps with Tocqueville in the 1830s, and it underpins much of the centralization of decision making in the national security state. Critics of democratic control of foreign policy making offer three basic points:

- Decisions about foreign affairs require expert knowledge that is unavailable to ordinary citizens. Only the president's elite advisers, who have access to secret information, are equipped to know what policy ought to be adopted. Too much influence from outsiders undermines the capacity for competent policy making.
- Democracy is incapable of prompt and decisive action. Foreign adversaries are able to take advantage of the policy conflicts that democratic debate over policy usually engenders. Centralized decision-making processes insulated from democratic controls allow clear expression of policy choices and quick action and prevent our enemies from exploiting disagreements.

- Centralized decisions facilitate continuity and long-range policy planning. This was a key concern of Tocqueville, who feared that a democracy had "little capacity for combining measures in secret and waiting patiently for the result."[75] Democratic pressures on policymakers create pressures for immediate gratification that often cannot be achieved in foreign policy.[76]

These are familiar accusations, but democrats can make strong counterarguments. In regard to the need for expertise in foreign policy, there can be little quarrel. Problems related to national security and relations with other nations, by their very nature, involve specialized information and benefit from the insights of experts. But is such expertise more or less likely to be brought to bear when decision making is highly centralized and confined to a small circle of advisers? The American experience over the past forty years suggests that highly centralized decisions are more likely than open, democratic processes to exclude relevant expertise. As the psychologist Irving Janis has pointed out, decision making by a small policy group is prone to a phenomenon that he calls "groupthink," in which independent critical thinking about problems is systematically excluded. In his now-classic study of the phenomenon, Janis found that a number of crucial American foreign policy failures, including the Bay of Pigs and the escalation of the Vietnam War, were subject to groupthink.[77] The George W. Bush administration's mistakes in Iraq—such as thinking that 100,000 troops would be enough to pacify the country—seem to be consistent with the notion of groupthink. In the cases of both Vietnam and Iraq, information and expert points of view that could have prevented serious policy mistakes were ignored by decision makers, who formed a tight little group reinforcing a conventional set of views. One antidote to groupthink is democratic participation in decision making, which naturally brings a variety of expert opinions to bear on a problem.

As for the need for prompt and decisive action in security crises, presidents and others in the executive branch have ample power to respond to emergencies and direct attacks on Americans. For example, when the World Trade Center towers were hit on 9/11, officials at the Federal Aviation Administration, without consulting any higher authority, made the unprecedented decision to ground all the thousands of aircraft in American airspace. No one would consider such an emergency decision, or a president's decision to respond to a direct military attack, to be at odds with democratic values. But most decisions regarding war and peace in the post–World War II period have not been made in an emergency context. Typically, there is plenty of time for democratic deliberation and congressional authorization before committing the nation to war.[78] The central decisions made so far in the war on terrorism—such as sending troops to Afghanistan or whether to attack Saddam Hussein—have been reached over weeks or months, with plenty of time for democratic deliberation.

Not only does deliberation not interfere with the need to respond quickly to emergencies, but it may also prevent policymakers from decisively pursuing foolish policies. In the Iran-*contra* affair, for example, Lieutenant Colonel North and his friends were decisive, but that decisiveness perpetrated an extremely unwise policy. More careful deliberation by Congress prior to the 2003 Iraq invasion might have exposed the poor intelligence regarding the Iraqi weapons of mass destruction that were the pretext for the war. The same could be said about most of the covert actions taken during the Cold War. Democracy may slow down policy action, but once decided, the policies openly reached are likely to be wiser and more supportable by citizens than those made by a handful of policymakers in secret.

Finally, there is little evidence that democratic societies are unable to support long-term policy initiatives. Empirical studies of public opinion and the experience of democratic nations show that public opinion in democracies can indeed sustain such initiatives.[79] The American public has been quite willing to support long-term foreign commitments, such as the postwar Marshall Plan for rebuilding Europe and the ongoing mission of NATO, when a convincing case for them has been made. So far in the war on terrorism, the public has enthusiastically supported military action against terrorists, even if it should produce substantial military casualties. Sustained support has been more problematic for questionable policy proposals, such as intervention in Central America, for which leaders have not been able to make a convincing case. The difference between the Marshall Plan and support for the *contras* was not the degree of "elite autonomy to support long-term policies" but the wisdom of the policies themselves. Leaders in democratic societies need not insulate themselves from public control to manage foreign policy effectively; instead, they need to develop policies that a democratic citizenry can support.

Repression

At the heart of American democracy, for most Americans, are the liberties guaranteed in the Bill of Rights. Freedom to say what you think, to organize politically, and to associate with whomever you wish are considered key elements of the American way of life. Unfortunately, the national security state has time and again put these fundamental liberties at risk. In the name of protecting society from foreign threats—usually from "communists," "subversives," and "terrorists"—government officials have spied on citizens, read their mail, intimidated them, discredited them, forced them from their jobs, and in some cases imprisoned them. As early as the 1790s, a few short years after the ratification of the Bill of Rights, the administration of John Adams passed the Alien and Sedition Acts for the ostensible purpose of protecting the new American nation from political ideas and agitation emanating from the French Revolution. As in subsequent experiences, the foreign threat from French revolutionaries was much exaggerated to justify this repressive legislation, and Adams's Federalist government used its provisions more often to harass its political opponents, the Democratic-Republicans, than to ferret out French subversives. Since then, during times of war or other periods when Americans have felt threatened, they have acquiesced to limits on their civil liberties and repressive government activities.

The period of the Cold War provides American history's worst examples of governmental efforts to repress free political activity. Ironically, at a time when the nation was supposedly mobilizing to resist an international threat to its freedom, the national security state was constructing an internal security apparatus that systematically robbed many Americans of their basic freedoms at home. Again, a foreign threat—this time it was communist subversion—was used to justify extraordinary and often secret internal security actions, but as in the 1790s, those actions were often directed simply at those who dissented from mainstream political views or at the political opponents of those in power. But the large police bureaucracies of the 1950s and 1960s made such covert activities more fundamentally threatening to the health of American democracy than they had been in the 1790s, when no such national security apparatus existed.

The core of the internal security component of the national security state was the FBI, and its architect was the agency's renowned director, J. Edgar Hoover.[80] Before World War II, the FBI had built its reputation on its success in combating such crimes as kidnapping and bank robbery and in battling gangsters such as John Dillinger. Its image as an apolitical law enforcement institution was a critical part of Hoover's strategy in building support for the bureau in Congress and among the public in the 1920s and 1930s. Hoover emphasized that, unlike domestic intelligence agencies in other countries, the FBI was concerned with fighting crime in association with local police departments, not monitoring political activity. This law enforcement stance undercut potential critics who feared that a national police organization might undermine civil liberties and democratic politics.

The bureau's experience in World War II profoundly affected its image and that of its director, however. In 1936, in anticipation of the coming military conflict, President Franklin Roosevelt had secretly instructed Hoover to begin systematic surveillance of "subversive" political groups, particularly groups friendly to Nazi Germany.[81] Interpreting his instructions quite broadly, Hoover eagerly began collecting information by such diverse methods as illegal wiretaps, mail interception, and break-ins. Although Roosevelt was most concerned about the activities of pro-Nazi groups, Hoover's own lifelong obsession with communist subversion ensured that equal scrutiny was focused on left-wing groups. Once the war began, the atmosphere of national crisis was used to justify such activities, as Hoover began to publicize the bureau's successes in capturing Nazi spies and foiling Nazi sympathizers. Its role of monitoring "subversive" political activity—which in the 1930s might have raised the concerns of civil libertarians—only expanded support for the FBI in the heat of war. No one worried about FBI surveillance, despite its constitutionally questionable methods, as long as it was directed against foreign enemies. By 1945, the public had come to admire Hoover and his FBI as leaders in the domestic struggle against our wartime enemies.

After the end of the war, Hoover identified a new set of foreign enemies to combat: communists. Thereafter, instead of being eliminated, the FBI's internal security apparatus was maintained and expanded as a permanent part of the national security state. Support for its continuation was assured in the atmosphere of anticommunist hysteria that developed in the late 1940s. Through the efforts of ambitious politicians such as Joseph McCarthy and Richard Nixon, fear of foreign communist subversion was shifted subtly to a concern about the "loyalty" of individual Americans. In 1947, under pressure from a Republican Congress and Hoover, the Truman administration initiated a security program that required government boards, with the assistance of the FBI, to review the loyalty of all federal employees.[82] Soon similar programs were established in state and local governments and throughout the private sector. Legislation was passed to provide a legal basis for the political surveillance of Americans: The 1950 Internal Security Act required members of communist and so-called communist front organizations to register with the attorney general, and it specified imprisonment as the penalty for failing to do so.

This law, along with the wartime Smith Act, which made it a crime to advocate the "violent overthrow of the government," allowed the FBI and the Justice Department to legitimize political surveillance as a law enforcement activity. A wide range of political activity was criminalized in this way. To investigate a political activity, the FBI needed only to label it "subversive" or claim that it was related to an organization supposedly advocating the overthrow of the government. Since it could discover whether organizations or individuals were violating either of these acts only by placing them under surveillance, the FBI used its discretion to justify monitoring any suspicious group—a category that included more and more groups as the years passed.

Under the auspices of its COMINFIL program, introduced to determine the degree of communist subversion in the United States, the FBI infiltrated thousands of organizations and kept files on thousands of individual Americans. Almost any liberal or left-wing group was sufficiently suspect to merit coverage by the COMINFIL program; such suspect groups included the American Friends Service Committee (the Quakers), the National Association for the Advancement of Colored People (NAACP), and the American Civil Liberties Union (ACLU). In the 1950s, about one-third of the FBI's entire investigative force (1,600 agents) was involved in such work, with the help of about 5,000 informants.[83] Group surveillance included warrantless mail opening, break-ins, and wiretaps. Secret files were created to maintain records derived from this illegal surveillance.

Not content simply to gather information about supposedly subversive groups, the FBI's COINTELPRO program involved itself actively in manipulating groups to influence and disrupt their activities. Through COINTELPRO, the FBI became an active force in muddying the political process. One of the most outrageous episodes involved a decade-long effort to undermine the position of Dr. Martin Luther King Jr. and his Southern Christian Leadership Conference (SCLC). Using as an excuse suspicions about the alleged communist ties of one of Dr. King's advisers—although Hoover's lifelong antipathy to the civil rights of blacks probably was a prime motivator—COINTELPRO leaked manufactured stories about Dr. King's personal life and financial affairs to the press and political opponents.[84] In the 1960s, similar efforts were mounted against the anti–Vietnam War movement, nearly all civil rights organizations, and critics of Hoover and the FBI. Justified as necessary to protect the country's national security, the COMINFIL and COINTELPRO programs became generalized efforts to monitor and disrupt any and all political groups that displeased Hoover and other FBI officials.

The FBI was not the only component of the national security state involved in repressing dissent and interfering in domestic politics. In the mid-1970s, a major congressional investigation led by Senator Frank Church, D-Idaho, and a separate investigation by the presidentially appointed Rockefeller Commission found that by the 1960s political surveillance of domestic politics had become routine in a variety of agencies.[85] In spite of an explicit prohibition against domestic activity, the CIA maintained Operation CHAOS to monitor the supposed foreign ties of domestic political groups, especially the New Left. The military services, under the cover of planning for civil disturbances, monitored a wide range of left-wing and dissident groups. Paralleling similar programs in the FBI and CIA, the National Security Agency operated its own mail opening and wiretaps of Americans. The Internal Revenue Service, in cooperation with COINTELPRO, targeted for audits and special treatment the tax returns of thousands of individuals because of their political activities, including Nobel Prize–winning chemist Linus Pauling and Los Angeles mayor Tom Bradley. Beyond these federal governmental agencies, the investigations found, many state and local agencies and police departments conducted political surveillance and disruption activities.

Following these revelations in the 1970s, all the agencies involved claimed to have reformed their procedures to forestall a repetition of the revealed abuses. Yet within a few years, the FBI was engaging in activities reminiscent of COINTELPRO. In the early 1980s, the FBI conducted a massive probe of the Committee in Solidarity with the People of El Salvador (CISPES) and, as it had often done in the 1960s, tried to justify targeting CISPES by reference to its supposed "terrorist" activities. But the FBI surveillance actually focused on legitimate political dissent in reaction to Reagan administration policy in Central

America.[86] After assimilating massive amounts of information about CISPES, the FBI was unable to document any instance of the organization's supporting domestic terrorism or any other illegal activity. The General Accounting Office reported in 1990 that the FBI launched nearly 20,000 investigations in the 1980s that involved monitoring "religious services, political lectures, and street demonstrations attended by people who were not suspected of any criminal activity or membership in any terrorist group."[87]

In reaction to the 9/11 terrorist attacks, the national security state largely cast off the restraints imposed by the Church Committee's concern for Cold War abuses and, once again, gave security agencies broad powers to monitor domestic political activity. In October 2001, Congress passed the USA Patriot Act, which broadly expanded the definition of who might be defined as a terrorist, gave the Justice Department new authority to detain suspected terrorists without charging them with a crime, and expanded the FBI's surveillance powers. Even before the legislation was passed, the attorney general had ordered the secret detention of hundreds of people—a number that would grow to nearly a thousand by the end of the year. Most were later released or deported, but while in custody all were denied the legal rights normally provided to an accused.[88] At the same time, the Justice Department issued new rules restricting detainees' access to lawyers and authorizing the recording of conversations between lawyers and clients. In May 2002, Attorney General John Ashcroft rescinded FBI regulations put in place after the Church Committee hearings of the 1970s to prevent the bureau from monitoring domestic political activities.[89] Although those regulations had often been flouted in the 1980s, as discussed earlier, this overt action signaled a new willingness to encourage the FBI to monitor and infiltrate domestic groups in the search for terrorists. Recent revelations suggest that in the name of combating terrorism the FBI is again engaging in COINTELPRO-like activities, such as infiltrating indiscriminately political activist groups, including Quaker peace advocates and animal rights defenders.[90] Muslims, especially, have been victims of massive FBI surveillance with agents infiltrating mosques around the country.[91] With the relaxation of restrictions on domestic surveillance and the mandate to root out domestic terrorist threats, the FBI investigated thousands of groups—most that posed little real threat. According to a former FBI agent, "You have a bunch of guys and women all over the country sent out to find terrorism. Fortunately, there isn't a lot of terrorism in many communities, so they end up pursuing people who are critical of the government."[92] In addition, as mentioned earlier, President George W. Bush admitted to authorizing a massive program of domestic electronic surveillance of Americans without obtaining court orders as the law requires.[93]

Some of the George W. Bush administration's more controversial actions were those concerning military tribunals and the treatment of persons designated "enemy combatants." In November 2001, President Bush issued an executive order to create secret military tribunals for the trial of foreigners accused of terrorism.[94] The order seemed designed to provide a forum for judging some of the al Qaeda terrorists who had been captured in Afghanistan and were being held at a detention facility at Guantanamo Bay, Cuba. To civil libertarians, military tribunals raised the specter of secretive, authoritarian courts that would be at odds with the basic commitment in American law to open and public judicial proceedings. In addition to such military detention facilities, the CIA established secret internment centers, the "dark sites" described earlier, for interrogating suspected terrorists, including one in a former Soviet-era prison in Eastern Europe.[95] Even more alarming to many, in spring 2002 the administration declared two American citizens suspected of ties to al Qaeda to be "enemy combatants," detained them in military custody without a specific criminal charge, and denied them any access to the judicial system. Although press reports suggested that there were strong grounds for detaining these two individuals, the administration's legal claim for such detentions was far-reaching—arrogating to the president the sole authority to declare an American citizen an enemy combatant who could be confined indefinitely in a military prison.[96] In asserting such a sweeping power, the president was asking Americans to simply trust him to determine—on his own and without trial—the guilt of such a suspect and to believe that he would use this power only against actual terrorists rather than against his political opponents.

At the same time, it became known that the George W. Bush administration also had secretly crafted a new military directive governing the treatment of prisoners captured in the war on terrorism. These new rules excluded persons designated as enemy combatants from the protection of the Geneva Convention and allowed harsh interrogation techniques, which human rights advocates claim included humiliation, degrading treatment, and even torture.[97] The new rules seem to have contributed to an atmosphere leading to abuse of prisoners in Afghanistan, Iraq, and Guantanamo Bay. The revelation in April 2004 of prisoner abuse at Abu Ghraib prison, including the publication of explicit photographs of US soldiers humiliating prisoners, shocked Americans and tainted the reputation of the United States throughout the world.[98] Critics of these policies, such as Republican Senator John McCain of Arizona—a former prisoner of war in Vietnam—argued that allowing prisoner abuse had undermined American credibility as a defender of freedom and endangered American soldiers who might be denied humane treatment in retaliation.[99] Even as Senator McCain and others in Congress moved to correct the abuses through legislation requiring adherence to the Geneva Convention and new military directives forbidding mistreatment of detainees, the Bush administration continued to insist on exempting the CIA from any such restrictions.[100] Although President Barack Obama has condemned the harsh measures undertaken during the Bush years, vowed to adhere to the Geneva Conventions, and signed an executive order to close the Guantanamo Bay detention facility, much of the repressive architecture the Bush administration established has become institutionalized as a part of the national security state.[101] His continued assertion of the state secrets privilege, continuation of the use of extraordinary rendition, and failure to close the Guantanamo Bay facility and other "black site" prisons reflects the inherent tendency of the national security state to maintain repressive measures in the name of American security.[102]

As with many actions taken since 9/11, the measures described here—whether the expanded surveillance powers of the FBI or the president's unchecked power to detain those alleged to be enemy combatants—may seem reasonable and necessary to some, when considered as defensive tactics directed against a terrorist enemy. But the history of our experience with the national security state, including the recent Iraq experience, should caution democrats that these measures are likely to be abused. As the Church Committee found in the 1970s, national security, whether in a "cold war" or as part of a war on terrorism, can become a blanket excuse for massive interference in democratic domestic politics. Individuals holding dissident or sometimes merely unusual political views may be spied on, intimidated, and prevented from exercising the opportunity to try to influence government. The ability of patriotic Americans to raise legitimate questions about various aspects of foreign and national security policy can be impeded. During the worst of the abuses of the 1950s and 1960s, the quality of American democracy was enormously diminished, and we must be on guard to ensure that the war on terrorism does not threaten it anew. Moreover, during the Cold War period, repressive measures undermined the nation's ability to deliberate openly and effectively about national security policies, resulting in costly mistakes in Vietnam and elsewhere. If the current war on terrorism is not to create similar transgressions of civil liberties or stifling of productive policy debates, the experiences of the past must be remembered and care must be taken to prevent their being repeated.

Distortion

The creation of the national security state has had a dramatic impact on the distribution of power and influence in American society. The civilian national security bureaucracies, the military services, and the defense industry (usually referred to as the military-industrial complex) have acquired an enormous amount of political power. For the past sixty years, that power has been used to bias public policy in favor of large levels of defense expenditures and an aggressive foreign policy. Even if one accepts the necessity for a substantial defense sector in the contemporary world, the self-interested pressures of the military-industrial complex have served to enlarge that sector beyond what it would otherwise be. Less-biased observers have to wonder whether most citizens would have chosen to build the immense defense establishment we now have without the pressures of this special interest. Partisans of democracy should be concerned that the political power of the military-industrial complex distorts in fundamental ways the operation of our democracy.

Since the creation of the national security state, the defense industry has been the nation's largest single industrial sector. A wave of consolidation in the weapons industry in the post–Cold War period, partly subsidized by taxpayers, now has created three gigantic firms—Lockheed Martin, Boeing, and Raytheon—that are responsible for most weapons production.[103] In addition, nearly all large US corporations, including such industrial giants as General Electric and General Motors, are involved in some defense contracting. More than 3 million jobs in plants located in nearly every American community are directly linked to defense spending.[104] The post–World War II decision to establish such a large defense sector has had profound consequences for our economy and for the structure of US industry. Unlike the economic models of most of our industrial competitors, who have much smaller defense sectors, the US investment in national defense has precluded making other important societal investments that would make our nation more competitive in the world economy.

In addition to its economic importance, the defense sector holds considerable political significance.[105] Because defense firms depend on governmental decisions for their business, they are very attuned to the need to exert maximum influence over government. They use their profits, earned from government contracts, to support lobbying activities and to contribute to the campaigns of elected officials. The defense industry is a major source of political contributions, providing $70 million to candidates between 1990 and 2002—more money even than was contributed by another industry well known for its campaign largesse, the tobacco industry ($45.5 million).[106] In many congressional districts, defense firms are major employers, and they expect Congress members to cater to their interests. According to a former Defense Department official, referring to the largest employer in Massachusetts, "[Raytheon officials] assume that the Massachusetts delegation will go along with even the most dubious Raytheon defense program because, 'What is good for Raytheon is good for Massachusetts.'"[107] The links to Congress are matched by links to the Pentagon, where defense firms can generally count on a friendly reception. Highly paid positions in the defense industry are usually available for retired military and civilian defense bureaucrats. The cozy links between Congress, the Defense Department, and the defense industry make for one of Washington's strongest iron triangles of influence.

The congressional clout of the defense industry has continued in the post–Cold War period, as it has campaigned vigorously for policies that expand arms sales. Industry lobbying has been very effective in getting Congress to fund weapons programs, even those the Pentagon does not want. For example, Congress has mandated the purchase of 256 C-130 transport planes since 1978 even though the US Air Force had requested only five![108] Not surprisingly, the

C-130 happens to be built at a Lockheed Martin plant in Marietta, Georgia—the district of former House Speaker Newt Gingrich. Other weapons add-ons have included extra Sikorsky Black Hawk helicopters, F-16 fighters, and even a $1.5 million helicopter carrier for the marines to be built in former Senate Majority Leader Trent Lott's home state of Mississippi. In May 2002, Congress overruled an attempt by secretary of defense Donald Rumsfeld to eliminate the $11 billion Crusader artillery system, now made obsolete by precision-guided bomb technology, after a massive lobbying effort by a coalition of companies involved in its manufacture. Senator John McCain estimated that unrequested congressional add-ons cost $2.5 billion in the 1998 Pentagon budget alone.[109]

Such superfluous weapons purchases create havoc in military budgets because Congress rarely adds the funds needed to operate and maintain the additional weapons systems. As a consequence, military leaders have to divert funds needed for other purposes, such as military pay increases and readiness training, to cover those costs. These skewed budget priorities have contributed to increased casualties in Iraq because Pentagon officials failed to invest in a sufficient number of armed Humvees and other military transport vehicles capable of protecting troops from roadside bombs. Paradoxically, excessive spending for military hardware thus creates shortages in necessary programs, and so an apparent need for even more military spending, a situation that Pentagon lobbyists have willingly exploited to expand overall spending.

These distortions in budget priorities, including continued funding of Cold War–era weapons systems, have continued despite new realities of the post–Cold War world. Even before the 9/11 attacks, many military experts were arguing for the need to adjust to the different kinds of threats, including terrorism, "rogue states," and ethnic genocide—as occurred in Rwanda—that the country would increasingly face in the twenty-first century. The strategy suggested for meeting the challenges of this new world required a military mission that would be closely tied to diplomatic, political, and economic actions.[110] And the kind of military force that would be needed for this new strategic environment was not at all like the kind of force that had been developed to fight the Cold War: massive infantry formations supported by expensive tanks and artillery systems, thousands of nuclear missiles on land and in submarines, state-of-the-art "stealth" bombers and fighter jets designed to counter similar systems deployed by an adversary, a national missile defense system, and the fleet of huge aircraft carriers. Despite the new strategic reality, entrenched Pentagon planners and their congressional supporters continue to advocate going forward with a long list of extremely expensive weapons, including the V-22 Osprey tilt-wing aircraft, the F-22 fighter, the Crusader artillery system, a new attack submarine, the F/A-18 fighter, a new nuclear missile submarine, and the Comanche helicopter.[111] These systems were designed to combat a major-power adversary, such as the former Soviet Union, and are not likely to be of much use against either terrorists or smaller "rogue states," or in counterinsurgency and nation-building tasks such as the post-invasion reconstruction of Iraq.

The case of the F-22 fighter, nicknamed the "Raptor," provides a good example of how the economic needs and political weight of the military-industrial complex promote ever more expensive and complex weapons systems even when there is no credible military rationale to justify them. Designed by Lockheed Martin and produced at a cost of $350 million each, this airplane originally was conceived in the 1980s to counter a planned advanced Soviet fighter, which was never built.[112] The Air Force intended the F-22 to replace its existing F-15 and F-16 fighters even though they remain superior to any other airplane in the world.[113] The United States now has a surplus of F-16s mothballed in the Arizona desert and is selling them to countries around the world, such as Chile and Poland. Rather than investing in a whole new fighter, several of our European allies are updating the F-16 with new electronics that provide advanced capabilities. As is typical for expensive weapons systems like the F-22, Lockheed promoted the project through massive campaign expenditures and lobbying and by spreading production among facilities in forty-four states.[114] After spending billions on 187 unneeded F-22s, Congress in 2009 finally voted to end the program.[115] Yet Lockheed had no need to be concerned about a decline in profits because one argument used to end the F-22 program was the high cost of the new Lockheed-built F-35 Joint Strike Fighter. The planned fleet of 2,500 of these newer jets was projected to cost $382 billion plus up to $1 trillion in maintenance costs over the life of the fighters.[116] To an even greater degree than the F-22, the F-35 contains complex electronics and stealth technology bound to cause immense cost overruns in the future and far more advanced than any potential adversary will match far into the future.[117] As they have done with F-16s, Air Force planners have proposed selling some advanced aircraft like the F-22 and F-35 abroad, creating the potential that they will become a threat to our own forces in future conflicts. As one critic noted in response to this suggestion, "We're in an arms race—with ourselves."[118]

Military sales abroad have been a growth area for the military-industrial complex, and defense contractors have lobbied hard for foreign policies supporting such sales. For example, only a few weeks after the end of the 1991 Gulf War against Iraq, the first Bush administration proposed the revival of a program to subsidize American arms exports to Third World countries, even though Saddam Hussein's war machine had been based on purchase of massive armaments on the world market. The arms export initiative was driven by the dependence of many American firms on arms exporting—a $16 billion component of the US economy. Even though arms sales were likely to contribute to future wars, the defense industry's addiction to such sales pressured the George H. W. Bush administration to recommend a revival of subsidies.[119] By 2000, the United States, the world's largest weapons supplier, produced one-third of all weapons sold worldwide. In

1997, the Clinton administration approved Lockheed Martin's sale of F-16 fighter jets to Chile—a decision that some believed would start a South American arms race.[120] To ensure Polish support for the Iraq War of 2003, the George W. Bush administration orchestrated a $3.8 billion loan to underwrite Poland's purchase of forty-eight F-16s from Lockheed.[121] These sales go forward even though American arms sold on the world market can end up being used against American soldiers, as occurred in both wars against Iraq. In Afghanistan in 2001, the ordnance fired at American soldiers by the Taliban and al Qaeda fighters—some of it made in the United States—had been purchased from international arms dealers. Such arms sales clearly illustrate the extent to which the military-industrial complex distorts democratic politics, making consideration of what is in the best interest of all citizens—preventing future wars—subordinate to the financial needs of the defense industry.

The F-35 Lightning II Joint Strike Fighter will assure massive profits for Lockheed Martin for years to come.

PRNewsFoto/LOCKHEED MARTIN AERONAUTICS COMPANY/Neal Chapman.

The design and production of unneeded weapons systems and subsidized sales to foreign countries create tremendous distortion in the federal budget. Continued high levels of defense spending come at the expense of investments in better schools, mass transit systems, renewal of our crumbling highways and bridges, a cleaner environment, and maintenance of the national parks system. All of these investments in the domestic economy would contribute to economic growth and greater prosperity for all Americans. But while our economic competitors around the world are making such investments, our inflated defense budgets prevent our doing so, thereby undermining America's future economic security. At the same time, high-cost weapons systems take away funds that could be used for homeland security—which may be even more important to our future survival. In an era when the threats the nation faces may come in the form of a bacterial agent delivered through the mail or a nuclear device hidden in a shipping container, more investment should be put into developing germ detection methods at the Centers for Disease Control and adding security measures at the nation's ports rather than wasting scarce resources on the F-22 and F-35. After 9/11, Americans realized that the failure to adequately fund security checkpoints at airports had made us more vulnerable than did any threat outlined on Pentagon drawing boards to justify expensive weapons systems. In the interest of protecting weapons contracts and the competitive status of the various military branches, the military-industrial complex promotes expenditures that may undermine both our economy and our real national security.

The increasing power of the military-industrial complex has meant an increase in the political power not only of the defense industry but also of the military itself. As Harold Lasswell predicted when the national security state was young, the role of military officers in American politics has expanded considerably over the past fifty years.[122] In spite of the American tradition of civilian control of the military, more officers have assumed government posts that are politically sensitive and that, before the rise of the national security state, would certainly have been occupied by civilians. In recent years, close presidential advisers, such as Obama's national security adviser General James Jones, have commonly come from military backgrounds, whereas such former soldiers were extremely rare in the White House prior to World War II. In a major departure from traditional civilian leadership of the CIA, Obama appointed General David Petraeus, military architect of the "surges" in both Iraq and Afghanistan, to be the agency's director in 2011. And as we will see, at the same time that soldiers have taken on important new roles behind the scenes, the elected officials they advise are less likely to have had military experience themselves. Civilian leaders have less capacity to evaluate professional military advice based on their own military experience.

Beginning in the 1990s, civilian control of American foreign policy has been further undermined as the Pentagon has developed its own worldwide diplomatic network parallel to that of the State Department.[123] The generals serving as

"CINCs" (commanders in chief) of the various theater commands around the world actively engage in diplomacy with the governments in their regions. One former CINC has characterized his role as equivalent to that of a proconsul in the Roman Empire.[124] Unlike the civilian ambassadors of the State Department, whose budgets Congress has reduced in recent years, the CINCs command enormous resources in their diplomatic efforts.[125] At the same time, because the United States no longer has a military draft, fewer civilians and fewer civilian public officials have had experience in the military. Some scholars have been concerned about a consequent, growing gap between civilian and military culture in the nation.

Since the 1970s, the United States has had a fully professionalized, career military for the first time in its history. In every major conflict in our past through the Vietnam War, most American soldiers, from lowly privates to the officer corps, have been civilians who joined to fight and then returned to civilian life at the end of the conflict. The result was a close interconnection between military service and the lives of ordinary citizens. With the new professional army, there are disturbing signs that that connection has been broken. Now that military service is a choice and not a civic obligation, fewer Americans have had the experience of military service. In fact, because the financial and educational incentives used to recruit young people are most attractive to those from lower-income families, today's volunteer force overrepresents economically struggling, working-class whites and minorities, especially those from the South, and vastly underrepresents the more affluent. Minorities now compose nearly half of the enlisted force.[126] America's military today, according to a recent *New York Times* article, is more likely "to resemble the makeup of a two-year commuter or trade school outside Birmingham or Biloxi than that of a . . . four year college in Boston."[127] In terms of demography and class, today's military is far from mirroring the country it serves.

The near absence of affluent Americans from the military means the absence also of the civilian political elites who are responsible for sending soldiers to war. Although as recently as the 1980s a large majority of members of Congress were military veterans, today less than one-third of members of the House and Senate have served in the military. Among the Bush administration officials who decided to invade Iraq, many, such as Vice President Dick Cheney, had not served at all or, like the president himself, had evaded combat in Vietnam through service in the National Guard. Increasingly, our professional military is subject to a civilian leadership with little experience or knowledge of military life.[128] The lack of firsthand experience may actually result in a more militarized foreign policy, since studies of foreign policy decision making show that military service is a major factor in reducing the propensity of civilian leaders to use force.[129] Moreover, given the class imbalance in the military, the political elites who opt to use force are asking for sacrifice from someone else's son or daughter rather than their own.

Not surprisingly, many in the military are beginning to see themselves as somewhat separate from the society they serve, producing a worrisome new civilian-military gap. Although civilian society holds the military in high regard, often seeing soldiers as exemplars of traditional values and virtues, some observers detect growing disdain within military culture for the decadence of civilian life.[130] Many in the military have begun to think that they are being asked to put themselves in harm's way on behalf of a society from which they are largely alienated. They see themselves as sacrificing on behalf of a "whiny self-absorbed society."[131] This has become a serious issue as casualties have mounted in Iraq and soldiers have been required to serve multiple tours of duty. As one former army lieutenant described the attitude of his troops in Iraq, "They feel like they're the only ones sacrificing . . . they say . . . it's me and my buddies over and over again, and everybody else is living life uninterrupted."[132] Perceiving oneself as bearing the burden of sacrifice for the nation may understandably lead soldiers to interpret their willingness to do so as a kind of moral superiority. In a 2003 survey of military personnel, two-thirds of respondents thought they had "higher moral standards than the nation they serve."[133] As retired Admiral Stanley Arthur summed up the problem, "The armed forces are no longer representative of the people they serve. . . . More and more, enlisted as well as officers are beginning to feel that they are special, better than the society they serve."[134]

Troubling evidence of this distinct military culture is the development within the officer corps of a strong partisan identity. A generation ago, a plurality (46 percent) of military officers considered themselves politically independent. Today that proportion has dropped to a minority (27 percent), while the proportion identifying themselves as Republicans has grown from 33 percent (which was comparable to Republican identification among the general public) to 64 percent.[135] Along with this increasing partisanship comes a reluctance to accept civilian control unconditionally, especially if the officer believes the civilian leader to be wrong. In a recent study, a majority of officers responding expressed the belief that an officer should insist that military views prevail in matters relating to the use of force and should resign in protest if they do not. As the same study pointed out, this view goes against American tradition:

> In the U.S. military there is no tradition of resignation in protest of dubious or unwise policies. . . . Union officers could not say in 1862, "We signed on to save the Union, not to free the slaves; we quit." George C. Marshall did not consider resigning in 1942 over the decision to invade North Africa, which he opposed. Resignation accompanied by protest undermines civilian control by giving a whip to the military ("do it our way or else").[136]

A military imbued with a self-conscious identity separate from that of civilian society might, in a time of crisis and in a situation in which it holds civilian leadership in contempt, consider taking an even more dramatic action than resignation in face of a policy with which it disagrees.

Crises in democratic systems always raise the specter of the military intervening directly to overturn democratically determined outcomes. Military coups against democratically elected governments are frequent and are a constant threat in many democratic systems around the world. Fortunately in the United States, the tradition of civilian control of the military and—in spite of the new attitudes toward civilian control just described—the broad support for the ideal of democratic politics in the military make that a relatively remote possibility. Still, although most of us would like to believe that "it can't happen here," prudent democrats ought to think about the potential for some future crisis to stimulate military intervention in domestic affairs. Signs of a growing civilian-military gap and the replacement of a military of citizen-soldiers with a self-consciously moralistic professional force raise a new challenge to our democracy.

Experience in most democratic countries indicates that professional armies are much more threatening to democratic politics in times of crisis than are conscript armies. Soldiers who are draftees, serving in the armed forces for only a short time, are much less likely to identify with their officers sufficiently to obey unconstitutional or undemocratic orders than are soldiers who regard the service as a professional career. That a conscript army is less likely to cooperate in a military coup than a professional one was illustrated in an attempt to overthrow the democratically elected French government in 1961.[137] In that year, a group of army officers rebelled against their government, in opposition to President Charles de Gaulle's intention to grant independence to Algeria, where the French army had been fighting a guerrilla insurrection for nearly a decade. The officers' plan was to consolidate control of Algiers and then to parachute into Paris and capture de Gaulle. In the first few hours, the plan went smoothly, as hardened professional paratroopers joined their rebellion. Soon, however, it ran into trouble because most of the draftees—the bulk of the army—refused to go along with the plot. Within hours of its start, the coup collapsed. The outcome would have been much different had the French army in Algeria been an all-volunteer force that shared its officers' contempt for political leadership. French democracy might have come to an abrupt end.

My intention in raising the example of the French experience is not to suggest that our professional army poses a direct threat to democracy. In the French situation, a particular history and the particular dynamics of the Algerian crisis produced the attempted coup. In addition, the willingness of French professional soldiers, as opposed to draftees, to participate in the overthrow of their government does not mean that American professional soldiers would react in the same way. What the French case suggests, however, is that if we are to have a large, all-professional military, we need to look out for the possibility that such an army might behave undemocratically in a crisis. To guard against that possibility, we need to devise measures to ensure our professional soldiers' continued loyalty to democratic values. We need also to think continually about institutional checks to ensure continued civilian control and to prevent military distortion of democratic processes. The armed forces, if they act in a unified way, are the only societal institution capable of eliminating democratic institutions in one blow. Democrats would be foolish to rely solely on the goodwill of soldiers for the survival of democracy.

Meeting the Challenge: Reform to Achieve True Security

Everyone agrees that the international security environment in which we live has changed dramatically in recent years. Even before the terrorist attacks of 9/11, the end of the Cold War had altered the way that the American nation interacted with the rest of the world. The United States is, overwhelmingly, the predominant power in the world—economically, politically, and militarily. As is documented in this chapter, no other nation-state even comes close to posing a significant challenge, let alone a threat, to American dominance. Nevertheless, the world is no longer a stable or a reliably safe place either for Americans or for the other peoples of the world. As 9/11 brought home to Americans, and as myriad intractable conflicts throughout the world bring home to their victims every day, the pressures of globalization; unfulfilled ethnic, national, and democratic aspirations; religious strife; and competition for resources foster a multitude of violent conflicts. As the predominant power, the United States often becomes the focus of the anger and hostility of those caught up in these many conflicts, and that fact makes national security as legitimate a concern for Americans as it was during the Cold War.

The national security state developed to fight the Cold War is increasingly unsuited to the conflicts it is likely to confront in this new security environment. Unfortunately, however, most of its institutions remain in place, along with their undemocratic aspects. The most important way to meet the challenge that today's national security state poses is to reform it to make it better address the kinds of security threats we face today and at the same time ensure that it reflects America's democratic values. Long-run success in making America secure will depend more on diplomatic, political, and economic measures that can weaken terrorist organizations and reduce the resentment of American power that fuels their hostility. To forge more nonmilitary instruments to promote national security, the Obama administration will have to overcome the legacy of the George W. Bush administration's hostility to international cooperation and the decline in American prestige around the world. Making the national security state more democratic by reducing its undemocratic defects—secrecy, centralization, repression, and distortion—will only improve its ability to respond effectively to our new security needs. As was argued earlier, democracy produces the best policy because it brings issues into the light for open discussion and deliberation. The knowledge and wisdom of all Americans will be needed to find the best ways to address the security concerns of today's world.

Among the many measures needed to democratize and reform the national security state, the following five seem to me crucial:

First, the five-decade drift toward centralization of war-making power in one man, the president, needs to be reversed. Too many Americans, including members of Congress and the news media, have acquiesced in the notion that the president alone can make the decision to go to war. In fact many Americans, even educated ones, seem to believe that the Constitution gives the president such power. Constitutional scholar Louis Fisher recounts his astonishment when, at a talk on war powers, a second-year law student demanded, "'Doesn't the Constitution give the president the power to declare war, subject to the advice and consent of the Senate?'"[138] When even those who profess to study the law can hold such erroneous ideas, a crucial step toward constraining presidential war power must be educating the public on what the Constitution actually says:

- The Congress shall have Power . . .
- To define and punish Piracies and Felonies committed on the high Seas, and Offences against the Law of Nations;
- To declare War, grant Letters of Marque and Reprisal, and make Rules concerning Captures on Land and Water;
- To raise and support Armies . . . ;
- To provide and maintain a Navy;
- To make Rules for the Government and Regulation of the land and naval Forces . . . (Article I, section 8)

In lodging the power to declare war in Congress, not the executive, the framers sought to ensure that there would be democratic deliberation among the people's representatives before the nation committed to war. There must be more discussion in classrooms, in the media, and in Congress itself about the value of such deliberation and the need for preventing the president from acting alone in matters of war and peace.

Under the separation of powers system, if the president is to be constrained and if decisions about war are to be publicly debated, the US Congress must be assertive in demanding its institutional prerogative to declare war. Its power extends beyond mere consultation. Presidents should be required not merely to consult with Congress before committing forces to battle but, except in true emergencies, to seek congressional authorization before acting—preferably a formal declaration of war.[139] For this reassertion of congressional authority to occur, members of Congress themselves must insist on restoration of their constitutional prerogative. In the recent past, too many have been so concerned about appearing unpatriotic in questioning presidential war plans that they have allowed the crucial power to declare war to slip from their hands. In addition, Congress needs to use its power of the purse and statutory oversight authority to rein in the president by threatening to deny funds for presidentially initiated military operations, rather than, as it has done in the past, meekly acquiescing to actions it does not fully endorse, only because it fears criticism for failing to support "our boys in uniform." As long as presidents know that members of Congress will be unwilling to withhold support when coerced in this way, they will have a free hand to place US troops in harm's way without concern for support from the people's representatives. When it comes to the war power, Congress holds the key to subjecting the president to democratic control.[140]

Crucial to more congressional power over foreign policy is less secrecy in national security matters. Congress must ensure that the ability of the executive branch to classify information is limited to matters that clearly must be kept secret. The broad powers granted to many agencies and individuals to create secrets must be curbed. President Obama should establish a national declassification center, something his campaign endorsed, to facilitate the process of declassifying government documents.[141] Only with less secrecy can Congress and the broader public participate effectively in guiding national security policy. As I have argued, broader scrutiny of the information and premises that inform national security policy will enhance the effectiveness of policy rather than impede it. Moreover, tighter restrictions on secrecy will constrain the natural tendency of officials to use it to hide their policy failures. The national security state can be held democratically accountable only if the public and its representatives possess the information needed to do so.

Second, the military-industrial complex that developed during the Cold War continues to distort national security policy, and it should be dismantled. The institutional bias in favor of expensive and nonessential weapons systems prevents the development of sensible security policies, including appropriate military strategies, for addressing current security challenges. Since World War II, the defense industry has been central to the US economy; millions of Americans depend on defense spending for their jobs and standard of living. As a result, domestic economic concerns rather than genuine security needs drive too much weapons development and associated strategy. Both reducing democracy's peril and formulating more appropriate security policies now require reducing the economy's dependence on the production of armaments.

Dismantling our militarized economy, however, must be done carefully. Because so many depend on defense jobs, careful attention must be given to the conversion to civilian production of industries now devoted to manufacturing expensive weapons systems. Without effective conversion plans, former defense workers will exert political pressure to maintain the national security state and its massive defense industry. The post–World War II alliance of defense industrialists, their workers, the military, security services, and defense intellectuals will conjure up new plans for expensive weapons systems such as a space-based missile defense. Such ruinous developments may be prevented if the defense industry can be converted to nonmilitary production. To do that will require a systematic industrial policy encouraging the development of such new domestic projects as high-speed rail systems or alternative energy systems rather than new generations of military hardware. The rapid dismantling of our Cold War economy might thus not only reduce democracy's peril but also have positive effects on the economy and standard of living of most Americans. Freeing workers from building unneeded tanks, fighter jets, and missiles, so that they can rebuild our economic infrastructure, would make the United States both more prosperous and more democratic.

Third, we need to revive the concept of the citizen-soldier.[142] The most straightforward way to do that would be to reintroduce the draft—most likely in the context of mandatory national service. All young Americans, men and women, between the ages of eighteen and twenty-five would be required to serve for eighteen months in the military, in homeland security, or in Americorps. In return for such national service, Congress could offer substantial college scholarships modeled on the GI Bill, with larger awards for those who opt for military service.[143] If these incentives did not produce sufficient numbers to meet military needs, unfilled military slots could be filled by means of a lottery. Such a system of mandatory service, with military assignments by lottery if needed, would eliminate the unfairness typical of the Vietnam era, when privileged students avoided the draft through a complicated system of deferments and exemptions. Renewing the draft for eighteen-month tours of duty would not eliminate the need for a core of volunteer professional soldiers serving longer enlistments to handle jobs demanding specialized tactical training and experience. But four to six months of training would allow draftees to handle many of the less-skilled jobs, such as guard duty, truck driving, or even some forms of combat. Soldiers in wars from World War II to Vietnam learned necessary combat skills within brief training periods.[144] Such a draft military would close the civilian-military gap, re-create a military that more closely mirrors society, and require the privileged to sacrifice for their country.

A key component of this return to a more citizen-based army should be an expansion of the Reserve Officers Training Corps (ROTC) on college campuses. During the Vietnam War, many colleges and universities eliminated their ROTC programs as a gesture of protest against the war. This wrongheaded response deprived many young people of access to the officer corps while they were completing their undergraduate education, and it denied the military the talents of these same young people. In this context, it is important to remember that drawing military officers from ROTC programs is conducive to reducing the growing gap between the civilian and military cultures. As products of a largely civilian educational system, ROTC officers bring different values and perspectives to the military than do those trained at the military academies. And the presence on campus of the students, faculty, and coursework of an ROTC program offers all students some degree of contact with the military culture.[145] In addition, the opportunity to study military history and strategy can increase understanding of military affairs, which is of importance to all democratic citizens. If the national security state is to be democratized, all citizens need to be more aware of military issues, and ROTC programs help to increase that awareness.

Fourth, future presidents must renounce the idea of preemptive, unilateral American military action, as exemplified in the Bush Doctrine, and instead rebuild the networks of international cooperation. After World War II, the United States was the chief architect of international institutions such as the United Nations, as well as of the growing body of international law aimed at restraining violations of human rights and aggressive military action. International law and institutions have served American interests well, while advancing human rights and justice around the world. The notion embedded in the ethos of the national security state is that America, basically alone, can guarantee world order. But in an international context of nearly two hundred sovereign states and myriad complex problems, such an approach can only lead to a weakening of American power and democracy. George W. Bush's radical repudiation of the traditional American support for international law and organizations endangers global stability and American security.[146] President Obama promised in his campaign a renewed commitment to diplomacy and international cooperation in American foreign policy, but many of his actions in office show a temptation, like his predecessors, to project military power unilaterally in the name of foreign policy objectives he deems desirable.

Finally, American foreign policy must be infused with democratic values and dedicated to promoting them. Too often during the Cold War, American policymakers supported repressive regimes around the world in the name of combating communism. Repressive dictators sometimes were considered more reliable allies than the democratic leaders whose loyalty to American priorities might waver. The temptation to rely on similarly nondemocratic allies in the war on terrorism must be resisted. The best policy for combating terrorism around the world is to promote democracy everywhere. Every one of the nineteen terrorists who commandeered the four planes on September 11th came from a country without democratic government. If we are to make the world safe from terrorism, we must work to eliminate the conditions that create terrorists. This effort will not be primarily a military one, but instead will require diplomatic efforts, economic assistance, and international cooperation. It will mean cultivating democratic forces everywhere, while also making sure that the United States of America remains, as it was when it was founded, an inspiration to all who believe in democracy. Working to meet the challenges that confront our own democracy will keep it so.

Thought Questions

1. Is too much secrecy necessarily a problem in a democracy? In what ways might open political debate place democracies at a disadvantage in international politics?

2. Chapter 1 argues that the separation of powers allows too little centralization of policy making in our government, but this chapter argues that when it comes to foreign policy, too much control has been centralized in the hands of the president. How can these arguments be reconciled, or can they?

3. Do you think Americans should give up some civil liberties, as in the examples mentioned in this chapter, to protect the country from terrorism? If yes, what liberties do you think it appropriate to sacrifice for the purpose? If no, how would you prevent terrorists from taking advantage of a free society to threaten the country?

4. Using the list under Selected Websites at the end of this chapter, follow up the status of a weapons system mentioned in the chapter, such as the F-35 Joint Strike Fighter jet, the Crusader artillery system, or the Osprey aircraft. What is its current status? Who is currently supporting it and who opposing? Is it likely to be canceled or ultimately produced?

5. America's professionalized, volunteer armed forces are presented in this chapter as a problem for democracy. However, in one respect—that of racial integration and equality—the US Army has long been more democratic than the rest of American society. How might the professional and even authoritarian character of the army have led it to promote integration?

6. Would you favor the revival of a military draft, as advocated in this chapter's conclusion? Why or why not? If you oppose the draft, would you volunteer to serve in the armed forces or leave such service to others? Why or why not?

Suggestions for Further Reading

Bacevich, Andrew J. *The New American Militarism: How Americans Are Seduced by War.* Oxford: Oxford University Press, 2005. A devastating critique of how Americans have allowed their foreign policy and their entire society to become highly militarized.

Clifford, Clark. *Counsel to the President: A Memoir.* New York: Random House, 1991. A thoughtful memoir by one of the architects of the national security state.

Fisher, Louis. *Congressional Abdication on War and Spending.* College Station: Texas A&M University Press, 2000. In this and the following book, America's leading scholar of presidential congressional relations details how presidents have come to make war unilaterally. He makes a well-documented argument that they have done so unconstitutionally.

———. *Presidential War Power.* 2nd ed. Lawrence: University Press of Kansas, 2004.

Halperin, Morton H., Jerry J. Berman, Robert L. Borosage, and Christine M. Marwick. *The Lawless State: The Crimes of the U.S. Intelligence Agencies.* New York: Penguin Books, 1976. A summary of the findings of the various investigations of the national security state, including the Church Committee's, conducted in the 1970s.

Hartung, William D. *Prophets of War: Lockheed Martin and the Making of the Military-Industrial Complex.* New York: Nation Books, 2011. A look at how one major arms manufacturer distorts American defense policy to assure itself steady profits.

Johnson, Chalmers. *The Sorrows of Empire: Militarism, Secrecy, and the End of the Republic.* New York: Henry Holt, 2004. A description and critique of how America acquired an empire.

*Kaplan, Robert D. *Imperial Grunts: The American Military on the Ground.* New York: Random House, 2005. A celebration of America's empire and the professional soldiers who protect it.

*Lord, Carnes. *The Presidency and the Management of National Security.* New York: Free Press, 1988. Lord, who served on the National Security Council staff during the Reagan years, argues here for greater centralization of presidential foreign policy power.

Mayer, Jane. *The Dark Side: The Inside Story of How the War on Terror Turned Into a War on American Ideals.* New York: Doubleday, 2008. A top-notch reporter documents the George W. Bush administration's excesses in the war on terror.

Packer, George. *The Assassins' Gate: America in Iraq.* New York: Farrar, Straus and Giroux, 2005. How a small circle of decision makers got the United States into Iraq and created a quagmire.

*Revel, Jean-François. *How Democracies Perish.* New York: Harper & Row, 1985. According to this author, democratic regimes are disadvantaged in their ability to conduct effective foreign policy.

Schlesinger, Arthur M., Jr. *The Imperial Presidency.* Boston: Houghton Mifflin, 1973. The classic study of the aggrandizement of presidential power over foreign and defense policy.

Theoharis, Athan G., and John Stuart Cox. *The Boss: J. Edgar Hoover and the Great American Inquisition.* Philadelphia: Temple University Press, 1988. A biography that reflects the numerous ways in which the FBI was used to violate the political and civil rights of Americans.

White, John Kenneth. *Still Seeing Red: How the Cold War Shapes the New American Politics.* Boulder, CO: Westview Press, 1997. A thoughtful analysis of the Cold War's continuing impact on all aspects of American politics.

*Presents points of view that disagree with the arguments presented in this chapter.

Selected Websites

www.cfr.org. The Council on Foreign Relations is one of the oldest and most prestigious of nongovernmental foreign policy organizations.

www.comw.org/pda. The Project of Defense Alternatives seeks to "adapt military policy to the opportunities of the new era."

www.csis.org. An influential think tank that provides support to the national security state.

Notes

Introduction: Models of Democracy

1. The models are based on those presented in C. B. Macpherson, *The Life and Times of Liberal Democracy* (Oxford: Oxford University Press, 1977). The names of some of the models and the descriptions of them differ from Macpherson's in several respects. Readers interested in Macpherson's more complete analysis are encouraged to read his book. Similar models are employed in David Held, *Models of Democracy* (Stanford, CA: Stanford University Press, 1996). Held draws as well on Macpherson, but he identifies a total of *nine* distinct models in democratic theory.

2. Ted C. Lewellen, *Political Anthropology: An Introduction* (South Hadley, MA: Bergin & Garvey, 1983), 18–29.

3. John V. A. Fine, *The Ancient Greeks: A Critical History* (Cambridge, MA: Harvard University Press, 1983), 383–441.

4. Held, *Models of Democracy,* 20–23.

5. Plato discusses democracy as part of his typology of governments in the *Republic* (London: Penguin, 1974). Aristotle's discussion of democracy can be found in *Politics* (London: Penguin, 1969), 115–16, 154–55. For a summary of the basic values of Greek democracy, Pericles' famous Funeral Oration is the classic source. It is reported in Thucydides' *The Peloponnesian War* (London: Penguin, 1972).

6. Held, *Models of Democracy,* 23.

7. Ibid.

8. Ibid., 14.

9. Montesquieu, *The Spirit of the Laws,* ed. David Wallace Carrithers (Berkeley: University of California Press, 1977), 176–77.

10. Jean-Jacques Rousseau, *The Social Contract* (London: Penguin, 1968).

11. The concept of representation itself antedated the American and French Revolutions. Many polities used representative assemblies prior to the late eighteenth century, but these earlier bodies, like the Roman Senate or the English Parliament, provided representation only to an elite portion of citizens. The assemblies instituted in the new French and American polities were different in that they were intended to represent the entire democratic citizenry. For a brief discussion of the history of representation, see Robert Dahl, *On Democracy* (New Haven, CT: Yale University Press, 1998), 22–25, 104–5.

12. *The Federalist,* ed. Jacob E. Cooke (Cleveland, OH: Meridian, 1967), 56–65.

13. The views of John Locke discussed here can be found in his *Second Treatise on Government* (Indianapolis, IN: Bobbs-Merrill, 1953); Hobbes's famous political work is *Leviathan* (Indianapolis, IN: Bobbs-Merrill, 1958).

14. Plato's *Republic* is an example of an earlier political theory that posits the "good" as the goal of political society.

15. Locke, *Second Treatise on Government,* 71.

16. Michael Margolis, *Viable Democracy* (London: Penguin, 1979), 32.

17. J. Samuel Valenzuela and Arturo Valenzuela, *Military Rule in Chile* (Baltimore, MD: Johns Hopkins University Press, 1986).

18. C. B. Macpherson, *The Political Theory of Possessive Individualism* (Oxford: Oxford University Press, 1962), 248.

19. These models are based on those found in Macpherson's *Life and Times of Liberal Democracy.* I have called Macpherson's "Equilibrium Democracy," "Pluralist Democracy."

20. Ibid., 34.

21. Ibid., 36.

22. *The Federalist,* 57.

23. Macpherson, *Life and Times of Liberal Democracy,* 48.

24. John Dewey, "Democracy as a Way of Life," in *Frontiers of Democratic Theory,* ed. Henry S. Kariel (New York: Random House, 1970), 14–15.

25. Ibid., 13–14. See also Ernest Barker, "Democracy as Activity," in *Frontiers of Democratic Theory,* ed. Henry S. Kariel (New York: Random House, 1970), 7.

26. John Stuart Mill, *Considerations on Representative Government* (Indianapolis, IN: Bobbs-Merrill, 1958), 55.

27. Alexis de Tocqueville, *Democracy in America* (Garden City, NY: Doubleday, 1969), 60.

28. The essential works by the authors presenting this argument are Roberto Michels, *Political Parties: A Sociological Study of the Oligarchical Tendencies of Modern Democracy* (New York: Dover, 1959); Gaetano Mosca, *The Ruling Class* (New York: McGraw-Hill, 1939); and Vilfredo Pareto, *The Rise and Fall of Elites* (Totowa, NJ: Bedminster Press, 1968).

29. Bernard Berelson, Paul Lazarsfeld, and William McPhee, *Voting* (Chicago: University of Chicago Press, 1954).

30. Ibid., 314.

31. Joseph Schumpeter, *Capitalism, Socialism, and Democracy,* 3rd ed. (New York: Harper & Bros., 1950), 269.

32. The best exposition of the democratic function of interest groups remains David Truman, *The Governmental Process* (New York: Knopf, 1952).

33. Robert Dahl, *Dilemmas of Pluralist Democracy* (New Haven, CT: Yale University Press, 1982).

34. For a thorough analysis of the events surrounding the writing of the Port Huron Statement and a thoughtful analysis of it, see James E. Miller, *Democracy Is in the Streets* (New York: Simon & Schuster, 1987). The complete text of the Port Huron Statement is included as an appendix in Miller's book.

35. There are a number of edited collections of the relevant articles. One of the best collections is Kariel, *Frontiers of Democratic Theory,* which includes important articles

by the leading participants in the exposition of more Participatory alternatives to Pluralist Democracy, such as Jack L. Walker, Steven Lukes, Peter Bachrach, Morton Baratz, and Christian Bay.

36. David Held, *Models of Democracy*, 3rd ed. (Cambridge, UK: Polity Press, 2006).

37. Joseph M. Bessette, *The Mild Voice of Reason: Deliberative Democracy and American National Government* (Chicago: University of Chicago Press, 1994).

38. James S. Fishkin, *Democracy and Deliberation: New Directions for Political Reform* (New Haven, CT: Yale University Press, 1991).

39. An example of such impatience was the Iran-*contra* affair during Ronald Reagan's administration. Several National Security Council officials, including Admiral John Poindexter and Lieutenant Colonel Oliver North, preferred to find illegal means to fund the *contras,* a group of Nicaraguans fighting the Sandinista government, rather than concentrate on convincing Congress of the need for such funding. See chapter 8 for more details.

Chapter 1: Separation of Powers

1. For a history of Americans' reverential regard for the Constitution, see Michael Kammen, *A Machine That Would Go of Itself* (New York: Knopf, 1986).

2. Gordon Wood, "Democracy and the Constitution," in *How Democratic Is the Constitution?*, ed. Robert Goldwin and William Schambra (Washington, DC: American Enterprise Institute, 1980), 12. For a detailed discussion of these state legislatures, see Wood's *The Creation of the American Republic, 1776–1787* (Chapel Hill: University of North Carolina Press, 1969).

3. James L. Sundquist, *Constitutional Reform and Effective Government* (Washington, DC: Brookings Institution, 1986), 19.

4. Max Farrand, ed., *The Records of the Federal Convention of 1787* (New Haven, CT: Yale University Press, 1966), 1: 26–27.

5. The classic attack on the elitist character of the founding is Charles Beard, *An Economic Interpretation of the Constitution* (New York: Macmillan, 1913). The now-classic critiques of Beard's view are Robert E. Brown, *Charles Beard and the Constitution* (Princeton, NJ: Princeton University Press, 1956); and Forrest McDonald, *We the People* (Chicago: University of Chicago Press, 1958).

6. Alexander Hamilton, John Jay, and James Madison, *The Federalist,* ed. Jacob E. Cooke (Cleveland, OH: Meridian, 1961), 349.

7. James MacGregor Burns, *The Deadlock of Democracy* (Englewood Cliffs, NJ: Prentice Hall, 1963), 36.

8. Sarah A. Binder, *Stalemate: Causes and Consequences of Legislative Gridlock* (Washington, DC: Brookings Institution, 2003), 81.

9. Alfred Stepan and Juan J. Linz, "Comparative Perspectives on Inequality and the Quality of Democracy in the United States," *Perspectives on Politics* 9 (December 2011): 844.

10. James L. Sundquist, "Needed: A Political Theory for the New Era of Coalition Government in the United States," *Political Science Quarterly* 103 (Winter 1988–1989): 613–36.

11. A thorough review of the political science literature seeking to explain divided government can be found in Morris Fiorina, *Divided Government* (New York: Macmillan, 1991).

12. Walter De Vries and V. Lance Tarrance, *The Ticket-Splitter: A New Force in American Politics* (Grand Rapids, MI: Eerdmans, 1972).

13. Gary C. Jacobson, *The Electoral Origins of Divided Government* (Boulder, CO: Westview Press, 1990), 105–36.

14. This logic applied to the creation of a bicameral legislature as well as the separation of powers. James L. Sundquist describes the famous breakfast meeting at which George Washington explained it to Thomas Jefferson: "When Jefferson asked why a second legislative chamber had been created, Washington asked, 'Why did you pour your coffee into your saucer?' 'To cool it,' Jefferson answered. 'Even so,' said Washington, 'we pour legislation into the senatorial saucer to cool it.'" Sundquist, *Constitutional Reform,* 22.

15. Ann Stuart Diamond, "Decent, Even Though Democratic," in *How Democratic Is the Constitution?,* ed. Robert A. Goldwin and William Schambra (Washington, DC: American Enterprise Institute, 1980), 37.

16. Americans are less satisfied with their health care system than are citizens of most other industrialized nations. Erik Eckholm, "Rescuing Health Care," *New York Times,* May 2, 1991, B12.

17. Theodore R. Marmor, *The Politics of Medicare* (Chicago: Aldine, 1973).

18. Camen, DeNavas-Walt, Bernadette D. Proctor, and Jessica Smith, *Income, Poverty, and Health Insurance Coverage in the United States: 2006,* U.S. Census Bureau Current Population Reports (Washington, DC: Government Printing Office, 2007), 18.

19. Theodore Lowi, "Constitutional Merry-Go-Round: The First Time Tragedy, the Second Time Farce," in *Constitutional Stupidities, Constitutional Tragedies,* ed. William N. Eskridge Jr. and Sanford Levinson (New York: NYU Press, 1998), 195.

20. Stepan and Linz, "Comparative Perspectives," 846.

21. Throughout the spring and summer of 1993, the press provided numerous accounts of the resistance Clinton faced from his own party. For a few examples of such articles, see Adam Clymer, "Single-Minded President," *New York Times,* April 3, 1993, 1; David E. Rosenbaum, "Clinton and Allies Twist Arms in Bid for Budget Votes," *New York Times,* May 27, 1993, 1; Rosenbaum, "Clinton Facing Threat of Revolt on Budget Plan," *New York Times,* July 28, 1993, 1; and Michael Wines, "The Joy of Being Undecided: Senators Bask in the Lights," *New York Times,* August 7, 1993, 1.

22. David E. Rosenbaum, "Congress Adopts Budget Proposal With Big Tax Cut," *New York Times,* May 11, 2001, A1.

23. David W. Brady and Craig Volden, *Revolving Gridlock: Politics and Policy From Jimmy Carter to George W. Bush,* 2nd ed. (Boulder, CO: Westview Press, 2006), 171–82.

24. Barbara Sinclair, "Congressional Leadership in Obama's First Two Years," in *Obama in Office,* ed. James Thurber (Boulder, CO: Paradigm Press, 2011), 89.

25. John E. Owens, "A 'Post-Partisan' President in a Partisan Context," in *Obama in Office,* 115.
26. M. Stephen Weatherford, "Economic Crisis and Political Change: A New New Deal?," in *The Obama Presidency: Appraisals and Prospects,* ed. Bert A. Rockman et al. (Washington, DC: CQ Press, 2012), 307.
27. Ibid., 307.
28. Ezra Klein, "Obama's Flunking Economy: The Real Cause," review of *Confidence Men: Wall Street, Washington, and the Education of a President,* by Ron Suskind, *New York Review of Books,* November 24, 2011, 12.
29. This account follows Tom Daschle, *Getting It Done: How Obama and Congress Finally Broke the Stalemate to Make Way for Health Care Reform* (New York: St. Martin's, 2010).
30. Barbara Sinclair, "Doing Big Things: Obama and the 112th Congress," in *The Obama Presidency: Appraisals and Prospects,* ed. Bert A. Rockman, Andrew Rudalevige, and Colin Campbell (Washington, DC: CQ Press, 2011), 208.
31. Jacobson, "Polarization, Public Opinion, and the Presidency," in *The Obama Presidency,* 109.
32. Sinclair, "Doing Big Things," 212.
33. Jacobson, "Polarization, Public Opinion," 95–96.
34. Brady and Volden, *Revolving Gridlock,* 206–7.
35. This description of the 2003 prescription drug legislation follows two accounts of the process: Brady and Volden, *Revolving Gridlock,* 184–88; and Jacob S. Hacker and Paul Pierson, *Off Center: The Republican Revolution and the Erosion of American Democracy* (New Haven, CT: Yale University Press, 2005), 85–93.
36. Paul Krugman, "The Deadly Doughnut," *New York Times,* November 11, 2005, A25.
37. Ibid.
38. Lori Montgomery et al., "Origins of the Debt Showdown," *Washington Post,* August 6, 2011.
39. Jonathan Chait, "Block Party," *The New Republic,* August 18, 2011, 2.
40. Damian Paletta and Matt Phillips, "S&P Strips US of top Credit Rating," *Wall Street Journal,* August 7, 2011, http://online.wsj.com/article/SB10001424053111903366504576491421339802788.html?mod=WSJ_hp_LEFTTopStories
41. Jeff Zeleny and Megan Thee-Brenan, "New Poll Finds a Deep Distrust of Government," *New York Times,* October 25, 2011, A1.
42. Eric Lipton, "Lawmakers Trade Blame as Deficit Talks Crumble," *New York Times,* November 21, 2011, A1.
43. In doing so, they were behaving no differently than they had in the previous decade, as argued in Morris Fiorina, "The Decline of Collective Responsibility in American Politics," *Daedalus* 109 (Summer 1980): 25–45.
44. Even the remarkable Republican capture, for the first time in forty years, of majorities in both the House and the Senate did not alter the power of incumbency. The new Republican majorities came about through the capture of "open" seats, where no incumbent was running. Incumbents, in fact, did quite well in 1994, winning reelection 91 percent of the time in the House and 92 percent in the Senate. Thomas Patterson, *We the People,* updated ed. (New York: McGraw-Hill, 1996), 344.

45. Kathleen Sullivan, "Madison Got It Backward," *New York Times,* February 16, 1999, A19.
46. The account of the S&L scandal follows that found in L. J. Davis, "Chronicle of a Debacle Foretold: How Deregulation Begat the S&L Scandal," *Atlantic Monthly,* September 1990, 50–66.
47. Ibid., 66.
48. The following account is based on Stephen Labaton, "Now Who, Exactly, Got Us Into This?," *New York Times,* February 3, 2002, sec. 3, 1.
49. Sean Wilentz, "A Scandal for Our Time," *American Prospect,* February 25, 2002, 20–22.
50. Leslie Wayne, "Enron, Preaching Deregulation, Worked the Statehouse Circuit," *New York Times,* February 9, 2002, B1.
51. Stephen Labaton, "Exemption Won in '97 Set Stage for Enron Woes," *New York Times,* January 23, 2002, A1.
52. Richard Oppel Jr., with Kurt Eichenwald, "Arthur Andersen Fires an Executive for Enron Orders," *New York Times,* January 16, 2002, A1.
53. This account follows that in Robert Kuttner, *The Squandering of America: How the Failure of Our Politics Undermines Our Prosperity* (New York: Knopf, 2008), 133–37.
54. The European system that comes closest to the American system is that of France. Its Fifth Republic constitution provides for both a president and a prime minister, with the president possessing independent powers over foreign affairs. Since 1958, however, when the constitution took effect, the same party has controlled both branches of government except in three brief periods (1986–1988, 1993–1995, and 1997–2002). In each of these periods, in what the French call "cohabitation," the government headed by the prime minister had, save for some consultation with the president, complete control of domestic policy and enacted his party's program into law. This was the case when Gaullist Prime Minister Jacques Chirac served in conjunction with Socialist President François Mitterrand from 1986 to 1988, and also when Socialist Prime Minister Lionel Jospin served in cohabitation with President Chirac between 1997 and 2001. In practice, the French system has operated more like a parliamentary system than a separation of powers system, even in periods of cohabitation. For more detail, see Vincent Wright, *The Government and Politics of France* (New York: Holmes & Meier, 1989), 76–98; see also Mark Kesselman et al., *European Politics in Transition,* 3rd ed. (Boston: Houghton Mifflin, 1997), 180–88.
55. This possibility is intriguingly explored in Joy E. Esberey, "What If There Were a Parliamentary System?," in *What If the American Political System Were Different?,* ed. Herbert M. Levine (Armonk, NY: M. E. Sharpe, 1992), 95–148.
56. Alan Cowell, "Impeachment: What a Royal Pain," *New York Times,* February 7, 1999, Week in Review, 5.
57. Guilt or innocence would, of course, come into play as a factor in determining the political viability of a prime minister suspected of criminal behavior. Under a parliamentary system, however, the legislature is not forced to perform the awkward quasi-judicial role that Congress must undertake in impeachment procedures—making, itself, a determination of guilt or innocence. In a parliamentary system, strong evidence of criminal conduct would most likely lead to resignation or removal of the

suspected minister—otherwise the party might suffer at the next election—but the truth of a criminal accusation would be, more appropriately, determined in court. Furthermore, depending on the circumstances, nothing would prevent a minister exonerated in a court trial from returning to active government service.

58. Two political scientists come to this same conclusion after a comprehensive empirical survey of presidential (separation of powers) and parliamentary systems worldwide. See Alfred Stepan and Cindy Skach, "Constitutional Frameworks and Democratic Consolidation: Parliamentarism Versus Presidentialism," *World Politics* 46 (October 1993): 1–22.

59. Alfred Stepan, *Arguing Comparative Politics* (Oxford: Oxford University Press, 2001), 156.

60. Fred W. Riggs, "Presidentialism: A Problematic Regime Type," in *Parliamentary Versus Presidential Government,* ed. Arend Lijphardt (Oxford: Oxford University Press, 1992), 218–19.

61. Robert Dahl, *Democracy and Its Critics* (New Haven, CT: Yale University Press, 1990), 155.

62. Ibid., 156.

63. Burns, *Deadlock of Democracy,* 40–41.

64. James Q. Wilson, "Does the Separation of Powers Still Work?," *Public Interest,* Winter 1987, 50.

65. For a more complete account of this failure, see William Hudson, *The Libertarian Illusion: Ideology, Public Policy, and the Assault on the Common Good* (Washington, DC: CQ Press, 2008), 119–52.

66. The list of books documenting Bush administration abuses has grown long. Two carefully researched and fair-minded accounts are, by a former official in the Bush Justice Department, Jack Goldsmith, *The Terror Presidency* (New York: Norton, 2007); and by *New Yorker* writer Jane Mayer, *The Dark Side: The Inside Story of How the War on Terror Turned Into a War on American Ideals* (New York: Doubleday, 2008).

67. Leon D. Epstein, "Organizing the Government: Political Parties," in *Mr. Madison's Constitution and the Twenty-First Century: A Report From the Project '87 Conference, Williamsburg, Virginia, October 1987* (Washington, DC: American Political Science Association, 1988), 20.

68. Some of the greatest names in political science have been advocates of strong parties, including one of America's first political scientists, Woodrow Wilson. Some major works advocating strong parties are Austin Ranney, *The Doctrine of Responsible Party Government* (Champaign: University of Illinois Press, 1962); E. E. Schattschneider, *Party Government* (New York: Farrar & Rinehart, 1942); Schattschneider, *The Semi-Sovereign People* (New York: Holt, Rinehart & Winston, 1960); V. O. Key, *Politics, Parties, and Pressure Groups* (New York: Crowell, 1958). For critical reviews of the issue of responsible parties, see Evron M. Kirkpatrick, "Toward a More Responsible Two-Party System: Political Science, Policy Science, or Pseudo-science?," *American Political Science Review,* December 1971, 965–90; Gerald Pomper, "Toward a More Responsible Two-Party System? What, Again?," *Journal of Politics,* November 1971, 916–40.

69. Committee on Political Parties of the American Political Science Association, *Toward a More Responsible Two-Party System* (New York: Rinehart, 1950).
70. Thomas E. Mann and Norman Ornstein, *The Broken Branch: How Congress Is Failing America and How to Get It Back on Track* (New York: Oxford University Press, 2006), 81–82.
71. David Lightman, "Senate Republicans: Filibuster Everything to Win in November?," McClatchy Washington Bureau, February 12, 2010, http://www.mcclatchydc.com/2010/02/12/84487/senate-republicans-filibuster.html.
72. Sundquist has little hope that either of these proposals would necessarily be effective in preventing divided government. See Sundquist, *Constitutional Reform*, 93–98.
73. These proposals can be found in Donald Robinson, ed., *Reforming American Government* (Boulder, CO: Westview Press, 1985).

Chapter 2: The Imperial Judiciary

1. Bruce Ackerman, ed., *Bush v. Gore: The Question of Legitimacy* (New Haven, CT: Yale University Press, 2002) provides several (mostly critical) essays on various aspects of the decision. For a favorable account, see Richard A. Posner, *Breaking the Deadlock: The 2000 Election, the Constitution, and the Courts* (Princeton, NJ: Princeton University Press, 2001).
2. Although federal justices served on the 1876 commission, it was the creation of Congress, not the judiciary.
3. For liberal celebrations of liberal judicial activism, see Ronald Dworkin, *Freedom's Law* (Cambridge, MA: Harvard University Press, 1996); and Peter Irons, *The Courage of Their Convictions* (New York: Free Press, 1988).
4. Mitchell S. Muncy, ed., *The End of Democracy* (Dallas: Spence, 1997).
5. Simon Lazarus, "The Most Dangerous Branch?," *Atlantic Monthly,* June 2002, 24–28.
6. Cass Sunstein, "What We'll Remember in 2050," *Chronicle of Higher Education,* January 5, 2001, 15.
7. Although federal judges are appointed, many judges at the state level gain their posts through elections. In some states, they are elected by state legislatures, and in others, directly by citizens. Forty-two of the states provide for election of at least some state or local judges. Henry J. Abraham, *The Judicial Process,* 5th ed. (Oxford: Oxford University Press, 1993), 34.
8. This example is based on an actual Supreme Court decision in February 2002. The mother of an elementary school student had sued the Owasso, Oklahoma, school district because some of her child's papers had been peer graded and the grades announced to the whole class. The Court ruled that the Family Educational Rights and Privacy Act did not forbid peer grading. Linda Greenhouse, "Practice of Students' Grading Papers Doesn't Violate Privacy Laws," *New York Times,* February 19, 2002, A16.
9. Abraham, *Judicial Process,* 270. Seventy countries give their judiciaries some power of judicial review, but in only six—Australia, Brazil, Canada, India, Pakistan, and Japan—do the courts come close to the power of the American judiciary.

10. John Hart Ely, *Democracy and Distrust: A Theory of Judicial Review* (Cambridge, MA: Harvard University Press, 1980), 4–5.

11. See, for example, Kenneth Janda, Jeffrey M. Berry, and Jerry Goldman, *The Challenge of Democracy*, brief ed. (Boston: Houghton Mifflin, 2001), 279.

12. Ibid.

13. Abraham, *Judicial Process*, 301. See also David O'Brien, *Constitutional Law and Politics*, 4th ed. (New York: Norton, 2003), 2: 23–27.

14. Abraham, *Judicial Process*, 312–14.

15. Alexander Bickel, *The Least Dangerous Branch: The Supreme Court at the Bar of Politics*, 2nd ed. (New Haven, CT: Yale University Press, 1986), 1.

16. O'Brien, *Constitutional Law and Politics*, 2: 31.

17. Albert P. Melone and George Mace, *Judicial Review and American Democracy* (Ames: Iowa University Press, 1988), 52.

18. Ibid., 61–62.

19. O'Brien, *Constitutional Law and Politics*, 2: 31.

20. Abraham, *Judicial Process*, 339.

21. This account follows James M. McPherson, *The Battle Cry of Freedom: The Civil War Era* (Oxford: Oxford University Press, 1988), 170–77.

22. O'Brien, *Constitutional Law and Politics*, 2: 1289–91.

23. Ibid., 2: 255–56.

24. Thanks to my colleague Neil Romans for pointing out this ironic juxtaposition.

25. Charles Hyneman, *The Supreme Court on Trial* (New York: Prentice Hall, 1963), 154.

26. Ralph A. Rossum and G. Alan Tarr, *American Constitutional Law: Cases and Interpretation*, 3rd ed. (New York: St. Martin's, 1991), 233.

27. Alpheus Thomas Mason and Donald Grier Stephenson Jr., *American Constitutional Law*, 13th ed. (New York: Prentice Hall, 2002), 261.

28. Lazarus, "Most Dangerous Branch?," 25.

29. Jeffrey Rosen, "The Unregulated Offensive," *New York Times Magazine*, April 17, 2005.

30. Simon Lazarus, "More Polarizing Than Rehnquist," *The American Prospect*, May 2007, 23–27.

31. Richard A. Posner, "In Defense of Looseness," *The New Republic*, August 27, 2008, 32–35; see also Justice Breyer's critique of the Heller decision in Stephen Breyer, *Making Our Democracy Work* (New York: Knopf, 2010), 164–71.

32. Ronald Dworkin, "The Decision That Threatens Democracy," *New York Review of Books*, May 13, 2010, http://www.nybooks.com/articles/archives/2010/may/13/decision-threatens-democracy/.

33. This history of abortion follows the account in Deborah R. McFarlane and Kenneth J. Meier, *The Politics of Fertility Control* (New York: Chatham House, 2001), 34–38.

34. O'Brien, *Constitutional Law and Politics*, on *Roe v. Wade* (1973), 2: 1237.

35. Michael J. Perry, *We the People: The Fourteenth Amendment and the Supreme Court* (New York: Oxford University Press, 1999), 159.

36. Quoted in ibid., 166.

37. The Court had struck down a commerce clause extension of minimum wage laws to states and cities in 1972 in *National League of Cities v. Usery* but had reversed itself in *Garcia v. San Antonio Municipal Transit Authority* in 1985.
38. Mason and Stephenson, *American Constitutional Law,* 266.
39. Herman Schwartz, "Supreme Court Assault on Federalism Swipes at Women," *Los Angeles Times,* May 21, 2000, M1.
40. Mason and Stephenson, *American Constitutional Law,* on *United States v. Morrison* (2000), 187.
41. Ibid.
42. Ibid.
43. Ibid., 189.
44. Schwartz, "Supreme Court Assault on Federalism."
45. Rachel E. Barkow, "More Supreme Than the Court? The Fall of the Political Question Doctrine and the Rise of Judicial Supremacy," *Columbia Law Review,* March 2002, 302.
46. Ibid.
47. Larry Kramer, "The Supreme Court in Politics," in *The Unfinished Election of 2000,* ed. Jack N. Rakove (New York: Basic Books, 2001), 107.
48. O'Brien, *Constitutional Law and Politics,* 2: 75.
49. Thomas Grey, quoted in Ely, *Democracy and Distrust,* 9.
50. Quoted in O'Brien, *Constitutional Law and Politics,* 2: 79.
51. Quoted in ibid., 2: 81.
52. Quoted in Ely, *Democracy and Distrust,* 11.
53. This example comes from Justice Antonin Scalia, a self-proclaimed strict constructionist and originalist. Quoted in O'Brien, *Constitutional Law and Politics,* 2: 82–83.
54. John F. Stack Jr. and Colton C. Campbell, "The Least Dangerous Branch? The Supreme Court's New Judicial Activism," in *Congress Confronts the Court: The Struggle for Legitimacy and Authority in Lawmaking,* ed. Campbell and Stack (Lanham, MD: Rowman & Littlefield, 2001), 107.
55. David O'Brien, "The Republican War Over 'Judicial Activism,'" in *Congress Confronts the Court,* 76–77. See also Jeffrey A. Segal and Harold J. Spaeth, "Supreme Court 5 Are on Power Trip," *Newsday,* February 21, 2001, A31.
56. O'Brien, "Republican War," 77–78.
57. Ely, *Democracy and Distrust,* 43.
58. See ibid., 43–72, for a thorough review and critique of the sources of fundamental values. See aso O'Brien, "Republican War," 86–96.
59. O'Brien, "Republican War," 93.
60. For a classic articulation of the dangers of relying on the wisdom of elites, see Niccolö Machiavelli, "The People Are Wiser and More Constant Than Princes," from *The Discourses,* excerpted in *Ideals and Ideologies: A Reader,* ed. Terence Ball and Richard Dagger (New York: Longman, 2002), 27–29.
61. Ely, *Democracy and Distrust,* 75–77.
62. Ibid., 105–34.
63. Ibid., 135–79.
64. Linda Greenhouse, "Court Had Rehnquist Initials Intricately Carved on Docket," *New York Times,* July 2, 2002, A1.

65. Quoted in Christopher Wolfe, *Judicial Activism: Bulwark of Freedom or Precarious Security?* (Lanham, MD: Rowman & Littlefield, 1997), 99–100.

66. Robert Kagan, "Adversarial Legalism and American Government," in *The New Politics of Public Policy,* ed. Marc K. Landy and Morton Levin (Baltimore: Johns Hopkins University Press, 1995), 88–118.

67. Ibid., 98–102.

68. Mark Tushnet, "Democracy Versus Judicial Review," *Dissent,* Spring 2005, 59–63.

69. Mark V. Tushnet, *Taking the Constitution Away From the Courts* (Princeton, NJ: Princeton University Press, 1999).

70. Robert Dahl, *How Democratic Is the American Constitution?* (New Haven, CT: Yale University Press, 2002), 153.

71. Stephen G. Breyer, "Our Democratic Constitution" (Harvard University Tanner Lectures on Human Values 2004–2005, Cambridge, MA, November 17–19, 2004). For an expanded treatment of Breyer's views, see his book, *Active Liberty: Interpreting Our Democratic Constitution* (New York: Knopf, 2005).

Chapter 3: Radical Individualism

1. Kay Lehman Schlozman and Sidney Verba, *Injury to Insult: Unemployment, Class, and Political Response* (Cambridge, MA: Harvard University Press, 1979), 191.

2. The army recruiting slogan "An Army of One" similarly reflects the individualist ethos.

3. Samuel P. Huntington, *American Politics: The Promise of Disharmony* (Cambridge, MA: Harvard University Press, 1981), 23–30; see also Seymour Martin Lipset, *The First New Nation* (New York: Basic Books, 1963).

4. Gordon Wood, *The Radicalism of the American Revolution* (New York: Knopf, 1991).

5. Alexis de Tocqueville, *Democracy in America,* ed. J. P. Mayer (New York: Doubleday, 1969), 506–8.

6. Cited in Herbert McClosky and John Zaller, *The American Ethos: Public Attitudes Toward Capitalism and Democracy* (Cambridge, MA: Harvard University Press, 1984), 112–13.

7. Herbert Gans, *Middle American Individualism: Popular Participation and Liberal Democracy* (New York: Oxford University Press, 1988), 2.

8. Mary Ann Glendon, *Rights Talk: The Impoverishment of Political Discourse* (New York: Free Press, 1991), 9.

9. Tocqueville, *Democracy in America,* 506.

10. Ibid., 692.

11. Ibid., 511.

12. Ibid., 287.

13. Robert N. Bellah, Richard Madsen, William M. Sullivan, Ann Swidler, and Steven M. Tipton, *Habits of the Heart: Individualism and Commitment in American Life* (Berkeley: University of California Press, 1985).

14. Ibid., 6.

15. Ibid.

16. Ibid., 6–7.

17. Ibid., 198.

18. Ibid., 206. Bellah also identifies a third conception of politics—"the politics of the nation," related to "high affairs of national life" such as war and peace.
19. Ibid., 200.
20. Ibid., 201.
21. Gans, *Middle American Individualism*, 1–22.
22. Ibid., 71–72.
23. Ibid., 15.
24. Frances Fitzgerald, *Cities on a Hill: A Journey Through Contemporary American Cultures* (New York: Simon & Schuster, 1986).
25. Gerald Marzorati, "From Tocqueville to Perotville," *New York Times*, June 28, 1992, E17.
26. Jane Gross, "In Simi Valley, Defense of a Shared Way of Life," *New York Times*, May 4, 1992, B7.
27. Ibid. Both quotes are from Simi Valley residents.
28. For a thoughtful exposition of the libertarian view, see David Boaz, *Libertarianism: A Primer* (New York: Free Press, 1997).
29. Congressman Paul Ryan's libertarian approach to solving America's fiscal problems can be found on his website: http://www.roadmap.republicans.budget.house.gov/. Ryan, who chairs the House Budget Committee, drew on these ideas in his 2012 budget proposal that passed the House in spring 2011.
30. The 2000 Libertarian presidential candidate, Harry Browne, earned nearly 400,000 votes, coming in fifth in the nationwide popular vote. The Libertarian Party platform offers a précis of extreme radical individualism: "We, the members of the Libertarian Party, challenge the cult of the omnipotent state and defend the rights of the individual. We hold that all individuals have the right to exercise sole dominion over their own lives, and have the right to live in whatever manner they choose, so long as they do not forcibly interfere with the equal right of others to live in whatever manner they choose." Quoted in Lyman Tower Sargent, *Contemporary Political Ideologies: A Comparative Analysis* (Belmont, CA: Wadsworth, 1993), 188–89; for a comprehensive philosophical defense of libertarianism, see Boaz, *Libertarianism: A Primer.*
31. The issue positions of the Libertarian Party can be found at its website: http://www.lp.org/.
32. Paul Brace, *State Government and Economic Performance* (Baltimore: Johns Hopkins University Press, 1993), 9–13.
33. Douglas Preston, *Cities of Gold: A Journey Across the American Southwest in Pursuit of Coronado* (New York: Simon & Schuster, 1992). This fascinating book is only incidentally about cattle ranching. While retracing the route that the Spanish explorer Coronado took in his search for the seven cities of gold, Preston befriends several Arizona ranchers who educate him on the problems related to the use of public grazing land in the West today.
34. It is also possible, sometimes, to solve the problem of the tragedy of the commons by changing a common pool resource into a private one. It is conceivable that the ranchers in this example might choose this solution by fencing off pieces of the common grazing land for each family. The ranchers would then graze their own cattle on

only their own private land and would derive full benefit from wise management of it. Although changing common pool resources into private property can be a solution, it is not always possible or economically desirable. Some common pool resources simply cannot be privatized. Clean air and water are the best examples; they cannot be "fenced." In some cases, even though you might be able to privatize a common pool resource, it would be more desirable not to. This seems to be true with ranching in parts of the American West today. One has to own vast amounts of land to support cattle on open grazing land. The cost to purchase and manage (buying and repairing all that fencing!) so much land is high. For many ranchers, the investment needed to ranch is much lower if common (public) grazing land can be used. Many readily accept collective regulation of their herd sizes rather than bearing the expense of owning private land. In addition, to return to the imaginary case of families on a common grazing land, even if they were to opt to solve their problem through privatization, this would be a *collective* solution—they would have to agree collectively on how to divide the land and formulate a set of laws of private property to govern its ownership. As the republics of the former Soviet Union are now discovering, creating a system of private property where there is none can be a daunting collective endeavor.

35. Isaiah Berlin, *Four Essays on Liberty* (Oxford: Oxford University Press, 1969), 118–72.
36. Robert Putnam, "The Prosperous Community: Social Capital and Public Life," *American Prospect,* Spring 1993, 35–42.
37. Ibid., 36.
38. Ibid.
39. In fact, social capital allows people to overcome even personal animosity on behalf of common tasks. Daniel Kemmis describes how the intense dislike of his mother for a neighbor never got in the way of her working with him in barn raisings on the Montana frontier. See Daniel Kemmis, *Community and the Politics of Place* (Norman: University of Oklahoma Press, 1990).
40. Bellah et al., *Habits of the Heart,* 84.
41. Thomas A. Spragens Jr., "The Limitations of Libertarianism, Part II," *Responsive Community,* Spring 1992, 45–47.
42. Glendon, *Rights Talk,* passim.
43. Ibid., 9.
44. Robert Dahl, *On Democracy* (New Haven, CT: Yale University Press, 1998), 48–50.
45. Glendon, *Rights Talk,* 12. This contrasts sharply with Canadian naturalization ceremonies, which emphasize "getting along with one's neighbors."
46. Benjamin R. Barber, "The Reconstruction of Rights," *American Prospect,* Spring 1991, 44.
47. Ibid.
48. Glendon, *Rights Talk,* passim. See also Amitai Etzioni, *The Spirit of Community: Rights, Responsibilities, and the Communitarian Agenda* (New York: Crown, 1993).
49. Etzioni, *Spirit of Community,* 9.
50. Ibid., 3.
51. *College Students Talk Politics,* prepared for the Kettering Foundation by the Harwood Group (Dayton, OH: Kettering Foundation, 1993), 42.

52. Glendon, *Rights Talk*, 47–75.

53. Etzioni, *Spirit of Community*, 3.

54. Glendon, *Rights Talk*, 64–66.

55. This is happening in Missouri and Wisconsin, where pro-life and pro-choice groups are working together to help women with unwanted pregnancies. See Tamar Lewin, "On Common Ground: Pro-life and Pro-choice," *Responsive Community*, Summer 1992, 48–53.

56. David Price, "Our Political Condition," *PS: Political Science and Politics*, December 1992, 682.

57. Quoted in ibid.

58. Jeffrey Goldfarb, *The Cynical Society* (Chicago: University of Chicago Press, 1991), 4–6.

59. Richard Morin and Claudia Dean, "Poll: Americans' Trust in Government Grows: Confidence in Government More Than Doubles Since April 2000," *Washington Post*, September 28, 2001.

60. Robert Putnam, "Bowling Together: The United State of America," *American Prospect*, February 11, 2002, 20–22.

61. Ibid., 22.

62. Quoted in Lawrence F. Kaplan, "American Idle," *New Republic*, September 11, 2005, 21.

63. Kaplan, "American Idle," 21.

64. Quoted in ibid.

65. Kaplan, "American Idle," 21.

66. Ibid., 22.

67. See www.realclearpolitics.com/articles/2008/11/obamas_acceptance_speech.html, November 4, 2008.

68. A call for a new communitarianism is found in Etzioni, *Spirit of Community*, passim.

69. Ibid., 253.

70. Ibid., 231–33.

71. Benjamin Barber, *Strong Democracy: Participatory Politics for a New Age* (Berkeley: University of California Press, 1984), 267–73.

72. Juan Williams, "Japan: A Case of Too Many Responsibilities, Too Few Rights," *Responsive Community*, Spring 1992, 36–42. In Japan, schoolchildren have been bullied by classmates and even killed for being too individualistic and not conforming to group norms. David E. Sanger, "Student's Killing Displays Dark Side of Japan Schools," *New York Times*, April 3, 1993, A1.

Chapter 4: Citizen Participation

1. APSA Standing Committee on Civic Education and Engagement, *Democracy at Risk: Renewing the Political Science of Citizenship* (report presented at the annual meeting of the American Political Science Association, Chicago, September 2–5, 2005).

2. Sidney Verba and Norman Nie, *Participation in America: Political Democracy and Social Equality* (New York: Harper & Row, 1972), 4–5.

3. Quoted in ibid., 5.

4. Alexis de Tocqueville, *Democracy in America* (Garden City, NY: Doubleday/Anchor, 1969), 68–70, 158–63.
5. Jacob E. Cooke, ed., *The Federalist* (Cleveland, OH: Meridian Books, 1961), 62.
6. Seymour Martin Lipset, *Political Man* (Baltimore: Johns Hopkins University Press, 1981), 87–126.
7. International Institute for Democracy and Electoral Assistance (IDEA), Voter Turnout website: http://www.idea.int/vt/.
8. In this chapter, the term "eligible voters" is used to refer to the age-eligible proportion of the population, a group that also includes some people over eighteen who are not legally eligible to vote, such as convicted felons or noncitizen residents (it also excludes Americans voting abroad). The Census Bureau measures turnout in relation to the total age-eligible part of the population because the agency has found it too difficult to develop an accurate count of all legally eligible voters, given the diversity of state laws regarding the eligibility of felons and the mentally incompetent and the difficulty of estimating the precise number of noncitizens in the population. Turnout data used in this chapter are from the Census Bureau unless otherwise indicated. Students will find that reported turnout may vary among different sources because of variations in the definition of the eligible electorate. The best estimates suggest that turnout figures would increase by about 3 percent (rising to about 52 percent in 1996) if measured in terms of only the legally eligible population. See William H. Flanigan and Nancy H. Zingale, *Political Behavior and the American Electorate*, 9th ed. (Washington, DC: CQ Press, 1998), 32–33; 1998–2004 figures are based on *Statistical Abstract of the United States: 2006*, Table 407, www.census.gov/prod/2005pubs/06statab/election.pdf.
9. Data on the 2008 election come from George Mason University political scientist Michael McDonald's United States Election Project website: http://elections.gmu.edu/Turnout_2008G.html.
10. The discussion of voter turnout is based primarily on two sources: Ruy A. Teixeira, *Why Americans Don't Vote: Turnout Decline in the United States, 1960–1984* (New York: Greenwood, 1987), 3–36; and Frances Fox Piven and Richard Cloward, *Why Americans Don't Vote* (New York: Pantheon, 1989), 3–25.
11. Teixeira, *Why Americans Don't Vote*, 15–21.
12. Sidney Verba, Kay Lehman Schlozman, and Henry E. Brady, *Voice and Equality: Civic Voluntarism in American Politics* (Cambridge, MA: Harvard University Press, 1995), 416–60.
13. Alan Abramowitz, *Voice of the People: Elections and Voting in the United States* (Boston: McGraw-Hill, 2004), 118–20.
14. Teixeira, *Why Americans Don't Vote*, 7–8.
15. Piven and Cloward, *Why Americans Don't Vote*, 17.
16. See ibid.; also Raymond E. Wolfinger and Steven J. Rosenstone, *Who Votes?* (New Haven, CT: Yale University Press, 1980).
17. Richard K. Scher, *The Politics of Disenfranchisement* (Armonk, NY: M. E. Sharpe, 2011), 85; for the 2004 election, see Curtis Gans, "Turnout Exceeds Optimistic Predictions" (press release), Center for the Study of the American Electorate,

Washington, DC, January 14, 2005; for 2008 election, see Curtis Gans, "African Americans, Anger, Fear and Youth Propel Turnout to Highest Level Since 1960," Center for the Study of the American Electorate (press release), Washington, DC, December 17, 2008.

18. Scher, *Politics of Disenfranchisement,* 87.
19. Ibid., 89.
20. Ibid., 89.
21. Ibid., 102.
22. Ibid., 103.
23. Ibid., 105. Despite the similarity to an unconstitutional poll tax, the Bush administration Department of Justice allowed the law to go forward.
24. Lizette Alvarez, "G.O.P. Legislators Move to Tighten Rules on Voting," *New York Times,* May 29, 2011, A1.
25. In addition to the Scher book cited above, the new voter suppression efforts are documented in Spencer Overton, *Stealing Democracy: The New Politics of Voter Suppression* (New York: Norton, 2006).
26. Harold W. Stanley and Richard B. Niemi, *Vital Statistics on American Politics: 2003–2004* (Washington, DC: CQ Press, 2004), 12.
27. Some scholars attribute the moderate rise in voter turnout that began in the 1930s and continued to 1960 to a renewal of political party organizations that occurred during the New Deal period. This renewal ran its course by the early 1960s, and a new wave of party reform further undermined political party organizations. Turnout, once again, began to decline. See Piven and Cloward, *Why Americans Don't Vote,* 122–80.
28. Gans, "African Americans, Anger."
29. Henry Farrell, "Can Partisanship Save Citizenship?," *American Prospect* (January/February 2009): 24–26.
30. Vanessa Williamson, Theda Skocpol, and John Coggin, "The Tea Party and the Remaking of Republican Conservatism," *Perspectives on Politics* 9, no. 1 (March 2011).
31. Teixeira, *Why Americans Don't Vote,* 78.
32. APSA Standing Committee, *Democracy at Risk,* 24.
33. M. Margaret Conway, *Political Participation in the United States,* 2nd ed. (Washington, DC: CQ Press, 1991), 8.
34. APSA Standing Committee, *Democracy at Risk,* 32.
35. Joseph N. Cappella and Kathleen Hall Jamieson, *Spiral of Cynicism: The Press and the Public Good* (New York: Oxford University Press, 1997).
36. Robert Putnam, *Bowling Alone: The Collapse and Revival of American Community* (New York: Simon & Schuster, 2000).
37. Verba, Schlozman, and Brady, *Voice and Equality,* 509.
38. Alexis de Tocqueville, *Democracy in America,* ed. Harvey Mansfield and Delba Winthrop (Chicago: University of Chicago Press, 2000), 180.
39. This is Putnam's own summary of the central finding of *Bowling Alone,* as described in Robert Putnam and Lewis M. Feldstein, *Better Together: Restoring American Community* (New York: Simon & Schuster, 2003), 4.

40. Putnam, *Bowling Alone,* 93–115.

41. Theda Skocpol, *Diminished Democracy: From Membership to Management in National Civic Life* (Norman: University of Oklahoma Press, 2003), 40–44.

42. Ibid., 108–13.

43. Putnam, *Bowling Alone,* 56.

44. Skocpol, *Diminished Democracy,* 153.

45. Quoted in ibid., 20.

46. Quoted in ibid., 107.

47. Ibid., 120.

48. Ibid., 119–20.

49. Archive of files from the Providence Chapter, League of Women Voters, 1940–1990, Political Science Data Center, Providence College.

50. Milton Greenberg, *The GI Bill: The Law That Changed America* (New York: Lickle Publishing, 1997).

51. Putnam, *Bowling Alone,* 277–84.

52. Skocpol, *Diminished Democracy,* 139.

53. Putnam, *Bowling Alone,* 49.

54. Everett Carll Ladd, *The Ladd Report* (New York: Free Press, 1999), 28–29.

55. Lester Salamon, *The Resilient Sector: The State of Non-profit America* (Washington, DC: Brookings Institution Press, 2003), 8.

56. Ibid., 15–23.

57. Putnam, *Bowling Alone,* 129.

58. Robert Wuthnow, *Loose Connections: Joining Together in America's Fragmented Communities* (Cambridge, MA: Harvard University Press, 1998).

59. Thomas Cronin, *Direct Democracy: The Politics of Initiative, Referendum, and Recall* (Cambridge, MA: Harvard University Press, 1989), 47.

60. Ibid., 197.

61. Harry C. Boyte, *The Backyard Revolution: Understanding the New Citizen Movement* (Philadelphia: Temple University Press, 1980).

62. Ibid., 64. For a more recent account of the activities of COPS, see William Greider, *Who Will Tell the People? The Betrayal of American Democracy* (New York: Simon & Schuster, 1992), 222–41.

63. Harry C. Boyte, *Commonwealth* (New York: Free Press, 1989), 90–91.

64. Mark Warren, *Dry Bones Rattling: Community Building to Revitalize American Democracy* (Princeton, NJ: Princeton University Press, 2001), 6–9.

65. Michael Cornfield, "Going Broadband, Getting Netwise," in *Divided States of America,* ed. Larry Sabato (New York: Pearson/Longman, 2005), 219.

66. Manfred B. Steger, *Globalism,* 2nd ed. (Lanham, MD: Rowman & Littlefield, 2005), 128–40.

67. For descriptions of several different virtual communities, see Steve Davis, Larry Elin, and Grant Reeher, *Click on Democracy: The Internet's Power to Change Political Apathy Into Civic Action* (Boulder, CO: Westview Press, 2002).

68. Michel Crozier, Samuel Huntington, and Joji Watanuki, *The Crisis of Democracy* (New York: New York University Press, 1975), 59–118.

69. Ibid., 113.

70. One best-selling American government textbook makes this argument its central theme. See Thomas Dye and Harmon Zeigler, *The Irony of Democracy,* 12th ed. (Belmont, CA: Thomson Wadsworth, 2002).

71. Jonathan Rauch, *Demosclerosis: The Silent Killer of American Government* (New York: Times Books, 1994).

72. Fareed Zakaria, *The Future of Freedom* (New York: Norton, 2004), 161–98.

73. Putnam, *Bowling Alone,* 49.

74. Skocpol, *Diminished Democracy,* 174.

75. Verba, Schlozman, and Brady, *Voice and Equality,* 49–96.

76. Russell J. Dalton, *Citizen Politics: Public Opinion and Political Parties in Advanced Industrial Democracies,* 2nd ed. (Chatham, NJ: Chatham House, 1996), 82.

77. Hedrick Smith, *The People and the Power Game,* produced and directed by Hedrick Smith (Chevy Chase, MD: Hedrick Smith Productions, 1996), videocassette.

78. Putnam, *Bowling Alone,* 245.

79. Thomas Byrne Edsall, *The New Politics of Inequality* (New York: Norton, 1984). These developments are discussed in more detail in chapters 6 and 7 of this book.

80. William Greider, *The Education of David Stockman and Other Americans* (New York: New American Library, 1986) documents the class bias of Reagan policies. As OMB director, David Stockman found it easy to impose spending cuts on programs for the poor but was prevented from interfering with probusiness programs and those benefiting the affluent, such as the Export-Import Bank and subsidies for private airplane manufacturers.

81. Piven and Cloward, *Why Americans Don't Vote,* 12–13.

82. Michael J. Graetz and Ian Shapiro, *Death by a Thousand Cuts: The Fight Over Taxing Inherited Wealth* (Princeton, NJ: Princeton University Press, 2005).

83. Piven and Cloward, *Why Americans Don't Vote,* 26–95.

84. For data on public support for more generous social welfare programs, see Benjamin Page and Robert Shapiro, *The Rational Public: Fifty Years of Trends in Americans' Policy Preferences* (Chicago: University of Chicago Press, 1992), 117–71.

85. Daniel Yankelovich, "A Missing Concept," *Kettering Review* (Fall 1991): 54–66.

86. Ibid., 59.

87. Richard C. Harwood, *Citizens and Politics: A View From Main Street America* (Dayton, OH: Kettering Foundation, 1991).

88. Ibid., 23.

89. Ibid., 17.

90. Thomas Ferguson and Joel Rogers, *Right Turn* (New York: Hill & Wang, 1986).

91. Heather K. Gerken, "The Case for Keeping Score," *American Prospect* (January/February 2009): a6–a7.

92. Gans, "African Americans, Anger."

93. Benjamin Barber, *Strong Democracy: Participatory Politics for a New Age* (Berkeley: University of California Press, 1984), 267–73.

94. Jeffrey M. Berry, Kent E. Portney, and Ken Thomson, *The Rebirth of Urban Democracy* (Washington, DC: Brookings Institution Press, 1993), 12–15.

95. Ibid., 13.

96. Ibid., 232–99.

97. "The Glue of Society: Americans Are Joining Clubs Again," *Economist,* July 19, 2005.
98. For a discussion of Tea Party use of Meetup, see Williamson, Skocpol, and Coggin, "The Tea Party and the Remaking of Republican Conservatism," 28.
99. The Kettering Foundation has published a number of booklets in connection with its National Issues Forums. See, for example, *The Health Care Crisis: Containing Costs, Expanding Coverage,* ed. Keith Melville (Dayton, OH: National Issues Forum, 1992). For information on the forums, contact National Issues Forum, 100 Commons Road, Dayton, OH 45459-2777; phone 800-433-7834.

Chapter 5: Elections Without the People's Voice

1. A study of new democracies throughout the world by a prominent social scientist uses the presence or absence of competitive elections as the sole indicator of democratic politics. See Samuel P. Huntington, *The Third Wave: Democratization in the Late Twentieth Century* (Norman: University of Oklahoma Press, 1991), 5–13.
2. R. K. Sinclair, *Democracy and Participation in Athens* (Cambridge: Cambridge University Press, 1988), 17.
3. Aristotle, *The Politics,* trans. T. A. Sinclair (Harmondsworth, UK: Penguin Books, 1962), 241. See also M. I. Finley, *Democracy: Ancient and Modern,* rev. ed. (New Brunswick, NJ: Rutgers University Press, 1985), 19.
4. Finley, *Democracy,* 22.
5. Benjamin Ginsberg and Alan Stone, *Do Elections Matter?,* 2nd ed. (Armonk, NY: M. E. Sharpe, 1991), 3.
6. Quoted in David M. O'Brien, *Constitutional Law and Politics,* vol. 1, 7th ed. (New York: Norton, 2008), 484.
7. Robert Dahl, *How Democratic Is the American Constitution,* 2nd ed. (New Haven, CT: Yale University Press, 2003), 15.
8. Sanford Levinson, *Our Undemocratic Constitution* (New York: Oxford University Press, 2006), 50.
9. Ibid., 58.
10. Levinson, *Our Undemocratic Constitution,* 57.
11. Douglas J. Amy, *Real Choices/New Voices* (New York: Columbia University Press, 2002), 2–3.
12. The example is adapted from Amy, *Real Choices/New Voices,* 34–36.
13. Quoted in Amy, *Real Choices/New Voices,* 52.
14. Two states, Maine and Nebraska, deviate slightly from this system by allowing election of individual electors by congressional district, with two electors (corresponding to the Senate portion of the total number of electoral votes) being chosen by statewide vote.
15. Gerald M. Pomper, "The Presidential Election: The Ills of American Politics After 9/11," in *The Elections of 2004,* ed. Michael Nelson (Washington, DC: CQ Press, 2004), 44.
16. Doris Graber, *Mass Media and American Politics,* 8th ed. (Washington, DC: CQ Press, 2008), 200.

17. Thomas Ferguson and Joel Rogers have developed the notion of the hidden election most fully. See their *Right Turn: The Decline of the Democrats and the Future of American Politics* (New York: Hill & Wang, 1986).
18. Ryan J. Barilleaux and Randall E. Adkins, "The Nomination: Process and Patterns," in *The Elections of 1992*, ed. Michael Nelson (Washington, DC: CQ Press, 1993), 30.
19. Ibid., 38.
20. Richard L. Berke, "Bradley Takes Early Party Prize: He Goes One-on-One With Gore," *New York Times*, April 20, 1999, A1. For the Bush campaign, see Don Van Natta Jr., "Aura of Invincibility Is Drying Up the Money Pool for Bush's Rivals," *New York Times*, June 10, 1999, A1. See also David Firestone, "Alexander Cuts Staff and Travel," *New York Times*, June 3, 1999, A19.
21. Marian Currinder, "Campaign Finance: Funding the Presidential and Congressional Elections," in *Elections of 2004*, ed. Nelson, 126.
22. Center for Responsive Politics, *2008 Election Overview, Incumbent Advantage*, http://www.opensecrets.org/bigpicture/incumbs.php?cycle=2008.
23. The FEC originally limited individual and PAC contributions to $2,000, but a recent amendment raised the limit to $2,500, which will be increased for inflation in odd-numbered election years. See the Federal Election Commission website at http://www.fec.gov/pages/brochures/contriblimits.shtml#fn.
24. W. Lance Bennett, *The Governing Crisis: Media, Money, and Marketing in American Elections* (New York: St. Martin's, 1992), 53.
25. David B. Magleby and Anthony Corrado, eds., *Financing the 2008 Congressional Elections* (Washington, DC: Brookings Institution Press, 2011), 171.
26. Ibid., 7–8.
27. Ronald Dworkin, "The Court's Embarrassingly Bad Decisions," *New York Review of Books*, May 26, 2011.
28. Barry C. Burden, "The Nominations: Technology, Money, and Transferable Momentum," in *The Elections of 2004*, ed. Nelson, 35.
29. Center for Responsive Politics, "Bundlers," www.opensecrets.org/pres08/bundlers.php?id=N00009638.
30. Michael Luo and Christopher Drew, "Big Donors, Too, Have Seats at Obama's Fund-Raising Table," *New York Times*, August 6, 2008, A1.
31. Nicholas Confessore, "Obama Seeks to Win Back Wall St. Cash," *New York Times*, June 15, 2011, A1.
32. Magleby and Corrado, *Financing the 2008 Congressional Elections*, 16–17.
33. Stephen J. Wayne, *Is This Any Way to Run a Democratic Election?*, 102–3.
34. Magleby and Corrado, *Financing the 2008 Congressional Elections*, 14.
35. Ibid., 307–8, 319.
36. Mike McIntire, "Under Tax-Exempt Cloak, Political Dollars Flow," *New York Times*, September 24, 2010, A1.
37. T. W. Farnum, "72 Super PACS Spent $83.7 Million on Election," *Washington Post*, December 4, 2010, A03.
38. Campaign Finance Institute (press release), "Non-party Spending Doubled in 2010," http://www.cfinst.org/Press/PReleases/10-11-05/Non-Party_Spending_Doubled_But_Did_Not_Dictate_Results.aspx.

39. Nicholas Confessore, "Campaigns Grow More Dependent on 'Super PAC' Aid," *New York Times,* February 21, 2012, A1. Confessore reports that Newt Gingrich's super PAC received nearly all of its funds from precisely three donors: Nevada casino owner Sheldon Adelson, his wife Miriam, and Texas billionaire Harold C. Simmons.
40. Magleby and Corrado, *Financing the 2008 Congressional Elections,* 293.
41. Campaign Finance Institute (press release), "All CFI Funding Statistics Revised and Updated for the 2008 Presidential Primary and General Election Candidates," http://www.cfinst.org/Press/Releases_tags/10-01-08/Revised_and_Updated_2008_Presidential_Statistics.aspx.
42. Center for Responsive Politics, *2008 Election Overview, Donor Demographics,* www.opensecrets.org/overview/DonorDemographics.php.
43. Finley, *Democracy,* 22.
44. Graber, *Mass Media,* 207. For a table documenting decreasing news coverage of presidential campaigns, see Marion Just, "Candidate Strategies and the Media Campaign," in *The Election of 1996,* ed. Gerald M. Pomper (Chatham, NJ: Chatham House, 1997), 85.
45. S. Robert Lichter, "Election Watch: Campaign 2008 Final," *Media Monitor* (Center for Media and Public Affairs) 23, no. 1 (Winter 2009): 2, www.cmpa.com/pdf/media_monitor_jan_2009.pdf.
46. Lear Center Local News Archive, *Local TV News Ignores Local and State Campaigns,* Norman Lear Center Interim Report, Annenberg School, USC, October 21, 2004.
47. Matthew Robert Kerbel, "The Media: The Challenge and Promise of Internet Politics," in *Elections of 2004,* ed. Nelson, 99.
48. Graber, *Mass Media,* 207–8.
49. Ibid., 207.
50. Ibid., 211.
51. Thomas E. Patterson, *Out of Order* (New York: Vintage Books, 1994), 69.
52. Ibid., 59–60.
53. James Fishkin, "Talk of the Tube," *American Prospect* (Fall 1992): 47. See also Just, "Candidate Strategies." For the 2000 and 2004 campaign sound bite, Center for Media and Public Affairs, *Election Newswatch Campaign 2004,* George Mason University, October 19, 2004, 7.
54. Kate Kenski and Kathleen Hall Jamieson, *National Annenberg Election Survey,* October 29, 2008, www.annenbergpublicpolicycenter.org/NewsDetails.aspx?myId=303.
55. Graber, *Mass Media,* 270.
56. Larry Rohter, "McCain and Obama Speak Off the Cuff, and Issues Arise," *New York Times,* July 11, 2008, A15.
57. Diana Owens, "The Campaign and the Media," in *The American Elections of 2008,* ed. Janet M. Box-Steffensmeier and Steven E. Schier (Lanham, MD: Rowman & Littlefield, 2009), 15.
58. Neil Postman, *Amusing Ourselves to Death* (New York: Penguin Books, 1986), 89.
59. Howard Kurtz, "Wall-to-Wall Levy Coverage," May 23, 2002, www.washingtonpost.com.
60. Kerbel, "The Media," 104.

61. Kathleen Hall Jamieson, *Eloquence in an Electronic Age: The Transformation of American Political Speechmaking* (New York: Oxford University Press, 1988).
62. Kerbel, "The Media," 92.
63. Owens, "The Campaign and the Media," 21.
64. The account follows that of Peter Drier and Christopher R. Martin, "How ACORN Was Framed: Political Controversy and Media Agenda Setting," *Perspectives on Politics* 18, no. 3 (September 2010): 761–92.
65. For a profile of Breitbart, see Jeremy W. Peters, "The Right's Blogger Provocateur," *New York Times,* June 27, 2011, B1.
66. Graber, *Mass Media,* 203.
67. Jay Rosen, "Playing the Primary Chords," *Harper's Magazine,* March 1992, 22–25.
68. Larry J. Sabato, *The Rise of Political Consultants: New Ways of Winning Elections* (New York: Basic Books, 1981), 13.
69. Quoted in Green, "Dumb and Dumber: Why Are Campaign Commercials So Bad?," *The Atlantic,* July/August 2004, 84.
70. George Stephanopoulos, *All Too Human: A Political Education* (New York: Little, Brown, 1999), 328–75.
71. Graber, *Mass Media,* 199.
72. Shanto Iyengar, "The Media Game: New Moves, Old Strategies," *The Forum* 9, iss. 1, art. 1, http://www.bepress.com/forum/v019/iss1/art1.
73. For two accounts of the Willie Horton story and the George H. W. Bush campaign, see Jack W. Germond and Jules Witcover, *Whose Broad Stripes and Bright Stars? The Trivial Pursuit of the Presidency, 1988* (New York: Warner Books, 1989), 10–15; and Sidney Blumenthal, *Pledging Allegiance* (New York: HarperCollins, 1990), 264–65.
74. Paul J. Quirk and Sean C. Matheson, "The Presidency," in *Elections of 2004,* ed. Nelson, 138–39.
75. Iyengar, "The Media Game," 3.
76. The Romney ad can be found at http://www.youtube.com/watch?v=EP2GsRzROF8.
77. Nicol C. Rae, *Conservative Reformers: The Republican Freshmen and the Lessons of the 104th Congress* (Armonk, NY: M. E. Sharpe, 1998), 40.
78. Rosen, "Playing the Primary Chords," 24.
79. Just, "Candidate Strategies," 90. For discussion of the 2000 debates, see Charles Babington, "Campaigns Matter: The Proof of 2000," in *Overtime: The Election 2000 Thriller,* ed. Larry Sabato (New York: Longman, 2002), 59; and Douglas Kellner, *Grand Theft 2000: Media Spectacle and a Stolen Election* (Lanham, MD: Rowman & Littlefield, 2001), 4–6.
80. Graber, *Mass Media,* 200.
81. Sean Wilentz, "Will Pseudo-scandals Decide the Election?," *American Prospect,* September 25–October 9, 2000, 49.
82. Paul J. Quirk and Sean C. Matheson, "The Presidency," in *Elections of 2004,* ed. Nelson, 139–40.
83. Owens, "The Campaign and the Media," 23.
84. Ibid., 22–23.
85. Ibid., 22–23.
86. Bennett, *The Governing Crisis,* 30.

87. Ibid., 7.

88. Sinclair, *Democracy,* 17.

89. E. E. Schattschneider, *Party Government* (New York: Rinehart, 1942), 208.

90. Lewis Lipsitz and David M. Speak, *American Democracy,* 3rd ed. (New York: St. Martin's, 1993), 326–27.

91. Walter Dean Burnham, *Critical Elections and the Mainsprings of American Politics* (New York: Norton, 1970), 133.

92. John H. Aldrich, *Why Parties? The Origin and Transformation of Party Politics in America* (Chicago: University of Chicago Press, 1995), 273.

93. Morris Fiorina et al., *Culture War? The Myth of a Polarized America,* 3rd ed. (Boston: Longman, 2011), 61–70.

94. John H. Aldrich and John D. Griffin, "Parties, Elections, and Democratic Politics," in *The Oxford Handbook of American Elections and Political Behavior,* ed. Jan E. Leighley (New York: Oxford University Press, 2010), 606.

95. Nancy Rosenblum, *On the Side of Angels* (Princeton, NJ: Princeton University Press, 2008), 108–62.

96. Two representative studies providing contrasting interpretations of partisan polarization are Morris P. Fiorina et al., *Culture War? The Myth of a Polarized America* (Boston: Longman, 2011); and Alan L. Abramowitz, *The Disappearing Center* (New Haven, CT: Yale University Press, 2010).

97. Paul J. Quirk, "Polarized Populism: Masses, Elites, and Partisan Conflict," *The Forum* 9, iss. 1, art. 5.

98. For a discussion of the roots of the Tea Party movement in decades-old Republican right-wing activism, see Sean Wilentz, "Confounding Fathers," *New Yorker,* October 16, 2010.

99. Philip Rucker and Felicia Sonmez, "Leaders on Short Leash in Debt Talks," *Washington Post,* July 9, 2011, A01.

100. Jacob S. Hacker and Paul Pierson, *Off Center: The Republican Revolution and the Erosion of American Democracy* (New Haven, CT: Yale University Press, 2005).

101. Steve Coll, *The Deal of the Century: The Breakup of AT&T* (New York: Simon & Schuster, 1986).

102. Ginsberg and Stone, *Do Elections Matter?,* 3.

103. Larry Sabato, *A More Perfect Constitution* (New York: Walker & Company, 2007), 26.

104. Amy, *Real Choices/New Voices,* 227.

105. The Media Policy Program of the Campaign Legal Center (which merged with the Alliance for Better Campaigns in February 2005) makes the case for the need for free broadcast time for candidates. See the center's website at www.campaignlegalcenter .org/FCC-198.html.

106. Bennett, *The Governing Crisis,* 206–11.

107. Joshua Green, "Clean Money in Maine," *American Prospect,* September 25–October 9, 2000, 36–38; see also Alan Greenblatt, "That Clean All Over Feeling," *Governing,* July 2002, 40–42.

108. Thomas J. Volgy, *Politics in the Trenches: Citizens, Politicians, and the Fate of Democracy* (Tucson: University of Arizona Press, 2001), 80–81.

109. Anthony J. Corrado, Michael J. Malbin, Thomas F. Mann, and Norman J. Ornstein, *Reform in an Age of Networked Campaigns: How to Foster Citizen Participation Through Small Donors and Volunteers* (Washington, DC: Campaign Finance Institute, American Enterprise Institute, and Brookings Institution, 2010), http://www.brookings.edu/reports/2010/0114_campaign_finance_reform.aspx.

110. Ian Ayres and Bruce Ackerman, *Voting With Dollars: A New Paradigm for Campaign Finance* (New Haven, CT: Yale University Press, 2002).

111. James S. Fishkin, *Democracy and Deliberation: New Directions for Democratic Reform* (New Haven, CT: Yale University Press, 1991), 1–3; see also his "The Case for a National Caucus: Taking Democracy Seriously," *Atlantic Monthly,* August 1988, 16–18. Fishkin tried out his idea for a deliberative opinion poll in Britain in April 1994. With the support of the Granada television network and the British newspaper *The Independent,* he gathered a random sample of British citizens together in Manchester to deliberate on the issue of crime. Portions of the debate were televised throughout the UK. Polls taken before and after the deliberation process showed that participants' opinions about crime changed significantly after the opportunity to deliberate about the issue. *The Independent,* March 9, 1994, 8.

Chapter 6: The "Privileged Position" of Business

1. Charles E. Lindblom first elaborated the "privileged position" of business in his now-classic *Politics and Markets: The World's Political-Economic Systems* (New York: Basic Books, 1977). This chapter draws liberally on Lindblom's arguments.

2. David Truman, *The Governmental Process* (New York: Knopf, 1951).

3. Besides Truman's work, another key case study from the period is Earl Latham, *The Group Basis of Politics: A Study in Basing-Point Legislation* (Ithaca, NY: Cornell University Press, 1952).

4. Truman, *Governmental Process,* 449, 486.

5. Ibid., 114.

6. For a good review of various critiques of Pluralism, see David Ricci, *Community Power and Democratic Theory: The Logic of Political Analysis* (New York: Random House, 1971). Ricci provides a bibliography of the major critical works.

7. Along with Lindblom, see G. William Domhoff, *Who Rules America Now?* (Englewood Cliffs, NJ: Prentice Hall, 1983); Thomas Dye, *Who's Running America? The Reagan Years* (Englewood Cliffs, NJ: Prentice Hall, 1984); Thomas Edsall, *The New Politics of Inequality* (New York: Norton, 1984); Thomas Ferguson and Joel Rogers, *Right Turn* (New York: Hill & Wang, 1986); James W. Lamare, *What Rules America?* (St. Paul, MN: West, 1988); Grant McConnell, *Private Power and American Democracy* (New York: Knopf, 1966); Kim McQuaid, *Big Business and Presidential Power From FDR to Reagan* (New York: Morrow, 1982); Beth Mintz and Michael Schwartz, *The Power Structure of American Business* (Chicago: University of Chicago Press, 1985).

8. One major study of interest group activity in Washington classifies the various groups involved in lobbying as follows: peak business associations, trade associations, unions, professional associations, farm groups, citizens' groups, and civil rights and

social welfare groups. Kay Lehman Schlozman and John T. Tierney, *Organized Interests and American Democracy* (New York: Harper & Row, 1986), 40.

9. Edsall, *New Politics of Inequality,* 124–25; Jacob S. Hacker and Paul Pierson, *Winner-Take-All Politics* (New York: Simon & Schuster, 2010), 116–36.

10. Rajiv Chandrasekaran and John Mintz, "Microsoft's Window of Influence," *Washington Post,* May 7, 1999, A01.

11. Schlozman and Tierney, *Organized Interests,* 67. Kay L. Schlozman et al., "Inequalities of Political Voice," in *Inequality and American Democracy,* ed. Lawrence Jacobs and Theda Skocpol (New York: Russell Sage Foundation, 2005), 55–57; Frank R. Baumgartner and Beth L. Leech, "Interest Niches and Policy Bandwagons: Patterns of Interest Group Involvement in National Politics," *Journal of Politics* 63, no. 4 (November 2001): 1191–213.

12. Frank R. Baumgartner et al., *Lobbying and Policy Change: Who Wins, Who Loses, and Why* (Chicago: University of Chicago Press, 2009), 200.

13. Ibid., 237–38.

14. Schlozman and Tierney, *Organized Interests,* 117.

15. Ibid., 293.

16. Darrell M. West and Burdett A. Loomis, *The Sound of Money: How Political Interests Get What They Want* (New York: Norton, 1999), 63, and on patching techniques, 61–62.

17. Center for Responsive Politics, www.opensecrets.org/overview/blio.php.

18. Center for Responsive Politics, http://www.opensecrets.org/bigpicture/blio.php?cycle=2010.

19. Michael Luo, "Changes Have Money Talking Louder Than Ever in Midterms," *New York Times,* October 8, 2010, A13; Nicholas Confessore, "Outside Groups Eclipsing G.O.P. as Hub of Campaigns Next Year," *New York Times,* October 30, 2011, A1.

20. Frank J. Sorauf, *Money in American Elections* (Glenville, IL: Scott, Foresman, 1988), 311–12.

21. Quoted in ibid., 313.

22. Quoted in Lamare, *What Rules America?,* 110.

23. Thomas B. Edsall, "Putting Political Reform Right Into the Pockets of the Voters," *New York Times,* December 15, 2011, C6.

24. Thomas R. Dye, *Top Down Policymaking* (New York: Chatham House, 2001), 100–101.

25. Anthony Faiola, Ellen Nakashima, and Jill Drew, "What Went Wrong," *Washington Post,* October 15, 2008, A01; Harold Meyerson, "Pal Around McCain," *Washington Post,* October 6, 2008, A15.

26. Center for Responsible Politics, http://www.opensecrets.org/industries/background.php?cycle=2012&ind=F.

27. Center for Responsible Politics, http://www.opensecrets.org/industries/totals.php?cycle=2010&ind=F.

28. Alec MacGillis, "In Cantor, Investment Firms Have Voice at Talks," *Washington Post,* July 26, 2011, A12.

29. Robert Pear and Richard A. Oppel Jr., "Election Gives Drug Industry New Influence," *New York Times,* November 21, 2002, A1.

30. Robert Pear, "Medicare Law Prompts a Rush for Lobbyists," *New York Times,* August 23, 2006, A1.

31. West and Loomis, *Sound of Money,* 58–59.

32. Ibid., 39.

33. Elizabeth Kolbert, "Special Interests' Special Weapon," *New York Times,* March 26, 1995, A20.

34. Chandrasekaran and Mintz, "Microsoft's Window of Influence," A1.

35. Edsall, *New Politics of Inequality,* 117–20.

36. Mark Crispin Miller, "What's Wrong With This Picture?," *The Nation,* January 7, 2002.

37. Eric Alterman, *What Liberal Media? The Truth About Bias and the News* (New York: Basic Books, 2003), 14–27.

38. Paul Farhi, "What NBC News Failed to Mention About GE," *Washington Post,* March 30, 2011, C01. About a week after the story broke and after numerous media commentaries on its failure to cover the story, NBC's *Nightly News* finally reported on it—taking pains to give the GE side.

39. The argument in this section follows Lindblom's summary of his position in "Democracy and the Economy," in C. E. Lindblom, *Democracy and the Market System* (Oxford: Oxford University Press, 1988), 115–38. This article, written in 1983, provides a concise statement of the position he originally developed in *Politics and Markets* but also elaborates on certain elements in response to critics of his earlier work.

40. J. Allen Whitt, *Urban Elites and Mass Transportation: The Dialectics of Power* (Princeton, NJ: Princeton University Press, 1982), 45–47. Details of the involvement of such automobile interests as General Motors and Firestone Tire and Rubber in the destruction of America's trolley system were reported in a congressional investigation in 1974. See Bradford C. Snell, *American Ground Transport,* report presented to the Subcommittee on Antitrust and Monopoly of the Committee on the Judiciary, U.S. Senate, February 26, 1974 (Washington, DC: Government Printing Office).

41. Lindblom, *Democracy and the Market System,* 120.

42. There are now numerous accounts of the background to the 2008 financial crisis. One of the most readable is Bethany McLean and Joe Nocera, *All the Devils Are Here: The Hidden History of the Financial Crisis* (New York: Portfolio/Penguin, 2010).

43. Menzie D. Chinn and Jeffry A. Frieden, *Lost Decades: The Making of America's Debt Crisis and the Long Recovery* (New York: Norton, 2011), 113–19.

44. Gretchen Morgenson, "Secrets of the Bailout, Now Told," *New York Times,* December 4, 2011, B1.

45. Mike McIntire, "Bailout Is a No-Strings Windfall to Bankers, If Not to Borrowers," *New York Times,* January 18, 2009, A1.

46. Gretchen Morgenson and Louise Story, "In Financial Crisis, No Prosecutions of Top Figures," *New York Times,* April 11, 2011, A1.

47. Doron P. Levin, "G.M. Picks 12 Plants to Be Shut as It Reports a Record U.S. Loss," *New York Times,* February 25, 1992, A1.

48. Lori Montgomery, "Automakers Press High-Stakes Plea for Aid," *Washington Post,* November 19, 2008, A01.

49. Such threats are commonplace and are enormously effective. For example, in October 1991, the CEO of one of Rhode Island's largest manufacturers made a speech announcing that the corporation was considering closing down all Rhode Island operations if certain policy reforms, especially reduction of workers' compensation costs, were not enacted. Nora Lockwood Tooher, "Hasbro Warns It May End Manufacturing in R.I.," *Providence Journal,* October 29, 1991, D01. The next spring, the state legislature passed a major workers' compensation reform bill.

50. Philip Mattera et al., "Money for Something: Job Creation and Job Quality Standards in State Economic Development Subsidy Programs," *Good Jobs First,* December 2011, i, http://www.goodjobsfirst.org/sites/default/files/docs/pdf/wmt-study.pdf.

51. "Case Study of Boeing Co.," *Good Jobs First, 2010,* http://www.goodjobsfirst.org/corporate-subsidy-watch/boeing.

52. Michael Cooper, "With States Desperate to Keep Jobs, Companies Have Upper Hand, Report Shows," *New York Times,* December 14, 2011, A21.

53. Charles Wolfe, "House Votes to Abolish Farmland Committee Over Hyundai Concerns," Associated Press State and Local Wire, March 29, 2002; and Bob Johnson, "Hyundai Picks Alabama Site for $1 Billion Plant," Associated Press State and Local Wire, April 2, 2002.

54. Richard C. Longworth, "Government Without Democracy," *American Prospect,* Summer 2001, 19–22.

55. Joseph Stiglitz, *Globalization and Its Discontents* (New York: Norton, 2002), 21.

56. Lindblom, *Politics and Markets,* 202. See also Benjamin Ginsberg, *The Captive Public* (New York: Basic Books, 1986).

57. Lindblom, *Politics and Markets,* 203–6.

58. Alterman, *What Liberal Media?,* 23.

59. Hanna Fenichel Pitkin and Sara M. Shumer, "On Participation," in *Higher Education and the Practice of Democratic Politics,* ed. Bernard Murchland (Dayton, OH: Kettering Foundation, 1991), 107.

60. See Carole Pateman, *Participation and Democratic Theory* (Cambridge: Cambridge University Press, 1970), 22–44, for a discussion of these issues. The argument presented here is developed, in particular, in her discussion of the theory of G. D. H. Cole.

61. A number of recent works advocate the need to democratize business organizations if we are fully to achieve democracy in the United States. For a short, cogent presentation of this thesis, see Robert Dahl, *A Preface to Economic Democracy* (Berkeley: University of California Press, 1985).

62. Bennett Harrison and Barry Bluestone, *The Great U-Turn* (New York: Basic Books, 1988), 38.

63. Robert Reich, *The Work of Nations* (New York: Knopf, 1991), 46.

64. Ibid., 48.

65. Paul Krugman, *The Age of Diminished Expectations* (Cambridge, MA: MIT Press, 1992), 11.

66. Benjamin Friedman, *Day of Reckoning* (New York: Vintage, 1989), 188.

67. Harrison and Bluestone, *Great U-Turn,* 9.

68. Ibid., 8.
69. Ibid., 21–75.
70. Jeff Madrick, "Time for a New Deal," *New York Review of Books,* September 25, 2008, 65.
71. Robert Kuttner, *The Squandering of America: How the Failure of Our Politics Undermines Our Prosperity* (New York: Knopf, 2007), 133–37.
72. Faiola, Nakashima, and Drew, "What Went Wrong."
73. Jeff Madrick, "Enron: Seduction and Betrayal," *New York Review of Books,* March 14, 2002, 21.
74. David Barboza, "Ex-Managers Say Sham Deal Helped Enron," *New York Times,* August 8, 2002, A1.
75. William Bradley, "Enron's End," *American Prospect,* January 1–14, 2002, 30–31; and Peter Schrag, "Blackout," *American Prospect,* February 26, 2001.
76. Ien Cheng, "Barons of Bankruptcy," *Financial Times,* August 1, 2002, 1.
77. David Cay Johnson, "Stanley Hails Bermuda Vote, but Employees Cry Deception," *New York Times,* May 10, 2002, C1.
78. Reich, *Work of Nations,* 8.
79. Robert Hessen, ed., *Does Big Business Rule America?* (Washington, DC: Ethics and Public Policy Center, 1981) is a collection of essays, several of which argue this point of view. See especially the essay by James Q. Wilson.
80. David Vogel, *Fluctuating Fortunes: The Political Power of Business in America* (New York: Basic Books, 1989).
81. Ibid., 13.
82. Ibid., 7.
83. Richard A. Oppel Jr., "Negotiators Agree on Broad Changes in Business Laws," *New York Times,* July 25, 2002, A1.
84. Stephen Labaton and Richard A. Oppel Jr., "Enthusiasm Ebbs for Tough Reform in Wake of Enron," *New York Times,* June 10, 2002, A1.
85. Nelson D. Schwartz, "Power Shift Is Expected by CEOs," *New York Times,* November 2, 2010, B1.
86. Edward Wyatt, "Dodd-Frank Under Fire a Year Later," *New York Times,* July 19, 2011, B1.
87. Ben Protess, "Patrolling Wall Street on the Cheap," *New York Times,* May 4, 2011, B1.
88. Gretchen Morgenson, "Slipping Backwards on Swaps," *New York Times,* November 27, 2011, B1.
89. Ibid., 68–69; G. William Domhoff, *The Power Elite and the State* (New York: Walter de Gruyter, 1990), 273.
90. Quoted in Hacker and Pierson, *Winner-Take-All Politics,* 117.
91. Ibid., 116–24.
92. For analysis of the defeat of Humphrey-Hawkins, see Kay Lehman Schlozman and Sidney Verba, *Injury to Insult: Unemployment, Class, and Political Response* (Cambridge, MA: Harvard University Press, 1979), 336–46. For labor law reform, see Vogel, *Fluctuating Fortunes,* 150–59. For a general discussion of business power over labor issues during this period, see Domhoff, *Who Rules America Now?,* 276–82.

93. Vogel, *Fluctuating Fortunes,* 296–97.
94. This account follows West and Loomis, *Sound of Money,* 141–66.
95. Ibid., 143.
96. Ibid., 165.
97. John Kenneth Galbraith, *American Capitalism: The Concept of Countervailing Power,* rev. ed. (Boston: Houghton Mifflin, 1956).
98. Stiglitz, *Globalization and Its Discontents,* 5.
99. Michael Walzer, *Spheres of Justice* (New York: Basic Books, 1983), 295–302.
100. Quoted in ibid., 297.
101. Quoted in ibid., 298.
102. Ibid.

Chapter 7: Economic Inequality

1. Emmanuel Saez, *Striking It Richer: The Evolution of Top Incomes in the United States* (updated with 2008 estimates), accessed July 17, 2010, http://elsa.berkeley.edu/~saez/saez-UStopincomes-2008.pdf.
2. Edward N. Wolff, *Recent Trends in Household Wealth in the United States: Rising Debt and the Middle-Class Squeeze—An Update to 2007* (Working Paper No. 589, Levy Economics Institute, Bard College, March 2010).
3. Adam Weinstein, "We Are the 99 Percent Creators Revealed," *Mother Jones,* October 7, 2011, http://motherjones.com/politics/2011/10/we-are-the-99-percent-creators.
4. Howard Kurtz, "Wiped off the Map, and Belatedly Put Back on It," *Washington Post,* September 19, 2005, C01.
5. Timothy M. Smeeding, Michael O'Higgens, and Lee Rainwater, *Poverty, Inequality and Income Distribution in Comparative Perspective* (Washington, DC: Urban Institute Press, 1990).
6. Michael Walzer, *Spheres of Justice: A Defense of Pluralism and Equality* (New York: Basic Books, 1983), 285.
7. F. M. Cornford, *The Republic of Plato* (New York: Oxford University Press, 1945), 195–96.
8. Walzer, *Spheres of Justice,* 285.
9. Of course, one of the judgments democrats often must make is which decisions should be turned over to experts because they require special technical competence. As with decisions about political ends, there are no clear technical criteria for making such judgments; hence, democrats would say all people are equally capable of participating in deciding when to call on the experts. For an excellent discussion of the role of technical competence in democratic decision making, see Robert Dahl, *After the Revolution* (New Haven, CT: Yale University Press, 1990), 21–30.
10. Robert Dahl calls this proposition in democratic theory the "presumption of personal autonomy." See his *Democracy and Its Critics* (New Haven, CT: Yale University Press, 1989), 100–101.
11. Gordon Wood, *The Radicalism of the American Revolution* (New York: Knopf, 1992), 229–43.
12. Ibid., 232.

13. Ibid., 234.

14. Ibid.

15. Ibid., 239–40.

16. Ibid., 234.

17. Alexis de Tocqueville, *Democracy in America,* ed. J. P. Mayer (New York: Harper & Row, 1969), 50–58.

18. For comparative analyses of various social revolutions, see Barrington Moore, *Social Origins of Dictatorship and Democracy: Lord and Peasant in the Making of the Modern World* (Boston: Beacon Press, 1966); or Theda Skocpol, *States and Social Revolutions: A Comparative Analysis of France, Russia, and China* (Cambridge: Cambridge University Press, 1979). For analysis of more recent transitions to democracy in Europe and Latin America, see Guillermo O'Donnell and Philippe Schmitter, *Transitions From Authoritarian Rule: Tentative Conclusions About Uncertain Democracies* (Baltimore: Johns Hopkins University Press, 1986).

19. Walzer, *Spheres of Justice,* xiii.

20. Paul Krugman, *The Age of Diminished Expectations* (Cambridge, MA: MIT Press, 1992), 3.

21. Bennett Harrison and Barry Bluestone, *The Great U-Turn: Corporate Restructuring and the Polarizing of America* (New York: Basic Books, 1988), 134.

22. Kevin Phillips, *Wealth and Democracy* (New York: Broadway Books, 2002), 163.

23. All figures cited in this paragraph are calculated from Table 10 of the US Census Bureau, *Current Population Reports: Consumer Income,* Series P-60, No. 151 (Washington, DC: Government Printing Office, April 1986), 29.

24. Frank Levy, *The New Dollars and Dreams: American Incomes and Economic Change* (New York: Russell Sage Foundation, 1998), 189.

25. Lawrence Mishel, Jared Bernstein, and Sylvia Allegretto, *The State of Working America: 2004–2005* (Ithaca, NY: Cornell University Press, 2005), 3.

26. US Census Bureau, *Current Population Reports, Consumer Income,* Series P-60, No. 184 (Washington, DC: Government Printing Office, September 1993).

27. Gary Burtless, "Growing American Inequality," *Brookings Review* (Winter 1999): 32–33.

28. Frank Levy, *Dollars and Dreams: The Changing American Income Distribution* (New York: Norton, 1988), 63. The annual rate of productivity growth averaged less than 0.5 percent between 1973 and 1988—the worst performance in the twentieth century. See Krugman, *Age of Diminished Expectations,* 11–12. Why did productivity drop? According to Krugman, economists do not know; they can offer a "set of explanations . . . that are little more than sophisticated cocktail party chatter," 14. Levy has updated his analysis in *New Dollars and Dreams.* The analysis in this section is drawn from both works.

29. Edward Wolff, "The Rich Get Richer and the Poor Don't," *American Prospect* (February 21, 2001), 15.

30. David Leonhardt, "For Many, a Boom That Wasn't," *New York Times,* April 9, 2008.

31. Gordon Green and John Colder, "Household Income Trends During the Recession and Economic Recovery" (press release), Sentier Research, October 10, 2011, 2,

http://www.sentierresearch.com/pressreleases/SentierResearch_PressRelease_October_10_2011.pdf.

32. Alan B. Krueger, "Inequality: Too Much of a Good Thing," in *Inequality in America,* ed. James J. Heckman and Alan B. Krueger (Cambridge, MA: MIT Press, 2003), 2–3.

33. Mishel, Bernstein, and Allegretto, *State of Working America,* 3. See also Susan Fleck, John Glaser, and Shawn Sprague, "The Compensation-Productivity Gap: A Visual Essay," *Monthly Labor Review* (January 2011): 64.

34. Mishel, Bernstein, and Allegretto, *State of Working America,* 3.

35. Phillips, *Wealth and Democracy,* 163.

36. Daniel Alpert, Robert Hockett, and Nouriel Roubini, "The Way Forward," *New America Foundation* (October 2011): 7–9, http://newamerica.net/sites/newamerica.net/files/policydocs/NAF-The-Way-Forward-Alpert_Hockett_Roubini.pdf.

37. "Family Income Growth in Two Eras," in *The State of Working America* (Washington, DC: Economic Policy Institute, Oct. 14, 2011), http://www.stateofworkingamerica.org/charts/view/49.

38. Thomas Piketty and Emmanuel Saez, "Income Inequality in the United States: 1913–1998," *Quarterly Journal of Economics,* 118, no. 1 (2003): 1–39.

39. Emmanuel Saez, "Striking It Richer: The Evolution of Top Incomes in the United States," July 17, 2010, http://elsa.berkeley.edu/~saez/saez-UStopincomes-2008.pdf.

40. Paul Krugman, "For Richer," *New York Times Magazine,* October 20, 2002, 65.

41. Economic Policy Institute, "Economic Snapshots," July 24, 2002, www.epinet.org/content.cfm/webfeatures_snapshots_archive_2002_0724_snap07242002.

42. Peter Whoriskey, "The 'Lake Wobegon Effect' Lifts CEO Pay," *Washington Post,* October 4, 2011, A01.

43. Chuck Collins, Betsy Leondar-Wright, and Holly Sklar, *Shifting Fortunes: The Perils of the Growing American Wealth Gap* (Boston: United for a Fair Economy, 1999).

44. Dinesh D'Souza, *The Virtue of Prosperity* (New York: Free Press, 2000), 43.

45. Sylvia Allegretto, "The State of Working America's Wealth, 2011" (EPI State of Working America Briefing Paper No. 292, Economic Policy Institute, Washington, DC, March 23, 2011), 2.

46. Nicholas D. Kristof, "America's Primal Scream," *New York Times,* October 16, 2011, SR11.

47. Sylvia Nasar, "Fed Gives New Evidence of 80s Gains by Richest," *New York Times,* April 21, 1992, A1; Keith Bradsher, "Gap in Wealth in U.S. Called Widest in West," *New York Times,* April 17, 1995, A1.

48. The European data cited here are from a 1986 study but are comparable to the 1992 American data because of the relative stability of wealth distribution over such a short period. Edward N. Wolff, "How the Pie Is Sliced: America's Growing Concentration of Wealth," in *Ticking Time Bombs,* ed. Robert Kuttner (New York: Norton, 1996), 75–76. The 1992 US calculation is based on Collins, Leondar-Wright, and Sklar, *Shifting Fortunes,* Figure 6.2, 208.

49. Nasar, "Fed Gives New Evidence"; Bradsher, "Gap in Wealth."

50. US Census Bureau, "Poverty Status of People by Family Relationship, Race, and Hispanic Origin, 1959 to 2003," *Historical Poverty Tables—People,* Table 2, www.census.gov/hhes/poverty/histpov/hstpov2.html.

51. Carmen DeNavas-Walt, Bernadette D. Proctor, and Jessica C. Smith, *Income, Poverty, and Health Insurance Coverage in the United States: 2010* (US Census Bureau, Current Population Reports P60-239, Washington, DC: Government Printing Office, 2011), 14.

52. Bhashkar Mazumder, "The Apple Falls Even Closer to the Tree Than We Thought," in *Unequal Chances: Family Background and Economic Success,* ed. Samuel Bowles et al. (New York: Russell Sage Foundation, 2005), 80–99. See also Isabel Sawhill and John E. Morton, *Economic Mobility: Is the American Dream Alive and Well?* (Economic Mobility Project of the PEW Charitable Trusts, n.d.), accessed October 15, 2011, http://www.economicmobility.org/assets/pdfs/EMP%20American%20 Dream%20Report.pdf.

53. Alan B. Krueger, "The Apple Falls Close to the Tree," *New York Times,* November 14, 2002.

54. Bowles et al., *Unequal Chances,* 186.

55. Ibid., 18–22.

56. Paul Krugman, "The Sons Also Rise," *New York Times,* November 22, 2002, A27.

57. Gregory Acs, "Downward Mobility From the Middle Class: Waking Up From the American Dream" (Executive Summary, Economic Mobility Project of the Pew Charitable Trusts, August 2011), http://www.economicmobility.org/reports_and_ research/assets/pdfs/MiddleClassExecSum.pdf.

58. Krueger, "Inequality," 10. See also Larry M. Bartels, *Unequal Democracy: The Politics of the New Gilded Age* (Princeton, NJ: Princeton University Press, 2008), 15–16.

59. US Census Bureau, "CPS Population and Per Capita Money Income, White: 1967–2004," and "CPS Population and Per Capita Money Income, Black: 1967–2004," *Historical Income Tables—People,* Table P-1, January 13, 2006, www.census .gov/hhes/www/income/histinc/incpertoc.html.

60. Author calculations from US Census Bureau, "Money Income of Families—Median Income by Race and Hispanic Origin in Current and Constant (2009) Dollars: 1990–2009," *2012 Statistical Abstract of the United States,* Table 697, http://www .census.gov/compendia/statab/2012/tables/12s0697.pdf.

61. Thomas Byrne Edsall and Mary D. Edsall, "Race," *Atlantic Monthly,* May 1991, 54–85.

62. US Census Bureau, "Educational Attainment by Race and Hispanic Origin: 1969–2003," *Statistical Abstract of the United States: 2004–2005,* Table 213, 141, www.census .gov/prod/2004pubs/04statab/educ.pdf.

63. Sabrina Tavernise, "Recession Study Finds Hispanics Hit the Hardest," *New York Times,* July 26, 2011, A1.

64. Rakesh Kochhar, Richard Fry, and Paul Taylor, *Twenty to One: Wealth Gaps Rise to Record Highs Between Whites, Blacks and Hispanics* (Washington, DC: PEW Social and Demographic Trends, July 26, 2011), 23.

65. Michael Moore's well-known film *Roger and Me* documents this transformation.

66. Harrison and Bluestone, *Great U-Turn,* 117.

67. Neil Fligstein and Taek-Jin Shin, "The Shareholder Value Society: A Review of the Changes in Working Conditions and Inequality in the United States, 1976 to 2000,"

in *Social Inequality,* ed. Kathryn M. Neckerman (New York: Russell Sage Foundation, 2004), 403.

68. Howard Rosenthal, "Politics, Public Policy, and Inequality: A Look Back at the Twentieth Century," in Neckerman, *Social Inequality,* 875.

69. Alpert, Hockett, and Roubini, "The Way Forward," 5.

70. Fligstein and Shin, "Shareholder Value Society," 402–4.

71. Robert H. Frank and Philip J. Cook, *The Winner Take All Society* (New York: Free Press, 1996).

72. Timothy Noah, "The Great Divergence: Did Computers Create Inequality?," *Slate Magazine,* http://www.slate.com/articles/news_and_politics/the_great_divergence/features/2010/the_united_states_of_inequality/did_computers_create_inequality.html.

73. Mishel, Bernstein, and Allegretto, *State of Working America: 2004–2005,* 184–89.

74. Paul Krugman, *The Conscience of a Liberal* (New York: Norton, 2007), 132.

75. Ibid., 205–6.

76. Krueger, "Inequality," 4.

77. Thomas J. Kane, "College-Going and Inequality," in Neckerman, *Social Inequality,* 319–21.

78. Paulson, quoted in Bartels, *Unequal Democracy,* 29.

79. Mishel, Bernstein, and Allegretto, *State of Working America: 2004–2005,* 401–3.

80. Bartels, *Unequal Democracy,* 29–63.

81. Krugman, *Conscience of a Liberal,* 136.

82. Leslie McCall, "Explaining Levels of Within-Group Inequality in U.S. Labor Markets," *Demography* 37, no. 4 (2000), 415.

83. Claudia Golden and Lawrence F. Katz, *The Race Between Education and Technology* (Cambridge, MA: Harvard University Press, 2008), 89–125.

84. Two books that document the success of the conservative movement in the Reagan and George W. Bush eras are Walter Williams, *Reaganism and the Death of Representative Democracy* (Washington, DC: Georgetown University Press, 2003); and Jacob S. Hacker and Paul Pierson, *Off Center: The Republican Revolution and the Erosion of American Democracy* (New Haven, CT: Yale University Press, 2005).

85. Jacob S. Hacker and Paul Pierson, *Winner-Take-All Politics: How Washington Made the Rich Richer and Turned It Back on the Middle Class* (New York: Simon & Schuster, 2010), 65.

86. Hacker and Pierson, *Winner-Take-All Politics,* 56–61.

87. US Census Bureau, "Labor Union Membership by Sector: 1983 to 2000," *Statistical Abstract of the United States,* 2001, Table 637, 411, www.census.gov/prod/2002pubs/01statab/labor.pdf.

88. Hacker and Pierson, *Winner-Take-All Politics,* 52.

89. Jacob Hacker, "Privatizing Risk Without Privatizing the Welfare State: The Hidden Politics of Social Policy Retrenchment in the United States," *American Political Science Review* 98, no. 2 (May 2004).

90. Ibid., 242; Economic Policy Institute, "Real Value of the Federal Minimum Wage, 1950–2004," *EPI Issue Guide: Minimum Wage,* Fig. 1, January 2006, www.epi.org/content.cfm/issueguides_minwage_minwage.

91. Bartels, *Unequal Democracy,* 226.

92. Lawrence Mishel, Jared Bernstein, and Heide Shierholz, *The State of Working America* 2008–2009, Economic Policy Institute, Table 3.38, www.stateofworking america.org/tabfig/2008/03/SWA08_Wages_Table.3.38.pdf.

93. Claudia Goldin and Lawrence Katz, *The Race Between Education and Technology* (Cambridge, MA: Harvard University Press, 2008), 346–53.

94. Kane, "College-Going and Inequality," 337.

95. Goldin and Katz, *The Race Between,* 276.

96. Douglas S. Massey, *Return of the L Word* (Princeton, NJ: Princeton University Press, 2005), 25.

97. Mishel, Bernstein, and Allegretto, *State of Working America: 2004–2005,* 3.

98. Hacker and Pierson, *Winner-Take-All Politics,* 48–49.

99. "Trends in the Distribution of Household Income Between 1979 and 2007," Summary (Washington, DC: Congressional Budget Office, October 2011), 4.

100. Extensive summaries of this research can be found in Lawrence Jacobs and Theda Skocpol, eds., *Inequality and American Democracy* (New York: Russell Sage Foundation, 2005), chaps. 2 and 3.

101. APSA Task Force on Inequality and American Democracy, *American Democracy in an Age of Rising Inequality,* Report Summary (Washington, DC: American Political Science Association, August 2004), 11.

102. Martin Gilens, "Inequality and Democratic Responsiveness?," *Public Opinion Quarterly* 69, no. 5 (2005): 778–96.

103. Larry Bartels et al., *Inequality and American Governance,* APSA Task Force on Inequality and American Democracy Report (Washington, DC: American Political Science Association, 2004), 48.

104. Bartels, *Unequal Democracy,* 254.

105. Ibid., 279.

106. Ibid., 281.

107. Jeffery A. Winters and Benjamin I. Page, "Oligarchy in the United States?," *Perspectives on Politics* 7, no. 4 (December 2009): 739.

108. Ibid., 744.

109. Rosenthal, "Politics, Public Policy, and Inequality," 861–92.

110. William Schneider, "The Dawn of the Suburban Era in American Politics," *Atlantic Monthly* (July 1992): 33–57.

111. Edsall and Edsall, "Race," 84–85.

112. Robert Frank, *Richistan: A Journey Through the American Wealth Boom and the Lives of the New Rich* (New York: Crown Three Rivers Press, 2008).

113. Joseph Siglitz, "Of the 1%, by the 1%, for the 1%," *Vanity Fair* (May 2011), http://www.vanityfair.com/society/features/2011/05/top-one-percent-201105.

114. Richard Wilkinson and Kate Pickett, *The Spirit Level: Why Greater Equality Makes Societies Stronger* (New York: Bloomsbury Press, 2010).

115. Ibid., 175–82.

116. Nolan McCarthy, Keith T. Poole, and Howard Rosenthal, *Polarized America: The Dance of Ideology and Unequal Riches* (Cambridge, MA: MIT Press, 2006).

117. Goldin and Katz, *The Race Between,* 352.

118. Economic Policy Institute, *Living Wage: Facts at a Glance,* www.epi.org/content.cfm/issueguides_livingwage_livingwagefacts.
119. Bruce Ackerman and Anne Alstott, *The Stakeholder Society* (New Haven, CT: Yale University Press, 1999).
120. Richard B. Freeman, *The New Inequality: Creating Solutions for Poor America* (Boston: Beacon Press, 1999).

Chapter 8: The National Security State

1. Gary Hart, *The Minuteman: Restoring an Army of the People* (New York: Free Press, 1998), 6.
2. For a detailed account of the rise of the national security state, see Daniel Yergin, *Shattered Peace: The Origins of the Cold War and the National Security State* (Boston: Houghton Mifflin, 1977).
3. One little-discussed agency established by the National Security Act of 1947 is the National Security Resources Board, which is responsible for coordinating defense production.
4. Harold D. Lasswell, "The Garrison-State Hypothesis Today," in *National Security and American Society,* ed. Philip S. Kronenberg and Frank Trager (Lawrence: University of Kansas Press, 1973), 434. In this remarkable essay written in 1962, Lasswell evaluates the extent to which his 1935 prediction had come to pass. For the original essay, see "The Garrison State and Specialists on Violence," *American Journal of Sociology* (January 1941): 455–68.
5. Harold D. Lasswell, *National Security and Individual Freedom* (New York: McGraw-Hill, 1950), 32.
6. Miriam Pemberton and Lawrence Korb, *A Unified Security Budget for the United States, FY 2009* (Washington, DC: Institute for Policy Studies, September 2008), 8.
7. Quoted in Common Dreams Newswire, "Business Leaders Applaud F-22 Funding Cuts," July 21, 1999, accessed at www.commondreams.org/pressreleases/july99/.
8. Lawrence J. Korb, "Bush Is Inflating Pentagon's Budget," *Newsday,* January 29, 2002.
9. Benjamin Schwarz, "Why America Thinks It Has to Run the World," *Atlantic Monthly,* June 1996, 94.
10. Andrew J. Bacevich, *Washington Rules: America's Path to Permanent War* (New York: Metropolitan Books, 2010), 12.
11. Ibid., 14.
12. Ibid., 25.
13. Stanley Hoffman, "The High and the Mighty: Bush's National Security Strategy and the New American Hubris," *American Prospect,* January 13, 2003, 30.
14. Bacevich, "Washington Rules," 248–49.
15. John Mintz, "Homeland Agency Launched," *Washington Post,* November 26, 2002, A01.
16. Thomas Powers, "The Black Arts," *New York Review of Books,* January 4, 1999, 23.

17. U.S. Senate, *Final Report of the Select Committee to Study Governmental Operations With Respect to Intelligence Activities,* 94th Cong., 2d sess., bks. I–III (Washington, DC: Government Printing Office, 1976) [Church Committee Report]; see also Morton H. Halperin, Jerry J. Berman, Robert L. Borosage, and Christine M. Marwick, *The Lawless State: The Crimes of the U.S. Intelligence Agencies* (New York: Penguin Books, 1977), 13–58.

18. Jeanne M. Woods, *Ending the Cold War at Home* (Washington, DC: Center for National Security Studies, 1991), 5.

19. Tim Weiner, "C.I.A.'s Openness Derided as a 'Snow Job,'" *New York Times,* May 20, 1997, A16.

20. Scott Shane, "Since 2001, Sharp Increase in the Number of Documents Classified by the Government," *New York Times,* July 3, 2005, YT12.

21. Ibid.

22. Quoted in David E. Rosenbaum, "When Government Doesn't Tell," *New York Times,* February 3, 2002, WK1.

23. Daniel Patrick Moynihan, *Secrecy* (New Haven, CT: Yale University Press, 1998), 178–201.

24. George W. Bush, *Memo to Secretaries of State, Treasury, Defense, the Attorney General, the Directors of CIA and FBI,* The White House, October 5, 2001, www.fas.org/sgp/bush/gwb100501.html.

25. U.S. House of Representatives, Committee on Government Reform—Minority Staff, *Secrecy in the Bush Administration,* report prepared for Rep. Henry A. Waxman, D-Calif., September 14, 2004.

26. Dana Priest and William M. Arkin, "A Hidden World, Growing Beyond Control," Top Secret America: A Washington Post Investigation, July 19, 2010, http://projects .washingtonpost.com/top-secret-america/articles/a-hidden-world-growing-beyond -control/.

27. Ibid.

28. David Sanger, "In Address, Bush Says He Ordered Domestic Spying," *New York Times,* December 18, 2006, A1. For a concise analysis of the legal and constitutional issues surrounding the NSA wiretapping, see George F. Will, "No Checks, Many Imbalances," *Washington Post,* February 16, 2006, A27; see also Jane Mayer, *The Dark Side: The Inside Story of How the War on Terror Turned Into a War on American Ideals* (New York: Doubleday, 2008), 67.

29. Shane, "Since 2001, Sharp Increase."

30. Ibid.

31. Powers, "Black Arts," 20.

32. Quoted by Robert Dallek in testimony before the House Committee on Government Reform, April 11, 2002, www.fas.org/sgp/congress/2002/041102dallek.html.

33. This account of the Iran-*contra* affair is based on a series of articles by Theodore Draper in the *New York Review of Books:* "The Rise of an American Junta," October 8, 1987; "The Fall of an American Junta," October 22, 1987; and "An Autopsy," December 17, 1987. It is also based on Bob Woodward's account of William Casey's CIA in *Veil* (New York: Simon & Schuster, 1987). For further background on Central America and US policy, see Morris J. Blachman and Kenneth Sharpe,

"De-democratizing American Foreign Policy: Dismantling the Post-Vietnam Formula," *Third World Quarterly,* October 1986, 1271–1308; and Robert H. Trudeau, *Guatemalan Politics: The Popular Struggle for Democracy* (Boulder, CO: Lynne Rienner, 1993).

34. The arms-for-hostages exchange turned out in the end to be an enormous fiasco. On several trips to Iran, North and others discovered that the supposed "moderate" elements in the Iranian leadership had neither the power nor the desire to help obtain the release of the hostages. Even though their contacts had assured them that all American hostages would be released if arms were provided, North and his friends were able to obtain the release of only two hostages, and the hostage takers replaced these individuals in short order with additional kidnappings. It turned out that the Iranians that North dealt with had exaggerated their power in Iran as much as North himself had lied about his access to President Reagan. North was famous for inventing tales about his frequent meetings with the president, including weekends at the presidential retreat at Camp David that never happened. Reagan later testified that he barely knew who North was and had never had a private meeting with him.
35. Neil Sheehan et al., *The Pentagon Papers* (New York: Bantam Books, 1971).
36. Clark Clifford, "Memoirs—The Vietnam Years II," *New Yorker,* May 13, 1991, 45–83.
37. Frank Rich, "Freedom From the Press," *New York Times,* March 2, 2002.
38. See Mayer, *The Dark Side,* passim, for detailed documentation of these abuses.
39. Ibid., 175.
40. Charlie Savage, "Obama's War on Terror May Resemble Bush's in Some Areas," *New York Times,* February 18, 2009, A19.
41. V. Noah Gimbel, "Has the Rendition Program Disappeared?," Institute for Policy Studies, June 16, 2011, http://www.ips-dc.org/articles/has_the_rendition_program_disappeared.
42. Daniel P. Moynihan, "The Peace Dividend," *New York Review of Books,* June 28, 1990, 4.
43. Hannah Arendt, *Crises of the Republic* (New York: Harcourt Brace Jovanovich, 1972), 34.
44. Sheehan et al., *Pentagon Papers,* 234–306.
45. "Names of the Dead," *New York Times,* June 23, 2011, A8.
46. Thom Shanker, "2012 Pullback Worries Military Experts," *New York Times,* June 23, 2011, A9.
47. Elisabeth Bulmiller and Thom Shanker, "War Evolves With Drones, Some Tiny as Bugs," *New York Times,* June 20, 2011, A1.
48. V. Noah Gimbel, "Has the Rendition Program Disappeared?"
49. Bacevich, *Washington Rules,* 19–58.
50. Arthur M. Schlesinger Jr., *The Imperial Presidency* (Boston: Houghton Mifflin, 1973).
51. Louis Henkin, *Constitutionalism, Democracy, and Foreign Affairs* (New York: Columbia University Press, 1990), 30–31.
52. Louis Fisher, *Congressional Abdication on War and Spending* (College Station: Texas A&M University Press, 2000), 68.

53. Ibid., 67–108.

54. Theodore Draper, "Capturing the Constitution," *New York Review of Books,* May 7, 1995, 40.

55. Andrew J. Bacevich, *American Empire: The Realities and Consequences of U.S. Diplomacy* (Cambridge, MA: Harvard University Press, 2002), 142–43.

56. For details about the Gulf War decision process, see Michael Massing, "The Way to War," *New York Review of Books,* March 28, 1991; and Thomas L. Friedman and Patrick E. Tyler, "From the First, U.S. Resolve to Fight," *New York Times,* March 3, 1991.

57. In fact, in a speech several months after the war, Bush argued explicitly that he was not required to seek congressional approval. For a discussion and critique of Bush's argument, see Theodore Draper, "Presidential Wars," *New York Review of Books,* September 6, 1991, 64–74.

58. Fisher, *Congressional Abdication,* 78–79.

59. George W. Bush, *Statement by the President Authorizing Use of Military Force,* The White House, September 18, 2001, www.whitehouse.gov/news/releases/2001/09/20010918–10.html.

60. Elisabeth Bumiller, "President Notes Dissent on Iraq, Vowing to Listen," *New York Times,* August 17, 2002, A1.

61. Mayer, *The Dark Side,* 44–71.

62. Ibid., 64–65.

63. Quoted in ibid., 71.

64. Glenn Kessler, "U.S. Decision on Iraq Has Puzzling Past," *Washington Post,* January 12, 2003, A01.

65. Nicholas Lemann, "How It Came to War," *New Yorker,* March 31, 2003, 39.

66. Jim VandeHei and Juliet Eilperin, "Congress Passes Iraq Resolution," *Washington Post,* October 11, 2002, A01.

67. Karen DeYoung and Walter Pincus, "U.S. Hedges on Finding Iraqi Weapons," *Washington Post,* May 29, 2003, A01.

68. Bumiller, "President Notes Dissent on Iraq."

69. Bacevich, *Washington Rules,* 220.

70. Bulmiller and Shanker, "War Evolves With Drones."

71. Charlie Savage and Mark Landler, "White House Defends Continuing U.S. Role in Libya Operation," *New York Times,* June 6, 2011, A13.

72. Bruce Ackerman, "Legal Acrobatics, Illegal War," *New York Times,* June 21, 2011, A27.

73. The argument in this paragraph follows closely that of Andrew Bacevich, *The New American Militarism* (Oxford: Oxford University Press, 2005), 30–31.

74. See Jean-François Revel, *How Democracies Perish* (New York: Harper & Row, 1985), for an example of this sort of argument.

75. Quoted in Leon Wieseltier, "Democracy and Colonel North," *New Republic,* January 26, 1987, 24.

76. These points are made succinctly in Michael Ledeen, "The Future of Foreign Policy," *American Spectator,* June 1987.

77. Irving L. Janis, *Groupthink,* 2nd ed. (Boston: Houghton Mifflin, 1982).

78. Fisher, *Congressional Abdication*, 162–63.
79. Bruce Russett, *Controlling the Sword: The Democratic Governance of National Security* (Cambridge, MA: Harvard University Press, 1990), 52–86.
80. There are many good biographies of this fascinating individual. One that documents well Hoover's disregard for democracy and civil liberties is Athan Theoharis and John Stuart Cox, *The Boss: J. Edgar Hoover and the Great American Inquisition* (Philadelphia: Temple University Press, 1988).
81. Halperin et al., *Lawless State*, 95–96.
82. For a fascinating account of the political pressures that led to the federal security program, see the memoirs of a key Truman aide who set up the program: Clark Clifford, "Annals of Government: The Truman Years—Part II," *New Yorker*, April 1, 1991, 56–58.
83. Halperin et al., *Lawless State*, 107.
84. Ibid., 61–89. For evidence of Hoover's hostility toward blacks, see Theoharis and Cox, *The Boss*, 10. See also David Garrow, *The FBI and Martin Luther King* (New York: Norton, 1981).
85. Documentation for all these activities can be found in Halperin et al., *Lawless State;* and Athan Theoharis, *Spying on Americans* (Philadelphia: Temple University Press, 1978). Both books rely primarily on the Church Committee and Rockefeller Commission reports in documenting these abuses. (Theoharis was a consultant to the Church Committee.)
86. Gary M. Stern, *The FBI's Misguided Probe of CISPES*, Report No. 111 (Washington, DC: Center for National Security Studies, June 1988).
87. Woods, *Ending the Cold War*, 18.
88. Matthew Purdy, "Bush's New Rules to Fight Terror Transform the Legal Landscape," *New York Times*, November 25, 2001, A1.
89. Adam Liptak, "Changing the Standard," *New York Times*, May 31, 2002, A1.
90. Spenser S. Hsu, "FBI Papers Show Terror Inquiries Into PETA: Other Groups Tracked," *Washington Post*, December 20, 2005, A11.
91. David K. Shipler, "Extreme Measures," *The American Prospect*, November 2011, 46.
92. Colin Moynihan and Scott Shaw, "For Anarchist, Details of Life as F.B.I. Target," *New York Times*, May 29, 2011, A1.
93. David E. Sanger, "In Address, Bush Says He Ordered Domestic Spying," *New York Times*, December 18, 2005, A1.
94. Elisabeth Bumiller and David Johnston, "Bush May Subject Terror Suspects to Military Trials," *New York Times*, November 14, 2001, A1.
95. Dana Priest, "CIA Holds Terror Suspects in Secret Prisons," *Washington Post*, November 2, 2005, A01.
96. Jeffrey Rosen, "Private Enemy," *New Republic*, July 8 and 15, 2002, 14.
97. Human Rights Watch, "Torture in Iraq," *New York Review of Books*, November 3, 2005, 67–72.
98. Bacevich, *New American Militarism*, 66–67.
99. Eric Schmitt and Tim Golden, "Pentagon Plans Tighter Control of Interrogation," *New York Times*, November 8, 2005, A1.
100. Ibid.

101. Michael Abromowitz, Joby Warrick, and Walter Pincus, "Obama Under Pressure on Interrogation Policy: Some See Harsh Methods as Essential," *Washington Post,* January 10, 2009, A01.

102. Savage, "Obama's War on Terror."

103. William Greider, *Fortress America: The American Military and the Consequences of Peace* (New York: Public Affairs, 1998), 79.

104. Daniel Hellinger and Dennis R. Judd, *The Democratic Façade* (Belmont, CA: Wadsworth, 1991), 209.

105. Hedrick Smith, *The Power Game* (New York: Random House, 1988).

106. Center for Responsive Politics, "Defense: Long-Term Contribution Trends," www .opensecrets.org/industries/indus.asp?ind=D.

107. Lawrence J. Korb, "Defense, Industry, and Procurement," in *Business in the Contemporary World,* ed. Herbert L. Sawyer (Lanham, MD: University Press of America, 1988), 40.

108. William D. Hartung, "Military-Industrial Complex Revisited," World Policy Institute, June 8, 1999, http://www.bu.edu/globalbeat/usdefense/Hartung070299 .html.

109. Thom Shanker and James Dao, "Army Digs in Its Heels and Saves Howitzer Plan, for Now," *New York Times,* May 2, 2002, A16; and Judy Sarasohn, "Taking the Crusader Fight to Lawmakers," *Washington Post,* May 16, 2002, A23.

110. Jason Vest, "Fourth Generation Warfare," *Atlantic Monthly,* December 2001, 49.

111. Lawrence J. Korb, "Pentagon Still Frozen in Cold War Posture," *Baltimore Sun,* December 21, 2001.

112. Dana Hedgpeth, "Air Force Pares Request for Additional Lockheed F-22s," *Washington Post,* February 18, 2009, D04.

113. Tim Weiner, "Air Superiority at $258 Million a Pop," *New York Times,* October 27, 2004, C1; for latest F-22 production targets, see Ken Dilanian and Tom Vanden Brook, "Raptor in Dogfight for Its Future," *USA Today,* February 26, 2009, 1B.

114. Dilanian and Vanden Brook, "Raptor in Dogfight for Its Future."

115. S. A. Miller, "Obama Wins War of Wills to Halt F-22 Program," *Washington Times,* July 22, 2009, A03.

116. Walter Pincus, "Senators Question Pentagon on F-35s," *Washington Post,* May 20, 2011, A05.

117. Chalmers Johnson, *Dismantling the Empire* (New York: Metropolitan Books, 2010), 175.

118. Mark Thompson, "The Sky's the Limit," *Time,* March 24, 1997, 52; and Thom Shanker, "Acquisition Panel Approves $60 Billion Fighter Program," *New York Times,* August 16, 2002, A15.

119. Clyde H. Farnsworth, "White House Seeks to Revive Credits for Arms Exports," *New York Times,* March 18, 1991, A1.

120. John M. Brodeur, "In Washington, It's Never Farewell to Arms," *New York Times,* May 11, 1997, E16.

121. Leslie Wayne, "Polish Pride, American Profits," *New York Times,* January 12, 2003, C1.

122. Lasswell, *National Security,* 40. See also C. Wright Mills, *The Power Elite* (Oxford: Oxford University Press, 1956), 198–224.

123. Bacevich, *American Empire,* 172–80.

124. Ibid., 175.

125. Ibid., 178.

126. Bacevich, *New American Militarism,* 28.

127. David M. Halbfinger and Steven A. Holmes, "Military Mirrors a Working Class America," *New York Times,* March 30, 2003.

128. Bacevich, *New American Militarism,* 26.

129. Peter D. Feaver and Christopher Gelpi, *Choosing Your Battles: American Civil-Military Relations and the Use of Force* (Princeton, NJ: Princeton University Press, 2004), 207.

130. Ole R. Holsti, "Of Chasms and Convergences: Attitudes and Beliefs of Civilians and Military Elites at the Start of a New Millennium," in *Soldiers and Civilians: The Civil-Military Gap and American National Security,* ed. Peter C. Feaver and Richard H. Kohn (Cambridge, MA: MIT Press, 2001), 64.

131. Bacevich, *New American Militarism,* 23.

132. Bob Herbert, "An Army About to Snap," *New York Times,* November 10, 2005, A31.

133. Bacevich, *New American Militarism,* 24.

134. Quoted in ibid., 24.

135. Feaver and Kohn, "Conclusion," in *Soldiers and Civilians,* 461.

136. Peter D. Feaver and Richard H. Kohn, "The Gap: Soldiers, Civilians, and Their Mutual Misunderstanding," *The National Interest,* Fall 2000, 5.

137. Benjamin Barber and Patrick Watson, *The Struggle for Democracy* (Boston: Little, Brown, 1988), 226–30. See also John Steward Ambler, *The French Army in Politics* (Columbus: Ohio State University Press, 1966), 259–61.

138. Fisher, *Congressional Abdication,* 164.

139. Ibid., 170.

140. For a more extended discussion of how Congress can assert its war power, see Fisher, *Congressional Abdication,* 165–73.

141. Tara McKelvey, "You Can Handle the Truth," *American Prospect,* March 2009, 19.

142. The argument in this paragraph is derived from Charles Moskos, "Reviving the Citizen-Soldier," *Public Interest* 147 (Spring 2002): 76–85.

143. Charles Moskos and Paul Glastris, "Now Do You Believe We Need a Draft?" *Washington Monthly,* November 2001, 11.

144. Moskos, "Reviving the Citizen-Soldier," 82.

145. Feaver and Kohn, *Soldiers and Civilians,* 470.

146. For a carefully argued critique of Bush's unilateralism, see Stanley Hoffman, "America Goes Backward," *New York Review of Books,* June 12, 2003, 74–80.

Index

About the Author

William E. Hudson is professor of political science at Providence College, where he teaches courses in American politics and public policy. He currently serves as director of the Public Administration Program and was the founding director of the Feinstein Institute for Public Service. He is the author of *The Libertarian Illusion*, also published by CQ Press, and *Experiencing Citizenship: Concepts and Models for Service-Learning in Political Science* (with Richard Battistoni). Hudson has published numerous articles on public policy issues in journals such as *Political Science Quarterly, Polity, Western Political Quarterly, Economic Development Quarterly*, and *Policy Studies Journal.*

⑤SAGE research**methods**

The essential online tool for researchers from the world's leading methods publisher

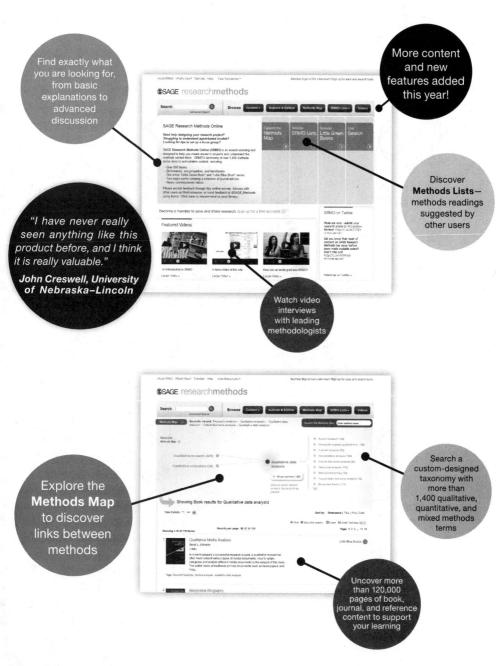

Find exactly what you are looking for, from basic explanations to advanced discussion

More content and new features added this year!

"I have never really seen anything like this product before, and I think it is really valuable."
John Creswell, University of Nebraska–Lincoln

Discover **Methods Lists**— methods readings suggested by other users

Watch video interviews with leading methodologists

Explore the **Methods Map** to discover links between methods

Search a custom-designed taxonomy with more than 1,400 qualitative, quantitative, and mixed methods terms

Uncover more than 120,000 pages of book, journal, and reference content to support your learning

Find out more at
www.sageresearchmethods.com